Kerwin Kay
Jill Nagle
Baruch Gould
Editors

Male Lust
Pleasure, Power,
and Transformation

Pre-publication
REVIEWS,
COMMENTARIES,
EVALUATIONS . . .

"**B**etween the covers of *Male Lust,* Kerwin Kay has swept together a fascinating chorus of voices testifying about the permutations of desire in men's lives. The feminist sex wars triggered the creation of a huge discourse about the pleasure and danger that lust brought to women's experience. Until now, there has not been a parallel outpouring of personal stories and critical thought about eros from the male perspective. Kay has been surprisingly successful at getting an awesome range of men to speak, with great intelligence and feeling, about this personal subject. Gay, bisexual, and straight men; transgendered men; disabled men; white men; and men of color add their pieces to the puzzle. This is a thought-provoking anthology with a variety of uncensored viewpoints that should interest anyone who cares about sexology, feminism, gender, psychology, or just that guy sitting in the chair over there."

Pat Califia
Author of *Public Sex:*
The Culture of Radical Sex

More pre-publication
REVIEWS, COMMENTARIES, EVALUATIONS . . .

"**G**oes beyond the clichés, and even beyond the alternative clichés, to break new ground."

Shere Hite
Author of *The Hite Report on Male Sexuality*

"***M**ale Lust: Pleasure, Power and Transformation* details the infinite varieties of sexual experience embodied in the lives of everyday people: men, boys, FTMs, gay, straight, bi, trans, aging, young, afraid, yearning, eager, ecstatic, painful, and confused. This collection of nearly sixty essays, memoirs, poems, political apologies, and debates is a wondrous look into the hearts and minds, groins and souls of the American male psyche. From Don Shewey's chronicle of being a sex worker to Max Wolf Valerio's experiences as a transgendered man getting off in a peep-show arcade, from John Stoltenberg's thoughts on sexual ethics to Steven Hill's remembrance of 'becoming a man' when he made his G.I. Joe beat up nelly Ken to 'get' Barbie, these pieces form a tapestry of male experience that is as complex, frightening, and moving as anything you will ever read. More important, the images and the ideas in these writings form the background and the context for a new way to talk about masculinity, gender, love, and desire that we are just now discovering. Not only an important addition to the literature of gender studies, *Male Lust*—brimming with terror and pity, the comic and the tragic—is a remarkable document of male humanity in all of its possibilities."

Michael Bronski
Author of *Culture Clash: The Making of Gay Sensibility* and *The Pleasure Principle: Sex, Backlash, and the Struggle for Gay Freedom*

"**T**hanks to the poets, priests, prostitutes, and philosophers of *Male Lust* who remind us that liberation starts with our bodies. And blessings to the fathers and sons, teachers and visionaries whose stories encourage us to heal the connection between our genitals and our hearts."

Joseph Kramer
EroSpirit Research Institute, Oakland, CA

Harrington Park Press®
An Imprint of The Haworth Press, Inc.

Male Lust
Pleasure, Power, and Transformation

HAWORTH Gay & Lesbian Studies
John P. De Cecco, PhD
Editor in Chief

Male Lust
Pleasure, Power, and Transformation

Kerwin Kay
Jill Nagle
Baruch Gould
Editors

Harrington Park Press®
An Imprint of The Haworth Press, Inc.
New York • London • Oxford

Published by

Harrington Park Press, an imprint of The Haworth Press, Inc., 10 Alice Street, Binghamton, NY
13904-1580

Cover photo © 1999 Steven Zeeland/Seadog.

Cover design by Jennifer M. Gaska.

Library of Congress Cataloging-in-Publication Data

Male lust : pleasure, power, and transformation / [edited by] Kerwin Kay, Jill Nagle, Baruch
Gould.
    p.   cm.
   Includes bibliographical references and index.
   ISBN 1-56023-981-6. —ISBN 1-56023-982-4 (pbk.).
   1. Men—Sexual behavior. 2. Sexual deviation. I. Kay, Kerwin. II. Nagle, Jill, 1964- . III. Gould,
Baruch.
HQ28.M35 2000
306.7′081—dc21
                                                             99-039462
                                                                     CIP

To the living memory of Allen Ginsberg

CONTENTS

Acknowledgments

This book would not have been possible without the help of an incredible array of people. For favors large and small, I thank Tommi Avicolli Mecca and numerous others at A Different Light Bookstore in San Francisco (www.adlbooks.com), Elizabeth Bernstein, Ahimsa Timoteo Bodhrán, Adrian Brooks, Ferrel Christensen, Anders Corr, Rebecca Fancy, Donna Flynn, Aurora Levins Morales, Bobby Lilly, Cleo Manago, Minoo Moallem, Lisa Montana-relli (whose editing suggestions were invaluable), Scott Noren, Wendy Ormiston, Jack Random, Michael Rosen, Gayle Rubin, Laurie Schaffner, Sara Schneckloth, Marcy Sheiner, Michael Shernoff, Mark Thompson, Carole Vance, and Layne Winklebleck of *Spectator* (www.spectatormag.com). I also want to thank the people at The Haworth Press, particularly my editor, John De Cecco, for their support and patience(!), as we brought this collection together.

I personally would not have been in an emotional position to address the issues this book covers without the understanding and love I found so readily given within the men's community. I wish to especially thank Cass Adams, Foster Goodwill, George Mathews, Kenneth D. Miller, Dan Pence, Vadan Ritter, Sten Rudstrom, Mark Silver, and Tom Smith for the critical support they offered throughout the years.

I am also grateful for the life support and inspiration I found within Boulder's queer community—an exceptionally high-quality group of people—and am especially appreciative for the friendships I have shared with Jim Davis-Rosenthal, Christopher DeWinter, Paul Krueger, Sue Larson, and Mark Nomadieu.

For their years of cheerleading, friendship, and support, I also thank Tracy Bartlett (you're *fabulous,* baby!), Gretchen Iverson, Priscilla Inkpen, Karin Kitely, Ali Luterman, David Marvin, Jim Sandler, Doug Wiese (dude!), and my dearest soul-sister Naneki Scialla. I thank also my teachers in Co-Counseling, Steve Bearman and Carin McKay, for their insights, commitment, and openhearted compassion.

The love and support I continue to receive from both my father, Bryan, and my mother, Kay, provides a deep reservoir of warmth to draw from within my life; I don't know how I can offer sufficient praise for such lifelong love, but I thank you both—ya done good!

Special thanks are due to both of my associate editors, Jill Nagle and Baruch Gould. I'm so glad to have shared the burden of this task with such playful and intelligent friends. The devotion and willingness they've displayed for all the tasks I've thrown at them have been of enormous help, and I thank them both for the excellent work they've done over the past many months. Without their help, this book would clearly not be as rich as it is; in fact, it might not even be done yet!

Last, I want to thank my two closest friends, Clare Corcoran and (again) Jill Nagle. The affection, humor, and intellectual insight both of you bring to me form the cornerstone of my life. I am scandalously grateful for your love and friendship. I love you both.

Kerwin Kay
www.mlust.com

Introduction

Kerwin Kay

Questions about sex are intimately linked to questions of power. For men, the connections between sex and power show themselves in an assortment of ways: the portrayal of sex as a competitive game, a matter of "scoring" and "bases"; the image of sex as an intrinsically desirable commodity, a reward offered to those who achieve, or who at least buy the right car; the valorization of the always-hard, always-ready dick. These same messages are repeated again and again, in innumerable forms and innumerable instances, and in their repetition, the lies become familiar, expected, and unremarked upon. *Of course* it's the hero who "gets" the hot babe; who would want a loser? In the wake of each of these linkages between sex and power, men (and those around us) suffer the consequences. We focus on performance rather than sensation. We pursue people we don't actually like, or who don't like us. We fear the soft cock, as if only hard dicks can feel, as if sex doesn't exist without penetration. We are damaged, yet the lies continue.

So real seems the untruth that it becomes possible to argue that men are simply biologically programmed to be "that way"—always hungry for sex, even "natural" rapists. But think of the force that suddenly comes to bear when the norm is disrupted: *faggot, pussy, wimp.* Think of the children thrown out of their homes for loving the "wrong" bodies, the blows that pummel vulnerable bodies, the unthinking hatred. Think of the silence that surrounds sexuality, the euphemisms that suddenly flower when we speak of sex, the prohibitions that even those engaging in the most normative, heterosexual, procreative sex face in discussing what they actually do, or what they desire. Think of the judicial system, its systemic bias against homosexuality (no adoptions, no legal rights for lifelong partners, generally no protection from outright job and housing discrimination). Think of a judicial system that not only favors heterosexuality but reserves its favor for specific types of heterosexuality: not S/M—that could cost you your kids; not polyfidelity—that could cost you your kids too; not for pay—that could cost you your kids *and* put you in jail. Think of the African-American, Latino, and Chinese men who have been lynched for the mere *suspicion* of looking at a white woman. Whatever biological ground our bodies provide, "male lust" is clearly a highly regulated—and therefore social—affair, shaped through a carefully deployed and nearly ubiquitous series of sticks and carrots. Removing these pressures, or adopting a different set, would radically change the way we think about the social/biological categories "male" and "sexuality."

Instead, society presents us with repeated variations of the same one-dimensional male character: he always wants sex, and sometimes he gets it. But while images of men pursuing sex abound, none of these sources shows us what these men truly seek, or what they actually find. Little information exists regarding the emotional realities of sex for men, a silence that extends over men's experiences in sex shops, with prostitutes, with S/M, in gay sex clubs, and even over men's experiences with simple flirting or long-term heterosexual relationships. Men have few examples to follow in creating sexualities that are both sensitive and self-assured, that successfully integrate concerns for social justice and emotional well-being. While mainstream pornography and pop culture offer numerous representations of male sexuality, the images offer little benefit—and much distraction—for men who need to explore the complexities of their sexual experiences.

This anthology seeks to break through the noisy silence surrounding male sexuality, to challenge the dominant images of men as unemotional sexual predators by revealing the wide spectrum of realities that lies beneath the surface. The iconography of "the stud" obscures vast terrains of male sexual experience, strangling men's voices with the false specter of "unmanliness." Men's accounts of sexual victimization, their stories of sexual shame and desperate longing, and even their tales of genuine joy and celebration have been silenced in favor of tired generalizations about men "always wanting some" and "just being that way." The truth of men's lives is kept well hidden behind a thick veil of "don't ask, don't tell"—a silence imposed lest the sexual and emotional truth overwhelm the fragile social fiction of "the real man." Yet how many notches on the bedpost can the sexual superhero mark before he must stop and ask what he's actually winning in this game? Where does he turn when he finds his image to be little more than an empty shell?

As we peer behind the false images, we see the challenges faced by men whose lives are far removed from the mainstream viewing screen, men whose relative lack of power makes them socially invisible, or who are seen as being somehow different from "ordinary guys." These processes of exclusion frequently turn socially marginalized men into "representatives of their kind" rather than individuals. For men who are oppressed, revealing one's life can thus become intimately bound to concerns about reinforcing prejudices or giving bigots more ammunition: a black man discussing his intense lusts or a gay man talking about his promiscuities invokes dangers that more privileged men never have to consider. As such men struggle to forge positive sexual identities, they must confront painful intersections of desire and oppression: white supremacist fantasies of hypersexuality, hyposexuality, or presumed perversity; heterosexist sentiments of disgust; erasures of desire imposed by societal expectations of people with disabilities or the aged; biofascist loathing for transsexual "freaks." Men who are not white, able-bodied, middle-class, or middle-aged; men whose self-identity does not match the box checked on their birth records; men who are in prison; men whose job involves sex—these men cannot pretend to separate their sexual lives from the prejudices, social regulations, silences, and threats of violence that shape their world. Different men wage their struggles with contradictory strategies: one gay man embraces same-sex marriage; another dives into the sexual underground. These diverse methods, however, let them challenge individually salient aspects of their common oppression.

Unlike marginalized men, whose social identities are constantly at issue (and therefore reinforced), privileged men move in a world where they constitute the ordinary. Because a privileged man's life is "unremarkable," he is less likely to know how his social position affects his life. A "white" man knows that he is "white," but he is likely to have little idea how this identity shapes his social world, much less his sexuality. He's rarely forced to stop and think about it. Any interpersonal or emotional difficulties he might have are thus made to appear as *individual* worries. This illusion of a fully autonomous self lets privileged men act with less concern about the social impact of their actions—they are more "free" than others. Yet, this freedom makes them less able to identify the links between their concerns and the larger social environment. Because of this hyperindividuality, itself socially constructed, privileged men are vulnerable to intense feelings of self-blame and isolation when something goes wrong. It makes them less able to understand how their lives relate to the lives of those around them, and less able to respond to the social forces that daily shape their lives.

The experiences of privileged men are, in fact, deeply linked to those of marginalized men. For every projection of sexual "perversity" onto a marginalized group, there are less noticed—but equally potent—rules established concerning "the norm." Heterosexual men are thus not only forbidden to have sex with other men; they are prohibited from sharing numerous forms of "overly intimate" affection. Likewise, white men are pulled between racial classifications that traditionally define them as "civilized," on the one hand, and contemporary trends emphasizing masculine potency, on the other. This shift partly explains the ongoing white appropriation of numerous African-American cultural forms, from rock and roll to hip clothing. Seen in this light, the possibility of treating another's experience as "Other" becomes less justifiable; the conflicts faced by oppressed men reveal much about the lives and thinking of those in power, and vice versa. Although we clearly are not all the same, our lives are indeed interconnected.

Understanding the effects of privilege and power is a critical factor in understanding male sexuality because men constitute a privileged class. Systems of power, such as male dominance, do not leave the powerful untouched. The very exercise and maintenance of power actively shapes the lives of the powerful. Even those occupying the uppermost positions within a society must exercise tremendous mastery over their own behavior in certain critical arenas, lest they rapidly lose their authority. The superstud with the ever-ready dick is admired and envied, yet the requirements of his position keep him tightly confined. Failure to achieve success, to come up limp, spells disaster. Men experience powerlessness precisely because they are expected to be in control, to be *real* men. The structures of male supremacy precisely define the contours of male "inadequacy" (for similar points, see Flax, 1987, and Palmer, 1983, among others).

Each author in this collection challenges the spurious image of the ultra-macho he-man in some way. These are voices that ask, voices that tell, voices that take risks in order to share. Some authors have chosen to use pseudonyms, realizing the harsh consequences that openly voicing their lives and visions would bring. Theirs are among the first voices to openly discuss men's experiences as survivors of sexual abuse and assault, to intimately detail men's struggles with sexual compulsion and self-destructive behaviors, and to share the experiences of men who work in the sex industry. They are some of the first male voices to celebrate sex rather than glorify it. They are the voices of transsexual men, men whose lives have afforded them a kaleidoscopic vision of gender and its ability to shift beneath our feet. They are the voices of women whose lives have been affected by male lust, whose insights as intimate outsiders offer another opportunity for understanding. They are not voices that all agree, and I have my own points of contention with some of them. Yet, each writer shares a willingness to reveal something about the male experience, to question that one-dimensional image of the superstud, and to ask for something more, something more real.

The essays, stories, and poems in this collection deliberately encompass a large scope. I have gathered together writings that represent a wide array of male experiences with sex and desire. Inevitably, there are gaps, even large ones, and no pretense is made that this work could offer any sort of definitive statement on male sexuality. Indeed, putting such disparate works together in one book highlights the extreme diversity of male desire, while hopefully drawing attention to the numerous social forces that shape, contain, and even produce "male lust." The writings are organized into four parts: *Challenges, Obsessions, Politics,* and *Inspiration.* Arguably, many pieces in one part could easily be placed in another—one person's obsession is another's inspiration, and vice versa—but these are the choices that made sense to us. A topic index is also included at the end of the book for easy reference. Given the sheer breadth of the writings, I do not expect that any comprehensive theory explaining male lust will emerge. I do hope, however, that the book will help foster a more sophisticated and fruitful dialogue concerning men and sex, one that acknowledges the tremendous variety of male experience and passionately seeks to join possibilities for lust and justice.

Ultimately, I believe men need this book. I know I once needed this book, desperately. I needed it because no one dared say these things, because shame and silence took up too much space in my life. This collection is my offering to you, my attempt to connect with you in someplace real, to challenge, provoke, and even tease you—to touch your heart. My hope is that your life will be nourished and enriched from reading this book, just as mine has been from bringing it together.

Blessings and goodwill upon you.

REFERENCES

Flax, Jane. 1987. "Postmodernism and Gender Relations in Feminist Theory." *Signs, 12*(4) (Summer).

Palmer, Phyllis Marynick. 1983. "White Women/Black Women: The Dualism of Female Identity and Experience in the United States." *Feminist Studies, 9*(1) (Spring).

PART I:
CHALLENGES

—1—

War Bonds:
Love and Lust on the Battlefield

Mark Mardon

> Aeroplanes drone; the tack-tack of machine-guns breaks out. But no light that could be observed shows from us. We sit opposite one another, Kat and I, two soldiers in shabby coats, cooking a goose in the middle of the night. We don't talk much, but I believe we have a more complete communion with one another than even lovers have. . . . In a half sleep I watch Kat dip and raise the ladle. I love him, his shoulders, his angular, stooping figure. . . .
>
> from *All Quiet on the Western Front*
> by Erich Maria Remarque, 1929
> (The novel, about World War I, became a movie in 1930.)

All through my youth, and especially as a teenager in Arizona during the late 1960s and early 1970s, I was addicted to combat movies. Perhaps I watched war pictures because I wanted to be close to my father, who had been an Army sergeant in the Pacific in World War II, and my older brother, who was a Marine corporal (later sergeant) in Vietnam. I craved intimacy with those two most important males in my life. But since my father was emotionally distant and never related his wartime experiences to me, I was forced to imagine what his life in the military had been like. War movies allowed me to perceive him as a hero, as somebody I could love.

My brother, by contrast, had been my lover before shipping off to war at age nineteen. I had been his plaything, his sex toy—soft, pliable, eager to please, and too scared to snitch on him for using me as he did (though, in

---

A version of "War Bonds: Lust on the Battlefield" first appeared as "Comrades in Arms: Love, War and Remembrance," in *The Nation,* July 5, 1993, *257*(1), p. 8.

fact, I had no inclination to reveal our secret). He was my opposite, my shadow: tough, aggressive, fearless, given to petty thievery and other mischief, able to build radio sets, catch rattlesnakes, and fix cars. Yet he had also been my protector, teacher, and refuge, looking after me tenderly, shielding me from our father's alcoholic rages, taking me with him on countless car/camping trips to explore Arizona's scenic backcountry, a landscape I came to equate with freedom and eroticism.

After he left for Vietnam, my brother's absence left a huge emptiness in my life that I desperately sought to fill. War movies at least allowed me to live the fantasy that I knew what he was living through in that faraway land, that I was with him vicariously, in a place I could hardly imagine, with men as tough and handsome and heroic as himself.

Though I watched them almost obsessively, I gave war movies little thought, at least before becoming a more discriminating moviegoer in the mid-1970s. Prior to that, I never intellectualized my viewing habit, nor analyzed what I was consuming. I simply immersed myself in mindless watching, which led me to identify closely and uncritically with a certain generation of actors and movies: Gary Cooper in *Beau Geste* (1939); Clark Gable in *Run Silent, Run Deep* (1958); John Wayne in *Sands of Iwo Jima* (1949); Glenn Ford in *Torpedo Run* (1958); Frank Sinatra in *None But the Brave* (1965); Henry Fonda in *Battle of the Bulge* (1965); William Holden in *The Bridge on the River Kwai* (1957); George Segal and James Fox in *King Rat* (1965).

Later, even as I was becoming more conscious of the reasons for my peculiar fascination, I continued to indulge in combat films, especially those about Vietnam.

It was only after moving to San Francisco in the early 1980s, to come out and enlist in the gay liberation movement, that I began to seriously explore what about those movies had so captivated me. I realized, in retrospect, that for a young homosexual male growing up in the repressed social atmosphere of Arizona in the 1960s and 1970s, war movies (along with their kin, westerns and prison movies) were my primary glimpse of what it might be like to live in close confines and emotional intimacy with other males. To gain the contact I desired with other men, it seemed, I'd have to fight wars with them.

During my youth, it was chiefly in war movies that I saw societally accepted depictions of male bonding. Men in these movies were closer to one another—both physically and emotionally—than in any other type of film I had ever seen, or than I had witnessed in real life. Indeed, time and again in combat scenes, men injured on the battlefield fell into embraces that would have been impossible were it not for the chaos of battle shattering social taboos.

Of course, for someone eager for explicit depictions of homoerotic love, the representation of male-to-male bonding in war films was always extremely tentative, mediated, and frustrating. Yet, from my perspective, starved as I was for affirmation (however slight) of the idea that men could love one another with honor and dignity, homoeroticism pervaded almost every movie I saw that focused on soldiers, sailors, or airmen in combat.

Even now, watching *Sands of Iwo Jima* for the umpteenth time, it's easy to understand why, as a gay teenager with raging hormones, I would devour the film (and so many others like it). It's filled with half-naked men exercising, flexing muscles, showing off, sleeping together, talking quietly one on one, prodding and probing one another's personal lives, exploring psyches, provoking outrage and earning affection in equal measures, commiserating over guys' personal losses, celebrating their victories. It's a veritable lovefest.

"War may not be the most intimate human relationship," wrote philosopher/psychologist Sam Keen in *Faces of the Enemy*, "but nothing except love moves us to take others so seriously, to explore their mind, their motives, give them such intricate attention. Warriors and lovers have much in common. In fact, war might be seen as a kind of homosexual ritual, a kind of perverse love affair for men who cannot love unless they can hit." Keen observed that "the sexuality of the warrior is a blend of repressed homosexuality and phallic assertion" (1986:131)

The bonds between men serving in the military at wartime may be termed "comradeship" or something else, but chroniclers of war often testify to such unions being the single most profound relationship in their lives. Legions of soldiers returning from war have attested to the fact that, as one retired Army colonel in Colorado recently put it, "at the height of combat action, men don't fight for abstract ideals like love of country, apple pie, or motherhood. They fight, and die, for each other" (personal communication, August 1992).

As Philip Caputo wrote in *A Rumor of War*, the relationship between buddies in war is, "unlike marriage, a bond that cannot be broken by a word, by boredom or divorce, or by anything other than death" (1977:58). Similarly, Vietnam veteran William Broyles Jr., former *Newsweek* editor and creator of the *China Beach* television series of the 1980s, wrote that during his tour of duty, he had been closer to his combat buddy "than to anyone before or since. We ate, slept, laughed, and were terrified together" (1984:58). That is why, he added, when the war was over, "something had gone out of our lives forever, and our behavior on returning was inexplicable except as the behavior of men who had lost a great—perhaps the great—love of their lives" (1984:56).

If movies, novels, and soldiers' personal diaries come close to conveying the truth, all of the most sensuous experiences possible for a man seem to be concentrated and heightened in war. The stretches of tedium endured at peacetime are broken with climactic shock effect, the bullets flying, the bombs bursting with white light, the bodies blowing to bits. No greater, more powerful orgasmic experience could ever be hoped for.

It is what follows the orgasm, though, that is most significant. It is the moment of collapse, of release, of love for your buddies flowing forth in a great gush, the sharpest, most intense emotion a man can feel. And it is this very emotion that men in war appear to be seeking.

The archetypal scene of male bonding in war stories is the moment when the protagonist sees a buddy hurt or dying. That's when the hero holds or caresses his friend, lets his love for him flow out, touching him, brushing the blood from his lips, pressing his cheek against his friend's, watching the life going out of him, and loving him as he may never love a man again. For that moment on screen or in a novel, all other action recedes—even if a battle is raging all around—as all attention is focused on an instant of tenderness.

It happens in a flash in *Sands of Iwo Jima,* when a young soldier falls amid mortar blasts and machine-gun fire. Another soldier kneels over him to place his hand on his chest, feeling for his heartbeat. The camera closes in on the dead man's face, showing it in sweet repose, with full lips seeming to invite a final kiss. The lens then scans down the soldier's torso till it stops to close in on a book sticking out of the man's jacket pocket, the title prominently displayed: *Our Hearts Were Young and Gay.*

A tell-tale moment occurs in *King Rat,* a film set in a Japanese-run prisoner-of-war camp and thoroughly drenched in homoeroticism. George Segal, as the shrewd, calculating, self-centered title character, sits awkwardly at the bedside of his only true friend in the camp (British actor James Fox, who exudes a powerful, androgynous allure), who lies unconscious from a bout of gangrene. When no one in the barracks is looking, Segal's character, otherwise undemonstrative, unemotional, and "manly," yet clearly captivated by Fox's sensitive, sensuous character, allows himself to lay his hand tenderly on his friend's hand, leaving it there till the camera cuts away.

War breaks down society's most rigid taboos. It allows men to glory in death and destruction, to be violently aggressive. It also allows them to weep tears of love over the men who are their brothers, masters, the ones they would like to become. At times, it lets them be slobbering, dopey, idiotic fools over other men, the very image they shun in peacetime.

That, I imagine, is why my brother rushed off to war, and why a great many other men like him must have been similarly motivated, even if they're not aware of the fact.

If most men's homoerotic urges do not easily well up from the cellars of their unconsciousness, it is because they are too deeply buried among the casks and cobwebs of the human psyche, in the darkness and dankness where the memory of the species is stored. It is in that moldy memory where the homoerotic roots of war are to be found.

Man-to-man intimacy is crucial to a healthy male psyche. If continually suppressed, this psychological need becomes convoluted and emerges some-how—too often in some strange, twisted form—into consciousness. This emergence can amount to a psychosis, including the horror of war.

Psychologists tell us that a large part of what motivates men to fight is fear and suspicion of the unknown, along with the deep-felt urge to defend that which is known and loved. Armies are formed by men who love one another, either in abstract or concrete ways. In defense of their love, they fabricate myths about other men in other armies whose motives are unknown to them and who must be considered a threat. The threat conceived in the mind becomes real and tangible, as accusations are made and warnings issued. Guns are raised against abstractions, not against other men.

From core military units—the platoon or squadron, for instance—there develops an inevitable hierarchical command superstructure, with layer upon layer of bureaucratic insulation from the root of the structure. But no matter how large and unwieldy an army grows, its psychological foundation appears to remain the same: men eager to be with other men for love and protection of their own kind.

The year my brother went off to war, my parents divorced. I moved with my mother to a new city and a new life. After one or two brief visits, I was not to see my father again for nearly twenty-five years (until he and my mother remarried in March 1995). My brother remains in the Marine Corps, a highly seasoned noncommissioned officer. I have not seen him since one of his leaves of absence from the Vietnam War (where he voluntarily performed two tours of duty). Nowadays, if I do watch a war movie—and I'm rarely tempted to do so—I can't help but think of my father and brother at war, of how they must have interacted with their fellow soldiers, how they must have loved and been loved by other men during what likely were the most intense periods of their lives. I flash back on photographs of my father from his war days. I see his all-American athletic good looks, his incessant sexy grin, the seductive way he'd thrust out his hip as he posed for the camera. Dad's wartime buddies must have been captivated by his devilish, erotic charm, while other men may well have resented it. The barracks, ship holds, and tents they shared must have been charged. I recall, as well, images of my brother, how he resembled our father, had inherited Dad's roguishness and virility. I remember how so often at night in our room, on the top bunk, he held me, nearly crushing me sometimes, as he worked both of us to orgasm. How he must have longed to be in a barracks bunk, wrapping himself around a body tougher, more angular, more resistant than mine—the kind of bodies so blatantly on display in war movies.

REFERENCES

Broyles Jr., William. 1984. "Why Men Love War," *Esquire* (November), pp. 55-65.
Caputo, Philip. 1977. *A Rumor of War.* New York: Holt, Rinehart and Winston.
Keen, Sam. 1986. *Faces of the Enemy: Reflections of the Hostile Imagination.* San Francisco: Harper & Row.

2

Elegy for My Father's Dick

Carol Queen

Well, I guess it's good they married each other after all.
Shame to ruin two families with 'em.

> Carol's grandmother, on Carol's parents

My father is dead now, and finally, at such a nonnegotiable and some-how reassuring distance, I can acknowledge and mourn the lack of sexual pleasure in his life. It's not something I ever would have done when he was alive: while he was living, I did not support his sexuality at all. Rather, I regarded every evidence of it as ridiculous, if not threatening—to my mother, if not to me. Maybe it was the incest taboo, inherited from the Puritan, paranoid culture of the 1950s, the decade into which I was born. Maybe it was my shame in him, for he did not carry himself like the kind of man entitled to success or pleasure. Certainly, in my budding and then flowering sexuality, I felt his scrutiny and resented it. In short, if I ever thought about it at all, I probably figured he had had more sexual pleasure than he really deserved.

I don't mourn that he is dead, not at all. It's easier to love him from this distance, easier to see him as a sexual being, even easier to communicate with him (sure, it's a one-way street, but hardly more than when he was alive). But my father's sexuality is a living issue to me now, these many years after his death, even as I forget the way his voice sounded and have to squint in my mind's eye to remember the way he looked—not in the photos I have of him, but day to day: the father of my childhood, my adolescence, my early adulthood. I was twenty-seven when he died and he was sixty-two; he lived just long enough to collect one Social Security check.

I cherish the photos, though, oddly, most of the pictures I have of him were taken long before I was born. I have his Army portraits, taken during World War II and sent home for his mother to display; I have snapshots from

Korea. I even have photos of his girlfriends, nameless beautiful women who seem more elegant in their 1940s hairdos than young women are today—though I'm sure they struggled just as hard for their experience, their sophistication, as I had to a generation ago, and as just-adult women do now. I wonder if they loved him, desired him, fucked him, or if he kept their pictures in a lifelong bout of impotent wishful thinking, the way some men keep signed Polaroids of porno stars.

I am twice as old now as he is in some of those photographs. They picture the dad I wish I'd known, the one I can imagine I do know—better, really, than I know the dad who was really in my life. He had just changed his name from Bill to Max. He had grown a mustache. He, the eldest child in his family, must have hit adulthood running, proud to be sent off to war, the last one, perhaps, that most Americans believed in. In his photos there is a charm, an engaging light in his eyes as he smiles at the camera, that I never remember seeing when he was alive. I know he smiled that smile for the pretty women whose pictures he kept, meeting them in Boise, in Denver, in Paris.

He saved all the photos and letters the pretty women gave him, and all the letters and cards he got from my mother before and after they married. He saved an empty box of Trojan condoms, doubtless the first one he ever bought (or the Army issued). I found it packed away with the letters forty years later, when I cleaned out his storeroom after he had died. He must have used the condoms and kept the box as a talisman. He kept no talismans from his later life, certainly none that were sexual. I fancy I can relate to young Max's memento and the life he must have been living to be inspired to keep it. It is my talisman now, as I explore the erotic world around me, as he was doing then. It is also the most concrete thing that links me to that great ineffable, his sexuality. I possess nothing at all to link me to my mother's.

When my father was alive, I believed, against all evidence, that I ought to feel more solidarity, more intimacy and likeness, with my mother. When I was little, I was Daddy's girl, wanting to wear his clothes and go where he went. My mother did not like her life, and with the healthy good sense of a little child, I did not want to be anything like her. Later, when the good sense of everyone in my family had been slowly eroded through our proximity to one another, I believed my father was my enemy in the class warfare that was my young understanding of feminism. I don't know that my solidarity ever did my mother much good; in fact, it was my father who actively solicited my solidarity, but I could not give it to him, partly because I blamed him for everything that was wrong with my family.

That he might be caught in a sexist snare just as certainly as my mother, I did not consider until many years later. I was quite sure my mother should not have been a wife; that he should not have taken on the burden of being a husband was something I did not bother to wonder about. That he was unhappy, I knew, but I didn't stop to consider why. I found him overbearing and bossy, a sad sack, a boundary-free zone. His emotional need for me felt incestuous and dangerous. I hated him for wearing his emotions on his sleeve. In the evenings, when my mother had passed out from the bottle or two of wine she'd drunk since getting home from work, he would come to my room and tell me stories, revealing too much, trying to solicit empathy I did not want to feel. Most of his stories were from the years before I was born, happier years. I resented his imposing on me a better family history that I could not share. I didn't want to learn any history. I didn't want to go backward. I wanted to get out of there.

I was the only one at home with a sexuality that flowed unstoppered. He had married a woman—my mother—who had been molested as a child. He adored her, I think, in the early years of their marriage—they read Shakespeare aloud in the park and wrote each other tender letters. They didn't have children until they were in their late thirties (and if being husband and wife was bad for them, being parents was worse). But the molestation made her a time bomb set, not to explode, but implode. By the time I was very small, she was an alcoholic—though he didn't know it until I sat him down and told him. I was about twelve and had lived with her that way for years; I was astonished (and contemptuous) at how surprised he looked. He had blinkered himself so as not to see the contradictions in his home, his marriage. She hated sex, though she probably never told him so, and neither of them had enough information or could communicate well enough to process the messages they were sending and receiving when he reached for her and she rebuffed or suffered him.

She did not tell him about her history of molestation until she was over fifty. They had been married for twenty years. She waited to tell him until the perpetrator (a family member we had often visited) was dead. By then, their chances for reviving and relearning sexual passion were dead too. He was embittered, diabetic, sick, and maybe impotent. She was distant, fuzzy, a vagued-out shadow.

She did not tell me about her history until years later. By the time I heard and assimilated this source of misery that was not my father's doing, he was dead.

Now I think my father's bitterness and short temper were tied right to his dick. And I wish he had listened when his dick spoke to him. I've always viewed complaints that adultery breaks up families with a bit of bemusement: my family could have used breaking up, or, at the very least, the relief of sexual and emotional tension that adultery would have offered. But there are no signs that Dad ever followed his dick out of the house—he certainly didn't sneak out at midnight, as I did as a teen, to chase his hormones down the road. Husbandhood, fatherhood, manhood à la the Boy Scouts ("to be square," they boasted in their pledge, "and obey the Laws of the Pack")—he took these things seriously, and his belief in them helped make him miserable. His empty Trojan box proved too weak a talisman in the face of a couple of decades of undiluted *Leave It to Beaver* expectations, though he never let it go. I wonder if he ever took it out to look at it, to remember the days he had tried hard to tell me about, when he was young like me and really alive.

I know that there is still a sentiment, shared even by some men, that men have too much sexuality—too much desire, too much access to pornography and other forms of sexual entertainment. There is one theory that states that the rush of sexual arousal in a man mimics the rush of rage, of murderous intent. This posits that rage is the basic state, sexual arousal a later development that overlays animal fury, and this seems to me debatable. But if rage is really the primal and primary emotion, I believe sexual desire civilizes it. And, in fact, it could as easily be the other way around, the rage rush a substitute for subsumed sexual lust. There was certainly rage in my house, a kind that was tied in knots, never really dissipating. My father mourned his truncated sexuality by exploding, a culturally acceptable way for a man to mourn. He learned this at his father's knee, or with a pack of teenage boys, or in basic training. As a very small child, I remember him as gentle. But manhood is supposed to harden a man, and he did not have the support, the skills, the vision, to shake off this cultural imperative.

He certainly did not avail himself, for most of his life, of sexual entertainment. I found no stash of pornography with his Trojan box. But when he was in his fifties, he spent several Saturday nights at the local art house's Midnight Movies watching *Debbie Does Dallas* (1979) over and over again, or sometimes *Behind the Green Door* (1972). He tried to take my mother to a showing in hopes she would get turned on—what possessed him to do this, I cannot even fathom, though I see well enough the hope he had that something might break the ice that sealed her away from him. But *Behind the Green Door* was too much, and she clapped her hands over her eyes: "Take me out of here," she demanded, probably the only demand she ever made, "right this minute!"—and he had to lead her out of the theater as if she were blind, for she would not take her hands away from her face until they were outside.

I think he must have continued to find her beautiful, desirable. I think he conceived of that doomed, ridiculous charade to try to awaken her again into his princess, the woman with whom he had long ago read Shakespeare. To me, she grew ever uglier with the ravages of alcohol and an empty life, but perhaps he saw through it, or did not see it at all, and found her as beautiful as any Marilyn Chambers. There is a degree to which he was a dreamer, and as his life neared an end (and as his cock, affected by diabetes, ceased to function), they seem to have rediscovered a hint of the romance they had once had.

But that was the price—his cock—and the romance they regained was a shadow of the richness of love and erotic passion I would wish them, or any couple.

And then he died.

My father lived long enough to know me as a queer—he was, after some initial discomfort, as supportive as I could want a dad of a dyke to be. I think he was tickled that someone in the family had a sexuality, a shot at sexual happiness. He did not live through the transition in me that, in fact, his death helped to provoke: in the crucible of my therapist's office, I confronted him, mourned not his passing, but his life, and began the work of atonement for hating him and his bitterness. At first it was literal, sitting his shade on a pile of pillows, as if we were at Esalen or some other therapy retreat, and saying things to him, letting out emotions I'd guarded forever. Daddy, I hate you. Daddy, I love you. Daddy, I miss you—though the squeaky voice that said these things belonged to the little girl who'd begun to lose him early, before puberty arrived to abruptly finish the process.

But soon enough, the conversations I had in therapy sent up shoots in the rest of my life, and a different landscape took shape. I began to fuck men again. I went back to school. I studied sexology. I began to write. I fell in love with a man, then another (very different from, yet indubitably connected to, fucking them). And at least one profound difference separated the men I loved and love from my father: they were sexual men, lived in their bodies passionately, knew what they wanted, and arranged to have as much of it as they could.

I also became a whore—for money, as is almost always true, but also partly because too much of my understanding of men was tied up in the noose of my father's thwarted sexuality. I had little intimate experience with men who listened when their cocks spoke to them, no experience at all with men who valued sexual pleasure enough to pay for it.

Yes, it had to do with my dad, but not as simply as you would think. Reconciling myself with the dearth that was his sexuality, and my mother's, led me to explore all the paths they never could. I work at Good Vibrations, a women-run sex shop, now. It is remedial work for my soul when I sell a vibrator to a woman who has never had an orgasm. It is equally remedial when I turn a trick: I remember my father and his secret reliquary, the empty box of condoms. Like ashes, fragments of my mother and father are scattered everywhere. I struggle with them in myself, but mostly I meet them in others.

If I could—if he were alive today—I would take the two hundred dollars my favorite client leaves me after we tumble, joke, fuck hard, and toss away the carefully tied-off condom. I would call one of my colleagues, one of the bright, feisty San Francisco whores whose company I am proud to keep, hand her those same Ben Franklins, and send her to try to revive Max. (I still do not know how I would revive my mother, long-dead Ophelia, but I think my father could have been reached, even after decades.) I would tell her to honor him, all his skin, his cock, his spark of life. If only he could have been handed a mirror that reflected back not a husband or a father—roles that, in the end, fed him little—but a lover. If only he could have remembered how that felt before he died.

My mother? Oh, she's another essay. They both bought a bill of goods sold by a culture that did not value sexuality enough to equip them for it, but that mandated they grow up, marry, multiply. They didn't ever question this trajectory, and I am the result, questioning everything. They left me with old photographs and with their lives to untangle and make sense of, like balls of snarled string. I'm glad to be in the world, sure, and glad I escaped the trap that snared them. But I am dancing on their graves.

3

Making Room for Roy:
A Survivor's Journey to Wholeness

John Ward

My family was not one that enjoyed being together. Family vacations, holidays, even the dinner table were, more often than not, endurance contests. It's no surprise that we did not record our discomfort with a lot of family photos. So, imagine my amazement when I found out, after my father's death, that he was a secret archivist of my boyhood accomplishments. My taciturn, absent father had carefully, lovingly, set aside and meticulously preserved— without a word to me—a collection of the evidence of what made him proud of me—my Phi Beta Kappa key, my dean's list medals, a handwritten copy of the speech I made when I was high school valedictorian. Among these trophies, almost by accident, were some photographs, including one that was taken when I was four, hugging my best friend Butchie, as if my life depended on it, and a portrait shot taken when I was about ten.

These days, I look at those pictures a lot, especially the one of the ten-year-old. I framed it, and it hangs in the bathroom next to the mirror, and, somewhere between flossing and the worried quotidian self-inspection to decide if I'm cute or not, or old or not, I see this little guy, with his eyes filled with glint and wonder and a big excitement about life.

This picture of who I once was is my gateway into the land of many chances, where linear time means not much, and where much is possible. The picture takes me wandering, sometimes just lost, sometimes trying to make a map of from there to here, trying to find the evidence that proves that I am, at long last, not guilty of betraying my life, that the bitterness and rage that so often have seemed to overpower me are but clouds mirrored on the gold disk of my heart.

Such a gift this picture is, such precious evidence of a feeling state and self-perception, so different, so still remembered, so real to me. Shortly after that picture was taken, I was raped. His name was Roy; he was about forty-eight; I loved him very much. He had a black 1950 Plymouth coupe, and I remember with pleasure his smell as he sat in the driver's seat and I sat alongside of him as we rode around, going to fancy restaurants, getting to order whatever I wanted. I don't remember the first time he put his hands on me, or how many times it happened. I remember that I didn't like it, and that I didn't want to lose him, and that there had to be a way to have him without that. There wasn't, really, and this was a very hard lesson for a little boy.

At some point, Roy disappeared. He worked at the lunch counter of the drugstore where I was the delivery boy, and one day I went in and he wasn't there. They said he'd quit. I thought he'd come and find me, but he didn't. As I look back, I think what happened was he dumped me for a more accommodating older kid named Frankie, whom I also longed for in my ten-year-old heart. Anyway, I went looking for Roy. I rode my bike to where he said he lived, but there was no such number. But I didn't give up hope. I kept my eyes open, and, sure enough, one day I saw his car, as I always knew I would. I was with another kid, and we made Roy take us to a drive-in and buy us burgers and fries and milkshakes. Roy and I saw each other a few times again—no more sex; he didn't even try—and I was happy. It broke my heart when my father told us we were moving far away, and I had to say good-bye to Roy. I can't remember how I arranged our meeting—I didn't have his phone number or address—but I somehow found a way to say good-bye to this man. He took me to a park in his car and we sat there in the dark, and I cried my heart out. If I could have figured out a way to dump my family and stay near him, I would have, but my ingenuity didn't stretch that far, and I was left with a sadness that I could tell no one about.

When I said good-bye to Roy at ten, I was not old enough or wise enough to know that I would spend my life, or a big chunk of it, learning what it means to me to have been with him and to have separated.

We moved, I and my family and my dog Rockie, away from Roy, far away from the world of that bright-eyed ten-year-old. I didn't know that the desolation I felt in the brand-new, treeless, boring, lower-middle-class subdivision where my father plunked us down was due, in large part, to the fact that I had suffered a grievous erotic wound, an initiation that was premature and incomplete. I just knew that my young life hurt and that I felt it to be somehow my fault.

As puberty came, I moved more and more into isolation. What was left of the open-hearted Midwestern ten-year-old couldn't survive in the tougher New York City world in which I now lived. To survive, I found a new, more acceptable persona, one that would make me president of the eighth-grade class, senior patrol leader, the smartest kid in the class. Meanwhile, I thought a lot about what happened with Roy. I couldn't leave it alone. I needed to make sense of it, to understand what it was he wanted, why anybody would want to do what he did, why I couldn't just be with him. One night, when I was about twelve or thirteen, I found myself in bed with a younger boy who was staying over. As I rubbed against his sleeping body, I almost cried aloud, "I understand, Roy; now, I understand."

Though it makes no sense to my logical lawyer's mind, I now see that the process of coming to understand Roy meant, according to the inscrutable laws of these things, that in some way I became him. In some inescapable way, I was of his lineage. As joined players in a powerful act, we were bound together in an exquisitely complex exchange. It mattered not at all, for the efficacy and force of the exchange, that, when it happened, I was ten and "innocent" by any standard. The story would play out in a predictable way, and indeed it did. Maybe, everybody works out a story in his or her sexual life. Even in the most circumscribed cultures, there must be inner, private dramas camouflaged in the mating ritual. Me, I danced the steps that I learned from Roy and from my shame-based parents and from the Catholic church of the 1950s. Of course, I could see none of this back then. All I knew was that it hurt.

I got raped again when I was thirteen. Tommy was my age, bigger than me, strong, beautiful, and well-developed. He didn't have to take me at knife point, but he did. I suppose you could say that Tommy initiated me into puberty, embarking me on an unwinnable battle with desire, trying to stay pure, longing to love another boy in innocence, feeling that I was just as unworthy of such a gift as I thought Roy had been.

When I was fourteen, I managed my very own first seduction. Jim was a freshman, and I was a sophomore. With the same, almost preternatural competence that I had had around Roy, I managed to get Jim to room with me on a school trip and to somehow have it accepted by him and the other guys sharing the room that it would be good if my bed and Jim's were pushed together. It was no trick at all to get my hands on Jim, with the surreptitious energy that I had taken from Roy. I was as excited as I have ever been when, feigning sleep, he came in my hand. The next day he wouldn't look at me, and I was in despair. I had wanted only pleasure and closeness. What had I done? What had gone wrong? I wonder if Roy had felt like that.

Where does a teenage boy who loves other boys go with feelings like I had? If he's really lucky, he knows and trusts someone who helps him see that it is right and fitting, and oh so sweet, to follow one's heart's desire with honor, no matter what the world says. Someone who helps him see that he doesn't have to sneak or be ashamed of the love and pleasure he offers or seek it in an underhanded way. There was no one like that in my life, and the only place I could think to go was confession. The first priest I knelt in front of was an outraged old man who kicked me out of the confessional. So I found a more sympathetic priest—Paul. I was fifteen and pretty cute. Paul was a lot like Roy. He paid attention; he bought me meals, and alcohol, and cigarettes. Like Roy, he was physically unattractive to me, and I didn't want to have sex with him. Like Roy, he dumped me when I wouldn't put out.

Through all this drama, I managed to be valedictorian of my high school graduating class, vice president of the student council, star debater, an acolyte at mass, and be drunk every weekend and at least one night during the week. It drove me crazy, trying to figure out what was real, my achievements in the outside world or the prison in my mind.

It all came to a head my first year in college. There was this guy; let's call him Joe. He flirted with me outrageously in the dining hall where we sat together, behavior that was so unheard of in that barren world of early 1960s Catholic schools that it shocked and excited me. One Friday night, I came home early from the bar and went to his room. He was in bed, but he invited me to sit down and talk. As he pretended to slumber, my hand wandered. He had an orgasm, and I left wordlessly. The next Friday, I was back again. This time, Joe got off easy again, but I didn't. After he came, he pretended to wake up, and he called me a cocksucker and threw me out of his room. Somehow, I managed to go back and face him the next day. He told me that he was not going to report me because it would just hurt my parents, but that I was a sick guy. In my heart, I agreed.

I got through the rest of that year at college by drinking every day and hiding and going from priest to priest, telling my story, begging for a forgiveness that I was not able to accept, deep in the drama, feeling a level of chronic psychic pain that alcohol deadened. I even went to Paul, the priest from high school, but he was too threatened to respond in an authentic way. Neither Paul nor any of the others whom I went to could say the words that might have helped: "Fuck the Church. The Church for you is a bad mother, keeping you stuck in a world of sin and redemption, victims and perpetrators, guilty and not guilty. Come home to your body, to the way of your nature, to the desires that call you and that, in the end, are your path to wholeness." They couldn't say those words, and, probably, I couldn't have listened.

I carried Joe around, as I had earlier carried Roy, through my twenties. I tried the witchcraft of Freudian psychiatry, a new start in the Peace Corps in North Africa, and a couple of years on the street as a draft evader during the Vietnam War. In the midst of all that, in my midtwenties, I fell passionately in love with a young man from Tunis. I felt a love so big that it made me proud, and made me pretty much able to tell people what I was feeling, even though, back then, nobody really wanted to hear about a man loving a man. Hassine, my beloved, was straight; my love was a disaster. He wound up getting a gun and looking for me. I probably deserved it, considering some of the awful things I did to him, like trying to get him busted by Immigration. But, for all the craziness of that connection, I learned that expressing my longing opened me to life in a way that I had never known, and always dreamed of, and made me feel whole. I learned with Hassine that my heart could be full. I could be something other than a loveless clown, even if I was being a fool, even if I was loving a man who couldn't return my love as a partner. Later in my twenties, I loved a heroin addict, Junior, and we planned to run away together to Canada. Junior robbed me and tricked me, and we hurt each other. It didn't matter; my love gave me a sense of being part of the community of humans that I didn't have otherwise. I suspect that Roy felt that way too, if ever he loved.

In 1970, I stopped using alcohol and drugs, permanently, and I came out as a gay man. Who can explain this psychic shift? Suddenly, all the antiwar marches, the music of the Beatles, the heroism of the drag queens who took on the police at the Stonewall Inn, the momentum of my own journey—all of it came together to create enough heat and light and juice for me to transform. It took a very rough year of drying out and getting off drugs, but there I was, twenty-seven years old, miraculously drug free, openly gay for the first time, committed to life, in some ways alive for the first time. There were a lot of firsts in my late twenties and early thirties: the first time I had sex without being drunk or stoned; the first time I had sex in a bed; the first time I went to a gay bar; the first date; my first boyfriend, then my first lover. How strange and exciting for all that to be brand-new at thirty! I thought I had left Roy far behind as I learned how to fuck and get fucked by Don, a man whom I loved and who loved me.

Needless to say, my story followed me into my relationship. Transfixed as I was by my visions of heaven and hell, by my story of victim and perpetrator, guilt and innocence, I was far from fully available for the musky, messy sweetness of life in an adult relationship.

I was thirty-seven when Don and I parted. Over the next ten years, Roy, who had been there all along, gradually came out into the open. About a year after Don and I stopped being a couple, Steve came along. I still get a tightness in my throat when I think of him. Everything I ever hoped love would be, and he picked me. This blond god of the upper middle class, he was the young Lord Krishna, and I sprinkled rose petals around the bed he shared with me. When he left me, really and truly desolate, after a summer of love, the jig was up. The time was at last at hand to face the fact that my relationship with Roy was still alive in me. More than that—Roy himself was alive in me in some way that I had up until then neither understood nor attended to. Now he insisted in a voice I did not recognize, but could not ignore, that I hear him, understand him, and, yes, in the end, embrace him.

The first signs of Roy's continued presence were, like him, shadowy and oblique. The modest but steady succession of wonderful men who saw what I had to offer and liked it ended for a while. Frustration and doubt gave way to desperation, and my body felt strange to me as it began to change into middle age. My loneliness began to feel sometimes unendurable, and that terrified me. Even more frightening, I could no longer deny that, despite the real work that the gay liberation movement had accomplished inside me, I still had a core belief that my desire to connect, particularly with a man who was younger, was corrupt. I began to notice that when I tried to make contact with a man, I would avert my eyes and clench my teeth and my anal sphincter. Words that told me I was tainted goods flashed in my brain, varied enough in format to capture my ongoing attention, constant enough to hypnotize: old, fat, bald, ugly, clumsy. I could have been describing how Roy felt about himself, but somehow, I just couldn't see the connection.

About seven years ago, after yet another wonderful man left me, I spent two weeks on a silent meditation retreat, praying nonstop for sexual healing. About three or four months after the retreat, Roy suddenly reappeared, unmasked. One bright, sunny afternoon, a bodyworker whom I was seeing moved to touch my face, and I was back in the car with Roy, ten years old, terrified, and completely out of my depth. The work could begin.

*   *   *

The awareness that Roy was still living with me did not at first feel like good news. I had minor car accidents, got traffic tickets, fought powerful urges to strike out randomly at strangers. One particularly bad day, after a sudden, uncontrollable fit of weeping in a restaurant, I thought pretty seriously about trying to get hospitalized. I didn't, but I knew that I needed to make some big changes.

The first thing I did was quit therapy. I sensed that this part of the journey needed to be truly mine, made in the company of others, but authentically personal in a way that the constant cues of therapy and my responsiveness to them made impossible. This story was about my heart and my dick, and I knew that I needed to keep it that way if the process was to unfold as it was meant to. What did The Buddha say? I asked everyone in the world how to end suffering, and no one could tell me, so I had to learn for myself.

I found a group of men, gay and straight, who got together once a week in the context of self-help and simply witnessed one another as they shared amazing horror stories. I felt listened to almost for the first time, and was hearing almost for the first time, as transformation swelled proudly in my breast, sitting among these heroes and shamans. I found a book for male survivors of sexual abuse. I used to carry that book around like a shield.

Characteristically, I would leave it behind somewhere about four times a week. Sometimes traveling all the way across the city, I would go and reclaim it. I was not going to lose that book. I went and talked to the man who wrote the book. I remember bursting into tears when I heard his voice during the telephone on the initial phone call, and crying more or less nonstop through my talk with him.

The body that I hated for so long in my struggle to banish all memory of Roy has become my patient, faithful friend and ally, eager to teach me. My body that holds the memory mark of Roy's uninvited touch on my hurt thigh, the fear of intercourse in my stiff, ungiving back and tight hamstrings—this same body, in its resilient generosity, has helped me to look again at the story of Roy and John and to see it in a way that offers some real hope and possibility for John, and, yes, for Roy. My body says to me, "Let the wounds you took from Roy, Roy's wounds, the wounds that I bear, be your gift. Let them teach you to dance." I answer my body by surrendering it to yoga, to martial arts, to vigorous physical exercise, to massage and bodywork and sacred sexual intimacy, and to life in community.

Slowly, very slowly, with many setbacks, a new way of seeing myself, and Roy, emerges from my practice. Holding myself as a victim has always been my stash. It has been my hidden, broken place of authenticity, of real tears and secret joys, the place in me that was filled with innocent longing, as well as the place that felt so corrupt that it left me isolated and untouchable. I have guarded my story with my life. To watch it take shape, change, and blow away on the wind, to scatter it like the ashes of my dead parents: this has not been easy. But it has been necessary.

My contact with Roy was crushing and overwhelming and unquestionably damaging. At the same time, it is the particular way that I got initiated, and in that way, it is—hard words to say and hear, but true—a gift. Moreover, it is a gift that carries a responsibility to the giver, to Roy. When I began to write this piece, some months ago, it was with the intention of casting out Roy, and ridding myself of the feeling, carried from my experience with him, that my sexuality was that of a perpetrator and that my lovers were my victims. I now see that it is not possible to evict Roy, and, truth be told, I do not really wish to do so. Like any dance, the dance I learned to do with him can be graceful or clumsy, healing or toxic, or a mixture of all that and more. If I choose at this point to call it the dance of perpetrator and victim, I do a disservice to Roy and limit myself. There is no real freedom for me if I spend my life defining myself as not Roy. It is neither sick nor terrible nor dangerous for me to offer him love now. To extend to Roy my compassion and regard does not mean that I will impose myself on others sexually, start looking for teenage boyfriends, or passively suffer inappropriate advances. Quite the contrary—by honestly recognizing that we are connected, that no one is outside the web, I give my support to a healing process that softens my experience of the world and makes me less of an aggressive force.

I have known for a long time in my work as a lawyer that the adversarial model of dealing with sexual abuse simply does not work. It feels like the beginning of great liberation to realize that the same is true in the life of my soul. There is a way for me to live as a good sexual citizen, and even to wear the smile of satisfied desire, but only if I am willing to love Roy and to accept the lessons that he has to teach. The work of doing that is the hardest I have ever done. The way constantly curves back on itself; hope fades from sight often; my longing for love and intimacy often seems doomed to frustration, overwhelming me and anybody who might possibly be available. But there is no turning back, and no more turning my back on Roy.

—4—

Out of Isolation

Frank Moore

A mat is on the otherwise bare performing area. Harsh bright lights. Jim lies in his world of the mat.

I lie here in my universe of the mat, my bed. I always have been here, lying in my universe forever, forever. My mat, my pillow, my sheet, my blanket . . . for countless force-fed meals, enemas, baths, shaves, haircuts, pissed-on sheets . . . many, many harsh-lighted days, many, many semidark nights. Outside my universe there are bony fingers, blotch-skin creatures. Sometimes they invade my universe . . . the sickly sweet-smelling ones. They "take care of me" . . . they handle me like they handle my pillow. Their voices are high, loud, flat. Sometimes they lie on beds beside mine, moaning and crying for alone many many, then they get quiet and others of them carry the still ones away. There are always new ones, but they are always the same. There are different bony fingers who invade my universe, who strip me, probe me, stretch me until it hurts . . . do strange things to me, like rubbing ice on my body then brushing me hard. They talk to me in funny ways . . . loud and flat. They say, "We are doing this for your own good." They don't think I understand what they are saying. I don't understand most of their words. But I understand enough. I understand I am not a Mister, a Mrs., a Miss, a Nurse, a Doctor. I understand I am not bony fingers. They can keep their universe of bony fingers. I am not going out of my universe of the mat. I understand enough. A long long when I cried out, they made me numb. I do not like being numb. In my universe of the mat, I am not numb. But they said crying out was not "appropriate behavior." I do not think appropriate behavior is good.

Everything that is not appropriate behavior makes me feel. But I understand enough to stop crying when the bony fingers are around. Stop making any

"Out of Isolation" first appeared in *The Cherotic (r)Evolutionary,* April 1999, *1*(8).

sound, any move when they are around. They stopped making me numb. I understand enough. I discovered a way of rubbing myself that makes me warm, makes me feel good. Bony fingers slapped me away from feeling good. Not appropriate behavior. I understand enough. I do appropriate behavior in the harsh light when they are around. I am still, quiet. In my universe of the mat. I do not even look into their world. I am busy creating within me. But when the harsh light goes and the semidarkness comes . . . when only the still or moaning bony fingers are around . . . I move, I laugh, I cry, I rub my body and good feeling comes. Not so loud or so much that the harsh light, the bony fingers, and their numbness come back. But just enough. And by rubbing, I know I am not bony fingers.

In the harsh light, they treat me just like my pillow. They change me just like they change my pillow. Always fast, like they need to move on. Sometimes, the special bony fingers, the prodders, stand over me and say I should come into their universe, what they are doing to me will help me. They talk like they talk to my pillow. Why should I want to go into their world of grays, where everyone wears white? In my universe of the mat, I lie on smooth, warm softness and create the brightest colors and the sweetest sounds to surround me. But I am not worried. Bony fingers never really believe I ever can enter their universe.

I only wish I was not the only soft fingers. . . . I wish there was another soft fingers in my universe of the mat . . . someone to share in the bright colors and sweet sounds . . . someone I could laugh with, cry with, move with, share good feeling with . . . someone who would be with me on the mat, touch me not like touching my pillow, not like pulling things out of me or to make me different. But just because we are the only soft fingers in the universe of the mat.

There is a new prodder. Do not look at bony fingers. But catch sight of same white. Miss Roberts talking to a pillow called Mr. Merrill. Same words about "to make you better." But sound of voice is somehow different, softer. The touch is still changing the pillow of me. But not bony fingers! I sneak a peak. Same white, but different. The skin is soft like my skin. The smell is almost like my smell. Almost enough to try to open my universe to this new soft fingers. But words came, the same words as bony fingers. The prodding soft fingers strips me bare just like she is changing the pillow of me. Easier to probe my pillow of a body. The prodding fingers does the same hurting "make you better" exercises on me as the other bony fingers before. And then the going somewhere else fast. And the touching the pillow of me, instead of touching me.

When the soft fingers and the harsh light were gone, I cried louder than before. I do not care if they make me numb. Maybe numbness is better if soft fingers are the same as bony fingers; if soft fingers also want me to go into gray and white, if soft fingers does not want to be with me, then numbness is better.

Soft fingers keeps coming back. At first, rushing to somewhere else, trying to pull me into the gray universe. I know how to fight against that bony fingers trick. But I like her soft warm skin touching me . . . like my soft warm sheet under me. Sometime soft fingers forgets about helping me, about making me a better person. For that moment, we are the only ones in the universe . . . together. Then soft fingers remembers the bony fingers and starts touching me like a pillow again.

But the moments of being together grow. I like when she forgets and makes mistakes and comes closer into my world. I like when she just sits on my mat . . . on our mat . . . and just looks at me, just listens to me. I feel more and more like I can show her my moves, show her my sounds. I like when soft fingers became Jane and I became Jim. I like when Jane just lies on the mat and we just look at each other, listen to each other, even when we really don't understand what meaning . . . but we feel. I like it when Jane starts making her own noises, not just bony words. I like when Jane holds my hand. I like when Jane comes into my world of dim light, when she wears colors bright, soft, smooth flowing . . . not bony fingers white . . . and even her hair is flowing strangely soft. I like when Jane comes wearing the colors soft even in the harsh light. I like when Jane makes the harsh light go away for a while, when Jane rocks me, when Jane rubs my head. I like when Jane slowly takes all the colors off. She is soft everywhere. She lies next to me on the mat. She makes soft sounds and soft moves, just like me. She is just like me now. Two soft fingers on the mat. I like when Jane lets me rub Jane's back, when Jane calls me Jim. I like it when we are in our universe of the mat sharing not appropriate behavior . . . laughing, crying, making good feeling come. Rocking or holding hands made different good feelings come together, making soft sounds together, together making good feelings come.

But suddenly Jane was gone. I was alone in happiness. Jane would come back into the happiness with me on the mat. So I was happy.

But when Jane came the next day, she was in bony white. Jane had become like bony fingers again. She said what we were doing was not appropriate behavior. She used words like romance and sexual that I did not understand. Jane left. The numbness came back without the bony fingers giving me anything.

Jane came back as bony fingers. I kept rising out of the numbness in hope whenever Jane came, but then fell deeper and deeper.

Jane came. I could not hold the crying back. I cried in the harsh light. Then Jane cried too. She made the harsh light go away. She came back into our universe of the mat and rocked me. Jane told me to teach her the noises and the moves of our universe of the mat. Now I have another soft fingers, Jane, on the mat, in the universe with me, together with me.

Together we can expand the universe beyond the mat. Jane can bring other soft fingers in. The bony fingers begin to fade. I can see, begin to see colors beyond the mat, begin to hear laughter beyond the mat. Jane says she and I together will explore the universe that is outside. She and I are happy.

5

Mapping My Desire

Sandip Roy

They didn't even kiss on Indian cinema. The lovers would draw closer and closer. The camera would zoom in. The audience waited with bated breath. The hero swooped down for the kiss. The camera skittered away to show nodding flowers and cooing birds. The shrill voice of the female playback singer burst into tremulous song. The magic moment was over.

The old movies had The Woman and The Other Woman—the kind you sowed your wild oats with. The Woman was demurely dressed, often in light colors, to symbolize her chaste beauty. The Other Woman wore dark clinging dresses with plunging necklines. She smoked cigarettes and had names such as Miss Rosie and Miss Lovely. She danced in the dens of evil smugglers—her padded bosoms heaving, her sequined skirt flying up to show her hefty thighs. Men growing up in India were torn between these two poles. They knew they were supposed to marry the virtuous woman in her pale saris. But oh, when the music started and the vamp wiggled onto the screen, they couldn't help throwing money at her. I was even more confused. I was interested in neither woman. I was ogling the hero. But all the heaving breasts and pouting lips kept getting in the way.

The problem with Indian cinema was the hero did not have to be handsome or young. Or more accurately, he could go on being a hero long after he was neither handsome nor young. So while each year seemed to throw up a fresh crop of nubile heroines, I was growing up with some of the same heroes my parents had seen on-screen. A popular matinee idol apparently buttoned his collar to hide the signs of age creeping up his neck. Another one wore a toupee. And, a third gave up a losing battle against his paunch. It didn't matter—they were men.

"Mapping My Desire" originally appeared as "Mapping My Desire: Hunting Down the Male Erotic in India and America," in *Looking Queer: Body Image and Identity in Lesbian, Bisexual, Gay, and Transgender Communities,* edited by Dawn Atkins, published by The Haworth Press, Inc., Binghamton, NY, 1998, pp. 271-275.

"Hmmm," said my great-aunt peering at the new baby, "he will be dark."
"Well, at least he is a boy," said my aunt. "It doesn't matter so much."
The market was full of herbal pastes guaranteed to make my sister fairer.
"Don't go out in the sun like that," admonished my mother.
"Try this new cucumber paste," suggested my aunt.

I, on the other hand, was a boy and my parents were putting me through the rigorous manly paces of tennis and swimming—all guaranteed to burn my skin a dark brown. But as long as I studied engineering or medicine it did not matter. Not that men were devoid of all standards of beauty. If a man managed to be tall and fair, he was automatically considered handsome as well—sort of a package deal. We all knew this harping on fair skin was archaic and nonsensical, a ridiculous hangover from a colonial past. In the abstract, we could theorize about how foolish it was. In practice, every Sunday, the newspaper matrimonial ads would be offering "Fair, 5′3′′, educated (MA), slim" women to doctor/engineer husbands. The darker ones were described as having "lustrous" complexions. The ones that said nothing about complexions tried to compensate with litanies about singing abilities and domestic skills.

Everyone knew the British had imposed a whalebone corset of Victorian morality around our hot-blooded, tropical selves. Before the British came, women did not wear blouses with their saris. The more diaphanous and sheer a sari was, the more its worth. The British, shocked at such tropical licentiousness, brought in blouses and petticoats. Everyone knew that our old texts and sculptures were replete with illustrations of sex in every possible form and permutation. Yet even today, India as a nation is not ready to lift the antiquated 100-year-old, antisodomy law that the British imposed on us and have themselves revoked in Britain. We know what we once had, or at least have some idea of it, but we have become too used to living in our corset.

In the West, for better or for worse, the media have in the last few decades produced images of desirability in males just as they have always done for women. Those Calvin Klein and Soloflex ads are probably in large part responsible for men feeling the need to go to health clubs and strap themselves into Nautilus machines and heave and pump and check the mirror every day for the first signs of a budding muscle or flattening abdomen. In India, we laughed at men who looked into the mirror too often. The only male models I could identify were the Wills Filter man (a ruggedly handsome type who drove Jeeps and smoked Wills Filter cigarettes) and the Zodiac man (who posed wearing only Zodiac ties). Apart from a few coat-hanger types who modeled what was always called "suiting and shirting," the only other men were mustachioed ones who marveled at their wives' cooking with XYZ brand of sunflower oil.

In India, the family was the most important institution; it dominated our lives and determined their course. For me, being gay was similar to betraying the family. It wasn't their rejection I feared; it was more whether my father would be able to hold his head high again. What would the neighbors say? Being gay was almost an act of selfishness—after all your selfless parents did for you, is this their reward in their old age? Coupled with the shame of being gay was an embarrassment about desiring men. Desiring men not for the jobs they had, not for their economic potential, but for their male beauty. It had been branded into our heads that beauty was a word that went with females, sunsets, and paintings. Beauty was an "unmanly" thing for men to concern themselves with. And here I was, a little freak, turning around to look at men on the street, missing my stop on the bus so I could follow some stranger a little while longer.

It was uncharted territory—this wilderness of male eroticism. But I was learning to look, to draw my own maps, and to chart my own desire. I was looking at college boys in faded jeans and the way the jeans clung to their asses. I was looking at those grainy ads of long-haired men in old tattered copies of *Rolling Stone* at the United States Information Services library. I was looking at the vegetable sellers and their sweaty bodies stained teak brown by the sun. I remember the boy bathing at the tube well on the street—the coppery brown slopes of his back and shoulders, the hard wet planes, the sleeping muscles in his arms, and the surprising fullness of his chest—clad only in a pair of faded torn underpants, his sex straining the threadbare fabric. How acutely I memorized the grace of his interlocking muscles as he poured a bucket of water over himself and his hand with those thick, coarse fingers burrowing under his pants to soap himself. His skin wet and brown, his hair in his eyes, the ballet play of his muscles as he vigorously rubbed himself dry—he remains frozen in my memory in an electric shock of unabashed youth.

It seemed to me that just as I needed guidelines in every sphere of life, so I needed pointers in my desire. Were hairy chests sexy? Dark skin? Mustaches? Recently, I came across an old cardboard box stuffed with the scraps of images I had torn from magazines—an underwear ad, a group of laughing youths in swimsuits advertising some cola, a row of bare-chested hill tribals in shorts—these were all I had by way of building blocks for the construction of desire.

I thought that in America it would all be different. We would know—the papers, the magazines, the gay porn would tell us what was sexy, what was not. And I found they did—only too well. After countless interchangeable films of smooth-skinned boys with brown-blond hair and tan lines on their butts fucking each other, I was ready to turn back to my cola ads for stimulation. And, what there was by way of erotic images for Asian men was corroded by the dubious politics behind their creation. Who made it and for whom? Was this exoticization or plain exploitation?

I remember a little glossy book of photos of a young Indian man on the beach. His name was Arjun, and he emerged from the ocean, wet and glistening and inviting. It was one of the first unabashedly male-erotic images I had seen of an Indian man in an Indian setting. Yet, because the pictures were taken by one Wolf Nikolas, about whom the book said nothing, they raised many disturbing questions. Who was Wolf Nikolas? How did he get Arjun to shed his clothes for the camera? Did Arjun know his wet body was on sale in every gay bookstore in the West? Later, I found that Arjun was well aware of what he was doing and had also secured Nikolas's help to emigrate from India. But every time our desirability is framed in the lenses of someone from outside our culture, these prickly questions will arise and haunt our desire.

So I was quite pleased to see a calendar on Asian men by an Asian photographer. Here at last we were on safe ground; we could unabashedly wallow in our desire without fearing we were playing into the hands of colonialist, exploitative, keeping-Asian-boys-as-pets, white men. The pictures were superb—buff Asian men liberally coated with glistening oil dallied in various stages of undress on rocks, under palm trees, and in gardens ablaze with tropical flowers. The foreword explained that this calendar hoped to shatter the stereotype of Asian men as passive, geeky nerds with smudged glasses and hunched shoulders. Another Asian man leafing through the calendar with me exclaimed, "Wow, these pictures could be right out of some fancy Western catalog. I mean these models are just as good." He meant it as a compliment, but it sent shivers down my spine. I looked at those pictures again; this time I noticed the perfectly straight aquiline noses and the smooth, tanned, oiled skins. I had hoped that by controlling the camera we would be controlling the definition of erotic. But that definition had been set long ago by others; these pictures were just trying to live up to it.

While the high-society models on the catwalks of Bombay aimed for the high cheek-boned, long-necked look of their counterparts in the West, in films, especially in South Indian cinema, the women often tended to be well-padded. That is how a woman's appeal was defined there—big-breasted and wide-hipped. While it is true that these women had no say in the way their sexiness was being defined for them, at least that definition came from the land and was not pirated out of glossy, foreign fashion magazines.

I saw a line drawing of two men sitting in a field. One was sitting behind the other, his hands resting on the other's shoulder and thigh. The men wore *dhotis,* which had ridden up to their thighs. They had turbans on their heads. In the distance was a little village temple with a three-pronged *trishul* spire. I looked at their turbans, the plain bangles called *karhas* round their wrists, and the amulet around the one's neck. They showed no distended organs as with the drawings of Tom of Finland. Yet the picture was unbelievably sexy. They were sexy because of the *dhoti,* the *trishul,* the *karha*—small everyday objects, so intrinsically Indian, it is difficult to find words for them in English. As with those objects, the eroticism in the image was untranslatable.

In the gay magazines of the West, which I lusted for in India, there are many sexy men. The pictures are artfully taken; the bodies have been sculpted in gyms. The pool or the beach the men are posed near could be anywhere. In the effort to make their appeal universal, their sexiness has been deodorized of the piquant smells of their particular cultures. They have been carefully deculturized and homogenized in the American melting pot.

But the men in my drawing are unmistakably Indian. Their sexiness stems not from their looks; they are not even naked. They are erotic because to look at them is to remember the hot, unrelenting, blue sky of an Indian summer. To look at them is to remember those lazy, sluggish, summer afternoons spent lolling half-dressed on the bed waiting for the first dark, pregnant clouds of a thunderstorm. I can once again feel the first fat, warm drops of rain. I can smell the rich, earthy odor of the parched ground as it soaks up the rain. I can taste the sticky juice of the mango running down my chin.

These men are exciting because I recognize them. They are exciting because they have not been stripped of their cultural context. They are exciting because their Indianness has not been carefully airbrushed out of them in order to make them "sexy." In fact, they are sexy *because* their roots are showing and the artist, instead of being embarrassed by them, has chosen to celebrate them. And in doing so, he has given me the image that I have been searching for—Indian *and* erotic—unabashed, unapologetic, uncensored.

6

Razors and Roses

Tommi Avicolli Mecca

whatever it is
it's still stirring
been stirring for too many years
been churning and sometimes chewing away
at what remains of me
there are feelings left
they bark bite
hissss
at inconvenient times

suddenly twelve again
and hiding in the back of the yard
thinking of pretty space boys
in ships made of wishes
I lose myself in their long black hair
later it's Joey shirtless and bronze
at his window across the alley
beckoning me with almond eyes
and a hand that slides slowly down his body
to a place I can't see
or Ant'ny in the dark one night
so scared after touching his cock
I take a long bath to scrub off the sin
I can't confess it
convinced God the father can never forgive
such a heinous crime
like Papa never forgives me
for running off that afternoon he tries
to teach me to walk like a man

only what's biting now is not the
pain of longing for boys I could not have
or Papa wanting a son I could never be

it's waking in a New Jersey bed
with a man I barely know
living here to escape Papa's rage at finding out
I'm nineteen and queer
the August sun's between my legs
leaving puddles of blood
Someone's fixing his tie in the mirror
"Am I gorgeous or what?"
I'm a lump of panic
"You'd better get a move on if you want a ride"
I scream from the bathroom: "Take me to the hospital!"
staring at brown red splotches
Rorschach nightmare all over the toilet paper
"It's only a cut," Someone's saying
only a cut
the day the kid in homeroom stabs me with a pencil
yelling: "I hate faggots"
too scared to see the nurse
that night refusing dinner
hiding in my room
hoping the lead reaches my heart
and bursts the damn thing
I'm ready to die

in New Jersey on the toilet
remembering flesh pounding into me the night before
the way Someone laughs when I say
"You're hurting me"
"He's playing hard to get," he tells a neighbor
he invites to join in
I want no part of this threesome
I say, "I'm going to bed"
But drunk they follow me into the bedroom
Someone climbs on me
"Take it in your mouth"

it's not Ant'ny
not the sweet taste of a young boy
not a classmate saying, "Come on, let's do it again,
nobody's watching"
though God is always watching
the nights and days large with him
I want to take Ant'ny again
I want him to hold me in a million arms
but I'm racing to my house whispering over and over
out of breath to God the father and creator
I'm sorry I'm sorry

to Someone that August night
I'm sorry, it hurts
he doesn't stop
like God never stops punishing me

most of my life longing for boy body next to mine
lying in a field or by a river
sun in our faces
no words
needing to strip and crawl into this other flesh
surrender
but I fly the white flag too many times
when the words inside are sharp
I swallow them every time
saying "yes, sister"
when she tells Mamma I act too much like a girl
I want to spit these words into her face
and watch her blood form rivers down her cheeks

my cheeks to the air
"Constipated for days," I tell the doctor
"I had to force it out this morning"
protect the man who says he loves me
protect the boy who stabs me with a pencil
I am always falling or colliding into things
they stop asking
they know
everyone knows

no one knows that at eighteen
Sal tells me we can't do it no more
for months wrestling on the kitchen floor
while his family's out
touching hard-ons and each other's lips
when he says we have to stop seeing each other
I sail a razor blade on red waters across my wrist
panicking and running out of the house to walk
the night like some damn zombie
intent on fading into oblivion
but the space boys let me lick their hairless bodies
and lay my head in their dark crotches
they're purring and smelling of roses

there are no words left
no feelings
I am sitting here at a computer screen
that leaves scrambled messages
there are ghosts in my attic
an occupying army
I know every soldier's face
when I hear them call my name
I fall to my knees
boy flesh to be beaten and used

this time
I put razor blades in my teeth

7

Movie Stars and Sensuous Scars

Steven E. Brown

Valentine's Day, 1992. Seven of us gathered in our living room, in front of the fireplace, as Lillian and I celebrated the formal union of our lives together, in a quiet, romantic wedding ceremony.

Not quite a year earlier, we went out for the first time. It wasn't a date. I was still new to California and hoping to make more friends. We went out to dinner. And talked with ease. Much of it about relationships. We were both recently removed from entanglements more problematic than fun. We shared that neither one of us ever wanted to get married again. In fact, we weren't even certain if we wanted future relationships. And if we did get involved, we most definitely did not want to live with the other person. We were both quite clear on that point. We talked about our dream houses. They were exactly the same. Right down to living by ourselves. Alone. And we liked it that way.

A month later, we were living together. A year later, we sat in front of the fire in our cozy living room getting married. In so many ways, we are your average couple of the 1990s, born in the early 1950s. Like other baby boomers, we married in our early twenties and divorced in our early thirties. Between us, there was one child—perhaps less than average. We both worked. We struggled to survive on the incomes we generated. We liked similar music and movies and meals. We were comfortable in similar social situations.

But we were also unlike many of our peers. We both had significant disabilities. Lillian used either a crutch or her wheelchair to get around. She has this mysterious, exotic disability that doesn't have a name. Born with dislocated hips and hyperelastic joints, she's had over twenty disability-related surgeries and spent about seven years of her life in hospitals. She has plenty of scars to show

"Movie Stars and Sensuous Scars" first appeared in *MAINSTREAM: Magazine of the Able-Disabled,* February 1997, *21*(5), pp. 26, 28, 31. It also appeared in *Voyages: Life Journeys*—Poems by Steven E. Brown, published by the Institute on Disability Culture, Las Cruces, NM, 1996.

for it. The arthritis that results from her condition causes her lots of pain—to which I relate. My disability, Gaucher's disease, a genetic, metabolic condition, showed up first when I was six. I am missing an enzyme that breaks down fatty cells. In my case, the cells that don't disperse wreak havoc throughout my body. I have broken just about every bone you can think of—some of them often. Pain and disability is part of our everyday lives.

Movement of any kind is often a challenge. When Lillian moves, she will sometimes come to a complete stop. All she has to say to me is "my ankle." I wait. I know that eventually the ankle will do whatever it must do and she will be able to move again. Other people are startled. Why don't I do something? What can they do? People want solutions. We are much too hurried to await the rhythms of our bodies. We, too, are impatient. But we also know there is nothing to do but wait. So we do.

This dissonance impacts every arena of our lives. Sometimes, more often as we age, sexual contact presents difficulties, which is unfortunate because Lillian is one of the sexiest people I know and easily the most compelling, desirable lover that I've had. When we make love, in whatever fashion, she is all there, and I have learned things about myself that I never knew before— how sensitive my nipples are, how exquisite it feels to have her fingers, her tongue, playing with their points.

Writing, even thinking aloud, about sexual play demonstrates growth. I recall a moment of disbelief more than twenty years ago. I'm in my late teens and dating the girl who would become my first wife—the person with whom I lost my virginity. She says she just had the most amazing experience. There's some guy in one of her classes who's doing a survey about people's experiences with masturbation. While walking across the college campus, stopping whomever he might encounter, he talked with a guy who claimed he had never masturbated. The surveyor didn't believe the guy, but he was insistent. My wife-to-be didn't believe it either, until I said I was that person, and I never had masturbated.

Not that I didn't like fondling myself, holding my penis until it swelled with male lust. But I had never gone beyond that moment. Never come. In fact, I had several experiences with intercourse before achieving my first orgasm.

Somehow I had grown up a prude. It doesn't really make any sense. My family is not particularly prudish. But I was, and to a degree still am. I've had to make conscious choices to overcome a shyness about my body, about touching and being touched.

Don't get me wrong. I like sex—since that first moment of feeling another's body, her sweat, her smell, her hair. My first wife and I were together for about a decade. The sex was good. When we parted, I missed it. Since she had been my only partner, I was still shy about looking for other partners. My prudishness reasserted itself.

Older, I believed that one of the ways to reestablish some of the self-esteem of a lost relationship was to plunge (figuratively and literally) into another's arms—to show that it could be done. I was in a group for people newly separated. I linked with another member. We went out a couple times. We had sex. I was disappointed. Sex without passion generated from more than two bodies meshing together did not satisfy me. Maybe it was my old prudery, maybe my personality, but I listened to my heart. I looked for more than one-night stands.

My ex-wife and I divorced for many reasons. One had to do with my awakening disability consciousness. Not my disability—that had always been there—but an awareness of my body; my disability had been expressed in the context of the negativity and humiliation that matched the stereotypes of the body beautiful being the ideal. That was beginning to change. I became alert to my body as a magnificent example of the resilience of humanity. My atrophied muscles, which had shamed me since my teenage years, no longer seemed a badge of failure. My body had survived surgeries and inflammations and many broken bones—and worked. In fact, I began to learn that, not only did I like my own body in ways I could not have dreamed of before I came to this disability consciousness, but I was considered by many to be sexy. Oh, I had been called handsome for years, but I dismissed it: flattery from family and friends. But when I started to like my body, I started to believe people were telling the truth. And if I could be sexy with this mangled body, perhaps others could be as well.

I started to seek women with disabilities to date. There was a level of communication that we did not have to establish with each other that always occurred with nondisabled people. Instead of awkwardly learning about my disability, we could immediately ask about each other's physical limitations, needs, and desires.

I dated a woman with a hearing impairment and another with cystic fibrosis and another who used a wheelchair. Sex with each of them was good. I no longer worried about the inadequacy of my body. I became comfortable with myself.

When I met Lillian, I had more confidence in my ability to be a lover. But, I had much more to learn. Although I'm the writer, it's ironic that I'm the one writing this essay. She's the expert. She's the one who has taken courses on sexuality and disability and taught it all over the world.

One exercise she does is to ask an audience to imagine the perfect lover. How tall? How short? How round? How narrow? What is the color, texture, length, feel, and smell of the hair? Is the face narrow or round? What color are the eyes? Are the eyebrows thick, thin? What is the shape of the ears? She continues working down the body in similar fashion. She gets very specific and often shocks people when she asks them to imagine the lover's pubic hair and genitalia. Is the hair thick or thin? Coarse or smooth? If it's a man, is the penis long? Thick? Circumcised? If a woman, are the walls of the vagina large? Small? Is the hair neatly shaved and groomed? Untouched? She continues asking specific questions down to the toes. When she finishes, people have a specific fantasy image of a physically perfect lover. She then asks the audience to think about how many people they have been attracted to who fit their descriptions of their imaginary lovers. Usually not too many. These days she uses me as an example to say that she never thought she would be attracted to a tall, slender man. My own fantasy lover has always been a woman with red hair, yet I've only dated one such woman in my life.

Our images of perfection come from magazines, books, movies, television, which are themselves fantasies. How many of us have seen our movie screen idols up close? If you have, you know that most of the time they do not meet their screen images of perfection. Somehow we forget about tricks of makeup, photography, editing, brush overs, and all kinds of techniques that make us look different from reality. Yet these figures of make-believe become our sexual icons.

People with disabilities who have obvious and subtle differences from our movie star fantasies often feel left out in the cold when it comes to looking and feeling sexy.

When I train, I sometimes ask for positive and negative stereotypical descriptions of people with disabilities. I get long lists. Most often, sexuality is not on either list, until I ask about it. We have bought into the stereotypes ourselves that we are asexual or hypersexual, but very often we forget to think of ourselves as sexy.

Many of the most attractive, sensual people I know are ones with disabilities. I think of a woman I once longed for. She had gorgeous brown hair with lots of curls and a curvaceous body. The fact that she was paralyzed made no difference. After months of working up the courage, I finally asked her out. We met for dinner and I was ecstatic. We seemed to have a good time. As we said goodnight, I asked her out again and she agreed. She never showed up for that second date. In fact, she didn't remember it. As it turned out, she was probably drunk or drugged the whole time we were out. She barely recalled that we had had a date. I still found her physically attractive, but I no longer had a desire to date her. Her disability didn't get in my way. Her lifestyle did.

I share this story because what it says to me is that people with disabilities are like everyone else when it comes to love. We all need and want it. We search for romance in a variety of ways. Sometimes it works; sometimes it doesn't.

Disability, in and of itself, is neither a deterrent of sexual longings nor any kind of automatic repellent against prospective suitors. People with disabilities, like everyone else, desire romance and love, touching and feeling. Some people, I suppose, would be less surprised to discover we are sexual and romantic beings than they would be to consider us desirable. But, if we would spend a moment to think about standards of beauty, we would realize they can change drastically from generation to generation, society to society, or culture to culture. In late-nineteenth-century America, for example, a beautiful woman was generally far heavier than today's slender models. Clothes, hairstyles, skin tones, and other characteristics of beauty have changed often during my relatively short life span.

Some individuals with disabilities exude sensuousness and sexual desirability more than their nondisabled counterparts. Some don't—just like intelligence, athleticism, creativity, and all of life's characteristics.

About a year ago, I met a woman at a workshop. Shortly afterward, we met again at a national conference. One of the highlights of this annual conference is a musical social. As someone who loves to dance, I make it a point to attend the event. This woman was also there. It was her first experience among a lot of people with disabilities in such a social situation. She concluded after her evening there that people were looking to score just like in any other social situation. She also noticed the dynamics you see everywhere else: sometimes people were mutually attracted; sometimes they were not. Still, there were a lot of different people on that dance floor and in that room with many diverse disabilities who had no trouble projecting themselves—or being perceived—as highly desirable—and desired—sexual human beings.

The stereotype of people with disabilities is that we are weak, dependent creatures. Those of us who live with disability know this to be untrue. Indeed, the opposite is more often the case. We are strong, fiercely independent beings. We have had to be to survive in this hostile environment in which we find ourselves.

This holds true in love and sexuality as well. When Lillian does trainings in sexuality, she describes sexual pleasure and the numerous ways we attain it. My favorite story is about the person with paralysis who comes when stimulated on a sensitive spot on their elbow. Their elbow? Yes, we have all kinds of erogenous zones. Most of us just don't know how to find nontraditional ones.

My body has changed since I first began this essay. My hands hurt more often now. I cannot please my wife, my lover, in ways that we are used to. But I can encourage her to touch herself. I can make noises of pleasure, reflecting what I feel as I hear her breathing change when her states of consciousness evolve. I can hold her and use my tongue to let her know that I am with her still. I can show her I love her by sticking around while she finds pleasure in her touch, her fantasies, her husband by her side. We continue to experiment to discover what works.

Isn't that what sex and love and romance and life are all about?

—8—

Porn Star?

Geoffrey Karen Dior Gann

I was doing drag shows once a week in a seedy little dive when one of the other drag queens, Chi Chi LaRue, asked me to be in a porn video. I had to think about it. First, I was confused. Why would anyone want to see a drag queen in a porn video? I didn't understand it. Gay men would want to see a man, and straight men would want to see someone who was all woman under the dress. I didn't yet know that many people are sexually interested in cross-dressing and in transsexuals and transvestites. Then I had to think about actually being in the video. I hadn't even seen more than three or four porn videos in my life. I didn't know that much about it. It seemed very risqué. My parents certainly wouldn't approve, but then they were Republicans; they did lots of things that I didn't approve of either. I decided that I didn't care what anybody else thought; I thought that it was okay, and that was all that mattered. I decided that anybody who watched porn but would judge me for being in it was a big hypocrite and the person's opinion certainly didn't matter to me. I decided to try it. Anyway, I would be in drag, so if I decided never to do another one, no one would ever recognize me.

Once I said yes, Chi Chi (who turned out to be a big porn director) asked me if I liked women too. I thought about it. I hadn't been with a woman for a few years, but it was mainly because I had no idea how to approach them or deal with them. Men were easier. I said, "Sure, why not? If I'm going to be having sex in makeup, a wig, and high heels in front of a camera crew and anyone else who might buy the movie, why not? I might as well go all-out."

We did the photo shoot for the box cover a month before we shot the video. I ended up in Las Vegas at the Consumer Electronics Convention signing autographs on that picture before we even shot the video. One of my friends commented that this was the only segment of the entertainment industry that could make you a star before you even shot a film. On the day of the photo shoot, I met Sharon Kane, the woman who was going to be with me in the video. I fell madly in love. I also met Tony Davis, a gay porn star whom I would later date. He was bringing a friend of his to meet Chi Chi,

Joey Stephano. Joey would later be lovers with Tony, Sharon, and me (separately usually) and become one of the most famous gay porn stars ever. We lived together at one point, and Sharon, Joey, Tony, and I were later often referred to as "the porn brat pack." We went everywhere together and were always noticed by the press. As the others got wilder and more into drugs, I just couldn't keep up. I dropped out of the circle, and we all went our own ways. Sharon is still a good friend. Joey eventually died tragically from a drug overdose.

Chi Chi had noticed my interest in Tony and decided to put him in the video. My very first scene, however, was a solo jack-off scene. I was in drag in a bathroom with what I thought was a straight camera crew watching me jack off and shove my long, pink, fake fingernails up my ass as I spread it for the camera. I felt like a complete freak show, certainly not sexy. When I was finished, I discovered that most of the crew were actually gay and they all said that my scene looked great. My second scene in the video was a three-way with Sharon and Tony. I felt a little more relaxed then, although it was a long time before I felt totally comfortable having sex in drag. The drag itself just wasn't a turn-on for me, but when I finally realized and understood that it was for other people, performing was easier.

The second video I did was a gay video, out of drag. While, on the one hand, I certainly felt much more physically comfortable not having to wear a wig or high heels, on the other, I felt much more exposed and vulnerable not being able to hide behind the makeup. I was very flattered to think that someone thought I was attractive enough to want to see me out of my clothes. I thought that some how I had fooled people into thinking that I was attractive but I knew the truth. I thought I was very ugly and had a bad self-image. I hated my body and did not take off my shirt in that first video. Much later, after I had worked out a lot and became more muscular, I noticed my own attraction to slim guys and realized that a lot of people had been attracted to me all along; I just hadn't noticed it before.

As the videos and the years went on, I faced many difficult issues. I was becoming very famous in drag, yet I didn't feel that that was really me. For a couple of months, I felt jealous of myself, jealous of this person, Karen Dior, who didn't even really exist. I had created her, and now I was jealous. I eventually was able to integrate the drag as part of me and realize that I was still me no matter how I was dressed. I realized that I would attract different people if I were dressed in leather rather than a preppy shirt and slacks, and so I decided that it wasn't so odd that I attracted different people when I was in drag.

Another difficult issue was that I felt, at times, sometimes within moments of each other, like the ugly duckling and like the swan. When I was doing a video, that crew treated me like I was a star, as did my fans. On the other hand, most of my friends were porn stars and actors and models. Next to them, I often felt like chopped liver. How can you compete with the most beautiful people in the world? I was angry at people for judging my value based on my looks, but I caught myself doing the same thing to others. I was wracked with guilt. Was physical beauty a blessing or a curse? A reward for good karma or a punishment for bad? I noticed that beauty could open so many doors. I also noticed that many people who perceived me as beautiful didn't see the real me at all. They only saw the outside. Many of my gorgeous friends were miserable, and all of them felt insecure about their looks. If these people felt insecure, what must other people feel? Maybe it truly would be a blessing to just be plain and fat and living in Iowa or somewhere. If I could just be happy and satisfied wouldn't that be better?

I have finally come to terms to some degree with the issue of looks. I realize that, to me, the way people look isn't the most important factor in determining my desire for them. Their personalities, the way they move, the way they think, and many other things are more important, but physical appearance is a part of it. I've become less obsessed about the way I look. I try to look as good as I can and leave it at that.

Being in videos has given me many opportunities for sex—both with men and women. It is pretty wonderful. You don't have to wonder what is going to happen. You both know why you are there: to have wild sex with a very attractive person. And you get paid. It's a pretty good deal, especially the women, at least for me. Until recently, I had dated only one woman in the past ten years. I just didn't know how to approach them. I'm sure a lot of men can identify with feeling terrified of rejection. Doing a porn video is like being handed a woman on a silver platter. Only recently have I developed the self-confidence and serenity to be able to approach people, men or women, without much fear of rejection. It's not that I am never rejected; it just doesn't bother me as much. I go on.

Once I finally dealt with those issues, I was able to settle in and enjoy what I was doing: having sex for other people to watch. The thought of it was totally erotic to me. Eventually, every part of filming a video started to turn me on, the bright lights, the smell of coffee brewing, and all the people standing around. I noticed that doing those things which, for one reason or another, some part of society said were "bad" really turned me on. It was like being naughty and flaunting it in front of the cameras. A man dressing in women's clothes was bad, for example, and it was just as kinky for a gay man (which is how most people thought of me) to lick a woman's pussy. Even getting fucked has some stigma among fags, as though the bottom is "more gay" and therefore less acceptable in polite company. Eventually, I was getting cucumbers shoved up my ass and fisting transsexuals. My natural tendency to want to shock was in full swing. Even though I haven't been in porn videos for a few years, I am tempted to come back just to get double fucked, or perhaps gang-banged in a sling by twenty-five guys.

I eventually stopped performing in porn videos because it just wasn't fun anymore. I felt as if I had done it all. Gay videos, straight videos, bisexual videos, transsexual videos—I was even in the Adult Video Hall of Fame. Although I am certainly not shy about people watching me, sex has become more personal and intimate than before. I wanted it to be just for me, just when and how I wanted it. I learned a lot during those years: I learned how to act, and now I get parts on television and in movies. I started directing videos, and I still have fun doing that. More important, I learned to love and accept myself and my body. I learned that sex is totally innocent. I learned how to have sex with women and even how to flirt with them, and, believe it or not, I recently had a girlfriend for six months. Not what I would have expected when I started out a shy, gay, drag queen.

—9—

If I Were a Straight Man . . .

Malcolm Lowry

da da da da da da da da da da da da da da dum . . .

You could say I was singing that once upon a time. Not that I ever wanted to be one. It's just, I was deep in the bosom of fundamentalist Christianity, and I believed it and practiced it more than most people could imagine. No, you don't understand. I wasn't just fanatical, I was downright obsessive. Every action, word, even thought literally revolved around my faith. I grew up with it. I knew nothing else. And I was incredibly sheltered.

This was my life at twenty-one, except for this nagging . . . this . . . what was that? It took me no less than a year and a half of turmoil just to give it a face and a name—I was gay.

In my faith, of course, being "homosexual" was regrettable, and "acting on it" was excommunicable, not to mention eternally damning. As for me, I knew absolutely nothing about being gay. So after having done everything I could to change myself (without success), I turned desperately to a trusted church leader and family friend for guidance.

God never gave a commandment without making it possible to keep, so I wasn't sure why no one else had ever found an answer, or why all gay people seemed to just "fall away" from the church. That wasn't going to be me! I was also amazed that straight people seemed to be so weak, almost not daring to speak about homosexuality. We were obviously here! The time for an answer had come. I would find it and share my findings with the world. People everywhere would stop fearing gay people, and gay people would stop running away from God in perceived helplessness.

So you can imagine my excitement (and relief) when the church leader told me of a breakthrough, state-of-the-art therapy in Salt Lake City that had an alleged 66 percent success rate, rather than the abysmal 2 to 3 percent its psychologist claimed other therapists were getting—2 to 3 percent? Horrifying!

No matter that it cost me thousands of dollars, depleting my savings and forcing me into significant debt; no matter that it caused me to give up two years of vacation time and work many of my days off to build up weeks worth of shift trades. This is the Lord we're talking about here! No holds barred. Little did I know, it would also involve heart-wrenching scars for life.

So off I trotted, south to the United States from my native Canada.

The first thing that happened was a test, an evaluation, an actual grade of my homosexualness versus heterosexualness—all done on computer. Now that was cool! I wanted all my friends to take that. I scored 38/42 in arousal/attraction toward men, 12/42 toward women. Gawd, get scientific.

But now for the real technology—biofeedback!—a technopsychology whereby a client can actually be taught to regulate his/her own heart rate or other autonomic functions. Arousal is just that, an autonomic function. Teach it to increase in response to one stimulus and fall in response to another. Teach yourself to be aroused by women. Cool! Why had nobody ever thought of this before?

Wait a minute! You want me to what? Get pornography? When I masturbate—and I will masturbate—I am to make sure I think of women, especially just before and during climax? Imagine my confused face. I had hoped to participate in some aspects of my faith while visiting, which would not be appropriate if I were to do that. I had never masturbated before. I didn't even have a wet dream until I was eighteen. Did I say that my every thought revolved obsessively around my faith? I said that. Okay.

"I didn't tell you to masturbate. I only told you that you would, and that when you do . . ." Ooh, shades of gray! I sure wasn't used to that! To masturbate or not to masturbate! To show faith in the power of God's commandments or participate in the therapy 100 percent! Well, God only knew, my life was already gray all over. I was here to find out if this therapy was going to work. I would participate 100 percent.

This was just the beginning. Now I'm going to tell you what else goes on, all the gory therapeutic details, but first, all straight guys reading this have to make a promise. As you read this, you have to imagine that you're in this therapy yourself. You are now making every possible effort to change; you will now become gay. Not temporarily, but for the rest of your life. Your goal is to learn to love sleeping with a man for the rest of your life. What? You think it grossed me out any less than you? Get over it. Humor me here. Now you can read on . . .

Dr. X leaves the room while I slip a malleable metal clip onto the head of my penis. From the clip extends an electric wire through which travels the telltale measurements of the clip's size. If I had any secrets before, they were no longer mine! Before my eyes (and his) was a digital readout of my arousal level. One ear of a headphone gave auditory feedback as well, with faster, higher-pitched beeps for greater arousal and slower, lower-pitched beeps for lesser arousal. The other ear received the sounds of the pornographic videos.

He would display a straight video, and I was to "find some button" inside to attempt to increase my own arousal; correspondingly, I was to "find some button" to reduce my arousal during the gay videos. He said the button was generally different for each person (argh . . .). Dr. X, also a devout member of my sect, made it clear, however, that there was no easy way to change, if it was going to be possible at all. I was sobered—and shaken.

My first exposure to pornography was blatant intercourse. Being a curious cat, I was very aroused, and Dr. X was very pleased (at the same time, I was rather grossed out . . . and was that all this sex stuff was? How boring). Next, it was time for my first gay porn. Well, if I had been curious before, here was home base, and I'd never been there! As I watched, the arousal meter hit the roof. And I waited . . . and waited . . . until it was over. All I had seen was a couple of guys walking around, saying nothing, looking at each other a couple of times.

"What was that?" I asked incredulously.

"A pick-up scene."

"A what?"

"A pick-up scene. That's all most guys can handle the first time."

"What's a pick-up scene?" I'm thinking to myself, but I thought better than to ask. I guess this guy thinks all gay men hang out trying to pick each other up all the time. Do they? I dunno.

Fast-forward a couple of weeks. Now for the real work. Typical session: Dr. X takes me through straight porn, to the unbearable heights of arousal, then abruptly switches to gay porn, at which point I would be expected to find my "button" and, miraculously, turn it all off.

If that weren't bad enough, a couple of months later, I think he started to get nervous. It was nearing the end of my time there, and suddenly he recommended electroshock aversion treatment; administered directly on my arm, the electric shock was intended to make the arousal less desirable through "negative reinforcement."

We had actually tried this once early in my treatment, but Dr. X had allowed me to control the intensity of the shock, and to press the button myself whenever I thought it helpful. He obviously didn't think I was using it often or intensely enough. This time, *he* took the controls. Sitting behind me out of my view, he pressed the button again and again, increasing the intensity more than I ever would have. I thought he would *never* stop pressing that button.

Finally, I turned around and shouted, "Would you stop that?!!"—fire in my eyes. That was as close as this timid kid ever came to violence. I'm sorry; I'm just not into pain. Needless to say, he didn't keep that up very long.

Yes, this did actually happen—and as recently as 1983! It's probably still happening today, in a neighborhood near you.

Well, actually, electroshock was Popcorn Playhouse compared to the most painful experience of all. About midpoint through the therapy, I fell hopelessly in love with my first love, another Christian actually. I had had no idea how overwhelming and gripping—and warm—that experience could be. Although there was no sex, Dr. X informed me that none of what we were doing in therapy would work unless I ended that association.

Ultimately, I saw no choice. Dr. X had admitted that to fail at this therapy would make it likely I would leave my faith. He didn't even have to tell me that leaving would cost my eternal happiness; I knew. So, I phoned my friend and ended it. I had never felt such pain, and don't think I ever have since. God, God, I groaned helplessly all night. I couldn't even cry. Not once. I felt so demolished, so alone, so horrified. Where was God? That night, I felt the innocence and excitement of my youth slip away.

A few months later, I returned for more treatments. Dr. X had a new, kinder, gentler strategy: hypnosis. I'm not even sure what that was supposed to accomplish, but it did help calm me down.

The results? Oh yeah, there were results. I was now scoring 36/42 women, though still 37/42 men. Yes, I could even make myself aroused by women—me! But the arousal was not warm or loving; it was passionless, lifeless, cold. The kind that says, "Let me get it off, baby" rather than "I can't get enough of you, baby; let's stay together, please." Perhaps Dr. X had never heard that the brain is the biggest sex organ in the body.

On my last day, I told Dr. X I was scared; I had seen virtually no reduction in arousal toward men. I was shaking. My eyes pled for reassurance. Without flinching, he looked at me and replied, "If I were you, I would be too." I was devastated, and my heart shrank in shame, and I had never felt such hopeless trepidation in my life. What had I done that was so wrong? For the first time in my life, I felt adrift, with nowhere to go. I was terrified for my eternity.

After returning to Edmonton, I did notice that the hypnosis seemed to be helping. It wasn't helping me change to be straight, but it did seem to help me cope with the misery and horror of burying who I really was, of denigrating my essence. I felt horrified at the prospect of never, ever sharing the preciousness of life with someone I really cared to be with. Forever. I knew that if I did, I would sacrifice my eternal happiness, and knowing that in advance, there would be no way I could be happy. I felt so irrevocably trapped!

I remember well the day I realized this. It was the kind of indescribably glorious sunny day we only dream about in Vancouver, but wherever I looked, all I could see was blackness. I didn't see a way that I would ever be able to experience anything but pain ever again in my life. At that moment, I lost something. I lost my desire to smile, or to have anything to do with anyone. Not because I didn't get what I wanted; I just saw no way in the whole world to ever be happy again. At that moment, I lost . . . myself.

* * * fast-forward * * *

Years of inner torment, and painful recovery later, I've actually enjoyed a few years of peace, happiness, even excitement. I'm so happy I decided to stay alive. I'm so worth it.

The only thing that kept me alive during the years that I still believed in my church was a funny thing a gay friend, also in the church, told me. He said, if the church were true, and I committed suicide, then I would be a murderer, which was worse than homosexuality; I would be better off to just be gay, he reasoned, enjoy it for fifty years, and die happily, reaping the same eternal unhappiness. Although his logic was questionable, and I never could have pulled his scheme off happily, and I knew it, it did keep me alive.

Nowadays, I've kept my earlier promise to myself. I refuse to let the world think that I am less than anyone else because I am gay, or that I am asking for special rights when I ask for equality. I experience profound joy and spirituality discovering my own meaning and fulfillment in life, and helping others do the same.

Most of all, I have many, many wonderful friends, most of them straight actually. Recently, one of my straight friends asked me out on a "date"— in front of some women friends of mine. You should have heard them cluck. He calmly defended himself. I felt so honored—by all of them. I love my friends!

Lately, there has been a resurgence of claims of a cure, of successful change. Yet, I can't think of a single aspect of the happy life I just described that I would like to change.

What, I must ask, constitutes a cure? Tying a Bible around the groin every night to prevent masturbation? Torturing oneself with visions of smelly worms at moments of arousal? Running hymns obsessively through one's mind hoping the thoughts will be washed away? Some fleeting erection I had once when looking at a woman after months of agonizing therapy? A wise Christian woman once wondered why I was so afraid of hell—wasn't I already there?

The therapy I endured took more faith, hard work, and painful mind changing than anything I had ever done, and I had done plenty! I loved the Lord with all my heart. I gave everything to the Lord—more than I ever thought I could. And where was He? Looking back, I don't believe He was there, and I don't believe He was absent. The only sense I had consistently through that whole experience was that, for me, to be straight was of another world—I may as well have set off on a hike for the moon.

Do you have a gay child? Don't try to suppress who she/he is. Why not have faith in your child? Why not teach him/her the same types of values about dating and sex you would teach your straight child? Doing otherwise will only hurt your child—and your relationship.

Trust me, your child's homosexuality is not going away.

Confessions of a Pregnant Husband

Howie Gordon

After examining my wife, the good doctor calmly assured us that our sex life could continue until very late in the pregnancy. "Unless, of course," he said, "you should encounter some discomfort."

Well, I knew he was going to say that. I'd already read it in all the books. I was just stalling for time. My wife looked over at me apprehensively. I could not meet her gaze. Under a smiling mask, I was a man in a panic trying stubbornly to bluster my way through the confusion.

"Well, yes, doctor," I should have said. "We have encountered some difficulty in our sex life. We don't have one anymore, and I think that I'm about to explode!"

I didn't tell the doctor that, however, and my wife joined me in the conspiracy of silence. Unwilling to play our little psychodrama in public, we made a good show of being the happy couple as we gathered our things and left his office. He was actually the wrong kind of doctor anyway. Looking back, we didn't need an obstetrician gynecologist for her body, we needed a psychiatrist for my head.

It was the fifth month of our first pregnancy. The problem was that I lost my lover to my child, and the kid wasn't even born yet. Welcome to parenthood. It's not what you would imagine either. *I was the one insisting on no sex!*

Can you believe that? I sure couldn't. It made no sense to me at all. I was so horny I was ready to burst. Oh, we still slept together in the same bed, but we didn't touch anymore. When her foot would drift over and touch mine under the covers, I'd pull away. I knew that I was nuts.

How did I allow myself to get twisted into a human pretzel of such conflicting emotions? I wasn't sure, but I knew it had gotten to the point at which I couldn't find the nose on my face without a Seeing Eye dog. Sex and pregnancy—there was the joker that just about destroyed our whole marriage.

In the beginning of our first pregnancy, it was all juicy strawberries and fresh whipped cream. After twelve long months of embarrassing testing and awkward attempts at trying to conceive, my wife and I had finally received the good word that we were going to have a baby. We glowed.

First were all the wonderful and exciting phone calls to our parents, relatives, and friends. Soon, the International Hand Me Down Baby Network began leaving gifts at our front door. We had to sign up for doctors and classes. The baby's nursery had to be planned. Construction and painting had to happen. We felt like it all had to be done by tomorrow because the baby was coming right away. It was a time bursting with creative energy.

This initial euphoria eventually yielded to a more practical approach as we settled down to pace ourselves for the nine-month marathon into parenthood. We wanted the baby. We were going to have the baby. We felt blessed.

Prior to any thoughts of children, my wife and I were on a once-a-day frequency of sexual contact. You know the old saying about wine: "A day without wine is like a day without sunshine"; well, we pretty much felt that way about sex. It was the highlight of the day. Orgasm was very important to both of us. Variety was always part of the program, and we shared responsibility for orchestrating our fantasies into mating rituals.

As our sex life continued into the pregnancy, however, subtle changes began taking place. In deference to the pregnancy, we seemed to have our sex more and more her way. I had the task of remaining passionate without offending her rapidly changing body. At first, I thought nothing of it. Like most pregnant spouses, I suppose, I had never loved my wife more.

As the weeks passed, however, sex became more and more difficult for me. Instead of increasing her arousal, my touch frequently made her flinch. It was not a pleasant experience for either one of us. I became hesitant about touching her. Her breasts became so sensitive that a stiff breeze seemed to be able to make her jump. Her body's need for orgasm totally disappeared. All of our old, well-established sexual rhythms and patterns had simply been thrown out the window. To my shock, guilt, and disappointment, the more my wife's belly grew, the less interested I became in having sex with her.

Some years later I read a newspaper column written by a psychologist of obvious wisdom, but whose name I unfortunately forget. This guy had clearly been through pretty much the same thing himself because he hit the nail right on the head. His thoughts were, in a nutshell, "The man feels responsible, even to an irrational degree, for having made his wife pregnant. Because of this, he is even more vulnerable to her feelings of resentment. Whatever goes wrong in the pregnancy appears to him to be his fault."

BINGO! . . . and when it came to sex, I had lots and lots of desire, but less and less for my wife. In fact, I started having more and more fantasies about other women. I found myself mentally undressing them in elevators, daydreaming about the neighbor's breasts, and wondering, inappropriately, about my wife's friends without their clothes on. I wasn't acting on any of these impulses, mind you, but the guilt was still enormous. It seems my timing couldn't have been worse.

As our sexual encounters at home became more and more like another chore that I had to perform, I simply started to withdraw from her. Hell, I had just finished twelve months of incredibly passionless, medically directed technical sex in order to *get* pregnant. Now that we were finally there, I just didn't want any more exercises in obligatory sex. The thrill was gone, and I was having trouble faking it. Naturally, being a man, I kept all of this to myself, while the frequency of our sexual intercourse dwindled.

The nameless psychologist understood all this. I paraphrase: "Although he may wish he could be angry or show some outward sign of resenting the intrusion of the pregnancy, he must remind himself of his own responsibility for it. . . . No one seems to care what a father-to-be is going through. His wife or mate has her hands full with her own adjustment. Her parents and his are concerned with her. All their friends ask her how she's feeling. . . . All his loneliness and his resentment about being displaced can get turned in on himself."

Whoever this guy was it's a shame I didn't have him for a tennis partner at the time. I could have saved both my wife and myself a whole lot of grief. As a writer, I turned to my private diary for moral support:

> Frankly, chums, I'm ready for a long boat ride to the Ukraine. My salad has been tossed so much lately that it's starting to look like guacamole. On the darker side of pregnancy, it is awfully hard to be Sir Galadad, the perfect husband, on a twenty-four-hour call. It's been five months and I have ignored every call of the wild that has come my way in the name of decency, true love, and the nuclear family . . . but I'll tell ya, kids . . . the gas shortage has come home. I feel like I have three kind words left for my wife and they are, "See you later!"
>
> I'm ready to go to Europe and come back after the baby is born. This doesn't seem too real to me as a possibility, but not much does these days except service—husbandry service. The biggest surprise of the pregnancy so far is how turned off I am to sex with my pregnant wife.

It was the pattern in our relationship that if one of the partners hit some kind of sullen bump and withdrew his or her affections, he or she was allowed about three days to work it out alone. It was usually me, and at the end of that time, my wife would do the confrontation and ask the appropriate questions.

We would try to act like the best friends that we were and create a "back room" where we could both go to find out what "they" were doing out there with "their" lives. It was a concept that had worked well for us in the past, but this time around, the results were not as great.

I met her first attempts at understanding me with stiff-armed rejection. When she continued pressing, I finally confessed that I had absolutely no desire left to have any more sex with a pregnant woman. I said that it just turned me off completely.

Did you ever hear words coming out of your own mouth that you couldn't quite believe yourself? That's where I was stuck. It was like ice fishing on a frozen lake without any hole. I was arguing passionately, like I knew what I was talking about, and yet, I couldn't quite find the way to get at the real fish underneath the frozen surface. I didn't let it stop me, though.

There's an old phrase in psychology that "in stress, we regress." Well, believe it. I found myself dusting off my old 1960s and 1970s antimonogamy speeches. As you might well imagine, my wife turned to utter mush. She was not overly thrilled to hear that I was actually entertaining the idea of having other lovers at this particular point in our relationship.

I felt like a total slime, but I really didn't know what else to do anymore. I was exploding internally. Desperation was talking. I just wanted her kept at arm's length. I continued to seek comfort in my journal:

> This pregnancy has my responsible-mate button turned up to 99.9, and my wife has gotten very used to it. It's only five months down and four to go. Even then, the old ways are over. There's no return to normal. We're going to be having a baby living around here. It makes me dizzy. I'm just doing a lot of head shaking and hanging on.
>
> I could use a weekend of oblivion with a couple of Las Vegas hookers, and what I get are more natural childbirth classes and books about newborns. My life is one giant should. I've been doing pretty well on all the tests, but, seriously folks, I'm ready for a break. The problem is that my wife doesn't get any breaks. She can't put her belly on the shelf and say, "I'll be back Monday," . . . so I'm shamed into sticking with it too.
>
> I don't know what we're going to do about sex. Putting myself into a pregnant woman is one of the most redundant experiences I have ever encountered. I have no taste for it. They say that love can move mountains. Well, it better . . . because unless our sex trip gets a little bit more harmonious. . . . I hate to even think about it . . .

Obviously distressed, my wife could not long endure my stubborn requests to be left alone, sulking and spewing poisoned ink. When she decides that she wants to probe my insides, there aren't too many forces in the known universe that I can use to stop her.

One day in the midst of all this, she just announced that she plainly refused to accept my right of privacy in this situation any longer. I responded by putting an ashtray through a picture window to keep her at bay. Whoa, Nellie! I was clearly losing control. It sure gave me a lot to think about as I cleaned up the pieces and replaced the window.

I didn't know what it was. There was help out there, I guess. I don't know why I didn't seek it. I guess it stemmed from some kind of patriarchal bullshit about being the bottom line . . . the buck stops here . . . and all that. A man was supposed to be able to take care of his family. A man was supposed to be able to take care of himself. I was failing miserably on both counts and trying hard to ride out the storm.

The ashtray through the window alarmed us both. It revealed the depth of my chaos and the passion of my frustration. My wife's resolution after much argument, pain, and grief was to accept my proposal that we weren't going to have sex again until after the baby was born. This was supposed to be a victory for me. I don't think so. It was dumb.

It was the hollowest victory that I had ever tasted. It made absolutely no sense to me at all. A murky distance developed between us. It was like back in the old days when we were courting and we still kept secrets about other lovers from each other. Our whole relationship seemed to be on trial.

Despite her tears and over her protests, I arranged to go have myself a weekend of sex with a hooker-type I knew. I thought of it as just calling the plumber to get my pipes cleaned. My wife didn't think of it that way at all. She was crushed. In the past, she would have just gone out, picked up some other guy, and matched me tit for tat. With her swollen belly, it wasn't like she could play the bar-hopping game for awhile.

When the time came for my lustful tryst with "the plumber," I ended up canceling. I called my own bluff and came up empty. I didn't really want to have sex with another woman. I was in enough trouble already. We passed that weekend in some kind of suspended animation, barely talking to each other.

Then one day, not long after, it all mercifully just came to an end. Maybe I had a nocturnal visit from Sigmund Freud or the nameless psychologist in my dreams. I don't know. The truth was that I just woke up one morning late in that difficult fifth month and very sadly missed our love.

She was still sleeping and I had to go off to work. I stood there for awhile watching her sleep. Her breathing was fitful and uneasy. I tried to imagine what the baby looked like napping in her belly. A warm flood of emotions washed over me. Perhaps a chiropractor spirit was working on my spine. Something that was badly out of whack was falling back into place. I wanted to hug and kiss her all over. It had been too long. I had loved this woman above all others so much that I had made her my wife. Now, she was carrying my child. I popped. The tears came, but I had to go to work. I left her this note: "This is the part where he totally panicked. I love you. I'll see you later."

When I got home that night, I swallowed a lot of pride and confessed all my sins. I was tired of all the constant worrying about the pregnancy. I was incredibly scared about us having a baby. And most important, I was angry at the way the pregnancy had dealt her such a controlling hand in all our acts of intimacy.

A powerless man does not many boners make. You can quote me. I explained that I couldn't quite seem to put together my lust with her pregnant body. I was lost in some kind of Madonna-whore complex. The Madonna was going to have my baby, but the whore had been the object of my desire. I just couldn't conceive of a pregnant whore. When my fantasies dried up, I had withdrawn in frustration. Well, love found the way to smash all that to bits. I loved my wife and I loved our having a baby. I just got a bit lost in the jet stream of such a miraculous comet.

When it came down to the nitty-gritty of our having sex, we had to throw out what almost ten years of being lovers had taught us. We had to go back to square one and learn how to touch each other all over again, if we were going to get through this pregnancy thing without destroying our marriage. There were grateful hugs and tears.

That night, my wife put on some very trashy negligee and we laughed and squealed like we hadn't done in months. Me and my pregnant whore were going to make it. Love had us laughing again. We were ready to go on.

You know, most people think in terms of the nine months' time of the pregnancy as what it takes for the baby's body to develop, but the lovers need that time, too, to begin becoming parents. There is such a wondrous bubble of intimacy that surrounds the creation of a new life between a man and a woman. Old ways are exploded and new ways must be found.

We grew into something way beyond the basic lust that it had taken for us to start our baby's life. Our full energies seemed to be absorbed in making each other feel safe and ready to become parents. It was clear that the nine months do more than just grow the baby. One marvels at the Creator's master plan, and rightfully so. We jumped our five month's hurdle and just kept right on going. As the due date approached, we were appropriately terrified.

We were going to do natural childbirth and all that, but when the first labor pain hit, all those ideas went flying out the window. She wanted the pain stopped. They held her off medication until she was seven centimeters dilated. It took forever. My wife labored over thirty hours with that first kid. I lived and died ten times. Labor was like watching God have sex with my wife, and I didn't know if I was going to get her back dead or alive when He finished with her.

My wife was utterly magnificent. She rode through those long hours like a mare at full gallop breathing hard in the moonlight. The end of this spectacular journey brought us a 7 lb 5½ oz baby girl. It actually became kind of addictive. We had two more pregnancies and two more kids. Turned out, we did it fairly well and it took some doing to climb back down off the baby-making bandwagon. We decided that raising three children was plenty, and we've all moved on with our lives. The kids, now sixteen, fourteen, and twelve, are thriving.

Now in the sexual evolution of growing older together as a couple, my wife and I have run into a whole batch of other problems. "Life is trouble," wrote Kazantzakis in *Zorba the Greek,* ". . . only death is not. To be alive is to unbuckle your belt and to look for trouble" (1952:101). And though my wife and I have certainly had our fair share of trouble, we are still together and still working hard to find the way to keep the flames of passion burning. Love finds the way.

REFERENCES

Kazantzakis, Nikos. 1952. *Zorba the Greek.*

11

Shadows in the Mirror

Manó Marks

I try not to spend too much time looking in the mirror. I can't see myself. There's a face, two eyes, and a mouth, surrounded by a messy mop of hair. I don't know who it is, or what lies behind it. I am an alien to myself. I live a life abbreviated by a fog. It's as if I've only lived eighteen years. The other ten are gone. Only vague recollections remain: a birthday here, a scraped knee there, a shadow, looming up in front of me, confronting me with its shapelessness, its void.

The memory of fear haunts me, takes me by surprise, ripping across the screen of my mind. Voices, images interrupt my day, my night, the dance of sex and love. Random associations and reverberations of times long ago. I am sitting at a table, and this really hot guy is across from me. He smiles and takes my hand, and I smile and take his.

Come here.

The shadow must cross my face, but he doesn't see it; he doesn't hear the voice either. I am not giving him my full attention. He lets go of my hand. Before I know what happened, the date is over.

I lie next to him, his body pressing me from behind. That's how I like it, that's how I've always wanted it. I snuggle close and smile, feel the warm cum drying on my now cooling body, feel the slowing breath of a lover who wraps his arms around my chest, feel his slowly softening cock against my butt. And I feel young, so young, slipping, deeper, lighter . . .

It's dark, and cold. I lie on the bed waiting, waiting. I can't move, it's not allowed. Finally, almost as a relief, he lies down behind me, his body so much bigger, and he reaches between my legs. I start to cry. Softly—so he won't get mad . . .

The tenth time I run these scenarios through my head, I put down the phone and decide not to call "that cute guy." Or I turn away when he tries to catch my eye. I look inward, trying most of all to forget there are people out there who might want me, might want to touch my body.

I want you to COME HERE.

My lover doesn't always know when a bullet races through my brain, knocking loose a word or a sound that fills my head. When she says, "You're so beautiful," I hear an echo, filled with power and age, tearing his voice through my soul. I blink, shake my head, and look away. "No," I say, "I'm not."

I feel the rush to anger, the rush to fear, the total consuming rage bubbling up every time I feel the choking grasp at my throat, the shadow of a hand on my cock, and the need to scream, to rage and throw myself against a wall, again, again, the burbling, inarticulate, all-consuming, all-unknowing crap of the universe pouring over my head, splashing down my body, and filling the room around me, burying my feet, knees, hips, moving toward my face, and there is no exit from this room, though I struggle and struggle to find one, frantic to save myself from drowning. In shit.

I am not beautiful. To be beautiful is to be vulnerable, more vulnerable— to walk with the stranger that is myself. To let someone touch me is to see and hear an overlay of him, of them, over the hands and voices of my lovers.

Quickly, I bite down on my hand. I can't scream; I won't scream. I don't want him to get angry. What if someone heard? What if someone heard?

I don't know what all my triggers are. I don't know who my nemesis is. As I gradually follow the connecting links and lift the smallest of veils, a mystery remains, a poignant reminder that I am alone. Every day. With a stranger.

Sexual trauma lives deep in my soul. I can't help the triggers, and the pain. Neither can my lovers, and those who want to be my lovers. The time comes when I have to make the choice. Do I tough it out and not tell them about the abuse, fearing that a trigger will freak them out? Do I tell them beforehand and risk rejection because of it? Every woman whom I've told about the abuse has been very supportive, still wanting to be my lover. Every man I've told has run from me, with one exception—a man who took so much control, so much power, that I ran from him. So I grit my teeth with men, and hold on tight with women.

What should I do? Wait until therapy has sorted out my past, awakened a new consciousness, and brought about a Nirvana of sexual understanding and happiness? I can't wait that long. Sex is part of who I am. In some ways, the abuse has fostered that, centered my attention on sex, on sensuality, centered me in my body. Only, I'm not in my self.

The fear never quite leaves. With men or women, there is an intensity of fear, of anguish that it will happen again. Is this unreasonable? What do you think? Would you tell me I'm being unreasonable?

It happened again, with someone I trusted very much, whom I loved and honored deeply. By someone—not just someone—a friend. He seemed to be a safe person, a man with no violence in his soul.

I love you. I'm sorry. I've just been self-destructive recently, drinking a lot. I'm sorry. I love you. I think this can bring us closer together.

At least with him I remember what happened; I know where I was and who attacked me. I know his roommate went to sleep on the couch that night, so he could rape me while I was dead drunk. I know that I stopped him, woke up with him on top of me, with me undressed. I know I left, and I can curse his name, even though I can't drive by his house.

He used to joke a lot.

Don't. Stop! Don't—stop! Don't stop! Don't stop!

I'd look away. I still have to, when I remember him. Some jokes aren't funny.

12

In the Body of a Man

Jamison Green

In the year that I was fourteen years old, a new family lived in the house next door to mine. I have no recollection of the adults, nor of the family name, but I remember the girl, Linda, and what her presence did to me and to the other boys in the neighborhood.

Linda was sixteen. She went to a private school, so we only saw her coming and going, and we never had much chance to get to know her. No other girl in the neighborhood was like her. She had thick, wavy dark hair that just brushed the top of her shoulders. She had breasts that looked heavy, firm, and round—handfuls, we called them. "Look at those handfuls," we'd say, as she walked from her father's car to her front door. She never glanced at us. She ignored us as we moved off the road when her parents drove through our ball games. We stood aside and stared at her, holding our best rebel poses. "I'll bet she's got hair on her pussy," Jeff said once. That did it. He gave us all permission to expose our lust.

When we couldn't gather enough boys to compose opposing teams, or when we grew weary of sports or war games, we would sprawl beneath the big redwood tree in my front yard and talk about what we'd like to do with Linda: kiss her, squeeze her titties, pull her panties down, smell her pussy, pull her hair to see her neck arched, exposed, make her touch our dicks, watch her tits wiggle, stick our cocks in her. We wanted to see her undressed, and we dared one another to hide in the bushes outside her window, to climb up in the branches of the bushy cypress that shielded her bedroom from the sun. I was the one who did it. Tommy went with me, but he never climbed up high enough to see in. I saw her in her white slip, her white bra, and pale yellow panties. I was terrified that she might see me, so I scrambled down before she turned.

"In the Body of a Man" first appeared in translation in *Cupido*, February 1998, issue 2, pp. 16-21.

"I saw her," I whispered to Tommy as we ran out of her yard.

"Well, does she?" Jeff asked later. "Does she have hair on her pussy?"

"Yeah," I said, grinning like a dog. "She does."

"Damn," he said. "I wish I'd seen that. How come you get to be the one who sees her?"

" 'Cause I'm the one with guts," I sneered.

I was also the one boy with a female body, the one destined to have a tighter angle on women's lives than most men can ever reach, destined to transition physically from female to male and psychically from boy to man. I was both cursed and blessed.

In that time of awakening lust, my boyhood was secure, but an awareness was descending on me that my dream of attaining manhood was fading, as the realities of female adolescence imposed a cruel fate on my developing body. My status among the boys in the neighborhood as a leader, as an equal (if not occasionally superior) team member, as a strong arm and strong will, was legendary. The difficulty for me, and for Jeff and Tommy and the other boys, was that as we were growing older, our worlds were being populated with many other kids who didn't understand who I was, didn't realize that I was the power hitter, that I was the best wide receiver, that I was the superior strategist in battle, and these cretins from the surrounding neighborhoods made the boys from my neighborhood feel stupid for permitting what those other boys thought was a girl to participate in their sacred rituals and games.

It wasn't until roughly two years later—when I was nearly sixteen—that I was finally barred from the neighborhood equivalent of the boy's locker room in a pileup at the scrimmage line, when Tommy gave my own tit a squeeze and shouted, "Hey, she's got 'em! She's gonna be a girl after all!" Mortified, I extracted myself from the pile of boy bodies, dragged Tommy up to standing, punched him hard in the stomach, and angrily stomped home, vowing they'd never get another chance at me like that again. That was the last "conversation" Tommy and I ever had. Of course, I would soon have my driver's license, so screw them. I had bigger plans, much wider dreams than could be sustained by those meaningless neighborhood games, and male lust was still very much a part of the picture.

There were girls I had my eye on: Suzie, Diane, Vicky. . . . I observed the adolescent mating dances they all engaged in with various boys, I listened to their critiques of the male sex (as I was able to do for much of my adult life, ensconced as I was within a female body, my presence overlooked when conversations among women turned erotic), and I watched how those boys gravitated toward the objects of their desire—"Oh, he's so stupid," they would say, and laugh—boys were like meteorites caught in the magnetic pull of powerful planets—"All he thinks about is himself"—and once they entered the girls' attractional fields there was no escape. Inevitable disaster lay ahead because the road to adulthood is paved with disappointment. Every single one of them was on a collision course with the crushing weight of adolescent emotions. I observed it all from a safe distance.

In that awkward time of physical maturation, it is often difficult for a boy to know what he likes: Was it the girl he was looking at that made him hard, or the female voice that he was hearing on the radio? Was it staring at the teacher's breasts? Did the televised kiss arouse him, or was it the sudden, unbidden memory of the Big Boobs magazine he saw in the liquor store? Boys tend to go with what the moment offers, except in cases of extreme peer pressure, when they would rather do what other boys think best. Watching everyone else back then confirmed in me the notion that I was not like anyone else. I was a boy hidden in a girl's body who would someday, somehow—though I didn't know how—grow up to be a man. I couldn't imagine how it would happen. I couldn't pull my own cock to manifest my manhood; I had to find and express my maleness in other ways.

I spent a lot of time driving around, listening to the radio, imagining a woman next to me who loved me, who would want to kiss me and stroke my body. I didn't think too much about genitals. I knew mine were not right for me, and I didn't think it would ever be possible to make them right. I was eighteen before a woman ever kissed me and let me squeeze her breasts, but I was hooked on the concept of taking a woman in my arms and ravishing her, while simultaneously providing her protection, long before that first Linda, who briefly lived next door, had ever pointedly ignored us as she sashayed in conscious tantalizing motion across her own front lawn. But when that first kiss finally came, I knew my penis was alive inside me.

The first two women I had long relationships with were both heterosexual. They were attracted to men, and really did not understand why they found themselves drawn to me. While they knew I had a female body, they both acknowledged that it was the male in me with whom they had fallen in love. The first one suggested that I have a sex change so I could finally be a man, and I still did not know that this was truly possible, so I told her, "Only crazy people do that," and insisted that she never raise the issue again. We broke up after three years, and she continued to date men. The second woman I was with frightened me when she told me she wanted to have my babies. Oh, I was flattered, all right. I knew she was saying that she trusted and valued me, that she wanted to merge with me in that deep, life-and-death way. I believed I could never give her children (sperm banks were a thing of the future then), and I would therefore always be a disappointment to her. Ultimately, our paths diverged due to different life goals, different paces, different drives. She continued to date men, while I decided to give lesbians a try.

I don't pretend to know what women feel when they are horny, or if a woman's horniness is the same as her experience of lust. I only know what I have felt, and what has always been consistent for me when I think of physical pleasure is my desire to place myself inside a woman, to feel the difference in her skin—her smoothness, her resilience, as opposed to my muscled rigidity—the wetness of her mouth, of her vagina sucking me in where I can swell and expand and exercise my life away.

All the driving around I did as a teenager was the perfect metaphor. I was a heat-seeking missile looking for that chink in a woman's armor. If I could have reached inside myself and pulled my hidden penis out, my desire would have been so much more obvious. As it was, I learned self-restraint. I could not allow my lovers to touch the female genitals I hid beneath my jeans: at least, there could be no penetration, not of me. That was too female. Eventually, my escapades among lesbians fizzled out like so much lesbian bed-death, initial passion resolving into deep friendship with waning sexuality, on my part, and frustrated desire to be with a woman, on the part of my partners. Being with me was not being with a woman, and so it never worked out, though I tried for over twenty years because I loved these women. But I had lost sight of lust, and a woman who is not desired in her partnership becomes filled with longing and resentment.

In the mid-1970s, I discovered that female-to-male transsexual procedures were possible and acknowledged to my then-partner and several friends that I was probably transsexual, that I felt I was a man, and that I believed I would be happier with my life if I had a male body. But I was also a feminist who believed that there is nothing inherently wrong or inferior about women, and women should not be restricted from activities, pursuits, or wage structures simply because they are women, and this led me to believe I owed it to the women of America to stay in that female body and prove that women could do whatever they wanted to do, as I believed I could do—and was doing. I also was not so sure I trusted the medical establishment, since doctors defined transsexuals as pathetic victims who needed their expert help in order to function in society, and I was functioning very well, thank you. I did not see my transsexualism as pathetic, nor myself as a victim, and I did not want to be forced to say such things in order to receive treatment.

I was also not so sure that the treatment itself wasn't dangerous. I spent about ten years doing casual research into transsexual treatments and outcomes, while I faced my own gradual awakening to the basic reality of my life: that I was psychologically stuck being a teenage boy because I was never going to grow up to be a woman. It simply wasn't psychologically possible. The only way I could grow up was to become a man, and at age thirty-eight, having fathered one child using donor sperm and watching my partner's belly swell with the growth of our second child, I realized I desperately needed to grow up. I had no choice anymore. What I didn't fully realize about the transition process from female to male was that it would take me back to that point in my adolescence where I had shut down and give me a second chance at life. It would revive my lust.

Testosterone fuels the sex drive for both men and women. Men have—on average—about ten times as much testosterone in their systems as do women, however. This doesn't mean that women's sex drive is less than men's—other factors contribute to the gestalt of desire, and these factors vary among individuals. In my body, the initial effect of testosterone was that it allowed me to feel "normal" for the first time in my life. It allowed me to feel calm, balanced, centered, the absolute antithesis of the clichés about 'roid rage and testosterone poisoning. And once I got comfortable with that feeling, once I started to relax and accept that my natural self was finally being affirmed, along came libido.

It was the most amazing thing, this new libido. It came pushing out the front of my body like an engorged cock, and it made me feel connected to my body as I never had before. My own penis started to grow—that is, my clitoris became enlarged, eventually to the size of a small penis—and after about a year, I had a cock I could grab onto. For the first time, I could imagine a woman giving me head. I could relate to my body as a locus of sexual pleasure, emanating from my genitals and spreading through me and beyond, out into the universe of female flesh and orifices.

Penises do lie. Sure, it's obvious when a penis is erect, but there's no reliable way to know what that erection means. An erect phallus is the most consistent visible symbol of desire that humanity has managed to agree upon cross-culturally. Yet it is possible for a man to feel romantic or erotic, sexual or lusty without creating an erection. My own erections are not so obvious unless I'm naked or in my shorts, since my penis is small, but my erections are spontaneous, and I both relish them and crave release from them the same as any other man. But it is not a penis that makes me (or anyone else who has one) a man. A man's penis is a specialized and much appreciated part of his body, nothing more. Without it, a man would still be a man. With it, if he's lucky, he's a man who can urinate in a standing position, deposit sperm close to a cervix, and enjoy orgasm—important activities, no doubt, but not the essence of being a man. There are certainly other ways to do all of those important things.

I marveled at my penis in the beginning; like an adolescent boy, I was delighted with my own performance. I was able to make love with my partner twice before she told me she was no longer interested in me; she used the fact of my transition as a rationale for the dissolution of our thirteen-plus-year relationship, while she hid from me the truth of an ongoing affair she was having with another woman. She used my intention to finally change my body as an excuse to mask her own betrayal.

I did not have partnered sex again until I was forty-two years old, had been through surgical sex reassignment so that I had balls to back up my cock, and had nearly weathered the full second psychological adolescence that transsexual people are privileged to endure. Meanwhile, I masturbated, as most young men do, while emotionally vacillating between despair at the loss of my partner and elation with the growing congruity my body and soul were achieving. I fantasized women on their knees before me, begging for my cock in their mouths, and I watched and felt my penis swell in response to the mere suggestion that they might offer me their tits and spread their legs. I would jerk myself off, reveling in the powerful release of my own energy, and then remember I was alone and sink into depression, much as my diminishing organ collapsed and lay forlorn across my ever-bulging silicone implant-filled scrotum.

It was male lust that saved me, lust that kept me centered in my body, kept informing me that I was alive and that I could go on. That burning drive to stick it into something, into someone, reminded me that there was life beyond a failed relationship. Gradually, I began to notice again that women existed in the real world, outside the pages of the pornographic magazines that I kept beside my bed, in my car, to feed the craving to feel good again for just a little while, for just the time it took to respond to the stirrings, to stroke them into hardness and milk them for all they were worth. Gradually, I began to see that real women were starting to notice me, express some interest in me. I was shy, still shaking off the remnants of that second adolescence, but I had to recognize that women were seeing me as a man at last, not as a boy, not as a lesbian, not as an androgyne, but as a bearded, hirsute, solid physical man with something to offer them.

The first time a woman did suck my cock, I was amazed by the feeling of it, by the sheer joy she gave me as she swirled her tongue around my cock's head, as she slid her lips along its shaft, as she looked up and smiled at me, pleased with herself. Her breasts were more than handfuls, and she enjoyed every inch of her body under my touch. We fed each other's fantasies, satisfied each other's hungers, and began to build a life together based on our separate, mutual lust.

I still don't know what a woman feels when she is horny, or if her horniness is the same for her as lust, but for me, lust is still the drive to make myself feel good. I know I feel best when I am pleasuring myself with a woman who loves me, pleasuring her because I love her, because it stirs more lust in me to see and feel her pleasure, the pleasure that she takes from me.

We feed each other. We are the circle of life and death. Sex between us is communication, an opening to the past and the future, a way of expressing everything, of purging the demons from our psyches, of redeeming our souls while all time is suspended. Sliding my male body against and into a woman who wants me, who loves me, is what makes all this possible for me.

Lust, as expressed through a male body, through a masculine psyche, is often characterized as something to be loathed, feared, and even ridiculed. Yet, we celebrate lust when it is expressed in the name of altruistic passion for a just political cause, or when it is displayed in passionate outrage against injustice, when it is nonsexual, chaste. If the penis can lie, then lust can be chaste. Lust is a craving and a desire to feel good. Sexual lust is only one way to express the many types of motivating desires and cravings that occupy our minds, our souls, our nervous systems. We are complex organisms, multisensate, multiprocessing, constantly striving for balance in a world that inundates us with stimulation, with obstacles, with conflicting social goals. Whether our efforts are worthwhile is for ourselves alone to judge in this lifetime, and for history to judge in its turn. As men, men whose bodies and psyches contain, and are sometimes driven by, complex and simple lust, we must negotiate a world full of judgment and limitations. We must use lust to serve both mundane instincts and higher vision, and if we can learn to appreciate what our lust can do for us, we stand a good chance at attaining that balance.

My balance point has been between my body and my psyche, between my masculinity and my attraction to female bodies. For other transgendered or transsexual people, their balance points may be in different places. One thing I have learned from going through the transition from female to male is that making assumptions about people based on their appearance is usually a gross error. We don't know who we are talking to—ever! When we think about bodies, about gender, about sex, we never really know what another person looks like, feels like, likes to do, unless we ask and get an honest answer. Even then, the answer may be true only for the moment, or for some discrete part of time. Transsexual people are often burdened with the notion that we reinforce gender stereotypes, that we "buy into" the binary gender system. Then the state of transsexual bodies is used to represent disruption of that system in films such as *The Crying Game*. It seems we can never get it right—either we buy into the system, or we are tearing it apart, making people vomit up their fears.

I don't care what people think about my penis, or about the fact that I was long ago treated as a girl. I don't care whether people think I am reinforcing gender stereotypes because I am a heterosexual man, or if they think I am bravely accosting the gender apartheid system because I've broken the barriers and lived on both sides of the gender fence. I care about living honestly and passionately, without fear or shame, and that means being unafraid to relate what happened back when Linda and her family moved out of our neighborhood.

*   *   *

I sailed past on my bicycle, watching the movers load up the giant van. Linda was standing on the corner, away from the gruff, sweating men who labored under her mother's irritated command and her father's aloof wariness. I couldn't help looking at her, and she stared straight back, telegraphing a message to me. Somehow I knew she wanted to talk. I turned around and pedaled back, stopping at the curb.

"Where are you moving to?" I asked. "Chicago," she said flatly.

"You don't want to go?"

"No. I never want to go. We move almost every year, and I hate it."

I nodded. Chicago was so far away from San Francisco that I could hardly imagine it.

"I saw you," she said. I was confused and gave her a quizzical look. "Why did you do it?" she asked. Instantly, I knew what she meant. I felt like running; I must have flushed deep red.

"You saw?"

"In the mirror."

I smiled stupidly, embarrassed both by what I had done and by how she had caught me.

"Why did you do that? Why did you want to look into my room?"

"I don't know," I said in a panic. "I guess I was just curious about you."

"Well, it was nasty and rude."

"I'm sorry . . ."

"My mother thought you were a girl, but I think you're a boy. If you ever grow up, maybe you'll understand what a hurtful thing you've done."

"I didn't mean to hurt you."

"It wasn't that you looked that hurt so much," she said. "It was that you stole that look and ran away. I always watched for you to come back, but you never did."

I was speechless. I wasn't sure I understood.

"Linda! Come in here, please," her mother called from the doorway.

"I'm sorry," I said again.

"Just don't ever do anything like that again," she said, turning away toward the house.

That was the last time I saw her, and the beginning of a lifelong effort to practice the art of communicating with women through any and every means possible.

—13—

Finding My "Yes!"

Jeannie Zandi

One day in line at the bank, I watched the men look at the women—some openly, some furtively, some glancing, some lingering. I noticed how the men were standing—both feet planted on the ground, sturdy, with their heads held high. I was standing with my weight on one leg and my arms crossed, with my head tilted slightly downward. The other women stood similarly. I decided to stand like the men and try looking at them the way they were looking at us, to see what it would be like. I put my feet flat on the floor, stood up tall, and felt the strength in my body. I immediately felt that I took up more space and that I was much more noticeable.

So I looked. For a moment I had a giddy glimpse into a wholly different world, a world where I could linger over the form of any man and not fear for my safety. But, feeling more visible, I felt more afraid. If I stood this way, I might be challenged, said my body. It felt dangerous to take up this much room, to even look at the men for very long, never mind linger over their forms. If one saw me, he might think I was "interested." If he thought I was "interested," he might approach me. He might not leave me alone—after all, I invited it. If he thought that I wanted it, he might take it.

I imagined what it would be like to have the strength to back up this stance, to be one of the physically more powerful sex, to be a member of the group that won arm wrestling contests, knew how to fight, did the raping, instead of a member of the group that was most often raped. I imagined that I belonged to the group who owned most of the businesses, held most of the political offices, played on most of the sports teams on television. As I tried on this persona, I thought that if it were mine, I would feel safe looking at men with open admiration and lengthwise glances, knowing I would likely not be hurt physically for it, that I wouldn't be inviting something I couldn't handle.

I remember a seven-year-old girl at a school where I worked. A bully told her to move as they stood in line after recess. Her eyes blazing, she asserted,

"Oh yeah? Make me!" Her fierceness was beautiful, uncrushed, as mine was at that age. A wave of grief and protectiveness engulfed me, as if I were looking at the last lovely specimen of a vanishing wild species. Not until I was pushed down repeatedly by boys when asserting myself, not until I was punched by my brother when I was winning an argument, not until a boy who liked me had his friend hold my arms while he threw a basketball at my stomach for not wanting to be his girlfriend, not until I consciously and unconsciously absorbed the violence to women did I hide that blaze in my own eyes, did I adopt a less visible, less powerful posture, did I lose touch with my own powerful "NO!" in the face of boys and men who attempted to coerce me. The rules for winning were based on who had might and power, and I didn't. So by the time the lust of young men came my way, it felt mostly like a threat, though I liked the attention. I felt by then that there was something about being male that made one more valuable, and if I couldn't be one, at least I could get the attention of one, and the way to do that was by appealing to them sexually. And though I wanted some attention, I didn't feel equipped to make things go the way I wanted them to once I got it (thus the ambivalence my male friends are confounded by in women: dressing and acting sexy, but cooling off upon approach).

As I grew older, I found that directing a gaze, never mind an admiring gaze, could instantly attract attention that I didn't know how to handle. No one taught me how to say "No," or that I had at least a 50 percent interest in what might happen between me and a man sexually, never mind how to physically protect myself in case I attracted the wrong kind of attention. Not only were men stronger and more comfortable being pushy, but it seemed their lust came on so fast, furiously, and insistently that I generally didn't have the time or space to find my own desire, or to even know that slowing down was what I needed.

On top of this, it felt as though men were trained to be sexually intimate by "stealing" something from us. I felt that I was so busy fending them off to create the room I needed to show up that the space seldom developed for me to actually meet them with my own desire. I felt that my job was to protect my vulnerability and sex from male lust until I was sure I was safe.

Many of my male friends and lovers complain that men do all the approaching, sustain all the rejecting, wear their desire on their sleeves. How vulnerable! It seems to them a privilege to be female—to wait and watch, to absorb the flattering attentions of the other sex, to pick and choose. But what I realized, standing tall in the bank line, was that leaving the approach to men is not simply a quaint custom, but a time-tested survival strategy for women. We can begin to match the power of men's physicality with the power of not showing our hands until we know we are safe. No matter how good a man looks, unless I know something about his life, his clan, his nature, his habits, I am not going to leave myself open to his advances, when the reality is that he has the ability to overpower me. So, as he approaches, I coolly size him up for capability of treating me well, without betraying my own attraction.

Some of this seems wise; some seems old and outdated. After all, I'm a strong and smart liberated woman. I've taken self-defense classes. I know how to set limits. And though my physical safety is not in my conscious mind when I interact with men, my mind readily conjures up visions of male lust turned violent whenever I walk alone in the dark, or during any interaction that feels a little strange. Every report of rape, abduction, or battering slips quietly into my psyche and forms a knot of fear and protectiveness there. It generates a low and constant unconscious hum, reinforcing the undeniable reality that, as a woman, I am physically vulnerable to men.

Despite this hum, there came a point in my life when I grew tired of my timidity. I had explored my fierceness and power long enough to feel the confinement of my emphasis on safety and protection. Though I sensed a real need for intelligent caution, I felt my lack of risk taking had left part of me undeveloped, and to grow there, I would need to see just how able I was to negotiate in the realm of lust. I wanted to develop a sense of mastery and forward movement myself, to claim my juiciness, and to flood my life with passion. Consciously, I was ready to rock and roll, to be open, loose, a slut, even if it meant facing rape or even death, just to be free.

So I decided to do a little sexual exploration. For a summer, I forced the girl-child I felt I was into the world of sex. I courted men's lust and met it as openly as I could, to learn how to maneuver in a trial by fire. The forthright conversations I had with the men I attracted helped me find my balance in the dance of sexual attraction and negotiation. It was incredibly empowering. I interacted with many men, just so I could find out where the line of danger really was, so I could sharpen my discernment and claim sex as my own.

I allowed myself not to be careful, not to mete out my passion in safe and controllable chunks, not to wait and wait until a man proved his trustworthiness, but to want him, to meet his approach, and to respond with my own. I then experienced the way men's lust could be life-giving instead of life-denying, a gift instead of a force that was trying to take something away from me. I risked my safety for this nourishment, for this raw material that, when joined with my own, contributed to something we were building together.

The strength of men is a blessing and is beautiful, when it is used to build, to love, and to protect. When it is used to steal, to bully, and to get one's way without regard for the wishes of others, it destroys the fine fabric of trust that is necessary for the beauty of the physically weaker to unfold (not that all women are physically weaker than men!). Still, as long as we live in a world of male violence, I do not believe that my sex will be able to offer the depth of giving that we have for the world, especially those gifts that lie in our most tender places—nor do I believe that the gifts which lie in men's most tender places will come forth and be offered either.

Not all men I've known have been coercive, and I feel sad that well-meaning men absorb a lot of rejection, suspicion, and shaming because some men rape, because so many men are socialized to believe that the only way to find intimacy is to coerce, steal from, and force themselves on women. I am also sad for the level of damage that is done to our lovely men to create such behavior. I would love to show my own lust and would love to engage the lust of men, without caution, playfully, openly. I certainly do much more than I did. Give me a world without violence, and women's juiciness would flow out to dance with the lust of men. In the meantime, girls need help in preserving and developing their fierceness, so that in trusting their "No!," they can find their "YES!"

—14—

Does Colorless Hair Cure Bisexuality?

Tortuga Bi Liberty

The fact that we are sexual beings until the very end of life, is seldom appreciated. . . . Now if men and women need each other to be fully human, and need to interact and relate to each other for their own self-esteem and self-identity, then we have to be compassionate and wise in creating, for old people and young people together, new life-styles that make it possible for old people to have some kind of sexual expression.

Maggie Kuhn, founder of Gray Panthers (1974:4-6)

When it comes to oral sex, I take out my teeth, honey, and you're going to get a blow job that'll take you on a trip.

Betty Dodson, masturbation artist and teacher (in Grant, 1994:254)

When I was young, the Beatles sang, "Will you still need me, will you still feed me, when I'm sixty-four?" For most elders, society replies, "You may get fed. You *won't* get touched."

I came out as bi around age twenty-one and interacted with bisexuals during two decades in the swingers' movement. Yet I had little experience with organized bi groups, as such, until the 1980s, when I joined San Diego's Bisexual Forum. Most meetings were formal discussions, and participants included adults of all ages. Moving to San Francisco in the 1990s, I found a different format—informal, cruisy, "bi-friendly" gatherings in a hip coffee-house, with many conversations going on at once. This decentralized style allowed for small talk, for individuals getting to know their peers, and for

---

This essay is dedicated, in deep admiration, to Betty Dodson. Special thanks also to Bill, Boats, Jan, Lorelei, Naomi, Tuppy, et al.

seeking by singles or by polyamorous couples. Here, the age distribution was markedly different—almost everyone was in their twenties or thirties. At a typical monthly gathering, with thirty people or more, perhaps three or four were in their forties (and some of these older members were pioneers who had joined much earlier, having been accepted then as young persons).

Sitting isolated among them, in my midfifties, white-haired, I perceived (and thus presented) myself as "too old"—obsolete, ugly, boring. People would lean around me to talk to a younger person. My own failure must be blamed on myself alone, yet I wonder *where were all the other gray-haired and white-haired bisexuals?* Does age "cure" bisexuality? Or lust in general? Or the need to socialize? My guess is that grey-haired bi singles do indeed exist, but don't often hang around this youthful group, as they rarely see their peers there. Perhaps each senior bi might try once—spending an evening alone in the crowd, without realistic hope. So each might give up and turn instead to sexless (noncruisy) pastimes. Or place personal ads. Or cruise the Net, where nobody knows you're a toad. Or, saddest of all, just sit home alone, wishing. Lonely isolation such as this can contribute to depression, bitterness, and self-hatred.

In the current climate, age segregation prevails. Most younger people avoid informal socializing with unrelated old singles, especially in sexy or cruisy or intimate or nude contexts. "We very rarely see a bar or a night club with an age range from sixty to seventeen in the cities," says Michelangelo Signorile. "We don't see that kind of mixing" (in Fertig, 1997). Sexual disgust and fear may even prevent young men from *talking* with old men, about anything at all, including nonsexual topics.

"There is a sexual attitude that permeates, and it cuts off the opportunities for exchange and expression of ideas," explains Jack Matlock, seventy-five, of San Diego. "There is open rejection, with comments . . . like 'that tired old queen.' . . . I know from experience in gay AA [Alcoholics Anonymous] that when the younger guys come in, and you start talking to them . . . and try to pass on what you've learned, they're thinking, 'He's going to jump my bones any minute'" (in Planck, 1997).

Novelist William Mann found older queers to be nearly invisible in the United States and Canada. Mann tells the story of Hank, who found a bar he liked in Boston: "Then I heard a young man call it a 'trolls' hangout. I had never realized until then that younger gay men would ever consider me a troll" (1997). In San Francisco, one bar, with large picture windows and an older clientele, is mocked as "The Glass Coffin." Within gay youth culture, oldie often equals moldy. Some young HIV-positive gay men, only in their twenties, were quoted as "joking," "At least we won't have to grow old and ugly" (in Valenzuela, 1995).

In the age game, gay men fare worse than het men, lapsing into middle age before thirty-five and acquiring senior citizen status by forty-five. E. Rogers says, "We think of older gay people as vampires, out to prey on our youth, obsessed with recapturing their own youth through sexual domination of a younger person" (1978). Honestly though, it's not all that much different with womyn. At fifty-five, I must learn to avoid womyn who are younger than me. How much younger? I'm not sure, but I risk being seen as the proverbial "dirty old man" if I guess wrong. If I cannot quite resist worshiping the forbidden nymph of forty, then I must be sure there's a pane of glass between her and me, or a camera lens. I must be voyeur, not participant. I must learn to hide my illicit yearning to put my tongue where it's no longer wanted—where it swam so happily in early days. I must learn how to conceal my absurd desires, impossible dreams, and "inappropriate" fantasies ("inappropriate" is the strongest curse that bureaucratic jellyfish allow themselves to mutter). I must act my age. I must be realistic. I must imprison my desire in a newly built closet. I must learn to be content with memories of real life. As for the ensuing half-life, or afterlife, I must hope for stoic nonhope. I must seek Buddhist nonseeking. To find peace, discard desire. Easy to say . . .

For overseas readers, let me state what goes unspoken among Yanks: society, here, tries to erase the sexuality of certain classes of persons, including the old, the "unattractive," and the physically challenged. Most porn implies that only the fittest should fuck and suck. "Imagism" hurts not only most of the old but also many younger people who are seen as "unattractive." When I became gray and wrinkled, I was enlisted by society into this oppressed class of "uglies"—a self-despising minority that rarely dares to reclaim its name. "So many of us feel asexual, or are *made by society to feel asexual*" says Barry Corbet, editor of *New Mobility,* explaining why his "disability lifestyle" magazine publishes a sex issue each year (in Sipchen, 1997). In Victorian times, "respectable" womyn were also pushed into this category of erotically erased persons. Even today, womyn may suffer from antisexual ageism more than men.

Antisexual beliefs concerning elders didn't always exist, and still today many cultures honor May-December marriages. Today, however the United States seems particularly obsessed with sexualizing youth and desexualizing elders. In a time of rapid changes driven by technology, the knowledge and beliefs of most Yank elders obsolesce even faster than their bodies, depriving them of their former reputation (admittedly overhyped) for mature wisdom. But even before you speak, people react to one's appearance (image) and to one's *perceived* age (this becomes significant if you look younger, or older, than you really are). Most people won't bother to evaluate your personality or your mind if they're already turned away by your appearance. "As they see you," warns a Spanish proverb, "so they treat you."

Please don't get me wrong. I'm *not* preaching to the young. I'm *not* asking them to confess bias. And I'm *not* asking them to modify their tastes, choices, preferences, attitudes, or behaviors. Most young persons really *cannot* "just say yes." They can't erase emotional or aesthetic revulsion by sheer force of idealistic will. I deplore all attempts at ideological bullying or PC guilt-tripping. Earnest attempts at emotion reform usually backfire anyway (as when a leftist Berkeley commune tried to "smash monogamy" swiftly, instead of nurturing polyamory softly, slowly). I preach to my peers, the old, and to those who soon will join us. I ask them to *seek old partners,* actively—to affirm their own worth by valuing, pursuing, and seducing their equals. *Lustful old people can, and must, liberate one another.*

Finding havens from ageism might be a little easier in the gay community. Older men in several cities have created "prime-time" organizations for gays and bisexuals over forty. When I attended my first G40+ meeting in San Diego, I felt waves of camaraderie and mutual respect within the room full of older men. If young men despised us, so what? We were happily busy, cruising one another and valuing one another. We soundly applauded a man who exclaimed "Limp dicks have feelings, too!"

There are magazines that praise the sexuality of older gay men. I hope older lesbians and bisexuals will develop similar periodicals soon. I was so excited when San Francisco finally got a cruisy venue for bisexuals, similar to G40+, in Spring 1997: an e-mail list for "BiFocus40." In San Diego, there is even a group that helps older womyn meet younger men, and vice versa: "December/May Singles." D/MS follows the wisdom given by Ben Franklin to younger men, "In all your amours, you should prefer old women to young ones" (1961).

Turning sixty-nine, gay male journalist and San Diego leader Queen Eddie says, "I openly admit my age because I want people who are approaching fifty, or approaching sixty, to know that your life doesn't stop. You can still have fun and be active. As long as your body allows you to do these things, do them. Don't sit in a room and wonder what you're going to do tomorrow. Go out there today and do something" (1997).

REFERENCES

Fertig, Jack. 1997. "The Scene and the Circuit Equals Death: Signorile Takes a New Cause." *San Francisco Bay Times,* May 15.

Franklin, Benjamin. 1745. Letter to "My Dear Friend" (June 25), often cited as "Advice to a Young Man on the Choice of a Mistress." In Leonard W. Labaree, ed., *The Papers of Benjamin Franklin,* Volume 3. New Haven, CT: Yale University Press, 1961, pp. 30-31.

Grant, Linda. 1994. *Sexing the Millennium: Women and the Sexual Revolution.* New York: Grove/Atlantic, Inc.

Kuhn, Maggie. 1974. Grass-Roots Gray Power. In Paul Kleyman, ed., *Senior Power: Growing Old Rebelliously.* San Francisco: Glide Publications.

Mann, William J. 1997. "Gay and Gray." *San Francisco Frontiers,* July 17.

Planck, Corri. 1997. "Is There Life After 60?" *Gay & Lesbian Times,* January 30, issue 475.

Queen Eddie. 1997. "Just Ask Queen Eddie." *Update,* March 19.

Rogers, E. 1978. "Older Gays: Our Neglected Roots." *Alive,* 1(11)

Valenzuela, Tony. 1995. "HIV Positive and Twentysomething." *Gay & Lesbian Times,* December 14.

15

Doing Time

Thomas McGrath

I'm a twenty-five-year-old white male. To those of you reading this, such specifics may seem trivial, but from where I stand, they mean a lot. You see, I'm doing time in prison, not just any prison, but an extremely racial Southern prison. It's not like most other prisons. I've never even heard of any other prison like it. It's a state-run plantation, and the same attitudes that existed during the plantation days of the South apply today, here and now. I'm not racist, by no means; my faith prohibits it. I'm also bisexual. Now we have the ingredients of this semiautobiography of one male's lusts and his struggles with them.

Life in the prison environment does not afford me to be myself. For instance, you have to sit a certain way, walk a certain way, read certain things (childish crap), to be the macho MAN. If I sit and cross my leg in a comfortable way, like you see many older men do, I'm told that I'm sitting wrong. If you don't act the MAN, you are talked about (really, you get talked about no matter what). No one says anything directly. You *never* come right out and say to anyone that he is effeminate or doing something "like a woman," unless you are looking for trouble, or the person is weaker in strength or mind than yourself, or the person is a female-acting homosexual (which I will get to later). I'm very compassionate toward people who are in need, and this, too, is considered by the majority as a female trait. It's people like me, though it's never happened to me personally, who have the hardest time in prison. (I'm also a first-time felon).

For someone young, like myself, it's hard to be *hard* all the time. When someone holds out a hand, especially someone who is possibly older in age or who has been doing time longer, we tend to grasp it and then we feel safe. We have some stability in our lives. We may talk into the wee hours of the night with this person and always "hang out" together, like people do on the street. This person may help you out, either by giving you things (food, coffee, smokes) or by helping you deal with problems on the outside that you can do nothing about. For me, it is my wife and children. You may not have any real way of returning the kindness that this person has shown you, so in your heart you feel obligated to do something. But what?

You may wash the "dishes" (plastic bowls, spoons, pot) after you both have eaten a meal. You may roll cigarettes for him, wash his clothes (usually he'll wash his own underwear). You'll do things to try to make his life easier, more comfortable, to show your appreciation for the things he's done for you. Eventually, you may become closer, and you may actually develop a physical attraction toward him. It may be mutual, and then the ice will be broken and the subject of sex will be brought up. He may ask you to masturbate him or give oral sex, whatever. Or you may ask to do it. This is only one situation I have observed during the five years I've been here. This is not the "Punk and his War Daddy" situation; it is *companionship*. I have seen this a few times and respect it to the fullest extent. It's based on mutual understanding and respect. I've seen short-timers commit other felonies because their companions have life and they wish to stay with them. I've also seen others leave and go out into the free world, but take care of their companions still inside.

As for myself, I don't have the courage to bring this type of companionship to blossom. I'm too much of a coward. It's too dangerous for someone like me to show my true self. I'm not about to work and slave for people I care nothing about, which is what happens when a homosexual or bisexual comes under the "administration" (protection) of one of the "organizations" (gangs) here. If I'm going to do something it will be for that person. I have to know a person and his or her habits. I'm just not into the sex thing for itself. There has to be something more to it. I'm this way with both women and men.

Most of the time, though, it's a "Punk and his War Daddy" situation. Let me familiarize you with the terms: "punk" and "boy" refer to the homosexual in the female role; the "war daddy" is in the male role and is the boss and protector of the punk/boy. He keeps the other prisoners, called "gorillas," "bears," and "hogs," from raping and abusing him, from taking the "boy's" stuff. The "daddy," also called the "man," can be bisexual; that is, he may have a wife or girlfriend outside. I've only seen two "boys" who were married, and one was just so he could best the woman out of her money. I see the homosexual men, both the "boys" and the MEN. The MEN are somewhat confused. Call them punks/boys and they want to murder you; they act the same if you call them homosexuals/gays. Let's face it, you can't play "pitch and catch" by yourself, and these people have a lot to learn when it comes to relationships of any kind.

Not all sex is rape, as I've shown earlier. But there are a few that I have seen, and I have had to remain silent. Yes, I know! But *I* must live with this regret, this haunt, not you. Rapes can be committed by force; that is, a deadly weapon, like a knife, is used or two or more individuals perpetrate it. A majority of the time, however, they are committed by intimidation. One or more men might display weapons and make verbal threats. For a person such as myself, I must always be one or two steps ahead of everyone else. I don't trust anyone in here too quickly, and *that* has saved both life and ass *more than once.*

When first-timers like me come into the system, we hear all kinds of stories—so many that it is hard to distinguish between truth and lie. Since being here, I know that anything is possible. But it is these stories, these "seeds" planted in the mind of the young men, that develop into the "flower of paranoia." You can get so scared that you don't want to speak to or be around anyone. I was like this in the beginning. After losing everything I cared about on the outside and realizing that I was alone, I developed an attitude that I wear as a "mask." It is *one* of the masks I often wear, especially when another prisoner tries to intimidate me. I've gained somewhat of a reputation for being "crazy" because of this mask, which enables me to be hateful and indifferent to the things that happen to others. All the while, underneath the mask, my very being weeps and fights for freedom, the freedom to express itself. It's like having a butterfly in a can. You'll never see it unless you remove the lid, but if you listen intently, you can hear its wings beating futilely against the can, trying to be free. I cannot remove the lid, not in here.

There are "gay" men who were homosexual on the street. They either place themselves in the female role or are forced into it. They refer to themselves as women and completely act out that role. They make panties and dresses, wear makeup, and fix one another's hair. Some are good-looking. I even have a real lust for one! He is very, very attractive and has legally changed his name to a woman's name. I dare say, I have true feelings for him, just as he is, and would commit to him, but I lack the courage to make any outright shows of affection. Besides, you just don't see a white "man" and a black "boy." You see, the race ratio in this prison is something like 97 percent black and 3 percent other. The majority would never give us any peace, and I would always be in trouble because I feel it is an insult to call a homosexual by anything other than his given or chosen name.

I've learned about myself that I am more at ease when around "companions" in here. I was the same outside when around gays and lesbians. I had gone through the "bashing" stage of these people, but was ignorant, and will use this time to apologize and sincerely ask your forgiveness. Back then, I was of "the majority," doing what the majority did and trying to fit in. It was not until I was put in prison that I started to read psychology and sociology and came to truthfully accept many things about myself.

Before I didn't have the understanding, so it was easy to go by the late propaganda preached in churches and talked about everywhere, the type of talk that makes homosexuals out to be some terrible device of Satan. People must come to realize that we give life to the words, the names, such as Satan. "Satan" is Adversity, which is a form of Hate, which is derived from lack of understanding, called Confusion, which is Fear, which is the lack of Reason in humanity. Thus, you have things like homophobia.

Who makes these rules and codes that say you can't have a male lover, perform oral sex, even with your wife or husband? Just who died and made this mass of idiots a Deity to dictate to me what I can do with my body? If I wish to put a stick up my anus, it's no one's business but my own. People, "the majority," mostly the wealthy, get together and decide what they do and don't like. And being that these people have power, they get what they want. All the while, they parade around with great pomp, but then they do the same things as we. Here, in the prison, like outside, "the majority" rules. But, as out there, you have rebels and deviants who will always refuse to accept the majority opinion and will buck the system.

There are too many concepts and not enough true doctrine. We have an abundance of knowledge, but we need to start understanding it, or we shall live and die in ignorance. From my own experience, I also know that we will never be able to comprehend others until we understand ourselves and accept who and what we are.

Peace, Love, Pleasure, and Respect

burnmarks, bleachstains,
n things that block the sun

Ahimsa Timoteo Bodhrán
(for the men who lovingly, who loving me, came after)

section I: burnmarks

eric

i hope i never see u again
i do not want u dead but i am not happy u r alive
i am not happy   eric
it has taken me a long time ta move on
ta forgive (bcuz I cannot forget)
u
for raping me
that night in january   13 months ago   in my dorm room
it has taken me that long ta write about it
it took me 5 months before i could speak again
before i could tell anyone anything about this
this memory u have burned inta my skin
the same skin u touched so many times as my boyfriend
n for the last time as my rapist
i didn't write about it   i didn't speak about it   for 13 n 5 months
i didn't forget about it   i didn't forget about it   n i can't forget about
it
i can't forget but i can forgive
i can forgive n i can move on now
n bcuz i can i will
i'll do what i can
which is almost everything
but forgetting u
n that night in january
n the memories u left
        burned inta my skin

section II: bleachstains

bleeding   still bleeding   i am still bleeding
eric
still bleeding
now across these white pages
n then across those white sheets
haven't even begun ta clot yet
gone n used up all my band-aids
cuz this wound too big
stitches don't hold   staples neither
went out n bought a mop for all the blood
but it can only hold so much
like a sponge it already saturated
n my bucket full

—there r things that stain deeper than clothes—
u a stubborn stain
feel kinda crazy sometimes like that macbeth lady
u a stubborn stain
permanent ink easier ta take out n less poisonness
my skin pink n raw   from scrubbin
from standin day after day in the same goddamn shower
water hot   almost scalding   it do no good
the flesh begin ta peel a bit
tear n wad up like used tissue paper
crumple n fold in upon itself

—there r things stained deeper than clothes --
the memory of u
stubborn like a toothache
no aspirin gonna ease this pain
        no suicide neither

section III: things that block the sun

baby
i'm sorry baby
didn't mean ta jump like that
forgot it wuz u for a moment
what?
naw there ain't no one else baby
u know that

no really
just
just bad memories that's all
      u know
      the kinda clouds that stick with u after a storm
      even tho it sunny out?
            yeah that kind
            the kind that block the sun
            yeah

baby?
aw nuthin
never mind
just come back over here n hold me for a while
      just
      not like that
      okay?
            yeah
            i'll b alright

17

Sex, Blindness,
and the Way of the Wound

William Thompson

As I sit down to write this, I found myself to be almost entirely at a loss and with nothing to say. It has only been in the last couple of years that I have even begun to get comfortable with my own sexuality, and it is still difficult to talk about. Comfortable, yes, but honest is perhaps a better term. My discomfort or dishonesty has been largely because of my blindness, which has impacted how I look at myself in relation to women, and even other men. When I was in my teens, I had friends to help me with the practical side of meeting girls—eye contact, body language, and other visual indicators were all things I needed to have explained. As an adult, I have learned to compensate for this lack of visual cues, such as hearing emotions by the way the voice resonates within the body. But these are practicalities, and, for me, sex and blindness has never been about practicalities. For me, writing about sex and blindness is about trying to reconcile my want for the erotic with the immovable fact of my blindness, my physicality always seeming to negate any kind of claim I have to an erotic life.

I lost my sight in a car accident when I was ten years old, so my blindness permeated my experience and understanding of sex from the very beginning of my adolescence. Losing my sight had never prevented me from doing the things I wanted to do: as a teenager, I skied competitively; I ran; I wandered all over town by bus and train. What I never did very well was to think about the impact of my blindness on me as a person. I certainly never thought about it in relation to sex. That connection never came until after nine years of marriage, when my relationship with my wife was already breaking down, and I could no longer maintain the illusion that my blindness had nothing to do with me both as a sexual being and as a man.

In the fall of my first year as a PhD student in children's literature, I was taking three graduate courses and teaching at the university in Edmonton. My wife and I had taken our kids—then four and two—to a water park. This place had a wave pool, water slides, a stereo, and what must have been a couple hundred kids all screaming at once whenever the waves began. I don't do well at places like this: it's hard to hear, and I had to hold my kids' hands just to know where they were.

My wife and I both were always afraid something would go wrong because of my blindness, and in fairness, it was my wife who took that on more than me. We wore a layer of tension around like a second skin, thickening us from the inside. In spite of the noise and confusion, however, things were going pretty well. Then, I took a turn going down one of the slides, and when I pulled myself out of the pool, there was incredible noise, with both the stereo and the waves going full blast—I couldn't hear a thing. My cane was somewhere on the deck, and without it, I had no way of knowing where I was. My wife was calling to me from the other side of a row of planters that bordered the pool, while a lifeguard was motioning at my wife for me to walk around the end of the planters. I stood there not knowing where to go, but also knowing that something was very wrong. Suddenly, my wife was crying, screaming, and swearing at this lifeguard. With no cane, I was as good as naked there on the deck, blind and deaf, for all I could understand of what was going on, experiencing a sick sense of being helpless. My wife's rage terrified me.

All that the situation really needed was for the lifeguard to come forward and show me how to get to where my wife was standing. I have no idea why the lifeguard didn't do this, but she didn't. My wife could have also come forward to help me, but she didn't want to leave the kids where they were. Still, it was my wife's rage that really struck me, evident in the disproportionately vicious stream of venom that she directed at the lifeguard. Her anger rooted me to the spot, even though I didn't really know what was happening. My response to the situation—that sense of being overwhelmingly blind and helpless—brought me to an acute awareness of something that was happening to both me and to my marriage.

By the time my marriage was breaking up, in January of that next year, I was feeling the heavy weight of years of not talking or even thinking about my blindness. I couldn't stop crying, and I couldn't put a name to whatever it was I was feeling. By February, my wife and I had split up. She and the kids stayed in the house we had been renting together, and I moved to a basement suite nearer to the university. Within five months, my life was a mess and I was living eight hundred miles from my kids.

The incident at the pool somehow ignited a whole host of insecurities. Standing there on the deck, I felt entirely unmanned—blind, exposed, and helpless—unable to move and unable to speak. And although I didn't understand why, at some level, my response to the overwhelming crises that erupted in my life got entirely channeled through sex. At the time, I cast it as a need for a relationship, but it really came down to sex—sex and my sense of self-worth, of which I had none at the time. Once I began to think about my blindness in relation to sex, I couldn't separate the two. All of the insecurities I felt about being blind, all of my feelings of helplessness and frustration seemed to be channeled into my feelings about sex. I felt neutered, repulsive to women in a way I had never felt before. I imagined any woman would turn away in disgust if I were to show any sexual interest in her. Lust was body, and my body was flawed. I felt ashamed every time I lusted after someone and told myself that I didn't deserve to have an erotic life.

In point of fact, women did reject me, though I think I set myself up through my own negativity. Many women initially responded to me; they were interested, certainly, but never in the ways I wanted. These women seemed to find me somehow less threatening than sighted men, at least until I showed some kind of interest in them. Rightly or wrongly, I told myself, it was my blindness that made me less threatening to these women, and it was my blindness that turned them off. The fact that no women responded to me fed my own sense of self-loathing, but it wouldn't have mattered if someone had responded to me or not. I felt cut off from the lower half of my body, and I put the blame on women for not rescuing me.

Part of the irony about all this was that I could relate to women—especially young mothers—in a way that I could never relate to other men. I became intensely interested in feminist thought during my years at school; this was, and continues to be, a genuine interest and concern, but at the time, I also somehow felt that having an interest in women's issues made me more nonthreatening—it seemed far removed from my own maleness. After I moved back to Edmonton and reestablished a week-on, week-off relationship with my children—something that helped bring my life back into perspective—I had that much more in common with the women I knew. They thought I was a good father. They respected me for being so involved with my kids, for doing the very things that they did for their own kids as a matter of course: taking kids to school, picking kids up from school, providing endless snacks, and running the bedtime show. But praise from these women was not what I wanted. I didn't want them to see me as a good father; I wanted them to see me as a potential lover.

Without being too aware of it, I began to use my blindness as a means of flirting with women. I tried to give my blindness an exotic appeal, despite the fact that I felt it was actually my blindness that turned women off the most. I felt compelled to play myself as the blind superdad, the guy who could be sensitive to his children's needs, bake cookies, and do a dissertation all at the same time. It wasn't as though the sensitivity was faked. I love my children, and I can bake great cookies. What was fake or dishonest was the way I used myself, my blindness, and even my kids to make myself more attractive to women. I felt as though I were living a lie; the truth was that I felt entirely at the mercy of my own lust and desperate need for approval.

It went on like this for a couple years, but nothing changed much. I stopped drinking, at least for a while; another relationship ended, and still nothing really changed. I continued to spin endless circles with guilt and shame and sex and self-loathing. It was like trying to cut a path through solid rock. Things started to turn for me when a friend, a female friend I might add, gave me an audio version of Robert Bly's *Iron John*. Bly's slightly nasal, oddly accented voice caught me immediately, and when he talked about the male wound, the wound that can proceed from alcoholism, disease, or disability, I felt myself grow still. It was like walking into a room that I always knew was there but had never entered, a place completely alien and entirely familiar. The image of the wound gave me a place to start, but the prospect of unpacking all that had been stored up was vaguely terrifying. Bly said that the way into the wound was through grief. Listening through the night to Bly speak didn't immediately change my life, but at least I could start putting names to the things that were making me crazy.

Bly got me thinking more concretely about my blindness. Thinking of myself as a blind person and as a blind man was difficult, at times even excruciating; it was a little like having to talk with someone I knew intimately but had avoided for most of my life. Although different people had talked with me through the years about accepting my blindness, I could never do what they seemed to expect of me. Acceptance felt like giving in, and I wouldn't do that. I had always resisted the measure of dependence that had been forced on me, but after reading Bly, I began to take an honest, if cautious, look at how I really felt about my own blindness.

Slowly, I began talking about my blindness whenever I needed. I began to feel more at home in my own skin, and I could actually feel myself unclenching. I came to recognize my blindness as a simple fact, as part of what makes me who I am. That was enough to get me started.

As I moved away from the self-loathing game, my way of sexually relating to women also began to change. It gave me a measure of humility, and I found that my frustration, anger, and helplessness were all my own. Even just knowing the exact source of those feelings helped me to relax with myself and around women. If I flirted, then at least I was doing it honestly. My feelings concerning my blindness have always intensified my feelings concerning sex, but finding the willingness to entertain some of the feelings related to the one has helped me, in turn, to feel easier about the other. As painful as that was, and as challenging as that still is for me at times, finding my way through this wound helped me to feel more at ease with my claim to the erotic, as well as with its claim on me.

—18—

Middle-Aged, Queer, and HIV Positive

Michael Shernoff

I'm a forty-seven-year-old HIV-positive gay man who has lived in the center of the HIV vortex since it descended upon my community. Most of my friendship group, the men with whom I expected to grow old, have died, as has my beloved partner, Lee. I wrote the first generation of safer-sex workshops for gay men and conducted these workshops on "Eroticizing Safer Sex" for more than 15,000 men all over North America in the mid-1980s.

During the 1970s, I lived in the sexual fast lane and really loved being there. My generation of post-Stonewall gay men came out in a culture that encouraged us to have sex with a stranger as casually as we might shake hands with a new acquaintance. Branded sexual outlaws, many of us embraced sex in a lusty and unapologetic way, creating a new politic rooted in the unending potential for male bonding through bodily pleasure. In those early years of the gay liberation movement, many of us discussed such topics as "Was monogamy an internalization of heterosexual norms?," "the politics of being exclusively a top or a bottom," "group sex," "leather sex," "drag," and so on. It was exhilarating and frequently a turn-on to be discussing particular sexual behaviors with other men, many of whom were intoxicatingly attractive. Looking back, I realize that part of my motivation for attending gay activist events was the hope of meeting and bedding some of the other activists. It was tremendously important and unbelievably validating to be talking with other gay men about sex, not to mention actually getting to have sex that often was emotionally rich, with an amazing variety of people. We placed a lot of emphasis on our right to do whatever we wanted with our bodies. We gave ourselves permission to experiment.

Before AIDS, cruising and searching for sex gave many gay men's lives meaning and focus. This is still true for a large segment of the gay population today, men of all generations. Time spent in the baths, sex clubs, or "meat rack" of Fire Island often had a primordial feeling of connecting to other members of the same tribe. For those of us in the process of developing cohesive gay identities, the energy of sexual possibility and actuality often became the core component of these identities, along with our political actions, organizing and building a queer sense of community. Positive connections to the gay men's community were bound up with our activism, our sexual adventures, and the emotional and friendly connections we forged simultaneously. While obvious parts of the urban sexual fast lane that had no more "depth" than the immediate satisfaction of sexual urges, the sexual climate also had a real celebratory aspect to it that was very healing, acting as a partial antidote to growing up in the homophobic culture of the 1950s and 1960s.

In this sexual free-for-all before AIDS, a steady supply of sex with unknown partners became a rite of passage for many "liberated" urban gay men, who saw sexual freedom and gay liberation as synonymous with no more repression, no more guilt or shame, no more hiding—being out and proud meant getting off as often as possible. I embraced this gay party ethos, as did nearly all my friends. It was practically unheard of for gay men to say anything negative about the gay sex scene. Those who felt alienated and intimidated by the hypersexual climate were afraid of being branded traitorous, uncool, homophobic, or erotophobic. Until recently, there was little, if any, exploration of the psychological fallout of fast-food, anonymous, "hit and run" sex, and few, if any, voices from within the community offered a counterpoint to the paramount position the urban queer sexual culture held in gay male society.

AIDS changed this earlier ethos, dramatically. Many men became justifiably afraid of sex. Instead of being an elixir of love and play, semen became equated with death. Many men stopped having sex or retreated into a monogamous relationship, hoping it would protect them from becoming infected. Partially in response to the fact that HIV is transmitted sexually, it is currently fashionable to trash the sexually free-wheeling times of the 1970s as nothing more than expressions of unexamined hedonism. In my mind, this sexual revisionism is dangerous, simplistic, and devalues an intrinsic component of early gay male culture. There was an incredible liberation and freedom in entering a place such as the Mine Shaft or baths where you could safely look at, touch, and sexually play with other men, without fearing that an admiring glance could be a prelude to being humiliated, fag-bashed, or even arrested. It also fails to note the profound connections that were made through sexual liaisons. Some of my best friends were men I met through an encounter that was initially sexual. I resent the backlash rhetoric that AIDS was a blessing in disguise for the gay community because it "made us" learn how to be more to one another than just sex partners. That is an insult to all of us who have lost so much and who continue to lose our lives every day to this illness, and an outrageously misguided take on the pre-AIDS gay sex scene. Gay men have always had deep friendships, loyalties, and love affairs—we don't just screw one another.

Similarly, many gay men have begun to identify themselves as being sexually compulsive and to refer to all the sexual activity in the pre-AIDS era as just that. I do not believe that being promiscuous is a mental illness. An often-repeated definition of a "promiscuous" person is anyone who is having more sex than the speaker. For many gay men, a high level of sexual activity is actually some kind of innocent, adolescent freedom combined with sexual experimentation. When some gay men talk about being sexually compulsive, what they really mean is sex that cannot be credibly taken as political liberation or personal ecstasy because it does not bring joy, cannot be controlled, and is used, just as alcohol or drugs, to assuage a nonsexual need. Certainly, some men act in ways that are self-destructive or destructive to others, and for some of these men, the support offered through twelve-step programs has helped them tremendously. But the labels "addict" and "compulsive" have the potential to (re)pathologize our sexuality. Many gay men flock to twelve-step groups, worried and anxious that they are "sick." All too often, my clients who go to these meetings come back convinced that their daily masturbation and frequent tricking prove they are "sex addicts." I simply don't see these actions as necessarily problematic. If they are not having high-risk sex or looking for a relationship, then what's wrong with these behaviors? It seems to me there is some plain, American Puritanism at work here—people who feel ambivalent about their bodies' ability to offer them pleasure through sex feel guilty, which leads them to conclude they are sick. How often is a gay man's ambivalence about the way he seeks sexual satisfaction really a screen for his own internalized homophobia?

At the same time, as I look back on the early days of my coming out into gay life, I question if all that erotic exploration made me happy. Being younger and emotionally unsophisticated, I often lacked any understanding of what propelled me to have sex. I remember, on more than one occasion, that while giving someone face, as much as I savored the taste and feel of the man's cock in my mouth, what I really needed was his affectionate touching and caressing of my head and shoulders. At that time in my life, I was unable to differentiate between my need for affection and my need for sex. In all honesty, I was barely aware that I had any emotional needs aside from those being satisfied by my numerous sexual escapades. Only with years of psychotherapy did I become aware that I was trying to have sex meet an enormous variety of needs that were often completely unrelated to sexual desire. When feeling horny or a simple desire to play with the other boys was what propelled me, I would generally have a wonderful time and afterward feel refreshed and nurtured. The problem was that I often found myself seeking sex when what I felt was lonely, bored, depressed, or sad. When needs other than sexual ones motivated seeking out sex, I generally came away feeling let down and dissatisfied, even when I had fun sex with several people. I eventually learned that when the need wasn't about sex, no amount of romping could ameliorate the uncomfortable feelings from which I was seeking distraction. This is a distinction I work on with my patients to help them learn how to sort out their motivations for themselves. I was not alone in confusing the sexual arena with a place where deeper emotional needs would be satisfied. Good sex is very intoxicating. Men in this society are notorious for thinking and feeling with our dicks and not being able to recognize needs for closeness, companionship, intimacy, and friendship. With all men being socialized to equate sexual "achievement" with self-worth, it is not surprising that the importance of sex increased exponentially in the all-male gay environment. Without the moderating influence of women, gay sexuality tended to become hypermasculinized. Some of the focus on sex in gay culture is a reaction against society's attempts to repress all expressions of same-sex love and sexuality. At a more subtle level, I think that society's shroud of silence around gay desire and men loving men has lead many gay men to forge part of their identities in the fire of hot anonymous sex with large quantities of men. Thousands of other men and I thus fashioned a component of our identities from the outside in, giving our desires and innermost longings true life in their undeniable physical enactment. Eventually, I began to examine having sex with strangers. Whenever engaged in terrific, mood-altering sex, I would wonder, "Is this my next husband?" It was terribly difficult for me to separate out the intense feelings that got stirred up in sex. Additionally, I generally wanted more from the man I was having sex with than just "hit and run" sex, even when I was in one of the venues where quickie sex was the clear agenda. A defining moment in my sex life occurred in 1980, literally, in the middle of an orgy. I was playing with several other men, each of whom would have been delightful on his own. In the midst of various sexual permutations—all great fun—I began to mentally balance my checkbook. Startled, I disengaged myself and sat down on the sidelines to ponder what had just happened. Moments before, I was living out a wonderfully complex fantasy, and then suddenly, I had gone somewhere else. Upon reflection, I decided that I simply did not want to be doing that at that moment. Something inside me had shifted; I got dressed and left chuckling and bemused.

There were also those times when quickie sex was perfectly satisfying. Yet, in hindsight, I see that something important was missing from all of those early sexual explorations: there was little, if any, exploration of the feelings we were having while being sexual. The separation of sex from feelings, and of sex from love, was almost institutionalized for certain segments of the emerging gay men's community, as it is for so many men of all sexual orientations. Even as gay men, many of us were not really able to integrate the feeling component of our lives with our sexual exploration. At the time, I didn't realize how desperately I wanted a relationship. Frankly, I didn't even know I felt desperate at all. I simplistically thought that sexual compatibility was the basis for beginning the relationship and didn't know the first thing about finding an appropriate man with whom to become involved.

I should be careful not to overstate my case. There was, indeed, a lot more going on than just sex. People were coming out, making friends, forging a community with political agendas, having affairs, and sometimes beginning long-term lover relationships, relationships that might or might not be sexually exclusive. I do not regret any of my past sexual behaviors. It was a crucial part of the evolution and growth of myself and thousands of other gay men to have had the opportunity to discover our sexuality and the erotic bonding that was a hallmark of that period. Increasingly, however, I am seeing the psychological fallout of having accepted a hypersexual definition of ourselves as gay men and as people. In splitting off our emotions from our libido, we may have done ourselves a disservice. Yet, at the same time, there is no denying that the sexual energy of the "meat market" was one important fuel for much of the good that happened in those years.

I know that I have learned a great deal from my sexual play with other gay men. As a younger man, sex was my primary means of being validated. It was also, and remains, just a hell of a lot of fun. Sex, and the pursuit of sex, was a primary recreational activity and means of playing. It is still one of the ways I get validated and play, but no longer the primary way. The shift is at least in part due to aging. Being in my late forties I no longer have the same energy available for sex that I once did. In all honesty, I'd have to say that sex occupied an inappropriately significant part of my younger life—too much of my life was bound up in sexual concerns and seeking sex. Being a middle-aged man with a satisfying professional, social, and emotional life as well, sex is now just one component of my life that I enjoy, and, as the anecdote at the start of this essay reveals, with which I struggle. But, all in all, the role and place of sex in my life now feels more balanced than when I was younger. I think this may be just a normal accompaniment of aging and—hopefully—maturing.

I still have powerful sexual attractions to large numbers of different men and relish the energy that results from these flirtations or encounters. Yet being, once again, single, at this point in my life, I prefer having at least some level of emotional continuity accompany being sexual. That is not to say that remaining sexually exclusive while I have been in committed relationships was easy or without struggles at times. Similarly, committing to engaging in

100 percent safer sex all the time has not been realistic. Over the past five years, I have engaged in unprotected sex during which I, as the infected individual, took my partner's semen during either anal or oral intercourse. This appears to pose little risk of transmitting HIV, as does a man performing oral sex on me as long as I pull out of his mouth before ejaculating. Receiving my lover's semen is an important and often spiritual act for me, one that I wish I was able to reciprocate. The general, as well as my personal, sexual landscape is a vastly different place than it was during my youth. Like thousands of other men of my generation, I mourn what was lost with the onset of AIDS. Most important, the lives, but additionally, the loss of sexual innocence, which today's young people cannot ever again know, as this deadly plague continues to find new victims.

What the Fuck?

Sara Sullivan

Men just want to get laid. It's common knowledge. "Men have one thing on their minds." "Men think with their dicks." Until recently, my life experience validated these stereotypes. While my earliest sexual experience was mine alone—fiery pleasure rushing up from my vulva as I ecstatically raced my red tricycle around in circles—I discovered my sexuality with others to be largely as a series of collisions with pushy male lust.

On a solo errand to pick up some mending when I was seven, the neighborhood tailor reached his long, skinny fingers between my legs and asked, "Does that feel good, little girl?," introducing me to my clit. When I was ten, my worldly fourteen-year-old friend gave me a stack of porn books, including *The Happy Hooker*, which I thought were nonfiction. I read them with great interest and no filter, absorbing information, misinformation, sex-positive attitudes, and sexist assumptions equally. A year later, I began to join in the kissing games popular in my neighborhood. Soon the kids called me a slut because I openly enjoyed kissing as much as the boys. I hadn't yet caught on that girls were supposed to pretend not to enjoy it, as if we were being coerced.

At age thirteen, I went out one day wearing a white Victorian-style shirt from an Indian imports store, the kind popular in 1974, and a simple choker, a leather string with a blue glass bead. I was small and thin for my age, with long, thick hair and big eyes. It was probably the first time I'd worn anything that showed the faint outlines of my new breasts. I heard catcalls for the first time, by three different men before I got home. I remember wondering why, barely daring to think that I might be sexy.

Around the same time, I began taking the dilapidated underground trolley to school. On almost every ride, out of the stifling crowd of winter-bundled torsos, something hard and smooth would press across my butt. The first time, I cried and didn't move, but after that, I would jab my elbow into the guy or stomp on his feet. Guilty and terrified, he would invariably scuttle away, as fast as he could in a jam-packed trolley. Child molesters were cowards, I learned. Soon I could recognize them by the furtive, greedy way they looked at me. I discovered that a certain facial expression kept them at bay. I would think, over and over, "If you touch me, I'll kill you!" while staring right into their eyes. My evil-eye kept them away, and sometimes made them run just the same as if I'd jabbed them with my elbow.

Who would have guessed the pretty, tiny girl on the subway was already a witch who could terrify grown men with her psychic power? Even I didn't know it or give my powers the respect they deserved. It was just survival, and unfortunately, I didn't have a choice. I didn't know how to turn that face on and off. I developed a tough shell and a deep distrust of people, men in particular.

By age fifteen, my body was hot and responsive, ready to ignore the past and hunt for the buried treasures of sex. But, while I was still a virgin, my sexy boyfriend date-raped me. My next lover, a dissipated musician in his twenties, belittled me for being too free-spirited in bed. One day I noticed that I simply wasn't horny anymore. I was curious and intrigued by sex, and still experimented with it, but lust had left my body. I felt defective. It seemed a cruel joke to have been given an especially sexy body, only to be burdened by the attention it received. I imagined how much fun I would have with all those slutty boys if only I could recapture the lusty joy I felt riding my little red tricycle.

This story is nothing new: bad men molesting girls, the difficulties of being a survivor, and so forth. Anyone reading this book is probably well aware of that particular downside of male lust. The story I really want to tell, however, is about what's happened now that I finally have my lust back. I genuinely like men, I appreciate their passion, and I'm ready to respond to some of their slutty invitations. So imagine my surprise to find that the man behind the curtain isn't a simple sex maniac after all!

Now that I finally match men's enthusiasm for sex, I find many men to be as fearful of female lust as the neighborhood kids were in the bad old days. Often they pursue sex as ardently as those boys pursued kissing, then call me a slut (or the equivalent) when things don't go their way. And I'm not talking about regular all-American guys, either. These are "hip" men, political leftists, artists, environmentalists, and feminists, who've been around long enough to have learned something about women.

A lot of men I've known have a hard time being real. Their inauthenticity can look like a sexist double standard or pseudosensitivity. Men often hide either their tenderness or their lust. It's the male counterpart of the virgin/whore dichotomy: the nice guy/stud dichotomy. The men who do show both tenderness and lust often act as if they own me, as if possession is the only context in which they feel safe letting down their guard. The scenario is predictable. We meet; we flirt; we talk. We get together for lunch, a walk, or something. We enjoy each other's company and flirt more. Maybe this time, maybe next time, I see the signs. He looks at me often in a hungry, nervous way. He's going to try to kiss me soon. (I love this part!) But do I want to kiss the guy yet? Or at all? Often the answer is, "Yes, of course!" (Now a word for those of you panicking about disease, the bogeyman of the 1990s—chill out. I'm a sensible person, and an expert on safe sex. So are most of my lovers, and the ignorant ones don't stay that way long. You probably get in your car even though you might be killed in a crash. I get in bed, seat belt on, and unless you're my lover, I don't want to hear anymore about it. Now back to our story.)

But maybe he's a can of worms I don't want to open. He hasn't asked if I have other lovers. He doesn't know how I view relationships. We're both grown-ups. We both know that we don't know the future. We're not making promises. We're not getting engaged or renouncing all other lovers. So I figure he must want lighthearted sex with no specific commitment.

Should I say, "No, let's wait"? I could do that. I have loads of willpower. Sometimes I do say, "Let's wait," yet soon they are at it again, touching me. I have needs too. Why should I have to be the one to provide all the "no" power? Providing willpower is a kind of "women's work," easier when my sex drive was damaged. But now my body is sexually alive again, and I like it. When the energy is raised, my formerly numb body is a conduit for magic electricity. I want to let it do its thing. I want to be in the moment as much as my lover is, not thinking ahead to all the consequences, not putting up roadblocks. If he needed me to be his wife before we had sex, he wouldn't be trying to have sex with me on the first date. So I don't need to break the flow of sexual energy by issuing a standard disclaimer, right?

Wrong, apparently. With many men, possessiveness kicks in shortly after sex, sometimes just after desire. Their sense of entitlement to have what they want from women, simply because they want it, boggles the mind. Their primary desire seems to be to have sex with me, but this is followed closely by a desire to make sure no one else does. The whole can of worms is presented through a smoke screen of romantic symbolism, which makes me suspect they are running a scam. Though they use words such as "commitment," their tone evokes images of control more than love.

So the same man who only weeks earlier was intent on seducing someone he barely knew, now claims that "sex implies commitment." Under questioning, he admits that he's "gotten laid maybe seven or eight times" in the past year, but insists that with each of these barely remembered women he was "open to commitment." He talks about "getting more serious," as if he believes it's what I've been waiting for all along. He seems to feel entitled to change the terms of our relationship at will and becomes scarily angry and insulting when I refuse to cooperate with his narcissistic program.

One lover seemed shocked that I had acquired my sexual skills and openness from having actual sex with actual men who weren't him and that I intended to continue doing so. I would have given up other lovers for this man, moved into his school bus, and had big fat babies, but he could never decide from one day to the next if he wanted to see me again. When he sent me an angelic white negligee for Christmas, it bolstered my impression that he wanted me to wait chastely for him, to prove my worthiness. Later, I heard through the grapevine that my old-fashioned loverboy had told his friends I was "promiscuous" (as if he wasn't!), as if it were some kind of moral disease. I finally got tired of his mixed messages and made him go away.

I did promise fidelity to one boyfriend in my rebirth-of-lust period, but he still got very angry with me when other men so much as looked at me. Of course, my appearance had attracted him, but he didn't want anyone else to take notice. I've been looked at my entire life, often in ways that threatened or distressed me. I'm not going to take the blame for it now that I relish it. His particular attitude is a traditional sexist one, which isn't surprising to find, except that it came from a quiet, highly educated artist with leftist politics and a feminist perspective. He seemed so sweet. I was sad to leave him.

A common theme here is the good old double standard. These men seemed to be inviting me to share in playful sex, but even if a woman will have casual sex with them, many men convince themselves she wouldn't do it with anyone else. They want to have sex with Sleeping Beauty, who at the moment of a kiss is suddenly transformed into a person with no life, a blank slate upon which the prince writes his desires. My frustration with the current state of my sex life is not just that I'm not getting enough good sex but that when I surprise men by being almost as driven by sex as they are, and then don't fall into a pattern of devoting my whole life to them, they seem to think I don't care about them at all. A few coldly belittle me, as if I have no feelings. One man attempted to punish my independence by cutting me off from sex, saying, "You can suck all the dicks you want, just not mine." (An hour later, he had changed his mind, but couldn't change mine. Sayonara, Sonny.) I guess this insensitivity stems from the virgin/whore dichotomy: the virgin is seen as helpless, sweet, and vulnerable, whereas the whore is seen as manipulative, cold, and invulnerable. I don't fit either model.

So it seems I'm being led toward the solution traditional feminine wisdom would suggest: "Since casual sex has negative consequences, just say no." Be a rules girl, and use my mojo to catch a man. But I don't necessarily want to catch that man! Commitment is too serious a business to blithely jump into. I can be much more miserable with a boyfriend than I could ever be without one. Lust surfaces quickly, but commitment takes time. There has to be a reason for it besides romantic convention and his desire to control me. Why can't we be friends, take time to get to know each other, and let things assume an organic shape? Why force the issue with an immediate demand for me to change my entire life?

I used to think all men wanted to get laid. Now, with more experience, I'd say most men want to get laid, but only on their terms. As I ponder various puzzling encounters with men, it occurs to me that since women often refuse casual sex, for many men, playful sex with women remains an untested fantasy. When they find a woman who wants it too, they finally bump into their own limits. Some panic and seize the double standard as a crude map to navigate uncharted waters.

The price of being a sexual trailblazer is the pain of being misjudged and whacked over the head with the virgin/whore billy club. When I am judged by a lover for saying yes to something he offered me himself, it breaks my heart. Sometimes I feel like the girl on the trolley, being assailed simply because her body is desirable, before she learned to scare men away. Still, I'm not going to hide my sexuality under a rock as I did as a teenager. I'm going to pursue good sex as greedily as men and find it where I find it. I'm pissed about all those lost sex years. I was robbed of my sex drive, now I have it back, and I want to nurture it. If I have to put up with some bullshit, so be it. I'll sometimes have sex with a sexy guy even if I know he's got character flaws or he's not as smart as I am. Why not? Men do that all the time. I don't need to define myself by whom I have sex with—I can have a roll in the hay with someone unsuitable as a mate. It's all for a good cause— keeping my energy flowing. And for the sisterhood. More women having more orgasms is good for all women!

I am grateful when men are honest and real with me—neither pushy nor pushovers, both sensitive and studly. I wish more of them could say, "Hi. I'm a complex being. I want your body. I want you to go out in the world and be treated fairly. I want to fuck you. I'm terrified of commitment, but I want to make friends, but I'm scared you'll force me to be your boyfriend and suck the life out of me. I'm also afraid you'll reject and hurt me. But still I want to fuck you! Now!" An unusually candid personal ad in the *San Francisco Weekly* says a lot: "Sensitive feminist by day, wild-eyed pirate by night, seeks fair maiden . . ."

Am I asking too much? Yes, I am asking for something new, something that doesn't fit the old mold, but does fit my needs. I want lusty friendliness without coerced commitment. I want us to have both the lust men are entitled to and the interest in the whole person that is expected of women. I want intimacy without ownership. But I'm running into a shortage of suitable partners. Some want to coerce me into a prison disguised as romance, some who fear being coerced into that same prison protect themselves by avoiding intimacy, and others who fear their own coercive potential are just not that available for hot sex. What's a slutty-but-sweet girl to do?

I claim my right to lust for lust's sake. I like men because they are fun, adventurous, resourceful, and playful. Many are good at solving concrete problems and lifting heavy stuff, and willing to thumb their noses at authority. In bed, they usually make up in enthusiasm what they lack in finesse. I want to learn from them, play with them, and take some of them up on what I thought they were badgering me for all along. It's payback time! Instead of fearing male desire, I say, "Work it, sister!"

20

Lion's Courtesan

Emil Keliane

All my life I have tried to fathom my own gender fate. In relation to other men, am I man or am I woman? As a developing homosexual child in Iran, I learned to adopt woman's sentiments concerning man and relationships; not a liberated, enlightened, independent woman's sentiments, but a subjugated woman's. I learned to feel and be inferior to man. I lay submissive and allowed him to penetrate me, thinking to myself, I am the courtesan he prefers most. But I knew better, that when he sank into my vagina, he descended into a hundred vaginas, simultaneously, and permeated our bodies with the same unisex lie. He did not distinguish my particular flavor, my own texture; he did not recognize the reverberations characteristic of my vulva, my womb. That I was lucky if he, with his eyes closed in ecstasy and self-love, distinguished the touch of my hair from that of his most prized Arabian!

Now in the States, I walk away from a tryst in the woods with a new him, who yet remains the old. With me, I take some evidence, some obscure token, a reminder: traces of blood on my pants from having scraped skin against stones and branches, underwear placed and forgotten in my pants' pocket, dents in my knees because I was taken from behind this time, the unique taste and scent of him upon my own person and in my mouth so that I must stop at a gas station for bottled water to gargle him out. A wasted attempt because it is not soap or water that wash a lover's scent—the saliva from his kisses that varied in intensity, the carnal recollections that survive in our bodies—but time and distance.

Later, he tells me he wants to fulfill a rape fantasy with me and a friend of his, but I say I am not yet ready; truth is, I do not want to. He asks me to narrate to him erotic memories from my past, but does not ask about love, romance. He wants me to disclose the erotic images that are conjured when I think of him privately. I refuse for fear of sounding forced and trite. The erotic talk only begins when we are deep in some dizzying act, and only then does it come easily, naturally, even imaginatively. I am so overcome by this dizziness that I can't help but embellish with white lies about my own brother fucking me when I was little, because perversity arouses him. These are stories from the unconscious really—that sex among young men was natural in Iran, clandestine, and prevalent. I construct fibs from already existing myths about men and homoerotic conduct in the Middle East.

Yet I cannot repudiate this man, this man who also dwells within, simply because he may possess tyrannical tendencies. In taste, in temperament, in identifying with and relating to others, and in general perception of the world I am two sexes, an androgynous spirit, and I refuse to betray either force that is existent within me. This is true not because I am gay but because I arrive from the intuitive and psychic womb of my father's and my mother's physiological imagination. I am androgynous because I am human. Ironic that in an attempt to integrate myself in a world adverse to homosexuality there would have to take place within me a heterosexual marriage of my male and female counterparts.

When I try to take him from behind I fail and lose my erection because I am not yet accustomed to, and comfortable with, the role of the aggressor. It is foreign to me, and the pressure to act causes temporary impotence. He instructs me instead to bend before him on the incline with my elbows planted into the fallen leaves, the crackling of which I don't hear because I am breathing deeply; I only hear myself breathing, concentrating to relax my essential muscles because they are inclined to tighten and to refuse him entry. He pushes against this blockade, persists despite the impasse I summon, and enters beyond my unwillingness. When the sound of his pelvis slapping against my buttocks ceases, I am overcome by a nameless shame. I feel strangely like an animal, without worth, and, ironically, he says he enjoys sex in the woods because it is "animalistic." When he grins, I cannot tell if, like a lion, he is smiling or panting.

A slipping in, a falling into, a traversal of barriers, and if only this would occur emotionally, spiritually. That day would just be religious! He lives always by the hunger and the appetite, always by the erection and the willing desire. The active, easy maleness. He can fuck and be fucked without effort, without meaning. But not I. . . . Once, I had only to stand before a mirror and say the words "I am gay"; that was all. But much to my surprise, the true challenge would arrive when I had to kneel before a man and struggle desperately to feel purely at one with my sexuality.

21

What I Learned
from One Mean Fucker

Martin Phillips

Most guys would be wisely timid about a rape confession. Maybe after too many drinks, one man might privately boast to another that he had succeeded in fucking someone without that person's consent. But being a male sexual assault *victim*, Oh dear! Not even a drunken man wants to tell that story. The subject brings to mind predatory priests or the movie *Deliverance* (1972), with its vivid rape scene and notorious pig-squealing humiliation. Is rape considered more degrading for male than for female victims? Perhaps so, in the minds of those who hold archaic beliefs about manhood and gender. These subtle attitudes linger and, in some sense, represent the triumph of the idiot. This graceless state of mind is part of the rape conditioning men possess; it is a pattern of learned social behavior.

Although I was initially shy about having been raped, I later came to realize it was actually to my advantage; it was like taking an advanced seminar on dysfunctional male sexuality. I've since worn that sordid historical fact like a badge. For I have glimpsed what is most frightening and disturbing about male sexuality, the sick side. I have felt it, the disease: it grabbed me by the balls; it fucked me. It was mean at first, threatening. When I presented no lethal threat, it was like I wasn't there. It could have been screwing anything, in brutal ecstasy. Yes, *ecstasy*. That is what, at the time, seemed so bizarre to me, that this big asshole of a guy was fucking me without my permission and he was quite pleased with himself. Naturally, I wanted to kill him.

However, he was just one incarnation of the malady, and although it is an individual act, rape is made possible by social conditioning. With regard to my own socialization, I remember how the bigger boys always had their way, especially in the boys' locker room. Everybody was in fear of someone, maybe not the same person. There were certain jocks who were quick to call someone else a *pussy*, usually as an insult. The guys who weren't jocks, but who were above somebody else in the pecking order, would call the rung below pussy.

Nobody wants to get beaten up by some bellicose moron. Fight back? Suppose a weaker boy somehow beats up a higher-rung aggressor? The victor stands over a bloody face and suddenly realizes the fellow on the ground was the guy he used to be; now he's the tough one looking down on another pussy. This hierarchical violence, explicit or implicit, helps maintain a complex system of power at every level of our panoptic nightmare. A society that punishes with violence, finds justice in violence, enjoys violence as entertainment, mixes sex with violence, feeds itself by violently killing animals, and rapes the earth as its daily business is a mean motherfucker.

We all like to think of ourselves as good people; even a rapist can project a confidence and self-satisfaction that suggests he holds himself in good esteem. My rapist was a fellow student at the University of Washington in Seattle. He was somebody I helped in a math class. Until he became my rapist, I would have described him as a nice guy, maybe not so bright, but he didn't seem mean, and although he may have had plans for me, such possibilities never even crossed my mind. It's not like I remember him treating me, or even looking at me, in a sexual way. Later, I realized he must have been. He was skilled at deceit; I was naive.

While a rapist may have a surprising amount of self-respect, the lust magnet is reduced to the solitary function of satisfying the rapist's momentary urge. Of course, the victim has desires and a will, but that fact is obliterated by the aggressor's sexual needs, which are only temporarily sated and which drive him beyond himself into the world of others as a marauding fucker, a sublime state of selfish transcendence. It seems odd that so many young men are somehow thwarted in their development, often rising only slightly above this elementary condition.

He fucked me with that familiar, repetitious pounding; he was lost in delirious ecstasy. In this way, there are similarities with hard-core crack addicts whose goodness depends on accessibility to the drug. In either case, the ultimate high is oblivion. The rapist is temporarily "gone," transported to a primordial state in which the most extreme transgressions against the rights of another being are irrelevant. All this seems particularly possible in men because of the single-sided nature of this chased moment: the remarkable independence of the male orgasm. Although womyn, too, can show signs of a twisted moral development and are certainly capable of "fucking over" others, they can never experience the same drugged, fuck-machine mode that a man can enjoy from a position of dominance bestowed upon him by his hard dick, regardless of the state of his object of lust. Female sexual abusers are becoming more common (if we are to believe the press), yet how many do it for ecstasy? Studies have claimed that womyn sexual offenders most frequently do it out of curiosity or spite or hatred.

As much as my rapist was mindlessly fucking me, he felt compelled to announce, "I'm coming!" It was mixed with a gurgling sound, yet the phrase rang with a *joyful* clarity. Although he spoke his good words with an unconscious, forced, guttural reflex, this fatigued phrase had a fresh sound, its meaning stripped of its cliché use. I'm sure he had heard this common phrase many times and was repeating it much as a cricket emits sound by rubbing its legs together, instinctively; it is an almost universal announcement made by human participants in sexual intercourse, male and female alike. Perhaps, in this respect, it is as meaningless as the outburst of semen, a gob of words that meant more to me than to my rapist, who spoke them with such masculine fervor. To whom was he speaking? To me? To God? To himself? Or was the purpose of these words to intensify his own experience, as he might very well do while masturbating? Or was that phrase an indication that he was vaguely aware of my presence? Perhaps he wanted to share his good moment with someone, anyone. When things go well for us, we are all generous, and that is just as true for a rapist. In fact (I'm almost afraid to say it), at that moment of his coming, I looked over my shoulder and noticed he appeared possessed by a desire that I, his object of lust, *enjoy* being raped. No doubt this is the dream of all rapists; there is probably nothing odd about it. I was the smiling cow on his carton of milk. Why shouldn't I be happy? He did everything he could within his limited abilities as a man to perform his God-given function. My contentment with his efforts would have transformed him from a ho-hum criminal into a butt-fucking Casanova.

In any case, he was deeply out of touch with my feelings and was, for the most part, self-absorbed in a grunting, staccato frenzy. We were both relieved when the last of his seed spurted into my bowels—the gift of his manhood was now mine; his all-important, urgent message was delivered. In the postcoital glaze phase, he became vulnerable and offered further startling revelations. I learned that his own sexual history included having been raped himself, that it had been his *initiation,* he claimed, into a *fraternity* whose good name I won't mention for fear of libel. He even went to the trouble of pointing out a related artifact that he kept on his windowsill—somehow I hadn't noticed it—his fraternity paddle in the shape of butt cheeks, with three Greek initials prominently carved into it. "Jesus," I thought to myself, "this rape thing is at the core of a university *institution*. It's clearly a more widespread cultural practice than I have been led to believe by our smiley-faced arbiters of social truth. These guys are being primed to run corporations; they're all getting MBAs!" Since that moment of divine understanding, I have often wondered if all of these university fraternities were, or still are, *filled* with queer-baiting, fag-fucking, motherfucking, girl-fucking, fraternity buddy-fucking *fuckers,* or if I had just stumbled on an anomaly.

One evening, by chance, he noticed me walking down University Way and picked me up in his mid-1970s Chevy Impala, on the pretext of having a beer. He told me he was taking me to his mother's house, but I never saw any evidence of her. Sitting in what was apparently his bedroom, we had just opened a couple bottles of cheap-ass Rainier beer. Just as simply as he had popped the cap off the bottle, he propositioned me for sex. It wasn't a sophisticated or even memorable statement of desire; it was just as dumb as a bottle cap. I said no; he lost it. Like a verbal non sequitur, his expression toward me was transfigured with anger and hate. It's not as if he verbally threatened me, or that he needed a weapon—it was all communicated with his eyes and his sudden, scary shift in demeanor. The fact that he was six inches taller and a hundred pounds heavier made all the difference. He just stared at me for a minute like he was going to hack me to bits after another swig of his beer. If he was bluffing, I couldn't tell. I was afraid to say anything and just looked around the room for a possible means of defense. He studied me. I knew some sick shit was about to happen; I had no idea what, but his look made me believe it included death. He told me to take down my jeans as he grabbed the Vaseline Intensive Hand Care lotion. I politely asked him what he was intending. "I'm gonna take a look at your ass. Don't worry, I just want to look at it while I jerk off." For some reason, it was believable, and far less severe than what I expected. He was obviously one fucked-up motherfucker. I wanted to believe his story; I was nineteen and had no problem with showing my ass.

Of course, once I complied with the initial command, any resistance was doomed. He began masturbating and simply moved closer. Even on his knees, he was towering over me, as he squirted the hand lotion all over his big, unsightly prick, stroking himself until he was good and hard. He made me stick my butt in the air and grabbed my balls with one hand to control me. It was smooth; he had done it all before. He was a goddamn *pro*.

Besides his fraternity brother confession, he made other remarkable statements. After the ordeal was over, he looked more sheepish and began to return to his other self. The sneer on my face made it clear that I had nothing but contempt for him: he was nothing more than the slime oozing from my bloody asshole. It was an odd role reversal. Two could play this look-at-my-face game. My tearful gaze was not threatening, but it actually made him feel defensive enough to provoke further rationalizations for his behavior. He tried to convince me that I would become like him, a sort of vampire rapist. He really believed his mythology. His rapist had told him the tale after raping him; he believed it, and, for him, it was true. So why the cold eyes friend? It got even more bizarre when he drove me home and was so friendly he dared to ask me if I wanted to see him again soon. Yeah, I wanted to see him immediately, *as compost.*

I never reported the rape because I believed he would eventually get off, find me, and murder me. I never even talked about the rape until a few years later, and that was with a male friend who had also been raped. I felt no one would really understand what it was like unless he or she went through something similar, and I never wanted anyone's pity. Then again, maybe I was just capitulating to socially fostered feelings of humiliation. I had many fantasies about buying a gun and stalking him. However, if I had actually killed the fiend, I'd be the one going to jail, not for a couple of years, but for life. As much as I wanted to vengefully obliterate him, it was playing his game, and I was going to lose. Besides, if what he told me was true, then there were plenty more just like him. As I continued to attend the University of Washington, I would occasionally see him standing around with some guys. It was a shock—he had friends! I wondered how many of them were rapists. When I would see him with somebody on campus, I would walk up to him and look at him like he was shit-cum so any innocent acquaintances might get the message. Then I'd spit and walk off without saying a word, continuing our dialogue of fluids.

He had told me he worked as a part-time mainframe computer operator in the Safeco building, but I only saw him near there once, many years later, in a three-piece suit. He looked like he was moving up the corporate escalator, another sleazy con artist. The last time I ever saw him was at a Womyn Take Back the Night demonstration on Capitol Hill. I was marching with some of my friends; he was standing on the sidewalk with some of his buddies. They were watching us pass by.

POSTSCRIPT

For many years, I felt a distrust of men who showed any sexual interest in me, even if I was attracted to them! I've had many male friends who were bisexual or gay, but my tendency to experiment has been reserved, limited to kissing and mutual masturbation, usually with other men who had, coincidentally, also been sexually assaulted or abused. I don't believe that having been raped "totally fucked me up." I have my own blind spots and preferences, like many people. At one point, one of my female lovers wanted to get into S&M, and I wasn't into playing either role, sorry. Call me boring, but it didn't appeal to me. Perhaps being raped for real at nineteen made acting out uninteresting. I've enjoyed sex that was fun for all involved, but what I loathe about fucking is when it's one-sided and sadistic.

PART II:
OBSESSIONS

22

The Monster in the Closet:
Men Who Molest Children

Paul Fleischer

"How could you work with those monsters?" This is the question that I both dread and eagerly await since doing my clinical psychology internship in a setting that, among other things, provides treatment to men who have molested children. My apprehension comes from the implications behind the question: (1) I must be a well-meaning, but dangerous, fool who helps to keep these sickos on the streets, or (2) I am, myself, some sort of sexual pervert, thus accounting for my compassion for men convicted of molesting children. Even minimal exposure to mass media makes it clear that the predominantly accepted "truth" in our culture is that men who molest children are monsters lurking in the shadows. They are subhuman, incurable predators who should be locked up, castrated, or killed. These are beliefs about which people feel passionately, and to question them in any way is to become suspect yourself.

Because of my experience working in therapy with both sexual abuse survivors and men who molest, I can offer a somewhat unique perspective. I have seen the incredibly destructive effects of molestation on the lives of both the survivors and perpetrators. It is because of its horrible impact that I have chosen to work with these men and to try to learn from them, as they have stepped out of the shadows and into treatment. In the process, they have taught me a great deal about themselves, our culture, and myself. What I have learned convinces me that we must move beyond easy scapegoating to examine some of the reasons these behaviors occur at such a high rate and to recognize how this culture produces people (especially men) who molest children. In fact, I believe the very process of scapegoating these men, of demonizing their sexuality and pretending that "they" are different from "us," is actually part of the very dynamic that supports child molestation. To be clear, I offer no excuses for sexually abusive behaviors: men who molest children must stop what they are doing and take full responsibility for their actions. At the same time, in much the same way that the monster in the darkness of a child's closet is recognized as a pile of dirty laundry when a light is switched on, the perception of these men as monsters also disappears as we allow the dark side of male lust and power in our culture to be illuminated.

I went into this work with some typical preconceptions and stereotypes about men who molest. I believed psychological research clearly showed that these men were truly different from other men. They were significantly more sexually obsessive, fixated, and/or sadistic than other men. They exhibited lower functioning and were socially inept. Many were incurable monstrous predators. Surely, this is what sophisticated psychological testing shows, right? Well, not exactly. Actually, not even close.

Despite countless attempts to discern specific offenders' characteristics— to distinguish "them" from "us"—the research demonstrates that there is nothing even close to a universal molester profile. What the studies actually show is that socioeconomic level, race, ethnicity, sexual orientation, marital status, drug and alcohol use, and prior mental health treatment offer virtually no indication as to which men will and will not molest a child. This lack of a common pattern was continually reflected back to me in my work: as with other men, perpetrators vary greatly in terms of intelligence, social abilities, backgrounds, and sexual preferences. Similarly, my work with survivors of sexual abuse revealed that many abusers do not fit the stereotypical "molester" profile. Men who molest are just as likely to be prominent members of the community as they are to be truly "deranged deviants" who live at the margins of society.

So why all the effort to emphasize the barely measurable differences that have been delineated? One possible explanation is that research publications are based on finding differences, so it becomes a smart career move to put this kind of spin on the material. Yet, I think there is much more to it than mere posturing. Researchers want what we all want: clear, definable differences between men who molest and those who do not. This kind of research is an act of hope: if we can identify molesters, we can protect our children. No matter how warped or monstrous or even pathetic these molesters turn out to be, we all feel safer when we can recognize them as "other."

Yet, if research that seeks to define this "other" is an act of hope, it is equally an act of denial. The possibility that men who molest children are not easily distinguishable from other men terrifies most of us. More frightening than some monstrous "them" is the fact that it is our neighbors, fathers, coaches, uncles, brothers, friends, sons, and business partners who are molesting the young in our society. To acknowledge that a sizable percentage of males raised in our society can do something as terrible as molest a child is to begin facing the atrocities we are capable of, as individuals and as a culture.

We feel the same fears and desires as children who just want their parents to destroy the monster in the closet and make them feel safe. Explanations about misperceptions and the unreality of monsters do not soothe children, and they do not easily soothe us either. We do not want to admit that the monsters we perceive are the product of the very real dirty laundry of split-off male lust and aggression in ourselves and our society. Letting go of our belief in monsters means having to recognize and take responsibility for the destructive aspects of our culture. It means having to experience the vulnerability of knowing that even the most horrific deeds that a person may commit are still human and are related to ourselves. Although scapegoating and witch-hunts provide a comforting sense of safety, this illusory comfort comes at the cost of not addressing the real problems.

Though we rarely count this cost, it is very high. Returning to the metaphor, if the parent destroys the child's pile of dirty laundry or forever locks it away to appease the child, both parent and child pay for this approach. Perhaps the most obvious cost is the monetary one: it is an expensive way to handle imaginary monsters. The other costs are more subtle and of more consequence: the child's belief in monsters is strengthened and his or her sense of powerlessness is reinforced. The child learns that fear of what lurks in the shadows is valid and that security lies in external protection. Yet, when the parent recognizes the dirty laundry is for what it is, it can be washed and returned to the child, who then reclaims it. When we stop trying to convince ourselves that men who have molested are monsters, we can begin to clean and reclaim the dirty laundry that is behind the monstrous image. We can begin to reclaim our sexuality and personal power and to find genuine security.

Yet it can be difficult and frightening to recognize that the molester's dirty laundry is also our own dirty laundry. For myself, it was disturbing to find that many of these men were not that different from me. While, as a therapist, I was pleased to be able to relate to them, a part of me felt more secure when sitting with the men who fit the stereotypes more closely. It was comforting to see how different they were from me. It was easier to attribute their molesting behavior to their otherness rather than acknowledging it might have some connection to me or my society. In truth, men who have molested offer a unique perspective into our culture's dirty laundry. Demonizing and "otherizing" them means missing a rare view into the dark side of male sexuality. Working with these men helped me see similar processes in myself, my other male clients, and in the greater culture.

The troubled relationship these men had with their own sexuality was only pulled out of the shadows of psychological defenses and secrecy because their molesting behavior had forced them into treatment. Otherwise, they would probably be doing what most of us do: continue, in isolation, to deal with the shame and confusion of sexual splitting. The splits in this culture's sexual attitudes, teachings, and behaviors are a profound effect of the patriarchal makeup of our society. Our puritanical roots are still powerfully evident in many of the themes within our families, churches, and even much of what the so-called liberal media offer as entertainment. The goodness of the spirit and the evil of the flesh (sexuality), the rigid gender roles for males and females, and the idea that sex is dirty and deserving of punishment are still deeply imbedded in our culture. These puritanical judgments act as foundations of shame and splitting: our sexuality is cast into the shadows.

As with anything else that is split off and pushed into the shadows, sexuality has gained an exaggerated power and importance. The result of sex being made into a devil is that it has taken on the importance of a god. The culture worships sex. It is idealized, objectified, and desperately sought. People (especially men) seek sex, not just as a source of pleasure, but as a source of power and worth. Patriarchal capitalism exploits this situation. The distorted power of sex sells, and, therefore, we are bombarded with sexual messages and imagery. This serves to both reinforce our overblown sexual desire and simultaneously trigger shame about having that desire. Sexuality becomes polarized and externalized due to the split between these two patriarchal forces.

The process of splitting, of casting that which we believe to be bad into the shadows, is so commonplace that we usually do not recognize that this norm is not normal. Molestation is an extreme (though painfully common) effect of sexuality being split off in our patriarchal culture. Demonizing men who have molested is just one more split. It encourages us to project all of our shame, fear, and anger about sex under conditions of patriarchy onto these easy scapegoats. It does not encourage us come to grips with and heal the larger problem. One of the most disturbing and frustrating parts of working with men who have molested children is seeing how the culture has, directly and indirectly, encouraged them to sexualize little children. While treatment programs are teaching that children are not appropriate objects of sexual desire, many marketing campaigns and movies are sending the opposite message.

One of the only consistent patterns I did see in these men was internal splitting and shame concerning sexuality. Part of them wanted it, needed it, and was even willing to make rationalizations in order to obtain it, while another part of them felt deeply bewildered and ashamed of these desires. Every one of these men whom I saw had some form of sexual shame and confusion. Each had split off part of his sexuality in one way or another, and it had come back as the monster it was feared to be. The men's shame was not just guilt about their offense; this shame preceded their offending behaviors. It was a more general shame about their sexual nature, and it seemed very familiar.

The destructive impact of shame cannot be overemphasized. Shame is the belief that who you are at your core is bad, wrong, or inferior. In the men with whom I worked, I saw that shame played a huge role in the development of their compulsions and other emotional difficulties. The harsh puritanical judgments about sex that these men had internalized served to feed their obsessions and compulsions in a vicious cycle. The greater their feelings of shame, the greater the internal pressure to escape through obsessing or acting out. Yet, the more they thought about or acted on their sexual desire, the more isolated and ashamed they would feel. They would then use the shame to try to control or destroy their sexual desires. This strategy brought only short-term relief at best, causing the cycle of shame and obsession to begin again. They would often feel weak, out of control, and disgusted by their lives. These men fall into the same trap as the general culture: wanting to fight and eliminate the demons rather than dealing with the feelings going on underneath. Judgment and condemnation merely serve to heighten their shame and make them less likely to seek treatment.

At the same time that puritanical messages about the evils of sex serve to shame us for being too sexual, patriarchal capitalism shames men for not being sexual enough. In an effort to manipulate people into being more productive consumers, happiness gets redefined as material reward, and sex becomes an objectified commodity used to entice buyers. Conventionally beautiful women become the ultimate symbol of male success, and we are taught to feel less-than if we do not live up to this James Bond/Playboy image. We "losers" in the game (pretty much all of us) are encouraged to escape our feelings of failure and impotence by living vicariously through highly sexualized entertainment, diversions that then reinforce our sense of failure.

Our natural sexuality becomes overdeveloped, warped, and is used to exploit us. Our natural desire for companionship and intimacy becomes subsumed by the promised fix of quick sex that is being sold to us. By giving us an impossible goal, a market niche is created. Both puritan-style and capitalist-style patriarchies function by making people feel insecure and then offering them an external source of validation. Men are left with an underlying sense of self-doubt and vulnerability, and very few tools to cope, beyond controlling one's feelings or competing more effectively. The hurt and sadness we feel, but cannot express, gets channeled into the few available emotional outlets: anger and sexual desire. Men act out these feelings on those who are vulnerable, and children are vulnerable. The molestation of children is one outcome of the insecure male's attempt to feel powerful, to replace that inner sense of self-worth denied him by society.

Just as the man who molests children needs to hear clear messages that molestation is wrong, he also needs help in forming strong social contacts that reinforce his inherent value as a human being, over and against the claims of puritan- and capitalist-style patriarchies. In my work, I have seen that men who molest universally lack the deep intimacy that might offer some counterweight to the insecurities created by the larger culture. In fact, the emotional isolation most child molesters experience is excruciating and intense, even among those men who appear to have "made it" in an outward sense. The sexually compulsive person is caught in a vicious cycle of wanting intimacy, seeking the substitute of sex, and then feeling more alone. When the objects of desire are children, the cycle is even more shame-ridden, intense, and destructive.

I see so much for us to mourn and change in our society. Yet our culture teaches that coercion and acquisition, not mourning, lead to transformation. Throw out the old and replace it with the new and improved and all will be right with the world. We react to men who molest with the very same response pattern that caused them to molest in the first place: We cannot tolerate the feelings they trigger about our society or our own vulnerability so we attempt to regain our sense of power and control by transforming these confusing and unpleasant feelings into anger and hatred. While men who molest attempt to feel powerful by turning children into one-dimensional objects of their sexual desire, we transform the men who molest into one-dimensional objects upon which we can act out our desperate need for security. We condemn those who molest and attempt to eliminate them, while continuing to foster and act on the very same compulsions that lead to molestation.

Molestation signals the degree to which we have split ourselves off from our desires, and the degree to which this process has warped love. Some men molest children, believing it to be an act of love. They fail to recognize that they are desperately attempting to meet their own needs: to fill their loneliness, quiet their shame, distract themselves from their pain and powerlessness. Many parents, politicians, and people in the community seek to socially brand, chemically mutilate, or even kill men who molest children, believing it to be an act of love for their children. They fail to recognize that they, too, are desperately attempting to meet their own needs: to soothe their fears, quiet their shame, distract themselves from their pain and powerlessness. Molestation and scapegoating are both rooted in fear and weakness.

True love requires courage and strength and is the only path to healing. Genuine healing requires accepting all parts of ourselves, recognizing our real needs, and attending to them appropriately. Much healing can come from recognizing "them" as a part of "us," from recognizing the situation as it is, without shaming either ourselves or so-called others. When we delve into the true issues surrounding child molestation, sexual violence, and sexual compulsion, we see the outcomes of a disowned sexuality common to many men. In understanding how we often divorce ourselves from our own desires, we can begin reclaiming the parts of ourselves that have been split off. We can begin to reclaim our sexuality and, in doing so, make sure that these parts do not take on monstrous forms. In healing, we can find genuine safety. When we love ourselves enough to clean up our own dirty laundry, to mourn and heal as we need, both our internal and external monsters will disappear.

23

Hypatia's Children

Thomas S. Roche

Hypatia: Alexandrian Neoplatonist philosopher [librarian of the Library at Alexandria], victim of 5th-century persecution of intellectual women. While she was driving to the academy where she taught, a gang of monks dragged her from her chariot, carried her into a church, stripped her, scraped the flesh from her bones with oyster shells, then burned what was left, all by order of St. Cyril, the city Patriarch. By making judicious gifts to civil authorities, Cyril and his monks managed to halt official investigation of Hypatia's murder. Cyril attained sainthood in 1882 when Pope Leo XIII canonized him "as a doctor of the church."*

Barbara Walker,
The Women's Encyclopedia of Myths and Secrets

In my personal sexual history, I've had to become a pioneer—but not to explore brave new worlds, at least not exactly. No, I've been exploring myself, carving paths out of the wilds of my subconscious, looking for some library of forgotten knowledge that will order and explain all my libido's demands. But the library has been burned to the ground, and my internal sexual world is undocumented, not only untamed, but untamable. I've dragged my more civilized self, kicking and screaming, through the red-light district urban jungle that

---

"Hypatia's Children" first appeared as "Hypatia's Finger," in *Black Sheets*, September 1997 (12).

*A few years later, the library at Alexandria was burned to the ground, all its knowledge lost. It is speculated that this was on orders of Justinian, the Roman emperor in Constantinople.

is my own desire—all the while hacking at the trees of knowledge with a surplus store machete. But exploring does not equal conquering, nor would I want it to. Trees of knowledge bleed, come, piss, shit—and they regrow faster than you can cut them. They grow fruit that tastes of bodily fluids. And each morsel of carnal knowledge makes me hungry for more.

My map of this jungle is constantly shifting, changing, transforming. And a pioneer, to me, is someone who effects a transformation, even as that transformation is affecting them. I've been thinking a lot about transformation lately, carving sonnets in my flesh to monarch butterflies, seeing black-leather chrome-studded rainbows over Alcatraz in the early morning. It's not really the kind of transformation sold in seminars at the Learning Annex, but I do admit to occasionally glancing through Learning Annex catalogs, looking for a way to discard this chrysalis of despair and sexual longing for an easy thirty-four bucks—twenty-nine for members. Of course, I also find myself staring at yuppies on the F-Market, wondering to myself what goes on inside them, what sort of soul could live inside a body, a persona, a social construction that appears, at first glance at least, to be so profoundly different from this one that I inhabit. I watched men, women, everyone else at San Francisco's Gay Day, wondering at the gap that divides gay and straight and bi, man and woman, African, European, Islander, American, Asian . . . wondering how the fuck I came to be here—how I came to live in this succulent miasma of creativity and longing, this city that devours caterpillars and spits out butterflies, or takes butterflies and clips their wings. In the city of St. Francis (probably a bestialist of some sort, which might explain a lot), where every manner of freak and malcontent is accepted, and even embraced, as long as s/he does it with style, there are some who don't have any style left, and sometimes they're lost in the transformation. I've seen wrecked souls, too, people hurting so bad you can feel it as they pass you on the street, and their transformations are as real as my own, as anyone's. The transformation of caterpillar into butterfly is no more or less a transformation, no less valid or important than the butterfly that hits the windshield of a Lexus doing ninety as it heads toward the toll plaza. Not everybody's so fucking lucky. Sometimes, things just don't work out. There are times I feel my own transformation taking me over, feel my body, my mind, my soul mutating into something . . . but what?

*   *   *

Half a lifetime ago, I sat alone in my bedroom handwriting my very first porno, a story about a World War I pilot captured and tortured by the Germans. I was confused at the curious mix of ecstasy and pain that seemed to be working through me. Afterward, overcome with self-loathing and guilt, I took the pages I'd written out back and set fire to them, watching them change from the products of my desires and fears, information that could destroy all that I surveyed, into charred, delicate, smoking membranes of deepest black—no longer dangerous to anything except dry grass, no longer an anthem of fourteen-year-old pain and longing. I wasn't ready. The wind came up and blew my story to fragmented pieces, scattering pinpoints of firefly light across the backyard. For a time, I felt purified. Even then, wrapped in my disgust and hatred and ignorance of my own hungers, I saw the irony, knew that that purification, that transformation, might be brought about by the writing as much as, or more than, the burning. But the terror that someone would discover what I'd written, discover this cancer growing within me, brought me into the backyard, disposable lighter in hand, time and time and time again, for years after that initial backyard Alexandria. More than once I burned a novel—not stories, but a novel, maybe a little short on plot and character development, but hundreds of pages of undiluted teenage male libido that I imagine might freak out the most diehard Web surfer, even today. Pages and pages of monster fucking, sex with demons, violent sexual murders, compulsory year-long servitude—men to women, women to men, men to men, women to women, and other—magic spells that would transform you from female to male and back again . . . and each time, the images returned to me no matter how I fought them, and I would find myself writing horny stories destined for the backyard barbecue. It was as if I were going into myself, finding this information, these images, these fantasies, bringing them out, and imprisoning them on the page precisely *so that* I could burn them, destroy them, decimate them, as if that would destroy what was going on inside me. As if I could burn and purify myself, as if, somehow, by burning these stories, I could transform myself into something . . . acceptable.

*   *   *

I spent some time involved with a woman who claimed, in so many words, that pornographers (like me) were responsible for all the childhood sexual abuse in the world. Even then, I snorted in disgust, but it took me years to get that accusative barb out of my flesh. The fact that six weeks after she told me that, six weeks after she made that comment, the woman decided she was a leather dyke and wanted to be a dominatrix didn't do a damn thing to heal me—after all, she was a survivor. Maybe this was some twisted evidence of the pattern incest creates. Who the fuck knows? Maybe her sufferings really were the fault of pornography—not that this possibility changed the texture of the fantasies that consumed me whenever I closed my eyes—if anything, it intensified them.

*   *   *

Locked in the hell of my own dreams, I wondered what the fuck was wrong with me, and what was wrong with the world that had created me—somewhere, deep inside, I filled with hatred for this thing that I threatened to become, for the beast that was locked within me. Sensitive New Age Guys did not fantasize about women being tied up and tortured against their will. Great Writers did not jerk off to images from *Man in the Iron Mask* (1976). Locked for years in a curious sort of death dance with my own passions, I seesawed between a sexy spiritual ecstasy and a self-important moral decay. I chewed the *Leatherman's Handbook* (1972) and *Macho Sluts* (1988), and the *Lesbian S-M Safety Manual* (1988) like stainless steel jellybeans, consumed gay male porn, and started writing it, too, not sure if I was bisexual or just a leatherboy locked in a straight man's body. Maybe somewhere in all that black leather faggotry was a place where sexual fantasies did not kill, where being a guy with a hard-on was not some sort of crime against the future.

*   *   *

I'm going to tell you about a recent moment when that desire was at its most dangerous for me, in its most frightening, yet liberating, manifestation. The party was one of those I frequently receive invitations for and rarely attend, a safe-sex and S/M party held in a local dungeon. I attended with a relatively new partner—someone I was newly bonded with after months of missed connections and fights. This was love in its purest form for me, and it was really my first attempt to do S/M in a primary relationship. My fantasies are, by turns, violent, frightening, intense, and hateful. My stories and novels are outlandish, kinky, and morbid. My sex life has been primarily vanilla.

My new partner was dressed in a Catholic schoolgirl's uniform. We had negotiated that I would be the "top," or the dominant partner, for the length of the scene. This scared the living shit out of me, since I had never really done S/M in a primary relationship, and I felt weird about tapping the vast sea of my kinky desires. But I was determined to play this scene to the utmost.

We found a corner of the dungeon. I grabbed her and forced her (though not much "force" was really used) into the most readily available structure, an upright cage just the right size for one person. I buckled cuffs around her wrists and ankles, padlocked her to the cage. I blindfolded her, but left her mouth free. I told her it was so I could hear her scream, but in reality, it was so I could kiss her.

And kiss her I did, as I took out my brand-new toy, a wicked-looking knife with a nine-inch blade. She writhed and squirmed as I opened her blouse and ran the tip of the blade over her flesh. I lifted her skirt and tucked it into her waistband so her crotch was exposed; then I cut away her panties with the knife and deliberately brushed her inner thighs with the sharp edge of the blade. I teased the blade into her mouth and she obediently licked it as if it were my cock. I brought the spittle-slick blade down to her breasts, pulling down the cups of her bra so I could tease her pierced nipples with the knife. By this time, I was unbelievably hard, excited and aroused, fascinated and focused on my partner's body as I almost never had been. She looked so beautiful, chained and helpless, dressed up in a way I'd never seen her. And every motion I made against her body—stroking her with the knife, rubbing my hands over her breasts, pinching her nipples, kissing her mouth with mine—caused her to quiver and squirm. I growled threatening comments at her—never abusing her verbally, but making it clear that I was in control and could do with her as I wished. I gripped her hair in one hand, pulling her head back and holding tight so I could be sure she would remain immobile. I looked at the pulsing line of her carotid artery. I touched it ever so slightly with the tip of my knife. I expected a faint moan from her lips, but such a thing would have been superfluous. Instead, there was only the frozen sensation, the knowledge in my partner and me that her life lay, in every sense, in my hands. I charged her flesh with the tip of my knife and then I thrust my body against her with kind of an explosion, as a release of static electricity.

The scene ended with me cradling and holding her, kissing her neck where a moment ago the tip of my blade had rested, a kind of intense catharsis for me despite the fact that neither of us had climaxed.

My partner told me that she had enjoyed the hell out of herself, and this was exactly the kind of play we'd discussed extensively and negotiated—but that's hardly the point. Which is to say, that's not why I'm telling you. The reason I relate that here is that at the moment when I held my lover's life in my hands, the moment at which she and I knew that one false move on my part could end her life, I felt more connected with my lover than I ever had. More at one with her, in an unbreakable union. But more important, I felt at one with my desire for her, the overwhelming, all-consuming lust I had felt since our first connection, the hunger that threatened to eat me alive—the burning desire to do her harm and do her well. The pleasure of control, of ownership, of feeling her spirit pulsing through my soul—this all came together to focus, in one frozen instant, all the need I had ever felt for her, and at one moment, it shuddered with a ripple through both our bodies and was gone.

It hardly mattered that the blade was less than razor sharp and probably *couldn't* have ended her life with the startling ease both she and I seemed to think it could. The spiritual energy, the tacit exchange of absolute power, was so tangible at that instant that it was just about all that mattered in the universe. It was as if, in that instant of need and utter satisfaction, all my horrifying fantasies of violence, coercion, and rape had all been transformed, by the fires of the aesthete's mind, into blazing jewels of utter and indescribable beauty.

It was of that moment I was thinking when later, as I kissed my lover in the tangled sheets of my bed, I told her, "You, my dear, are dangerous."

* * *

And my lover *is* dangerous, like every horny person is dangerous—like every hard-on or wet cunt is as dangerous as it gets, dangerous to the whole fucking structure of the world that says pleasure is bad. She is not dangerous to herself; rather, she is dangerous to *me* because I desire her so acutely in such instances as the one I described that everything else ceases to be and only one thing exists—the union between the two of us. She is dangerous because of *her* desire because *my* desire is what's dangerous to me. Dangerous to the part of my brain that says, "Getting off is bad!" Or, as John Preston described it, "How dare you even think those things!" Perhaps this was the side of me that burned stories for years, that tried to purge my own darkness with a seventy-nine-cent lighter and a can of lighter fluid. That side of me eventually lost the fight, of course, for the stuff of dreams is fireproof, and the books inside my head have pages laser-etched on chromium steel and bound in asbestos. Instead, I learned to write faster and faster, piling up porno quicker than I could burn it. Eventually, I discovered that if I stuck the stuff in an envelope and put stamps on it, people with titles like "Managing Editor" would send me back money. The rest is a rather sordid history, perhaps appropriate for a sleazier venue. But now when I write, I find myself going into another sort of backyard, where the fires are those which burn inside a laser printer, and the information I process from my sometimes inconvenient fantasies becomes a general consciousness for anyone who cares enough to read it. My writing is transformed, whenever possible, into someone else's fantasies. Is this really any different, to give my fantasies away to all of you, maybe because I'm not comfortable with them in my own head? I'm not sure I know, and I'm not sure I care anymore. Somewhere inside all of this navel gazing, amid the whirling cut-ups of noise and hallucination, is some sort of real truth, some core *piece* of what I am. Or maybe *pieces*, as in piece of writing, piece of gold, piece of my mind . . . piece of ass. Those pieces form a whole, maybe, somewhere, or maybe they don't. But with every story I tell, the transformation heightens, the ante is upped. My confidence grows, confidence in what drives me, what moves me, and what moves and drives *you*, my unfortunate victims, as well. The burning will always return—the shame, the longing—but nobody can burn my desires out of me. Because the moment of flame, of transformation, of destruction and rebirth is exactly *what I am seeking* when I go to those dark places inside me. I am seeking the wisdom that comes from purge, the phenomenon of clarity that only comes from destruction, from the burning.

In some Byzantium, some day, maybe today, maybe tomorrow, next week, next month, Justinian gives an order to his generals—put the library at Alexandria to the torch. And Hypatia laughs, a wicked, satisfied laugh, and gives that son of a bitch the finger, for she's a dangerous slut, a smart-assed pervert, the immortal bitch-goddess of carnal knowledge and unsavory hungers, and she knows, as all her children know, that flame cannot purify in this fashion . . . to Byzantium's horror; flame can only transform.

REFERENCE

Walker, Barbara. 1983. *The Woman's Encyclopedia of Myths and Secrets.* New York: HarperCollins Publishers, Inc.

24

I Wonder If My Great Great Toltec Grandmother Was Ever a *National Geographic* Centerfold

Jorge Ignacio Cortiñas

I act like it's me who can tell just by looking at them, but really I can tell 'cause they want me to know: the white faggots are like that. Most days I sell weed in the park, and from the spot I claim right by the footbridge I see them before they see me, walking up the grassy hill and staring at their feet. They won't look up till I mutter, Mota. Then I wait and see how they act.

They do shit that lets me know. They try to look under the bill of my cap; they smile when I hand them the weed; they say, Adios, or some shit like that and then stick around, like it takes them longer to walk away. If they want to give me stuff right away, a ride or a bag of speed, then I know for sure. That's the type of white man who will pay if I let him put his mouth on me. If there's nobody right by me, and if I feel like it, I say, Aiight, or Sounds good, and the guy will drive me someplace, someplace of his.

He'll kneel before me. He'll open his mouth to me, close his eyes, and bathe my scrotum with his tongue. This is what he pays me for. He'll take me into his mouth; he'll swallow me whole; he'll drink my sperm and believe that he knows me, believe that he can taste soil on the tip of my penis. When I cum, his eyes well up with sorrow, his hungry mouth like a little baby when they got no teeth. I stare down at the bald spot on his head, at his big-eye expression. Afterwards, my body feels spent and raw, his tasteless saliva shrinking as it dries on my skin.

Taking money from these men is easy. They hold out their money in the beginning, hoping I'll put it away real quick in my back pocket, three twenty-

"I Wonder If My Great Great Toltec Grandmother Was Ever a *National Geographic* Centerfold" first appeared in *Best Gay Erotica '98,* edited by Christopher Bram and Richard Labonté, published by Cleis Press, San Francisco, 1998.

dollar bills, all facing the same way, like all three Andrew Jacksons agree. I never say thank-you. That's for them to say into the silence of my poker face, a face I make look like I'm thinking of something else. They always say something. They want to. Some of them say, Thank-you, softly, like a prayer said by someone who's just realized he is wrestling with his faith. Some of them say it loudly, like they have already convinced you, but they're always afraid they haven't. Either way it's the same. When I leave their house I walk out the door and don't look back. I don't say nothing. My backside is taunt enough.

I always bathe afterwards, and change my socks and underwear, even if it's only 11 a.m., the day is just starting and I got no place to be. I never return their phone calls. Sometimes I listen to them, but I don't say I have. Then I call them out of the blue, tell them to be ready in fifteen minutes, have a bottle of Añejo, and the money ready, cash, up front.

It's harder to get them to buy me things. That takes time. Maybe I drop a hint. Most times they'll ask if they can help, like, is there something they can get me, something I need. I'm careful not to smile when I think about the full-length Fila bubble jacket stuffed with goose down that is way above the counter at Foot Locker, behind two employees dressed like referees and under the watchful eye of the security guard, where brown and black hands cannot reach it.

I tell this man to drive me out of my neighborhood, past my corner, where I might run into one of my crew. Keep driving, into the next neighborhood, where I just barely know people's names, but know enough to keep a low profile and not fly my colors. Drive, past mom-and-pop stores that sell canvas Carthartt jackets and polyester Ben Davis, to the Foot Locker, all windows and polished metal. When he gets me there, I make a beeline for the jacket, wait for the man to catch up to me, and then point with my chin and say only my size, Large.

He doesn't know I was there two days before. Considering my options. Trying the jackets on. Asking if they thought the inventory would hold out until first thing Sunday, when I can come back with this man and his stack of credit cards that he holds out like shiny glass beads.

I walk him back to his car but don't get in. On the sidewalk, mothers with small children swarm around us. He looks up with eyes that say he was expecting to at least suck me off this morning. I tell him I have to get to work. I lie because it's best to leave them dangling with their desire pent up and twisting, so that they begin calling over and over, ready to spend. I lie because I will always put myself in charge, show him and myself that it's me calling the shots, not him, the green he's got, or his appetite for men with a full head of hair. I lie because I know the kind of man he wants me to be, like men at home in a language he does not speak, men who care enough to shave, brown men who might cry when they're drunk and might even let you touch them while they close their eyes and think of someone else, in another country. I walk home, leaving this white man only the view of my black Fila jacket and my stagger, the stare of his mouth at my backside.

I know the man is looking at me, and I wonder how far I can drag his gaze with me, when I come up to this Norteño on the corner who also stares at me, hard. In another neighborhood, at another hour, the stare of this rival güey might mean something else, the way he locks onto my pupils, doesn't let go, holds me up to the streetlight, and shakes out my pockets to see if I'm afraid. But high noon on Sunday, flanked by his homies, his eyes are a dare, mad dogging me, asking why my jacket even looks blue, on his corner, and do I wanna start something.

The Norteño stands his ground, makes me take a step around him, and when he exhales a slow, 'Sup, I look straight ahead, and nod. As I pass him, my eyes rotate to the side and I just barely catch sight of his features, my height and looking like some kind of prince in his red forty-niners jacket, round Olmec face set in gangsta stone. I want to brush up against him. I want to think of something to whisper in his ear. But I only pick up my pace, because in the sunlight our eyes never meet.

25

Pornography's Child

Sy Safransky

I discovered sex in 1955, in a hatbox, in my father's closet. What a cache he kept there, beneath the gabardine business suits and woolen overcoats and wide, flowered ties draped like jungle foliage over a metal rack; the closet smelling vaguely of him, his cigars, his aftershave, and my mother's mothballs, although the books crammed into that hatbox had a different smell entirely: funky, spicy, foreign (written in English, they were published in France). For years, I imagined sex would smell that way too.

They were odd little books, crudely printed, as if on a press that hadn't been cleaned in years, the letters fat and smudged, the photographs grainy. And the prices! I don't know which astounded me more—what was in them, or the fact that they cost at least ten dollars each. I'd been amassing an enviable science fiction collection for fifty cents a book. It was inconceivable to me that anyone would charge, or my father would pay, that much money for something like this.

But there was nothing like this, was there? These stories and pictures puzzled and enchanted me. I studied the photographs the way a botanist might look at a plant he had no idea existed. I mean, it didn't seem quite real, though the evidence was compelling: all the naked bodies, joined hip to hip, or mouth to crotch, in threesomes and foursomes, in beds, leaning over chairs—apparently enjoying themselves, though that was suggested more by the text than the often bored and distracted faces. All this hothouse groping and moaning, long-voweled ahhs and ohhs—unbelievable, but here it was. People actually did this; at least, they did it for the camera.

I was ten years old, just starting the sixth grade, and had never been told a thing about sex. This was an era, remember, when *sex* and *education* did not roll off the tongue as if they were one word, but seemed to be at opposite ends of the universe, separated by worlds of ignorance and embarrassment and

"Pornography's Child" first appeared in *The Sun,* June 1985, issue 115, pp. 3-5.

denial. Like the lens of a telescope, these books let me see (and in such detail!) undreamt planets—though I was still unsure it wasn't just more science fiction. It took my classmate Eddie to ignite the real rocket of my curiosity, with the casual disclosure, on the P.S. 244 schoolyard, that "fucking makes babies."

Oh, the lightning leap my mind took, synapses quivering and bucking, revelation rolling in like a thunderclap: people really did do this; it wasn't just something they conjured up in France for my father's amusement.

I soon discovered that the pleasures the books so abundantly described were, after a fashion, available to me too—if not at the crossroads of male and female (which would have required a bit of social engineering beyond my capacity), then at the juncture, surely no less steamy, of my hand and my imagination.

For the first time since I was three, I started taking afternoon naps—in my parents' bedroom. It was, I explained, quieter up there. Of course, I hardly slept at all. I read and reread; in a lifetime of reading, have I ever come across anything so crude and so compelling? There was no pretense here of literature, of feathery description, of artful erotica. The only artistry was that of my own touch—the book propped up on the bed so both hands could be free, my fingers making a music all their own. Never mind the hack lyrics, between my legs, the symphony swelled and moaned, lifting me high and higher, teasing with a soft note, bringing me down with a groan.

Amazingly, I was never discovered. Or maybe it's not so amazing, as we always learn what we must to survive. In that household, stealth was as necessary as it would be to a hunter crouching in the woods—or, more to the point, to his prey. When it came to sex, none of us got downwind of each other. But that was true of most things. For all the arguing, the unrelieved histrionics, there was little real feeling expressed in my family. There were words, and more words, in two languages even (my father's parents, who spoke Yiddish, lived with us), but the language of pure emotion, the only language the heart understands, wasn't spoken. Instead of hurt honestly stated, there was anger; instead of anger, there was envy; instead of doubt, there was debate. Instead of sex, there was secrecy and silence. So I covered my tracks—indeed, I did a better job than my father had—put back the books, wiped off the stains.

Thirty years later, I'm still covering my tracks, but from whom? In a sexually enlightened age, why the secrecy about my longings, as if sex and pornography were the same and my dirty thoughts best kept in a closet? Why, after all the marriages and affairs, after all the sex—dry humps and sloppy wet reunions, puppy dog sex and shark sex, pinball sex, saintly sex, psychedelic melt-your-heart sex—why, after all this sex, am I still ashamed about sex? Why, when I look at a woman, does the guilt follow so quickly upon the desire that the two have become indistinguishable? Indeed, after all the women I've seen, in the flesh and in my own imagination, why am I looking at all?

*   *   *

In the current debate over pornography, I would be an ideal witness for either side. The civil libertarians could put me on the stand to wave the flag of freedom—and a patriot I am, ready to die for those jewels in the American crown, our First Amendment rights. The book burners, on the other hand, could simply take judge and jury on a tour of my ruins, letting the facts speak for themselves, letting my false hungers and false gods betray me. Step closer, your honor. Oh, sisters of mercy, gather round. Justice, raise your blindfold and look, if you can, at this sorry desolation: The mind turned into a Hollywood set, its windows taped over with stills. Women in every possible pose, in every shade of desire, wanting him, or coyly pretending not to, showing him what he wants to see, or shimmering for a moment in the distance, always out of reach, a mirage. But isn't it all illusion?

Look at him—once a boy who stared in wonder at the stars, who knew before any of his friends the names of all the planets—look at him, now trembling with anticipation over the darkened line where panties meet thigh. What does he see there with his tortured eyes? The violence, your honor! Not just to women—oh no—but to this young boy's soul, his innocence drawn from him as surely as he dreams of his seed being drawn out by one of those fancy French tongues. Now he's lived his dreams. He's fully a man. And what licks at him, my judge—my dark judge, my stern judge—is fire. Isn't he a victim too?

Victim, oppressor. It's a razor line between. A friend tells me he buys men's magazines so he can masturbate while looking at the pictures, but he feels guilty for supporting an industry that exploits women. I tell him that, once in a while, I buy those magazines too—sneakily, with an alibi prepared should someone I know see me in the store. We laugh, and I wonder if this is how prisoners laugh, fingering the bars. But aren't we the tower guards, too, peering down at the women in the yard? "It's a substitute for intimacy," he says. "A sorry substitute," I reply. "At least it's safe," he says. "Safe," I agree, "but less interesting than the real thing." He admits that even when there's a woman in his life, he buys the magazines. Well, I can understand that. I'm happily married, and sometimes I masturbate, but never happily. If I'm not, in my fantasy, exploiting a *Penthouse* model or a movie star or a friend, I'm surely exploiting myself, turning sex, once again, into porn.

Ah, the guilt. It's even more relentless than the horniness. Like an eager lover, it prods all night at the heart. And what, exactly, am I so guilty about? Is it my desire, or is it my denial of my desire, or both? One moment, I'll berate myself for my insatiable sexual appetite. The next, I'll malign myself for my mousy heart, for laundering my dirty thoughts with spirituality or fidelity ("sex is wrong except with *her*") instead of telling the world what I really worship and what I'm really married to: the pursuit of my own pleasure. But then I feel guilty for describing myself so crudely, and thus distorting my deeper longings, which sex only masks. Isn't that pornographic, too, to titillate myself with a version of myself barren of soul, as if *I* were the centerfold—a staple through the navel, the pages of my days sticky with passion's passionate lies?

Perhaps I'm being too hard on myself. We all make a pornographic movie of the world, objectifying ourselves, emphasizing fear instead of love, jerking off over images of comfort or fame or money or sex. We all read from the same lurid script: the newspapers airbrush reality, then package it in a formula not much different from that of the men's magazines; the schools deny the joy in children's bodies, using desks to tie them down, boredom to torture them; businessmen screw us. Where do we find the high regard for human possibility so notoriously lacking in hard-core pornography? And where do I find the man or woman whose sexual imagination isn't a little haunted too? So why this extra burden, this self-loathing, the exponential guilt? Who but me is booing me? And when I speak out, in my own defense, who but me is listening? It's a one-man show, on an empty stage—words, and more words— an act as lonely as sex with myself. I know the soliloquy as intimately as the woman spread out on the page or in my mind or in my bed—how hard it is to keep them apart!—yet no woman, no matter how hurt by this, has been less forgiving of me than I am of myself.

*   *   *

I can't remember why I looked inside my father's closet that first time. Maybe my father himself led me there, not consciously, of course, but simply by being who he was. His life led me there, to the dank of him, the jungle where his father had led him and told him to make it on his own, there beneath the leafy canopy that blocked out the light, there on the spongy ground crawling with unnamed fears, there with his big naked body he never loved, his dirty books and his dirty jokes, his domineering mother's dirty looks. He never made it out of the closet, out of the heat and stink of his mind. But with so much grief in there, he had to leave the door open just a crack. With so much confusion of jungle calls, he had to let out a little cry. Maybe I heard him.

Perhaps the only difference between us is that I've taken a step out of the closet. Denying my own wound has never gotten me anywhere except into deeper denials, which always creates suffering. Can you end suffering by legislating against it? Can you legislate against the past? Can you transcend it? For a while, I tried that, too, making God into a pinup, just one more unattainable object of desire.

It's said that we're compelled to live out the unfulfilled dreams (and nightmares) of our parents. In this observation, there's no blame, but no easy assurance, either. My father, like most men of his generation, dreamt of women's bodies, not their souls, yet blushed if he talked in his sleep: the women weren't to know. He feared women, but they weren't to know that, either. He split himself down the middle: on one side was the responsible, hard-working family man, on the other was everything wild and, because it was untrusted, seemingly savage. A deep wound separated the two worlds, and pornography was the balm he rubbed along it.

26

Dream: Initiation

Lou Lipsitz

My old father stands beside the used car.
There's a crack in the windshield, streaks of rust.
It's a souped-up Chevy, about '55,
been down the end of a lot of dirt roads.

He looks like a sixty-year-old teenager:
white t-shirt, sleeves rolled up, pack
of Luckies tucked in.

He's brought a little blonde for the initiation.
She looks sexy, but tough as nails.
Tight jeans and a blouse hanging part open.
Her look says: I won't be easy, but you
can get it if you're man enough.
I'll make your dick feel like a scalded
finger.

He lights a cigarette and stares at me.
He's motioning for me to come along.
My father, who hadn't touched my mother
in 35 years. He's telling me there's nothing
to wait for. Fuck what anybody thinks.
Fuck what you think yourself. Do
what you have to do. What any man
has to do.

"Dream: Initiation" first appeared in *Southern Poetry Review,* Summer 1995, *35*(1), pp. 37-38.

Then I open my eyes, erection
in my hand, messenger from the other world.
But my dream father and the little blonde
will wait. One day I will have to come
to her, barreling along this road
in an old car full of dust and the bitter need
to prove I'm a man.

27

Pumping Iron, Pumping Cocks: Sexual Activity in the Gym

Lawrence Schimel

Tonight I held another man's cock in my hands as he played with his nipples. I hadn't meant to engage in any sort of sex this evening, and in many ways, the encounter doesn't qualify as sex, per se, at least not on my part. It would be wrong to say that sex happened to me. I aided and abetted sex, but I did not have sex.

I'd gone to the gym and, after my workout, had gone to relax in the heat of the steam room. It wasn't very hot, the steam having begun to dissipate. I stared around me, deliberated where to sit among the half dozen men on the benches. I work out at the Chelsea Gym, an all-male, almost all-queer gym notorious for its frisky steam rooms. Often, I've had to deal with grab-first-ask-later queens attracted by my youth, as if youth alone equaled beauty.

I took a vacant corner spot and pretty much ignored my companions. Two of them separately stared at me intently as they stroked their groins, and I acknowledged that I was aware of their hungry intentions and disinterested. All heads turned whenever the door opened, and I, too, looked up at each newcomer, each new naked body—and also scowled at the rush of cold air each brought with him. The steam evaporated further. We waited. The spaces on the benches filled up. Men shifted to allow a newcomer to sit. A nice-looking, well-hung man took the empty seat next to me. At last, the jets kicked in, and the room filled with vapor. I closed my eyes, rubbed my tired muscles, as the waves of heat washed over me, easing tension.

When I looked up again, all of the other men in the steam room had paired off, their hands in each other's laps as they jerked each other off.

"Pumping Iron, Pumping Cocks: Sexual Activity in the Gym" first appeared as "Pumping Iron, Pumping Cocks: Sex at the Gym" in *Strategic Sex: Why Won't They Keep It in the Bedroom,* edited by D. Travers Scott, published by Harrington Park Press, Binghamton, NY, 1999, pp. 17-22.

The man next to me and I were the only two who weren't partaking, though his dick was hard and he'd been stroking it since this furtive sexual activity began. I found him to be the most attractive man in the room. I think, objectively, he was probably the most attractive man in the room. He had a nicely defined body, a cock with enough heft to it—he was the biggest of any of us, without getting into obscene or unmanageable sizes.

The pairs around us continued their motions, arms flexing. He fixed me with a look.

So, I gave him a helping hand.

Now, I can engage in sex without having an erection. I've done so before, and can have a very enjoyable time. I can get fucked without having an erection and have an enjoyable time of it. I can suck someone off without myself getting an erection and, again, enjoy myself immensely.

Tonight, however, as I am holding this man's cock in my hands and stroking him, I am hardly present in the act. I am in a private space, inside my body. I go to the gym to get out of my head. As a writer, I spend all day in my head, cerebrally, thinking, engaging the blank page, creating narrative, whether fiction, poetry, or essay, like what you're reading now.

He's got a very nice cock, I'd like to play with it again under other circumstances. But right now, it's not very meaningful. I'm tired; my body aches. I'm feeling not in the least erotic. I'd like someone to give me a massage, to feed me, and perhaps to hold me while I fall asleep. I'm not aroused and I'm not taking any pleasure out of jerking him off. Why then am I doing it?

Because he's attractive. Because I'm curious. Because I feel I should be responding to him, the situation.

Because I know I'll write this essay when I get home.

I've never fooled around before in the steam room, even though I've watched others do so many times before. I like being in the presence of sex, even without any intention of taking part. Sometimes, if there's an attractive man in the showers with me, I'll hope he comes into the steam room after me and fools around with someone so I can watch. Sometimes, later, in the privacy of my bed, I'll remember the look of him reaching over to fist his neighbor's cock with one hand and his own with the other. I'll remember and jerk off, at last giving myself permission to be turned on.

I'm never aroused while I'm there, watching.

The gym has a nonerotic boundary around it, for me. I go to the gym with an editor of mine—my workout partner—and so right away I am nervous about propriety. Sure, he's a gay man and has probably had sex in similar situations himself, but the idea of him coming into the steam room while I'm engaged in some sexual act causes embarrassment and shame in me.

Not because it's public sex—I wholly endorse that. But what is meant to be anonymous sex—quite different from sex engaged in under other circumstances—is no longer anonymous. (Arguably, sex at the gym is less anonymous than other forms of anonymous sex, since you begin to know these people whose workout schedules overlap yours, whom you see regularly over a span of weeks and months, and even if you never talk, there's a familiarity about them, a sense of knowing.) There is a confusion of boundaries between the chaste, almost-asexual (although politically sexual—that is, with a political sexuality) professional persona and the private, erotic, uninhibited sexual self.

The steam room of the gym is not a space designated for sex. Had I run into an editor—or anyone else I knew—at a sex club, a space designated for sex, I would not feel embarrassment or shame. I might be nonplussed, perhaps perturbed, at having to interact with someone I am unprepared to deal with, the way I begrudge running into certain acquaintances on the street and having to do the dance of pleasantries. But shame, when we were both obviously there for the same reason, and that reason was sex?

Tonight I am flirting with this taboo, with this fear of being discovered engaged in sex, that adolescent thrill of sneaking a parent's or older sibling's or friend's pornography to jerk off to.

A lot of people I know from the outside world come to this gym. And, since I spend so much time at home, alone, writing in solitude, these daily gym excursions have begun to provide me with a social network of casual acquaintances, people who are familiar, with whom I sometimes gossip. They are my equivalent of office friendships, and our relationships are casual—and nonerotic. Any of these people—there were a handful of them upstairs while I was working out—might come into the steam room at any moment.

Can I get off without getting caught?

But part of me wants to get caught. I am part of a community, and this stud I'm playing with is like a Trophy Fuck: whether its enjoyable or not, you take him home because everyone else wants him, and it improves your social standing to have bedded him. I want to be caught because I want the attention. And I want the attention now, not what I know I'll get from writing about this experience later tonight in this essay.

I want to be caught because some part of me wonders why my dick isn't hard, won't get hard, even now that I've decided to play with this man next to me, and I am trying to prove something to myself about my identity as a gay man, according to a set of arbitrary and amorphous, undefined external social rules about what it means to be gay. In the "straight" locker room in high school, I'd be embarrassed to have a woody while looking at another guy, but in queer locker room bravado, I'm embarrassed not to have one—especially doing what I'm doing. If we were in one of our apartments, I'd be unconcerned by all this social pressure and anxiety about acquaintances interrupting us and would therefore have an erection. I'd like to be in one of our apartments, where the acts we'd allow ourselves would be more extensive and enjoyable.

In the steam room, there is no such thing as foreplay. It is all speed, all animal sex. Men do not kiss in the steam room. Sex, for me, is less fun without kissing. Men do not really caress, not for the pleasure of rubbing bodies against each other, the intimacy of skin. One man might run his hand over another's thigh, but it is with hopeful inquisitiveness, or with the intent to get his neighbor aroused already so they can get off before someone comes in. Because anyone entering the room breaks up any and all action. Everyone freezes like rabbits caught in headlights. Hands drop whatever they're holding and cover crotches, trying to hide the erections that (hopefully) are too long to fit behind a palm.

It's curious to me, how these men will have sex in a public space—the gym—and yet are so self-conscious the moment they're reminded of the public nature of it, in the scrutiny of a stranger. This prudishness is somewhat practical: sexual activity in the gym is forbidden by the city's Health Department and thereby the gym's management. Memberships could be revoked if someone who works at the gym found them engaged in sex and reported it, or if other members complained. But the truth of the matter is, most of the guys who work at the gym don't care one way or the other, and the other members of the gym usually crowd around to watch whenever sex happens in the steam room, hoping they might join in, like a backroom frenzy.

The difference between these steam room jerk offs—or the more rare suck offs—and those of a backroom, however, lies in the nature of the space. The gym is not an arena intended for sex. It is not supposed to be happening there, and everyone is aware of this fact. When two (or more) men in the steam room begin to engage in sex, they are implicitly asking for the consent of everyone else in the room. Onlookers might not vocalize their consent for this activity to take place—although, alas, too often sex is egged on by onlookers whose sexuality is limited to lame and simplistic porno movie dialogue—but they have not withheld their consent either.

A newcomer has not yet had a chance to withhold his dissent, so everything comes crashing to a stop while everyone takes stock of one another and evaluates what is going on and how they should react. Surreptitiously, hands crawl back into neighbor's crotches, and the newcomer either watches or takes part or ignores what's going on.

In the steam room around us, men continue jerking each other off in pairs. The man whose cock I hold loses interest in my playing with him because I have so little apparent interest in it. Because he cannot reciprocate. My lack of arousal disturbs him, perhaps insults him, in the rules of queer locker room bravado. I should be hard and horny; I should be wanting him. I have a curiosity, nothing more. He shifts away from me. I let his cock fall from my hands, graciously stopping. He stands up and leaves the steam room. The pairs of men around us pause as the door opens—the glare of headlights— but then resume.

I am disappointed. I feel embarrassed, among these other men who are involved in their own pleasure. Because I did not finish off the guy I was playing with, the implication is that I was not doing a good job. I feel a twinge of shame: If I had given him more pleasure, he would have stayed until he came. If I'd been hard, he would've stayed until he came. I failed at sex.

But these thoughts evaporate, and most of my shame with them. I still feel that irrational social peer pressure, that I should've been aroused despite my anxiety surrounding my professional life. But I know that judging my "performance" is irrelevant to what passed between us. Things weren't clicking. We engaged in sexual activity because we were seated next to each other, not out of any desire for each other. I was not interested in having sex then, was engaging in it to ask myself an intellectual question: How far will this man let me go with him? And also, How far am I willing to go with him, in this situation?

But having proposed these questions and being in the moment with the answer, I was surprised to discover the answer—a *frisson,* like being confronted with a newcomer's scrutiny.

I return into myself. I glance at the men around me, as they build toward the grunting, messy climax of sex. My disinterest returns. The steam is dissipating again; the door is slightly ajar. I stand up, I leave the steam room. The guy I was playing with is not in the showers. I see him through the window as I pass the sauna, leaning over the man next to him.

I shower, leave.

I write this essay. Alone, in my apartment, I think about the scenario again—the feel of his cock in my hands, his initial eagerness as he twists a nipple as I work him, the thrill of doing this in public, my eagerness to be caught—and I am hard.

28

Odin's Horse

Jack Random

I've got Allen by the hair and I'm dragging him over to the bed. He's naked, unbalanced, hands cuffed behind him, and breathing hard from having his face slapped. I'm naked too, apart from knee boots, a motorcycle cap, and assorted straps that decorate my torso. Both our cocks are hard.

"Bend over bitch," I tell him, pushing him face down over the end of the bed. "Daddy wants that sweet little ass of yours," and I kick his legs apart, so that he's bent over at the waist, feet on the floor, ass spread open.

As I do it, I notice that my voice is thick with excitement, my heart racing. I feel like I'm flying inside my own skin—like riding that runaway horse when I was thirteen, not in control at all, just hanging on, balancing on the beast.

A little high-pitched moan comes out of Allen when I say the Daddy thing, escapes from somewhere deep inside his chest. It's what he told me he wants, for Daddy to want him that way. Not to be the little boy you understand, this isn't a molestation scene. No, he wants to be the real, grown-up, sexually mature, thirty-year-old Allen, and he wants Daddy to want to fuck him in the ass. To show Daddy that he's a good boy and a great fuck and deserves to be loved and accepted, forever and ever.

And I want to give that to him. Well, maybe not the "forever and ever" part, but this is a fantasy, and it's the fantasy that I want to give him. Be good, pass the test, pass the initiation, and Daddy will love you and say that you are a man after all—even if you want to be fucked in the ass.

It's burning in me, right down in the pit of my stomach as I wrap cuffs around his ankles. I'm moving fast, hands trembling a little as I run a rope through the bed frame and tie the ends to the cuffs. I pull the rope into a slipknot in the middle, taking up slack, forcing his legs further apart. I reach up and yank his cock and balls through the loop of rope and tighten it. Now, when he moves his feet together, the rope pulls his cock, distending his scrotum toward the floor. He looks so damn hot, bent over and helpless, all hard and panting, with his eyes squeezed shut.

This is my fantasy too. Putting him through this. Putting anybody through this. Like letting my demons out on a leash, I feel in and out of control at the same time—riding the beast.

I stand up between his legs and lay my cock in the open cleft of his ass, rocking my hips, letting him feel it rub up and down, the stroke of the shaft and the poking blunt tip.

"You want it, don't you boy?" I whisper, intimate.

He nods, unable to say it out loud.

"Say it." A little louder, threatening, "Say, I want your cock Daddy." And I reach down, stroking his cock a little. I feel it twitch. "Say, I want you to fuck me Daddy."

I want it too. I want him to call me Daddy and beg for my cock. Need him to do it, to recognize that in me and make it real. I've needed to do this my whole life.

As a boy, I couldn't ever figure out what it meant to be a man. When I saw my father, trying so hard to transcend his Okie roots and become Ward Cleaver, I came to the idea that our manhood was something that we could choose, that we had to invent for ourselves. I knew I couldn't be my father, couldn't get married and have a corporate job and try to make everything in the world fit into a bland little bottle. I wanted too much, needed too much that was different from him.

I was an unhappy kid, and I knew instinctively that if I was going to survive, let alone ever be happy, that I was going to have to find a way to take myself apart and put it all back together differently. Like the Norse god Odin, hanging himself from Yggdrasil, the World Tree, I needed to be ripped apart and to consecrate my own life. At least, that's how I tell the story now.

At the time, my late teens and twenties, it was mostly just about drugs and alcohol and motorcycles. I think I tried out, without consciously thinking about it, every silly masculine role offered by our culture that wasn't my father's. Anything I could put on and carry around with me as a shield from the unbearable terror of my own existence, and, of course, the frightening prospect of my bisexuality.

It took me most of my adult life, but I have an idea of what I want now. I want to reinvent manhood for myself—to show that I can be macho tough and still nurturing. I want to play out this scene with Allen all the way to the end—to get that charge of the arrogant, initiating, dominant male without letting it get out of control, into abuse. I want to be Odin the All-Father, the lawgiver, and also patron of poetry. I want, with leather and sex, to work the magic of the runes that Odin learned in nine days of agony on the tree.

Allen can't say it yet, can't ask me out loud for what he wants. He turns his head to the side and tucks his chin into his shoulder, even as he arches his back, offering his ass. It's good; it's sweet and hot, but it isn't what I want.

"You will say it, boy," I whisper, "even if I have to beat it out of you."

Moving away from him, I take the heavy flogger from its hook. I give it a few practice swings, warming up, letting him know what's coming. It's part of the game, to let him know what I'm about to do. When he didn't speak, he was letting me know, maybe without even knowing himself, that he wasn't there yet, that he wasn't in the place where begging for my cock would mean anything to him, where he would be giving me something real. It's a dance, playing this game. We're working together.

I swing the flogger in smooth figure eights, letting the tips snap against each of his shoulder blades in turn. Left, right, avoiding the spine. Allen lies still, getting into it. I start to increase the force of the blows, watching his skin turn pink and then red. My attention is focused, ignoring everything in the world but the two square feet of skin on his upper back.

The tails of the flogger are starting to leave welts now, starting to mark him. It seems to go on forever—the precise repetition of movement, the gradually increasing strength of the strokes. He begins to move a bit, and I start to whip him faster. His head comes up, stretching him out flatter on the bed.

I'm flying now, swinging the whip perfectly, watching his skin, judging how much he can take. I'm on the horse, and it's pulsing between my legs, ignoring the reins, but I know I won't fall. I'm calm inside my terror, just like I'm in control inside my sadism, inside my violent maleness, waiting for Allen to break, waiting for the moment when his begging for what he wants will mean what we both want it to mean.

He starts to jerk back and forth a little, making tiny grunting noises. I hit him harder, watching the first faint shading of the bruise that he will wear for days. My arm and the whip are the same, and I feel the tips touching his skin as if they were a part of me.

"Say it, boy," I snarl, starting to pant from the workout. "Tell Daddy what you want."

And he does say it then, sobbing it out from some deep place inside himself, letting the pain excuse the tears that he normally can't get at, begging to be fucked, calling me Daddy.

I drop the flogger and stroke myself hard again, watching his tearstained face as I put on the condom and the lube. I unhook his ankles and pull the slip knot from around his cock and balls. Twisting him violently by the legs, I roll him up and onto his back on the bed. He winces as his back hits the mattress, shifts slightly with his hands still shackled behind him.

Stroking myself through the latex, getting as hard as possible, I climb onto the bed and hook his legs up over my shoulders. His cock is heavy and pink, lolling half hard across his abdomen as I begin to work up into him. He's ready and open for me though; the bulbous head of my dick slides easily into the tight heat of his ass.

And then we're doing it, fucking each other as we look into each other's eyes. I'm thrusting and feeling how deep inside him I am. He's gasping, slack jawed with each thrust, as I drive his bruised back and shackled hands down onto the bed.

"Thank you, Daddy," he whispers. "Thank you for fucking me."

And that sends me over the edge. I come, sharp and hard and so suddenly that I haven't even got a second to think about it before it happens. I'm slamming away in him and then he calls me Daddy and I come, spine stiffening, breath stopped short in my throat, cock throbbing, all on the speaking of a single genuine word. Daddy.

Eventually, when I've recovered a bit, I pull out of him and uncuff his hands, let him stretch a little before I gather him in my arms and put his head on my chest.

"Jerk off for me, boy," I tell him, running a lubed hand up and down his cock. He does, and it takes less than a minute before he's pumping a huge load all over his stomach.

We lie together like that for most of an hour afterward, letting the sweat and come dry on our skin, talking softly, and every time he calls me Daddy, something in my heart jumps.

Men are like this, I've found. What we are, what we think makes us men, is something we carve out for ourselves—more than that, it's something we have to put into the eyes of other men. It isn't enough that I feel strong and loving when I'm holding Allen. I need him to see me that way, to think of me as Daddy, and to prove that he does. And it isn't enough for him; that I say I want him; he has to be sure.

Together, at least for tonight, we are finding our own level, mapping out our own kind of manhood. I am riding Odin's horse, the anger and violence that I've inherited as a man, but I can ride it and not let it run wild. Afterward, holding Allen and loving him, feeling as large and strong as the sky, I am reconsecrated in his eyes—ripped apart and put all back together again as just the kind of man I've always wanted to be.

29

Need

Justin Chin

In the small space of the bookstore booth, we fumble with the finesse of adolescents going for third base when the parents are due back from church choir practice at any moment. He clumsily kisses me; I grab his shaved head and press his face into mine, sucking on his tongue, all the while groping, pawing at each other's crotch and ass. He pulls off his jacket and lays it on top of mine on the small makeshift stool. I slip my hands under his shirt and play with his nipples while he unbuttons his shirt. As each button is undone, I can see the glint of ink on his chest. He pulls his shirt off, and standing there in the booth lit by unblemished porn bunnies faking their pleasure, he wraps his arms around me and kisses me again. This time, it's hard, slow, and deliberate; with his hand, he holds the back of my head and guides my mouth down past his chin, across his neck to his impressive biceps. This time, I see that he has a swastika tattooed on his arm. "Kiss it," he says quietly in my ear, his voice not menacing nor put on, and I place my lips on the dark lines on his flesh and kiss it. I let my tongue dawdle over it, while he tongues my ear like an eager puppy. He is covered with tattoos with no seeming connection: daggers, flames, evil eyeballs, a Gothic creature, stars, planets, a cartoon mouse, a hypodermic needle, backdrops. Nestled in these sprays of dark and color are two swastikas, one on each bicep, each sinister and gleaming in its bold simplicity. There is a more ornate swastika on his forearm that looks not unlike it was inspired by a fourteenth-century woodcut. For a minute, I think that maybe it is one of those Buddhist symbols unfortunate enough to look like a swastika, with legs that turn the wrong way, but buried in the map of his flesh is a flesh-colored cross made of two spikes, the negative space colored red, the center containing a diamond with a black squiggle

"Need" first appeared in *Drummer,* June 1997, issue 204, pp. 17-19.

like a single quotation mark, and further, dark elongated N, a crown with a sword piercing through it. I find a German word in gothic script just by his left armpit when I go there to bury my snout in his scent. We fumble with our trousers, hastily unbuttoning and unzipping, and push them down to ankle level. He looks at me dead in the eye and says, "Fuck me." He turns around, bends forward, and spreads his legs as much as the space will allow. Above his underwear line, above his crack, in a two-inch-high open-cut script, he has *White Power* tattooed unflinchingly across the fleshy bit of his lower back—a small tuft of sparse hair in the small of his back threatens the sentiment. I spit into my palm and grease up, spit into his ass crack and let the glob of saliva slide into his hole, and roughly shove my dick inside of him.

The territory of need brings us to strange places. It's a difficult decision when the chips are down and you're fucking. If push came to shove and the cards are in motion, would you fuck that neoconservative Republican or that spongy Baptist minister if you knew they were who they were, instead of tricks in some tricking spot—scuzzy trolls who would do in a snap, fucks that will get you out of jams and other serious shit. Like the time I was homeless in Honolulu, living in the 7-Eleven parking lot: I ended up tricking the local teamsters' boss with the hard, shiny, distended beer-gut, bad teeth, and constant flatulence, all for pizza and a good sofa. Would I do it different if ever I knew better? Like the good-looking trick who turns out to be one hell of a colonialist asshole, as if he lived in a Rudyard Kipling novel and I was to be his Mowgli: while lying on the floor with him rimming my asshole I let go a squishy spray of shit onto his face, made some excuse about lactose intolerance, and left while he sputtered to the bathroom. Like the old troll who lives in the darkest niche of the bathroom in the bar, giving blow to anyone who waves his dick in front of him: I come in and he's waiting for the next dick, and he grins toothlessly, asks if I want a blow job. I tell him I'm just there to piss the overpriced beer out. He snorts, says, "All these colored guys just love to get their dicks sucked, but hey, remember, no matter what color your dick is, cum is always white."

Then there is the time I fucked a guy who had a distinct fantasy. He wanted to play INS agent on border patrol. He even had the uniform for it. He told me he wanted to catch me crossing the border illegally, and then I'd be detained in a holding cell while I was questioned and taught a lesson about illegally crossing borders. His imagination is excellent and the role he played was worthy of an Emmy: I scampered across his bedroom as if his futon were a high wire doused with searchlights that would separate us and them, him and me, as if his brown carpeting were a dust road, a river; he pounced on me and asked for identification, for papers, and *I no speaking 'lish,* so he stripped me down to my BVDs, made me crouch doggy style on the bed, with my ass sticking in the air, while he stood behind, slowly pulling my briefs down. "Take that you stinking Mexican; take that back to your family," he squealed, as he came on my ass; then he pulled the briefs up and snapped the band so that his cum was squished inside my underwear. I'm putting on my clothes when he says, "I'm sorry. I know you're Chinese, but sometimes, I just get too excited." In some parallel universe, these thoughts might go through your shagged mind: "Why am I here? What is in it for me? Am I having fun? Are you having fun? Are we having fun? Am I playing along? Am I playing along right? Have I always been playing along? Am I right or wrong? Did I agree to this? Did I agree to all of it? Did I know what I was agreeing to? Did I agree to everything and anything and anyone? Is my brain a sexual organ? Are my guts, my spleen? Is sex just sex? Is cum a delicious creamy fluid emitted from the end of an erect (or sometimes un-erect) penis that I love more than oxygen?"

Someone once told me his theory about these interracial pig-fuck scenes: these colored boys let themselves be degraded because, somewhere inside of them, they feel they don't measure up, and they're secretly pleased that the white boys want them in any way. And somewhere inside these white boys, they believe that, or they don't question the balance, have never even thought of the question. "But what if the colored boy is doing the degrading?" I ask, but by then, we're fucking and not talking about politics and sex anymore. Was he a colored boy or a white boy? You decide.

When I fuck, it is not me that is fucking.

The porn boys on the screen, innocuous, shaved, and plucked muscle monsters with their vacant stares, are going at it beside the pool, but no one is paying any attention. He straightens up and turns around suddenly. "Do you like to play rough?" he asks. "Come on, punch me, kick me. Show me how," I say. He grabs my neck with one hand and slams me against the wall; with his other hand, he smacks me firmly across the head. He leans in and kisses me while grabbing and twisting my balls until my eyes water. He alternates between gentle strokes and rough scrapes; he chews on my dick like a puppy high on rawhide, until my hard-on has turned as flaccid as any seasoned tweaker's. He sticks his hand into my mouth. I suck his fingers, and he pushes them deeper in until I gag; he takes the spit and mucous-wet fingers and sticks them into my ass while gnawing at my tits. He turns me around and sticks his dick into my ass in one rough movement. There is a short sharp shear of pain, and I want to pull him out, clench my sphincter to calm down, but he's holding me tight, his muscular arm wrapped around me like comfort. *"Just ease into it,"* he says and I do. As he thrusts his dick in and out while still holding me, I lean forward and suck on the small ornate swastika on his forearm, which is in front of me. I'm not sure if I need to cover it with my mouth so that I won't see its troubling stare or if I just want to taste it. He's cooing, *"Yeah, that's good,"* over and over. I break out of his hold, his dick slips out of my ass, and I turn to face him; he leans forward to kiss me, and I punch him in the gut. He doubles over; in that position, he slouches to his knees, puts his mouth to my dick, and sucks away. I let him do that for a bit, then I raise my knee and shove him to the ground. He falls back and sits there while I stick my boot into his crotch, let his balls fall on the tip of my boots and bounce them up and down. While he is watching my boot playing with his dick, I backhand him across his face; he is caught unaware and his head snaps to the side. "Oh fuck," he groans. I pull him up, turn him around, spit into his ass and start fucking him again, while I hold onto his chest for support. He spreads his arms overhead and rests them on the wall for support, and the fleshy map of swastikas and SS symbols, indelible scrawls of our unspoken minds, a past and a present untold, a shaky future, map of everything that falls apart, bounce and quiver and mesmerize with each thrust. I pull out of his ass, and cum on his tattoo—White Power covered in cum. I smear my cum into the tattoo. He turns around, one hand masturbating; he uses the other to gently push me down to a squat, sticks two fingers into my mouth, pries it open, leans forward, and cums hard into my open mouth. I stick my tongue out to catch his full load. I stand up, grab him, and kiss him, and we pass his cum back and forth between us until it becomes indistinguishable from spit and tongues.

30

God Is a Bullet

Christopher Hall

I can first remember having erections when I was about four or five. They usually happened when I was outside, playing with my friends. We played a lot of games—War, Cops and Robbers, Cowboys and Indians—that somehow involved death. Dying was as inevitable as killing in any of these games, and I was very good at it: when the imaginary weapon of one of my friends tore into my body, I would let out a long cry of anguish, throw out my arms, and topple elegantly to the ground, moaning and wailing the whole way.

There was something about being dead that was very exciting to me. As I lay in the grass and dandelions, awaiting my resurrection, my crotch became tight and hot and a warm tingling sensation ran through my entire body. It caused a sense of wonderful confusion in me; although too young to understand sexuality, I did understand desire. I knew that there was something my body wanted and needed, but what exactly it was escaped me.

*   *   *

The process of becoming a man is very tied up with death. This truism has been studied in intimate detail by feminist scholars for the past thirty years, seeking to decode the scripts that drive so many men to seek their manhood through violence against women, children, and other men. There is no doubt that men are encouraged to prove their masculinity through physical attacks on others; the gun and the fist are the favorite playthings of boys, and the shift from pretend to the real thing is still seen as the ultimate rite of passage for males. However, the drive toward homicide that feminist analysis tends to emphasize is only half the story: for masculinity to function, an equally powerful drive toward suicide is just as important.

In truth, the definitive icon of masculinity is a strange fusion of John Rambo and Saint Sebastian; the ultimate demonstration of a man's virility is to be killed—violently and painfully—while killing his enemies. The male myth has promoted the idea that violent death is itself an expression of power—it is a sign of a man too strong to be dominated, too mighty to surrender his masculinity to another man. The only way this man can be conquered is through his total annihilation.

So death is presented to men as an ecstatic moment, one almost orgasmic in its intensity; the more the body is mutilated, the more agony the man suffers before succumbing to death, the greater the ecstatic moment. It is as though every bullet is a tiny packet of divinity that bestows grace unto its victim. This ethic manifests itself in countless icons: Butch and Sundance hurling themselves into a wall of gunfire rather than surrendering; Roland standing at the pass, choosing to fight an unwinnable battle rather than dishonor himself by calling for help; the Light Brigade, charging mindlessly into the Valley of Death; Obi-Wan Kenobi sacrificing himself to Darth Vader's blade in order to become even more powerful. If men are to be warriors, to march lock-step into battle for their superiors, then the urges toward homicide and suicide must be bred into a careful partnership; thus, men spend much of their lives hurting themselves and those around them, preparing for the real thing.

*   *   *

By the time I was in eighth grade, I had survived every brutality that children's minds could devise. Thanks to my classmates in PE, I had been conditioned to flinch at any sudden movement in my direction, something that gave extra amusement to the jocks. By the time I reached high school, I was completely isolated from my peers and my family and spent most of my time locked in my bedroom, listening to music and reading. My insides were a contorted mass of rage and self-hatred. Bloody fantasies of self-mutilation and mayhem consumed my mind at least as much as sex did. One day in my senior year, I stood in front of a trophy case, quivering with pain. I had just come to the realization that there was no possibility that I would graduate with the rest of my class that year. I had failed every value I had ever been taught; that truth was as cold and real as the pane of glass guarding the trophies, and I hated myself for it. My whole body burned and trembled. My face was sore with the effort of holding the tears in; I wanted desperately to release them, but I couldn't remember how. As I stared into the glass, I thought of what it would be like to put my fist through it. The idea had an almost sensual beauty; I wanted to feel the shattered glass rip into my skin and see my blood splatter across the gilded plastic statues. It would be a bright, clean pain, one that would sweep aside the dull gnawing sensation in my gut, if only for a few moments. Best of all, people would see it. The gaping wounds in my arm would scream all the things that I couldn't force past my lips. For several long moments, I held my fist in front of the glass, glaring at my reflection, trying to do it.

I didn't; some buried corner of rationality prevailed. I shoved my fist into my pocket and walked home, feeling sick.

I sometimes wonder if my decision was a victory or a defeat. I think that what that tiny piece of rationality told me was that if I did the deed, I would be forced to talk about all those evil things swirling around inside me. I would expose carefully hidden parts of myself, and that idea frightened me more than anything.

* * *

In our society, there is nothing less erotic than a penis; as an icon, it represents rape, war, and death. Male sexuality has not been destroyed, but in the cultural mind, it is a thanatological force, not an erotic one. A "phallic symbol" is a gun, a knife, a spear, a missile; the phrase is almost never taken to imply something that inspires life or growth. Few people would have the vision to see the pen I write these words with as the most important phallus in my life. Thanks to my ability to write, I can bypass my lips and speak through words instead of wounds.

Although sexuality is despised in both men and women, the practical manifestation of attitudes is very different. Whereas women are told to deny their sexuality, the nature of men is assumed to make them unable to maintain this level of purity; men are creatures of violence, and if a man is not allowed to satisfy his urges through marriage, womanizing, or whoring, he will be forced to satisfy them through rape. Male sexuality is acknowledged as normal, but it is not acknowledged as good; it is simply an unpleasant reality. The male sex drive is seen as a dark, predatory thing, not erotic at all, but a constant reminder of the core of violence that defines manhood. The cock is a thing devoid of grace or beauty, which poisons everything it touches. Men, even more than women, have a love-hate relationship with their genitals. Women can maintain their purity by detaching themselves from their sexuality and denying that they have pussies. There is no such belief about the penis. Men are perpetually faced with a paradox: if a man denies the power of his cock, he denies also his manhood, but to acknowledge it is to face an ugly, violent part of himself. Lust denies respect, and so men are faced with the idea that their very nature will always cause them to harm or demean the ones they hold dearest.

In this atmosphere, that men choose to define themselves through violence is not so very surprising; in fact, it could be no other way. In our old models of masculinity, desire and violence have been woven together so tightly that they are practically synonymous; sex is violence, and vice versa. One of the great tragedies of feminism is that theorists such as Andrea Dworkin have championed the immutability of this concept even more enthusiastically than the patriarchs who are so enamored of traditional gender roles. Dworkin and her followers (now thankfully decreasing in influence) decry the rates of violence against women as misogynistic genocide, but ironically promote a view of male lust that makes such violence inevitable.

Paradoxes such as this are the rule, not the exception, in sexuality, and the fact that most modern sexual ideologies refuse to recognize this represents a failure of integrity at the deepest, most vital level. We live in a binary society, one that values the ability to make clear, rational distinctions between on/off, good/bad, this/that, up/down, us/them, man/woman. When these distinctions cannot be drawn easily, it is horrific to us. The goal of mainstream sexual ideologies, whether feminist or puritan, has always been to construct models of sexuality that are wholly rational, civilized, and consistent. Puritan traditionalists try to define sex through rigid gender roles that adhere to biological sex and remain constant through each encounter (with your heterosexual mate for life, natch!). Feminist models conceive of sex in completely genderless egalitarian terms, with little role difference that is not dictated by anatomy.

At some level, I have always known that these models, which need to justify fucking as a means to some better romantic, spiritual, or reproductive end, are lies. I have always known my own sexuality to be a thing more complex and fluid than anything implied by these bloodless, arthritic ideologies. To fuck, passionately and honestly, is to enter a nexus point at which all the aspects of self—emotional, physical, intellectual, psychological, spiritual—meet and interact with one another. What we do in bed is a product of our whole selves, and so it is no more a rational thing than we are. To insist that sex should conform to the strictures of rationality is to deny the whole point.

I have felt the reality of these truths since the first time I had sex. It took a long time for me to articulate the reasons, but I knew instinctively that none of the different things I was told about sex when I was growing up satisfactorily described what I felt during sex. The first time I went down on a woman was an act of communion more intimate and real than all the wafers Father Taylor fed me when I knelt before him in church. To this day, I can think of no moment when I am more at peace than when I am kneeling in front of a lover, feinting and thrusting at her clit with my tongue. The sensation of her warmth trickling into me is overwhelming; I like knowing that part of her body becomes part of mine and that every beat of my heart is pushing her deeper into my veins. I feel vulnerable and powerful at the same time, and for a while, everything is healed.

Queers seem to understand these truths better than straights. Despite my own rather conventional sexual history, I feel a much deeper empathic connection to my friends with queer sexual tastes. Although we may not be attuned to the same erotic stimuli, I feel a very real sense of honesty between us because of the mutual acknowledgment of sexuality as a metamorphic process that can incorporate and transform the contradictions of everyday life. Queers also seem much more aware of the gulf between what happens in one's fantasies and what one desires in real life. One famous queer whose writings have taught me a great deal is the late gay pornographer John Preston. In his writings about gay S/M sex, Preston explored the inherent contradictions of sexual relationships. He showed, in powerful detail, how encounters that had the superficial appearance of torture and oppression could actually be liberating. In his essay "What Happened?" Preston wrote about his initiation into S/M sex and the moral importance that it assumed in his life:

> Fears and anxieties that had been long repressed forced themselves right up to the surface and demanded that I confront them. I remember learning to trust someone whose power over me was real. Yet the men who initiated me into S/M did so at my request, with my compliance, a stark change from the men and women who had abused me emotionally without my consent or even knowledge. The men I met in the dark underworld of S/M were not unwelcome authority figures forced on me in everyday society; they were men I chose myself, something that I had learned to accept and deal with. (1993:28)

This passage illustrates at least one very important truth about manhood and sexuality: in our society, men's relationships with the world are supposed to be sadomasochistic in almost every sense but the sexual. Our very identities as men depend on our willingness to take our proper places in hierarchies in which we submit to very real tortures and humiliations from those above us and pass those same abuses on to those below us. This lesson is repeated at every level of education, from the playgrounds and locker rooms at school to the workplaces where we are finally allowed to stake our claims to full adulthood. It is only when people choose their own roles, when they orchestrate elaborate parodies of the power structures ruling their lives that these power games are seen as corrupt and venal.

Part of this dynamic is due to the fact that the S/M games which Preston saw as so important to his life, violate one of the primary tenets of the Sacred Cultural Laws of Sex: sex, at most, should be a means to an end, not an end in itself. It can be used to further romance, to have babies, to reach some kind of New Age spiritual insight, but there must always be an excuse to justify fucking other than the orgasm. The idea that passionate, honest fucking can be a healing act in and of itself is alien to our traditional conception of sexuality. The utilitarian view of sex lies at the heart of the paradoxical relationship that men have with their cocks. The Freudians have the symbology backward: the gun/knife/spear is not a substitute for the penis; the penis is a substitute for the weapon. We are raised with the idea that our ultimate fulfillment as men will come, not through sex, but through combat. The de-eroticizing of the male body shows the priorities of manhood in our society. It can be depicted as a machine, a tool, a weapon, but very rarely as a sexual object. Whereas every aspect of the female body—lips, thighs, breasts, hips, ass—is inscribed with sexual implication, the cock is the only locus of sexuality on the male body. This is why men tend to center their sexuality so heavily around erection, penetration, and ejaculation: the cock is the one part of the male body that we are taught to associate with sex. Everything else—our muscles, hair, nipples—is neutered in the cultural eye. These things have values that can be measured and summed up in mathematical terms, as though they were nothing more than the results of a very sophisticated engineering project.

The neutering of our own bodies is key to the suicidal component of masculinity. During the last years of my adolescence, when my depression was extremely bad, I felt a deep cleavage between my mind and my body. At times, I had the distinct impression of being locked inside a machine, something which may have represented me to the outside world but which had no real connection to myself as I knew myself to be. Locked inside my skull, I might command my right hand to reach out and pick up a glass of water, and as it did so, I would watch the interplay of bone and muscle under skin as dispassionately as I would have watched a remote-control claw. It was during these times that it would have been easiest for me to mutilate or kill myself. I had little intuitive connection to my body, barely associated it with the idea of Me, and so physically attacking it seemed less horrible. It even seemed an act of liberation. My body, after all, represented a lie and kept my real self sealed away from the world. This is only the traditional masculine ideal taken to its extreme. It is this idea that makes it possible for us to be content as cannon fodder, to submit to the weird cycle of abuse and self-abuse that makes up so much of our lives.

This is another revelation I gained from reading Preston and other queer writers: in gay theory and culture, the entire male body is given sexual implication, not just the crotch. By eroticizing the body, they make it something greater than the sum of its parts. Lust, the true kind of lust that makes itself known in groin, head, heart, and every atom in between, encourages a holographic view of the body: the whole is implicit in each of its parts. Thus, to brush your lips against a lover's nipple, to inhale his scent and feel his heat, is to intuitively learn more about his essence than would seem to be inherent in any one of those fragments. Lust, far from being demeaning, is a humanizing thing; it is empathy at its deepest level. And although I don't feel the sexual connection to the imagery that Preston did, I do find it to be very powerful.

I find it powerful because it is only recently that I have begun to feel aware of the sexual potential of my own body. For a long time, I thought of my body as either pitifully inadequate or (at best) a physical nonentity, a thing that wouldn't arouse any passion, either positive or negative, in someone else. I've come to realize that neither of these ideas is true and that others don't necessarily see my body in the same ways that I do. My view of my physical self is becoming more nuanced, more attuned to small details of sensation and how they interact with the whole. I am, in short, learning to see my body as a part of myself, something that grows and changes in response to the path my life takes. It is more than a box of flesh wrapped around my real self.

These sound like simple (and even trite) truths, but, in fact, they represent very hazardous territory for a heterosexual man to navigate. In terms of a physical vocabulary of sex, heterosexual men are almost mute. Although women are taught a million different nonverbal signals to indicate sexual desire or availability, men have virtually none. The detailed familiarity with one's body that such a vocabulary requires does not fit with what a man is supposed to be; it is, at best, suspicious and, at worst, a sure sign of being a faggot. It makes one appear vulnerable and vain, traits that are feminine. Therefore, for a man to show a great deal of awareness of his body, to think of it as something other than an anonymous thing, is a form of self-castration.

* * *

It is important to me that my cock be considered an erotic thing. I do not deny the validity of death and destruction as an aspect of the phallus; after all, the power of sex comes from the fact that it has equal potential to annihilate or heal and that it demands an intricate understanding of yourself and your partners to avoid going the wrong way. This understanding, and the choices it implies, is the rawest available proof of our humanity.

But when that choice is denied, when the phallus is symbolic only of rape, murder, defilement, and arrogance, then humanity is denied as well. The only possible expression of humanity is the distorted sadomasochism we see in modern portrayals of masculinity, whereby a man's power is measured by the dual index of how much pain he can give out and how much he can withstand before going to his final, bloody death. Without the moral choice of the cock as an erotic thing, we move further from our humanity and deeper into the pit of self-loathing that we have been digging for God knows how many thousand years. And the deeper we go, the more logical the homicidal suicide of masculinity seems.

REFERENCE

Preston, John. 1993. "What Happened." In *My Life As a Pornographer and Other Indecent Acts.* New York: Richard Kasak Books, pp. 123-136.

31

Cock in My Pocket

Max Wolf Valerio

> I got my cock in my pocket
> and it's shovin up
> through my pants
>
> I just wanna fuck
> this ain't no romance

Iggy Pop
"Cock in My Pocket"

Sex is like a feast now, an absolute smorgasbord. I am in a porn store in the Tenderloin, almost by accident, on a whim while walking by. Suddenly I feel an insatiable rush—I grab through the magazines. There's all kinds of stuff: women over forty, fat women, girls who like to fuck big cocks, women in bondage, motorcycle sluts, white women with black men, black women with white men, Asian women with black and with white men, black and white women with Asian men, women with breasts so huge they can barely walk, women with tiny breasts, women dressed like little girls, snarling dominatrixes tying men up and stabbing their balls with stiletto heels, women being paddled over the knees of men or women, women being fucked in every conceivable and inconceivable position in almost any environment you could wish for— beaches, barracks, classrooms, cafeterias, crosswalks—and in the background of the store, on television monitors, women moaning in orgasm. And the other men there, all of us, we are all wolves, a pack of wolves, hungry, panting in excitement.

With a jolt I saw myself, there in the store with all those men, one of them. No one could have picked me out as being different in any way. Here I am, once a lesbian-feminist, now a hungry wolflike man in a porn store, browsing girlie magazines.

I go up to the counter and get five dollars worth of tokens for the video arcade, impatient. *Make that change fast, man. I've got to get off, now.* Up the stairs, into a booth—which one? In and out of doors in a hurry, some of the booths smell too bad, acrid from semen. Finally I get into one that seems clean and search for the knobs in the dark, lock the door shut. There, in the flickering light of the small screen, I undo my pants and reach for my clit, which is big from testosterone now—a small penis. Hold it between thumb and forefinger, stroke up and down, like a cock, up and down, fast. Flip through the channels with frenetic intensity.

* * *

There is a texture to my sexual fantasies that is different now. I was always more of a "top"—more dominant in my fantasies, aggressive, the pursuer not the pursued as female. Yet now, on the hormones, and fueled by the contrast of male and female bodies—that context of edge and vulnerability—my fantasies are more aggressive than ever.

* * *

Standing next to Debbie, a co-worker, at break time, I slide into an expanding sexual dream. Lately, we've been flirting, and suddenly she's standing at a nearly intimate distance. So close, in high heels and a black dress, tight and revealing of large, perfumed breasts—I can smell her fragrance, a sweet scent, flower petals crushed under the tongue of a bull. I watch her breasts move under the taut stretch of black, her nipples outlined and erect, her tits globes, wet melons. I imagine tasting them. In heels, she's teetering off balance, just a little. If she falls, I could catch her. Standing there, face to face with her in that outfit, I realize again the intensity of this new male sex drive, the aggression of it. I have to hold myself back to keep from touching her, a sheer effort of will, gritting my teeth. I want to fuck her so bad, grab her and throw her down on the floor and fuck her so hard she aches for days. This impulse almost overpowers my better sense. It's so strong, a rush of white lust from groin to gut to flaming solar plexus, a hard stretch of flame. The eyes of the bull inflamed and entranced by the red cloth. I have to stop and take stock. This feeling is different in intensity from what I'd known before, in its pleading for release.

No wonder guys lose it sometimes! I think at this moment, How can they not? In the beginning, I thought this a lot. *My god, if this is how men feel, how come they don't rape more often? Rape and plunder. Take.*

* * *

It is wrong to rape. I knew that before; I know that still. Any man who acts out these fantasies or impulses, no matter how strong, is committing a wrong act, an abominable act, and should be punished. Even so, I understand now the force of will it can take to keep from running wild with these feelings, the temptation.

Rape is an act of violent sex. Power and sex are entwined, joined in ancient communion within the brain, in the hypothalamus, seat of the id. Many people feel more powerful when they feel sexual; many people are turned on by other people's power or lack of power, their strength and perceived ability to vanquish and control, or their vulnerability, their fragility. This is as ancient as hunter and hunted, prey and predator, the abduction of Persephone by Hades, the tender romance of Beauty and the Beast.

I've talked to many transsexual guys, and they'll wonder out loud, If we had normal penises, would we rape? With that piece of meat dangling between our legs, so easy, so ready, and then watching and wanting these women. . . . One transsexual man, Tom, tells me that he got turned on when he realized that a woman he was walking behind was afraid of him. This was a new feeling, scary and strange. He didn't quite know what to make of it. This jacked-up sex drive freaked out one transman so much he stayed inside for his first few months on testosterone, afraid to go out, unsure of what he might do. In time, most of these sexual feelings become less intense—we grow into our new sex drive and learn how to deal with it. Even so, some transmen say in dark tones, half scared, drunk on libido and hallucinating sexual abandon, *I might do it, I could rape a woman; maybe I couldn't control myself.*

I wouldn't. I bet these guys wouldn't either. But the stuff we take, that virile hormone testosterone, grabs you by the edge of your scalp and holds you tight—you begin to wonder, and if *we* wonder, knowing what it's like on the other side of the threat, knowing how afraid and vulnerable a woman can feel, what must it be like for nontranssexual men?

Around this time, I went with my friend Aleister to the Exotic Erotic New Year's Ball, a colorful San Francisco cavalcade of costumes, bands, and naked people. There are no naked babes to be seen, oh maybe one or two, but mostly the naked people are out-of-shape pasty-skinned middle-aged men with leers smeared on their faces. I'm disappointed. Aleister and I wander around with beers in our hands, watching the celebration and the yuppie band playing soggy rock music.

At the end of the evening, a woman begins to masturbate with criminal glee. She looks as though she's in a trance state. She has on a red corset. She's yanked off her silk panties for the occasion, leaving them crumpled beside her. She pulls her breasts out and over her bustier and stares into the distance as she fingers herself. The light is dim and shines all over her body with a sticky, yellow glow. Men begin to gather around her, a crowd that grows from every angle, an approach of sentinels with transfixed faces, male animals driven by the sight of a female lifting her ass into the air, making anguished lustful cries.

A pack of men, muscular and with audible breath, breathing down on this lone woman touching her pussy with light, dancing fingers. She keeps on, circling her clit with an expert touch, finely honed, as though she's massaging a jewel. I walk closer; the crowd tightens around her, a noose of bodies. I realize all at once, *I am a man, drawn by hypnotic power to this woman, to watch her.* The men are tense with sexual feeling. I am one of them, turned on like being branded by hell's irons. I feel the surge of it, a force close to unstoppable.

We breathe down on her in that clamp of bodies, all the men now sweating, frantic with excitement. She begins to give one man a blow job, lips sliding up and down along the length of his pole. Everyone watches, tight, not moving, transfixed. "Let her breathe! Back up and let her breathe!" one guy's yelling from within the crowd. I keep watching myself and watching the crowd and watching her and feeling only a dim ability to control this strong urge. "Let her breathe!" The guys are not moving. What will happen? Then some begin to back up, just a step. The crowd's still chomping at the bit, close to pandemonium, reeling at the edge of mob violence. Tail Hook, panty raids, gang rape—men often commit acts in groups that they wouldn't otherwise do. It occurs to me that this is what those situations feel like, in the beginning, when they are contained, before all hell breaks loose—a vein of violence pulses beneath the surface. I can barely move back. I'm enthralled, held by fascinated lust and the thick movement of the group. I move back a few steps. I force myself with a mechanical effort *because it is right, because I have to,* sheer moral force.

It's breathtaking to watch this happening, to be in it and of it. A man in a crowd on the edge of . . . what? Doing what we could do and might do if we could get away with it. What were we almost about to do to that woman?

I walk with Aleister to the band area, shake off the arousal I feel. We stand for a while and watch the band, then walk home in blazing rain. My umbrella snaps in the storm, and I watch as it tangles up in the gutter, a maze of steel spokes and torn black cloth.

32

Missing Parts

Andrew Clark

On a warm summer day, I follow my next-door neighbor to his house. We are in a suburb of Hartford, Connecticut; the houses on our street are simple—ranches, split-levels, and small colonials. Most were built in the years following World War II. I live with my parents, my older sister, and my younger brother in a white ranch. My neighbor's house is a split-level. I have never been inside.

The time is the late 1950s. I am four or five years old, and when someone older asks me to do something, I do it. Chuck says he has something he wants to show me in his house, so I climb between the rails of the split-rail fence that separates our houses and follow him.

I am not sure of his age, other than that he is a teenager, much bigger than I am. We enter his house through the garage, which is empty of cars, and then go into the basement level of his house.

Chuck closes a few doors and I wait in the middle of the room.

"Do you have to pee?" he asks me when he comes back.

I say, "No."

"Do me a favor," he says, walking about the room. He points to his mouth. "Do it here."

I say nothing, and he comes over to me. "I'll show you," he says and lifts me up. He puts me down on a bench in the middle of the room. Moving quickly, and without asking, he pulls down my shorts and underwear and leans into my groin. I feel his warm mouth around my little penis. There is an undeniable shock of pleasure, not just from his mouth, but from being partially naked. The cool, damp air of the basement feels soft against the back of my legs and buttocks.

He walks behind me and reemerges at my left side. He lies down on the floor in front of me. His pants are at his ankles, like mine. His penis is sticking out. It's huge, its head swollen and purple. I have never seen such a thing before.

"Play with it," he says. I get down from the bench, and for a moment, I am confused as to what to do. I shuffle to the workbench, pick up a hammer, and shuffle over to Chuck. I squat down and tap at his penis with the hammer, as if it were a nail. I shuffle back to the workbench and pick up a saw. I bring the saw over and pretend his penis is a tree, sawing back and forth, but not touching it.

Chuck tells me to come to him. He reaches out and lifts me up, then pulls me down on his face. I look down between my legs and can see the bridge of his nose. My feelings are beginning to change. I don't know what is happening; I am a little frightened. Chuck is still gentle and playful, still a kid like me, but he is in charge, and leading me into areas that I know nothing about.

It is here that my memory is interrupted. When it resumes, I am fully dressed. Chuck is too. He gives me two Hershey bars with Almonds and strokes the back of my neck. I do not look at him; my head is down. I look only at the floor. "You won't tell anyone?" he asks. I shake my head no. "You won't tell your mother?" "No." I am sent home.

The final memory is of the backyard, walking home alone. I do not know who else is at home, how long I have been away, or whether I have been missed. I know that I would never tell anyone, particularly my mother. She would blame me. How would I describe what Chuck and I did? No. What had happened between us was our secret.

*   *   *

Thirty years later, a July day, I am taking my lunch in the cafeteria of a university near my place of work. I notice two boys at a nearby table. They are young adolescents, on the cusp of manhood. They are probably participants in a summer program the university sponsors for high school students. One of them draws my attention. He is of mixed race, most likely Asian and Caucasian. His eyes are dark, his skin smooth and delicate. He is a little young, a year or two shy of perfection. Still, what a joy to behold! Youthful enthusiasm radiates from his eyes and infuses his gestures. He is full of promise and hope.

When my lunch is finished, I walk to the trash can, passing his table. He does not acknowledge me as I pass. I leave the cafeteria, and when I am outside the building, I turn. Through the glass wall I can see his profile. I cannot leave; I sit on a nearby wall and watch.

Nearly half an hour passes before they emerge. They walk past me and I fall in behind them. He is oblivious to my presence and I can stroll along behind them unnoticed, but noticing. That is all I want, isn't it? To observe. They are walking toward a large set of stairs. My heart leaps in anticipation. If I position myself correctly, I may be able to see the outline of his underwear against his pants as he walks up the stairs. To learn that he wears underwear would be a great triumph, worth all the time I spent waiting. I do a quick assessment of his clothing. The prognosis is not good. His pants look to be made of denim, a heavy fabric that I have learned usually does not allow you to see that elastic band at the bottom of a pair of jockey shorts.

They reach the bottom of the stairs, and I quicken my pace to catch up to them. I do not go up the stairs myself, but step off to the side. Looking up, I have a perfect view of the side of his leg as he walks up the steps. As I had feared, the fabric is too heavy; I can discern nothing.

I give up at this point. He is probably heading back to a class. Finally, I have the willpower to force myself back to work. As I walk away, I am aware of feelings of excitement and engagement. What are the possibilities? My best chances lie with his joining one of the groups of boys playing Frisbee or soccer on their lunch breaks. It would be unlikely that he would actually remove his shirt, but there is the possibility that he might lift it up to wipe his face or cool off his body. If I were in the right position—a crucial if, I will have to carefully consider where to position myself—I might be able to glimpse his underwear. If I were extremely fortunate, I might actually learn two things: whether or not he is wearing underwear and whether or not he has a belly button. It has happened before, in a single instant, a brief lifting of a shirt; I learned both things about a particular boy. It is almost too much to hope for.

There are other things I could learn as well from watching a boy at play. If I were close enough, I might be able to see a pulse in the neck or across the stomach or chest. If I watch the throat carefully enough, I might be able to see a swallow. To know that a boy of such beauty has a beating heart, or has to swallow, would be of great comfort. In fact, there is nothing I couldn't learn about him that, in some way, wouldn't be comforting—even to see the blinking of his eyelids.

* * *

This was the world I found myself living in as an adult in my midthirties. I had a responsible career and was involved in a long-term relationship. On the surface, I appeared happy and adjusted. In reality, I lived two lives. I inhabited a parallel universe, speaking a second language in which I had been fluent since early childhood. When stimulated by something such as the high school summer program student, this other world threatened to overwhelm me. Its power only seemed to grow as I grew older. Instead of adulthood bringing a sense of order or control, I was confronted with a picture of myself lurking around school yards, hoping for a glimpse of white cotton fabric.

I was in therapy at the time and began to speak more openly about my other life. Al, my therapist, pointed out that I had talked very little about actually having sex with these boys, that my prime motive seemed to be finding things out about them. This was true. What I desired was to collect information. This required a constant state of vigilance, an unending scanning of the horizon for the right kind of boy and the particular situation in which I might learn something about his body.

As I talked more openly with Al about my feelings, a certain kind of logic revealed itself. There was an informal order, a hierarchy of curiosities. First would come underwear and the belly button, the two seemingly interchangeable in importance. If one of the two remained undiscovered, it was automatically elevated in importance over the already discovered. The next step up the ladder was more overtly sexual. I did not doubt the existence of the penis; my curiosities in that area had more to do with function. Was it a sexual organ? Did it become erect? The question became, "Was this boy sexual?" It was here that the logic of the process took a dangerous turn. The only way to answer that question was to engage him in some kind of sexual activity. If he showed no interest in such activity, then it only reinforced the suspicion that he wasn't sexual. Ultimately, the only way to answer the question was to force myself on him. So far, I had yet to cross that line.

At a certain point, Al asked some questions relating directly to my sexual abuse experience: "Did you see your neighbor's belly button? Was he wearing underwear?" The answer to both questions was no, but these questions intrigued me and gave me a glimmer of hope. Perhaps what I was experiencing was in some way related to what had been done to me. In fact, the connection between my present-day list of curiosities and the images I retained from the abuse was clear. If the boys I sought were present-day reincarnations of my neighbor, then I sought to know if they had those things which I didn't remember my neighbor having. The things I remembered him having, such as a penis, raised questions about function, not presence or absence.

It would be years, though, before I was ready to fully acknowledge these connections. What stood in the way was a source of considerable confusion and shame to me. My neighbor had abused me, but why didn't I feel any anger toward him? Why wasn't I repulsed by the bodies of teenage boys rather than drawn to them? The truth was I loved my neighbor and had spent a great deal of my life trying to be with those who reminded me of him.

* * *

Several years passed before the issue of sexual abuse came up in therapy. One night, I was watching television and saw two young women being interviewed on a talk show. They were describing their experience of having been molested as children by their father, a highly regarded professor. There was nothing in particular about the women's stories that I connected with, but I continued to listen. Suddenly, I found myself crying. The source of my emotions was clear to me; in my mind, I had a vague image of myself in the basement. For the first time since that day, a palpable feeling connected to the incident existed.

What occurred over the next few months was remarkable to me. As Al and I sorted through the memories, I was able to associate emotions with them. Toward the first part of the incident, the "sex games," I remembered the initial feeling of excitement, then an increasing sense of humiliation as the ritual became more bizarre. Regarding the final part of the abuse, when the little boy was paid for his services, I saw a child who was dazed and full of confusion.

One day I made a startling discovery. There was a clear difference in the nature of the images I had retained. During the first part of the abuse, the images were clearly defined. They originate as if they were coming from a child's eye. I was "in my body." In the second set of memories, the images were fuzzier and the perspective was from above. I was looking down on myself and my neighbor as he stroked my neck and gave me the candy bars. I was "out of my body."

The juxtaposition of the two sets of memories led me to believe that between the two parts of the abuse that I remembered, a traumatic event occurred. This was what caused the sensation of being out of my body. During this time, Al and I did some analysis of my dreams. In one of them, I was lying down and became aware of someone's presence next to me. I began to feel as if I were suffocating, and when I awoke, I was choking. I had no associations with the dream other than a vague sense that the other person in the dream might have been my neighbor. At one point, Al wondered if the dream was suggesting that what had occurred during the part of the abuse that I did not remember was that I had been forced to perform oral sex. I was wary of reading too much into dreams and said to him, "I don't remember being forced to perform oral sex." As I said the words, a powerful reaction swept over my body. It started in my legs and worked its way up. I had the sensation of being swept out of my body, taken away to a place above.

I waited for a more specific image, but nothing came. Still, I was left with a strong sense that something deep within me had been touched. The suspicion that I had been forced to perform oral sex was reinforced, as was the connection between the trauma, the loss of memory, and the sensation of being out of my body. The feeling I had just experienced was of being swept out of my body in an upward direction, toward the ceiling. It was from that perspective that all my final memories of the abuse came.

"Recovering" the memory of what had happened became my focus. Nearly a year after I had first experienced feelings about my abuse, something happened. I was lying on a bed in the afternoon, drifting off to sleep. Suddenly, I was aware of an image. The scene was the kitchen of my house in Connecticut. I was a young child, about the same age as in the memories of the abuse. Several concrete details, particularly the light on the ceiling, lent the image an air of authenticity. In the image, I was kneeling on a chair. My sister, who was almost three years older than I, approaches me with a can of whipped cream in her hand. I open my mouth and she puts the nozzle in my mouth and squirts. I am aware of the pleasing taste of the whipped cream, but also of a feeling of suffocation, as she has squirted too much. The image ends.

What was I to make of this? There was no doubt in my mind that this was a memory of an actual event. Was it a "recovered" memory, or just something I had never thought about for decades? Why had it come back now? Why, in the middle of this emotional work, during the exploration of the possibility of having been forced to perform oral sex, would I remember this scene? Was my mind playing tricks on me?

This was not how it felt to me. When I talked with Al about it, I had a tremendous sense of being helped along, an almost physical sensation of a guiding hand on my shoulder. As I talked, I broke down, and Al asked me if my tears were tears of fear. I said, "No." It felt more like they were composed partly of sadness at what had happened to me, and partly of relief. The relief came from the knowledge that what had happened to me was real, its effects long-lasting and powerful. My internal life and my "curiosities" were not just a result of my being crazy, but were rooted in my experience.

*   *   *

When I began therapy, I envisioned a dramatic change in which I would no longer have the feelings that drove me to start. My curiosities about boys' bodies would be replaced by the straightforward adult knowledge that we all share the same basic body. I thought I would find the exact formula driving my curiosities. What became clear was that there was no formula. What was constant and unchanging was the underlying feeling of confusion. Al would remind me that small children are naturally curious about the human body, and one of the ways in which they act on this curiosity is to compare their own bodies to those of others. That day in the basement, my natural child's curiosity was transformed into something dark and debilitating.

To have believed that I could be completely free of these feelings at the end of therapy was a misplaced hope, one that denied the complexity of our lives and the seriousness of what had been done to me. But, if the feelings remained, what did change? What allowed me to leave therapy after eight arduous years, feeling that I was no longer in danger and posed no danger to others?

First, I had a sense that my life had stabilized. I slowly let go of the fear that there existed in the world a teenage boy who could intervene in my life in the way that my neighbor did. For years, I lived in fear that I would develop an infatuation with someone that would be so strong as to wreak havoc throughout my life. I came to recognize that fear as the child's fear—a fear completely justified by what happened to him. Now there was the adult part to balance out the fear and recognize that boys were boys, not gods.

The second important factor was the development of a space between myself and the feelings with which I had struggled for so long. For most of my life, we had been inseparable. I was what I felt. Now there was some distance between the two, giving me the ability to step back from the feelings, see the connection to my abuse experience, and acknowledge that I had a choice whether to act on these feelings.

That space is vitally important. The child would live on, with all his fears and worries, but was no longer in charge of my life. That space is the essence of adulthood. It allows for choice and the acceptance of responsibility for one's life.

33

Differences

Greg Abrams

I am on another coast, in another phase of my life, standing in a checkout line to purchase underwear. My boyfriend and I are the same size, and we will share these sexy garments. I imagine his gnarly chest and hunky ass cheeks moving inside the cotton jersey shorts we both favor. I feel the first rush of blood fill my groin as I imagine biting his buns through the shorts, the flow of my saliva staunched by the soft, dry fabric.

Freedom surrounds this desire. I may go anywhere, demand anything of him. He needs no protection from me, and hence, nor do I, from my own lust, nor from his. We trust each other. The space between us invites the depth and breadth of our mutual fire. I will not consume him, nor myself. We are both too hardy for that. We will only heat, and heat, and heat. The only coolants are the faint echoes of distant whispers, long since banished.

Then, the young woman behind the checkout line. In an instant she imprints me, impinges upon my body. I could pin down the moment before my blood changed. A thousand things happened then, many of them contradictory. Already my head is feet above me, separating my thoughts from the raunchy, roiling demands my body is about to make. Already the very fact of my imminent desire fills me with a sense of shame, of unworthiness. Already I am preparing to be taken by a force I don't feel entirely comfortable with.

My eyes travel around the curves of her insistent breasts, straining through tight fabric. I envy the restraining undergarment whose frontal 'V' chronically squeezes the rounding orbs. The thin, orangey fabric of her T-shirt bunches slightly around her slender waist. She turns from behind the register to remove a hanger with a tailored men's shirt, and I glimpse her delicate hips, the saucy roundness of her ass cheeks, perfect as plums. Something heavy and opaque hangs over the whole frontal facade of my body, obscuring the blinding raw crackly lightning of my desire for this female form. Shame grows so easily in the gap between the electric impulses racing around my groin, shoulder, chest, mouth, the soles of my feet, and the placid affect I believe I must present. How many live this way, so many moments carpeted over by sweltering silence?

I surmise that you, the reader, are already rushing to judgment. I imagine that you believe that I cannot host these impulses toward women and simultaneously be an ally to women. I am projecting my deepest fears onto you. Thus, I want to defend myself, to tell you things that will redeem me in your eyes. (Of course, it is only my own internalized authority that can redeem me, but I entreat you to play the Other in my internal dialogue.)

Does it make a difference to know I care deeply about and have worked on behalf of women's issues? Does it make a difference to know part of me views my lust for women as a sacrament? And what of my own feelings of shame and unworthiness, the years of hidden adolescent desire, what place do they take in this equation? The sexual ease and confidence I have since attained has benefited not just me, but also many women. Does it make a difference to know women have come to me wanting sexual knowledge, secrets, instruction in the unknown and come away profoundly grateful for having swum in the pool of safety I create for them to explore their desires? It made a difference to them, to me, and, I believe, to the universe.

The feminism I studied in college brought me closer to women but complicated my raw desires. It was easier to have sexual relationships with men, who, aside from being more readily available, seemed to need less protection from sex. I came to see that this belief itself perpetuated a sort of sexism: women, like chastity, are good, vulnerable, and of course don't desire sex. Men, like sex, are bad, dangerous, and want it all the time. Sex, then, becomes something that bad, insensitive men impose upon good, fragile women. Men need restraint, women protection. In a rape culture such as the United States, paying attention to these dynamics is essential. Acting as if they exhaust the analysis of what it means to be in male and female bodies leaves no room for creating mutual pleasure.

Even as we identified these myths, my peers, both male and female, remained at a loss for how to act on their attractions for women, whereas the means to approach men seemed patently obvious. The old, tired stories remained stubbornly entrenched. When I asked a college girlfriend why she didn't act at all on her desire for a particular woman, she said, "I didn't want to come off like some asshole guy." I pressed for denial or confirmation of the tenets: men and sex are already bad, right? So pursuing sex with a man has a certain freedom, which is that the already bad man can't be defiled, right? Whereas, no one wants to do this bad thing to this good woman, who couldn't possibly want or enjoy it. In addition to patronizing women, this equation also leaves little room for men who feel pressured to have sex to decline without breaking script.

Part of women's script is the injunction to both invite and repel sexual attention. Or, perhaps more accurately, to invite the desire but repel its manifestations. Invite, repel; invite, repel. And what of my own experience of being desired? Are you still listening, gentle reader?

Does it make any difference to know that I, too, have had men fall at my feet? Does it make any difference to know that I have worked long and hard (and still haven't quite succeeded) to rid myself of the idea that sex is always ever an act of defilement done to good women by bad men, no matter the gender of those involved? Does it make any difference to know that I, too, am a woman, who just as often stands as object of this lust?

I, too, am a woman, who just as often stands as object of this lust. Greg Abrams is a pseudonym, and I must ask your forgiveness for having lured you into this thought experiment. But it is, after all, what this culture enjoins me to do, is it not? To lure and seduce, but ultimately fail to deliver on the promise, which redeems me as a Good Woman. But as an intellectual whore, my sin this time is only the utterance of the word, not the deed of the body. And my purpose is deeper understanding: understanding of the notions of Men, Women, and Sex, and how they affect us all. As desirers of women, we are unlikely bedfellows: straight men, dykes, bi folks of all genders—perhaps as arbitrary a uniting attribute as sexual identity itself. Yet, the equation hangs heavy, despite the differences.

Standing at the checkout counter in front of the beautiful cashier, I had lowered my eyes, only to see men's shoes. Where was the position for a woman-desiring woman? The representation of female desire is still in its infancy, especially compared to that of male. Desiring a woman sexually still makes me other than woman, sliding easily into the most obvious box of Bad Man. Thus, my boyfriend and I shared more than just underwear—we shared the stigmatization of the rush of blood inside them.

Until sexual desire from any gender, in the direction of any gender, takes its meaning from the respect and pleasure of all involved, and not from old scripts that both allow and perpetuate repressive/rape culture, the echoes of the bad man desiring the good woman will ring, fainter though we hope they grow, calling into question, perhaps ultimately forcing us to reinvent, the differences.

Jill Nagle

34

The Evolution
of a Sexual Masochist

David Elsop
Danielle Ephraim

DAVID'S STORY

Queen Linda, a *Vogue* model look-alike, stood imperiously erect in her spiked heels and bikini lingerie. She waved her long horse crop menacingly at me as I stood before her, naked and apprehensive.

"Stick your chest out, slave," she commanded. I quickly thrust my chest forward, offering her my sore nipples, which she had just released from the tight clothespins she made me wear while I cleaned her bathroom on my hands and knees.

With intense concentration, Linda began methodically cropping my tender nipples. I involuntarily flinched and caved in my chest. "You moved," she quickly informed me. "Don't move," she said sternly. "Stick it out." She hit harder, repeatedly. I struggled to stand still and failed. "I told you to stop moving." She emphasized the last two words with quick vicious cuts with the crop. I gasped for breath and fought to keep panic at bay. I wanted to flee, but felt frozen to the spot. The pain in my nipples was intense, and the leather crop sounded like gunfire in my ears. I watched her flushed beautiful face as she zeroed in with increasing frequency and power on my tortured nipples with deliberate, full, quick strokes. "Are you moaning? Be quiet. I don't want to hear any sound from you, slave. Not even breathing." I grasped on to her directives as best I could. I willed my self to yield to her, to become a receptacle for her energy. Without looking up from my nipples, she accusingly asked again, "Are you moaning?" "Yes, Mistress, sorry, Mistress," I whispered. Using all my willpower I kept my chest thrust out to meet her blows and watched silently in awe as she cropped me repeatedly.

Later, after visually ensuring my nipples were still intact, I gingerly dressed, left her workplace, and immediately wrote down the feelings the session evoked in me. Then I went home to my wife Danielle and told her in general about the session. A few days later, Danielle and I went together to our sex therapist. This pattern was repeated many times over a fifteen-month period as I explored my masochistic "nature" and Danielle and I struggled together to improve our relationship, sexual and otherwise.

I've been a sexual masochist for as long as I can remember. Most of my abundant masturbatory experiences have been either to fantasies or enactments of pain and humiliation at the hands or command of a woman or women, or to the image of worshipping superior women. The first orgasm I can remember occurred when I was swinging on a tire swing with my hard little penis painfully pinned up between my abdomen and the rim of the tire. I was about seven years old. I discovered that I liked the mixture of pain and pleasure caused by the friction and pressure of the tire against the underside of my penis. During this activity, which I repeated often, I imagined my beautiful, tall, blonde piano teacher, with whom I was infatuated, talking to me. In my fantasy, sometimes she would order me to punish myself for not practicing enough, for not playing to her satisfaction. The more I would suffer, the more she would be pleased. My goal became to please her at any cost. I would see her smiling with lipstick-glossed lips and smell her perfume as I arched my back and felt the painful crush of my body's weight upon my penis. Somehow, the more it hurt, the more excited I felt, until I came, throbbing with pleasure and release.

Over the years, I devised countless ways to cause pain/pleasure to my penis, and I created a panoply of masochistic fantasies to accompany my frequent masturbation. When I was old enough to be left home alone, I seized virtually every opportunity to masturbate to my masochistic fantasies and masturbated myself to sleep almost every night. Climaxing would not end my fantasy dominant's subjugation of me. She would just command me to begin again and would be pleased to know I would be a bit slower to climax the second (or third, or fourth) time around, and therefore could be made to endure more torture at her command. She always had me striving to please her more, and her demands often involved pushing my limits.

By my freshman year of college, I feared that my masturbatory urges were out of control. I would masturbate to climax five to ten times a day. I knew there was something out of balance about my sexuality and tried to eliminate the symptom—frequent masturbation—to effect a cure. I vowed to cut down, but never could reduce my frequency for long. I tried to notice what was happening in my life when I felt the strongest urges and realized that I was channeling all my anxieties, fears, anger, and guilt into masturbation. Knowing this, however, did not help me cut down one bit.

I did not reveal my masochistic desires to anyone until a few months into my marriage. I was twenty-eight when I first tried to talk to Danielle about my sexuality. She attempted to understand and was willing to act out her idea of what I desired. What she did was way off the mark for me. She also did not enjoy what she tried with me. She wished I had told her before we got married and said she would not have married me if she'd known. About this time, we got pregnant with our first child. We both felt hurt and rejected and uneasily ignored the issue. The outcome was many years of relatively infrequent and low-passion sex, and considerable resentment and dissatisfaction on both our parts.

I continued to have a very active secret masochistic masturbatory life using pornography. Off and on through the years, I used a P.O. Box to subscribe to magazines and pulp newspapers featuring dominant women and submissive men. I collected pornography, seeking pictures that fit my images of dominant women. I would periodically throw all my pictures away, sensing that my relationship with pornography was having a negative effect on my relationship with Danielle. I always wound up rebuilding my supply.

As our family grew from three to four, I continued to keep up a secret relationship with pornography and masturbation. I kept wondering if I would be happier in a relationship with a sexually dominant woman. My dilemma was that I loved Danielle and my children and did not want jeopardize my relationships with them. Yet I also felt a powerful pull to continue my masochistic sexual activities. I lived this double life for years, though the issue gnawed at me.

Over the years, I began to feel more pessimistic about my marriage and became more willing to risk losing it, or at least being "exposed," to Danielle. I think on some level (largely denied) I was very angry at Danielle and wanted to hurt her for her unwillingness to accept and respect my masochistic sexuality. I felt angry even though I knew rationally that I had misrepresented myself sexually until after we were married, even though I knew it was perfectly reasonable for her to have no interest in S/M. I felt trapped, and rather than address my feelings openly with her, I took some actions that I knew would enrage her if she ever found out.

On a business trip, I saw a prostitute and had her dominate me. I had hoped to learn something about this force within my life, something to help me decide to stay or leave my marriage. The outcome was inconclusive. I then wrote a letter to the postal box of a local dominant seeking an ongoing relationship, again with the hope I would learn something to help me resolve the issue. An indication of my desperation, poor judgment, and irrationality at this point is that I included some personal information, including naming Danielle and my children, in the letter, with the idea of letting the dominant know I was a "safe" person, not a threat to her.

I received no reply. Months later I got a phone call at home from a woman who claimed she mistakenly received my letter asking her to dominate me. She acted upset and asked me what she should do with the letter. I said, "Burn it, please." Instead, within a month, both Danielle and my feminist boss at work received a copy of the letter. Danielle was enraged and demanded I tell her everything I was doing. I confessed the episode with the prostitute and explained more about my S/M activities. Danielle and I entered counseling with a sex therapist. In a terribly embarrassing meeting with my boss, I told her enough about the circumstances of the letter and my life situation (including that Danielle and I were entering therapy) for her to let it pass. Danielle's and my fear that I would lose my job did not happen, but it was a very frightening possibility. Danielle thought the dominant had sent the letter. At first, I thought this unlikely, but I later reassessed my denial when I learned that the woman I wrote has a motto that includes heartlessly betraying the men that fall prey to her.

Seeing the prostitute and attempting to contact a dominant woman without discussing it beforehand shattered both Danielle's faith in me as well as my faith in myself. We both realized that I was not to be trusted to keep vows I made. I was humbled and humiliated to realize I was capable of taking actions that I think are not ethically sound. I vowed to be honest with her.

Marital counseling helped us talk more about our sexual differences, and to slowly rebuild trust. It also helped us stabilize and improve our sexual relationship to a small degree. I cut down considerably on my use of pornography, thinking it was making it more difficult to be intimate with Danielle. I stopped climaxing using pornography because sometimes I would not want to be sexual with Danielle because I had recently climaxed using pornography. But, despite the help counseling offered, we did not resolve any issues or break through to a significantly better place.

A few years later, the low-level marital dissatisfaction Danielle and I felt rose in volume again, too loud and painful to be ignored. I became convinced I would not be able to resolve this issue in my life without exploring it directly. I was just too strongly drawn to submissive fantasies. I was quite adamant with Danielle that I was, and would always be, a sexual masochist, and angrily insisted she accept me as such. I also talked with Danielle about my desire to see a dominant woman regularly.

Danielle considered my request, but also urged me to go to a different sex therapist with her, a woman who had written books about how to achieve healthy sexual relationships. Danielle and I agreed to stay married for two years, during which time we each could do what we pleased, as long as we addressed the consequences in therapy. No guarantees were made about whether we would continue to live together.

Danielle preferred I pay a professional sex industry worker rather than develop a personal nonfee relationship, so I began seeing a woman who worked at a "live lingerie modeling" business. Workers at the club could dominate clients within a strict policy prohibiting patrons from touching the models (and the models rarely touched the clients). That suited me fine. I did not want to engage in the close physical activities I enjoyed with Danielle, and there was plenty to explore within that limit. Danielle and I agreed that I would tell her every time before I went to see Linda and would let her know about every contact. In other words, no secrets. I agreed to bring my reactions and reflections to my S/M sessions back to therapy for analysis.

Our therapist made a critically important intervention with us at the outset by helping each of us remove shame from the picture. She helped Danielle express her feelings without shaming me, and she respected my need to engage in the activities I felt compelled to explore. She remained confident that we were both doing what was necessary to find our way to a healthier relationship with each other. More than that, she kept us focused on being honest, disclosing our feelings, and reaching down deep to our love for each other. She supported us to treat each other with integrity, as best we could, and to not shame each other when one of us faltered. Removing the shame enabled the process to proceed and unfold.

It was very helpful to me, though extremely upsetting, to see Danielle's pain and hear her anger. Even though Danielle's anger and fears scared me, I knew Danielle understood I needed to do what I was doing in order to (hopefully) become more loving toward her. Danielle's willingness to tolerate my exploration of S/M, and her support as I did so, absolutely increased my love for her. Her letting me go outside our relationship to do what I needed, paradoxically, drew me closer to her. The resulting closeness has been appreciated by us both.

I saw Linda for over two dozen sessions over a fifteen-month period. In the first six months, I would anticipate each session for days and be filled with fantasies of what she might do with me. I felt like a dam had burst inside me and a flood of suppressed masochistic fantasies came pouring out of me onto paper. I'd mail Linda these papers, wanting her to know my most personal masochistic fantasies. I encouraged her to do things that were fun for her, regardless of my desires or reactions. After a session, I would write down my feelings (as my therapist encouraged me to), especially the feelings I experienced as she dominated me. I would call Linda to "debrief" each session over the phone. I began to remember and write down incidents from my childhood that had the same feeling tones I experienced in the sessions, and I began to identify the same recurring themes in the copious fantasies I wrote to Linda.

As I candidly told Linda all my fantasies, I began to be very frightened she would not like me, would refuse to see me anymore, and would somehow be hurt by my bizarre fantasies. As this unfounded fear arose, I remembered many conversations I had with my mom about sexuality and boy-girl relationships when I was preadolescent and an early adolescent. She cautioned me often about how I needed to be absolutely certain I cared for a girl before telling her because girls can be terribly hurt by boys who change their minds. Since I felt I had no idea what love was, I ended up not telling any female I loved her until I was in college, and even then, I feared I was overstepping myself. My mom had no idea that I felt insecure with girls, and she unwittingly reinforced a denial of my vulnerability by stressing to me the inordinate power boys have to hurt girls. I believed her wholeheartedly and swore to myself never to hurt a girl.

In fact, my early experiences with girls were terribly unsettling to me because I felt so exceedingly vulnerable to them. I vividly remember the desperate longing and awe I felt for a third-grade beauty whose love I tried to purchase with gifts and favors. She accepted my gifts and treated me with humiliating disdain, leaving me terribly crushed and vowing to never be so exposed again. I closed myself off from truly feeling love and passion for a girl. Those dangerously vulnerable feelings of passionate attraction were relegated strictly to my masochistic fantasies, where I was compelled by a dominant woman to show them and to suffer for having those desires. At the time, my mom seemed to not have a clue about how emotionally devastating my experience with girls was, and she continued to cast male passion as villainous hurtful behavior.

The first six months I saw Linda, all the fantasies I related to her were of a masochistic nature. Then, unexpectedly, immediately after a particularly painful session, I surprised myself by having an entirely different kind of daydream. I was feeling quite vulnerable and a bit teary eyed, and remember thinking I did not want to be hurt anymore. I imagined Linda beginning to hurt me and asking her to stop. I imagined asking her if I could hold her hand and talk, and she said, "Yes." I held her hand, cried, told her I did not want to be hurt anymore, that I was afraid to be close to her, but wanted to be close to her, and that I wanted to figure out how to do that. I told her I was afraid I would fail if I tried. In the fantasy, she was flustered and uncomfortable and tried to get me to stop crying, while I just told her, "It's fine that I'm upset. It's just where I need to be." Within a few days, I was back to eagerly wanting her to dominate me again, but I sensed a shift beginning within me.

The part of me that wanted a genuine loving connection with Danielle slowly grew stronger, and the hold my masochistic fantasies had over me very slowly decreased.

The opening vignette of this chapter is from a session during this pivotal shift. As with every other session, afterward I processed my feelings and thoughts. This time I felt sad that I have a strong desire to be hurt by a woman. As I thought about the session, I realized that her commands were, in a sense, asking me to "disappear," to become nothing while she became everything. I was required to take anything she gave me, however painful, without any complaint—to endure anything to remain in her presence. I remembered the familiar humiliating feeling of being berated by my mom, and not being allowed to give my side of the story. I had to take it quietly, however hurtful. What I felt, what I experienced or thought did not matter; what mattered was my mom's view of reality. I learned over time to shut up and take it, not just from my mom, but in many of my childhood relationships.

I noticed with sadness that my masochistic fantasies contained little or no tenderness, yet I was clearly beginning to long for this warm nourishment. I began to actively question the ways I linked pain and pleasure. I questioned whether I have to suffer to get pleasure in my life, both sexually and other-wise. Do I deserve pleasure, freely given? How much suffering or work do I have to do to be allowed to enjoy myself? I looked at my tendency to obsessively focus on work and put off play, especially with those I love. It seemed to me that I had been raised to sit at a table with a feast on it (the possibility of reveling in healthy positive sexual delight with Danielle) and not eat, or at least eat only very politely and carefully, avoiding the most delicious dishes and eating only sporadically and modestly. Perhaps I can stuff myself while alone (masturbating), but I cannot thoroughly enjoy my-self. I must suffer in the process.

Over the course of my work with Linda, I went through a very gradual change. After the flood of fantasies burst forth, the flow subsided and my passion for masochistic sessions lessened. I wrote less, and I fantasized somewhat less. S/M shifted from being a major preoccupation to something I enjoyed but was not strongly drawn to. While there were still positive aspects to my sessions with Linda, the thrill slowly left. I found myself enjoying intimate time with Danielle much more than my time with Linda. I finally came to a point where I did not want to have any more sessions.

My explorations with Linda ended about fifteen months ago. Since that time, I experienced an unprecedented extremely stressful period at work and watched my masochistic fantasies spike upward during the most pressured times, accompanied by a slowly increasing desire to act on them. Finally, about a month ago, I went back for another session (with another woman,

Linda being gone), curious to see if I would find myself wanting to reinitiate regular sessions. The session matched my fantasies, but did not compare favorably to the intimacy I share with my wife. Since the session, I have felt no desire to return.

I think I have benefited tremendously by exploring my masochistic fantasies in a conscious way, letting myself connect the feelings evoked to feelings from childhood. Having a "neutral" and accepting dominant mistress, who did not bring her own needs and issues to our sessions, helped me keep focused on my issues. Her acceptance of my wildest fantasies and lack of judgment for anything I wrote or suggested was very helpful. Talking extensively with my mother and learning more about her has helped me reevaluate my childhood, my relationship with her, and the ways I have learned to deal with intimacy. I am grateful she was available, willing, and able to discuss the past with me. Having Danielle encourage me, talk with and listen to me, and struggle to understand me was essential. Working with a therapist who is comfortable with feelings and conflict, skilled in helping couples address radically different approaches to sexuality, and accepting of my explorations was also extremely important.

I've done a lot of grieving throughout this process. Grieving for the lost years of love and sexual passion with Danielle, grieving over the pain, loneliness, and neglect I experienced as a child. I've felt sadness about the pain I have caused Danielle through my betrayals and lies and my need to explore my masochism.

What if I were married to a dominant woman who loved me and respected my limits? What if this dominant and I were involved in the local S/M community? I suspect I would be writing an article extolling the virtues of safe, sane S/M sexuality in consenting adult relationships, using my relationship as a shining example. I just don't know. I do know that after the most painful sessions with Linda, a voice in me afterward, however small and weak, said, "Why am I doing this? This does not make sense. I don't want to do this." As the months progressed, the small voice of protest grew until my desire to continue was extinguished. I wonder what would have happened if Linda had been truly sadistic, manipulative, and desirous of magnifying my submission to her. Would I have developed an unhealthy dependence on her? Would I have let her really hurt me? I don't know, and the uncertainty is unsettling.

I feel more deeply connected to and in love with Danielle, in a way I did not know was possible. I have learned over and over that being honest with her, however painful to one or both of us, is the healthy route to take. For me, that truth still includes a strong pull toward masochistic fantasies, as well as a healthy uncertainty about what I might desire to do with that pull in the future. I've thought about writing S/M fiction as an outlet for my masochistic energy. I know it's important to keep an ongoing dialogue with Danielle about my internal masochistic life. At the same time, my sexual passion toward Danielle has a wider range than before my exploration. I look forward to seeing where our sexual energy goes together over the next ten or fifteen years. I'm particularly grateful Danielle gave me the freedom to explore my sexual masochism and continued to love me through the process. I'm grateful to be partners with her for many reasons and curious to see where our partnership leads.

DANIELLE'S STORY

I thought of him as my personal angel, bringing me loving warmth each day. He was my touchstone. He was a man with deep feelings, not afraid to cry, and a buoyant, silly playmate. He always arrived on his bicycle, wearing a bright blue vest and sandals on his feet.

I looked forward to a trip together to a remote resort: we would be alone; we would let our love carry us. By this time, I knew him well, and I felt a deep connection with him. I trusted him and welcomed his sexual energy. I could feel my longing in my tingling fingertips. But David shrunk from my passion. It was the first of many, many disappointments. "Maybe he's secretly gay," I thought.

Thus began our seesaw dance of avoidance of intimacy. One was up for love; the other was down on too much commitment. Teetering, we would change our roles frequently. Sex was sweet, but sporadic, which satisfied us both. I think the reason I was able to decide to move in with David was that I had recently been assaulted, and I was afraid to live alone.

Living with him surprised me. He seemed so near, yet so far, so open, yet so closed. I hadn't realized how orderly he was, or how central his need for control and predictability over his environment. My absentminded messiness jarred him. Though emotionally generous, his extreme independence meant that he rarely let me help him with everyday comforts, and he rarely offered the kind of casual support that I had expected. For instance, if he were making tea, he wouldn't think to offer me some. If he were fixing himself breakfast, it wouldn't occur to him to bring a bowl over for me. He seemed bound to the idea of ultimate independence.

This was only background noise, though. We found each other vastly interesting, amusing, sweet, and tender. He thought I was brilliant and complimented me frequently. He told me he loved me. Neither of us had a driving need for sex. I was relieved that, contrary to some of my friends' situations, my lover didn't pressure me in bed every night. We both liked to curl up beside each other.

He didn't like dancing with me; that bothered me. Moving my body to the music loosened my sexual desire, and it showed. He would withdraw, close his eyes, and dance solo to an invisible audience. "Don't look at me like that," he would say. Later, I would gingerly initiate sex. He wouldn't be interested. It dawned on me that he rarely responded when I initiated sex. The hotter I was, the more flaccid his response. I felt as if I frightened him. I wondered where his sex drive was. Why wasn't I attractive to him?

The night before our wedding, I was filled with love and passion. David was filled with love, but where was his passion? I said to myself, "Oh, he's just scared. Don't let it get to you. Give him room." Little did I know that I would still be saying this to myself years later, especially at times when I yearned for culmination of my sexual love for him. I began to warn myself weeks before special events like Valentine's Day, anniversaries, birthdays, or weekend trips: "Don't expect anything. David will pull back. Keep your expectations low." It was a masquerade. If I didn't disclose the depth of my desire for mutual sex, he might not shy away. I could play it straight and low key and might be surprised with some moments of mutual passion.

David had let me know several months after we were married, and shortly before our first pregnancy, that he had masochistic fantasies. I simply didn't get it. How could this guy committed to feminism and egalitarianism wish to have an unequal relationship? How could my compatriot in consciousness raising use pornography to jerk off? What about exploitation of women? Didn't his fantasy women look like models with tight-fitting clothes and high heels? Didn't he frequently express disgust at heels, makeup, and fashion as instruments of sexism? I didn't know how to integrate these strikingly opposite beliefs and desires in the same person.

How could anyone desire to be a slave? My strongest adult identity was closely tied to both personal and political liberation. I couldn't fathom wanting to be a slave. I had to work to *rid* my mind of intrusive images of holocaust torture; I couldn't imagine *choosing* images of enslavement. I didn't want to hear about it.

I completely missed the boat regarding the primacy of his sexual masochism. I had no inkling that his constant annoyance with me and his lack of interest in sex with me were directly linked to his masochism. I had no understanding that he had an enormous sexual drive, and that he was tremendously sexually active, just not with me. He wasn't active with anyone for the most part, just his pornography photos, video clips, clothespins, and incredible imagination. It took years before I finally understood that David believed his masochist identity was fundamental to who he was, and as permanent as his hazel eyes. He compared his sexual identity to homosexuality, not only in terms of society's disapproval, but also in terms of its immutability. He had a need to identify proudly as a masochist, but felt he couldn't risk coming out of the closet.

The differences between his sexual desire to please and serve a dominant woman and my real experience of living intimately with him seemed completely incompatible. First of all, he was turned off by my initiation of sex at least 95 percent of the time, unless I was playing at being someone else. Second, except in the area of traditional male roles, such as house renovation and maintenance, he rarely volunteered to extend his energy beyond meeting either his own personal needs or explicitly agreed-upon obligations, such as taking care of the children for a defined period of time. He was driven to accomplish, and his energy was focused like an arrow on achieving his goal. The dichotomy between his fantasies of ultimate submission and his real-life focus on meeting his current project timeline, to the exclusion of all else, disturbed me. While in his fantasies he lived to serve, in reality, I watched him lose his ability to be flexibly responsive to the intimate others in his life, including myself. We lived with a steady undercurrent of anger.

As our lives together became more and more strained, I felt strongly that David's masochism was symptomatic of some deep sorrow, some pervasive unhappiness. I knew that our lack of addressing the issue wasn't working. Our family structure wobbled. His relationship with our adolescent daughter pushed him into rages, as she tested her ability to powerfully assert herself. Whereas I was unable to fulfill his fantasies, it seemed as if she was perfectly fit for the role of Female Dominant; she was so comfortable with being in charge and ordering others around. I puzzled over his intense dislike for her personal power.

Though he had been interested in personal exploration for years, he was stridently unwilling to consider viewing his masochism as anything other than a healthy difference. He let me know over and over again that he considered sadomasochism to be a healthy, though societally suppressed, form of sexuality. I still had no idea how extensive his fantasy life was, how often he was hurting himself, and how much of his life energy was devoted to hiding and fulfilling his sexual fantasies.

In spite of my feelings, I learned that if I was initiating sex, and I wanted him to be hard enough to have intercourse, I would have to "play." I learned that I could play dominatrix without torturous images, imagining that I was a queen and he was the lucky one in my harem, here to please me. It had to be a pleasure that excluded any mutuality. Then he would get hard and excited. When I played this game, I left my body. I felt like Silly Putty picking up the fuzzy outlines of what I thought he wanted. I would often cry after orgasm, feeling so disconnected from the man I married.

I collected the mail one afternoon after work when David and our older daughter were at a movie. I eagerly opened the only real mail in the batch of bills and solicitations, my name and address handwritten on the envelope. Who could be writing to me? "Dear Mistress Eva," it began, in my husband's hand, and continued on to explicitly outline his willingness to devote himself to Eva's every wish. It was clearly a copy of a handwritten letter to his Mistress. He had, according to her wishes, included my name, the children's names and ages, our address, and his work address. I was stunned that he would expose me and our children in the pursuit of his sexual pleasure.

I visualized myself strutting into the theater, waving the white paper over my head, all faces turned to me as I poured out my rage against my betrayer, pointing to him and exposing him for a liar, a cheat, a hypocrite, and, most of all, a mammal without a real brain. It seemed to me that I finally understood all men. They are completely and mercilessly driven by whatever controls their sexual impulses. At that moment, all that was wrong with our relationship seemed tied to his penis-brain. His dishonesty and risky behavior were absolutely driven by his lust. I didn't recognize that my see-no-evil, hear-no-evil attitude was equally at fault. I had made it virtually impossible for him to let me inside his daily struggles and desires, nor did I recognize that I had eagerly selected a partner with little libido for sex with me.

So began my understanding of the secret life of David Elsop. Piece by piece, I came to understand the enormity of sadomasochism in his life. I learned about his visits to prostitutes, his extensive use of masturbation and clothespins on his penis and nipples, and his consistent, compulsive lies. I came to understand that his lack of passion for me was related both to his frequent masturbation and to his prohibition against sexual desire.

The sex therapist we visited as a result of this mailbox emergency helped us to strengthen the commonalties in our sexual lives so that David and I could, ostensibly, find more sexual satisfaction in our own marriage. But we remained miles apart. I still considered his masochism a symptom, while he considered it a sexual preference.

Several years later, on a holiday afternoon, he told me he wanted to work out at the gym. I expected him home for the traditional family evening meal. Instead, he arrived home at 10:30 p.m. and informed me that he had gone to a lecture on S/M sponsored by a local S/M support group. He invited me to begin coming to chapter meetings with him, explaining that he had decided to become active in the community. I slept on the couch that night and had a long talk with myself, between tears. The next morning, I told him that I had no interest in supporting his choice to join the S/M community. I was interested in supporting him to learn about S/M within the context of our marriage, and the only route that appeared feasible to me was to see a therapist who would explore the roots of his masochism. I was finally able to say, and believe, that I would leave the marriage if we weren't able to explore this issue directly, together.

So began the next chapter in our saga. We were blessed to find a therapist who was experienced, bold, and wise. She helped me to see my role in the subterfuge and lying: David had no option but to lie and hide when my attitude was to blame him. I needed to let him explore without shame. This was not easy.

I agreed to a two-year commitment to our marriage, during which time I would live in a form of suspended animation. His drive to be dominated was so strong, we decided that the best route was to actively explore it, with the guidance of our counselor. To survive his development of a sexual relationship with a dominant mistress, I needed to use my already well-developed ability to disassociate. As needed, I watched our situation as if it were a movie, analyzing and observing, but not feeling.

It seemed easier to me to accept this situation as if it were not in the context of a real-life relationship. So he researched and found a lingerie show employee who would dominate him without their bodies touching (much). I later learned that he had begun contact of this sort soon after we began discussing the possibility, but before our agreement to do so, and that, subsequently, he had lied to me about the frequency of his visits and minimized the intensity of his relationship with his Queen Linda. That's when I threw my wedding ring over the side of a boat. I showed him my grief with tears and rage and considered throwing him out of the house.

Our therapist, however, hailed the moment as a breakthrough: a willingness on his part to share the truth with me. While I viewed his confessions as an exposure of more lies, she commented on our new ability to confide honestly in each other. She praised David for his honesty and me for my display of feeling. Because of her faith, because we had previously made our commitment to work together, and because David was so willing to say, "Yes, I have turned a corner; I want to be honest with you," I held on for the ride. His expression of grief over his betrayal and his acknowledgment of the compulsive nature of his actions gave me hope. I also was able to recognize my part in making it nearly impossible for him to be truthful with me.

35

Power Lunch

W. C.

Three yuppies in striped power ties cut
a deal, watch us from the dark corner
of the restaurant, wish they could trade
places with me. No way. This isn't
arbitrage or junk bonds, but putting
yourself on the line and someone
taking you over it. Trust is a complex
issue that, in simplicity, may define
itself in a cold spoon of raspberry sherbet.
Open your mouth, Robyn, they are waiting
to observe your feeding; again and again
the submission of your mouth to the cold,
the way your tongue skates on the metal curve
before I remove it. The man seated with his
back to us drops his spoon, sneaks a look,
returns to the hushed conversation. Those
who observe with furtive glances, excitement
written on their mouths, know when they possess
power and when they are weak in its presence.

"Power Lunch" was originally published in *Growing Pains,* March 1992.

36

Listening to Lust:
A Conversation with Sonya Roberts
About Aural Sex

Siobhan Brooks

Sonya Roberts is a psychology student at San Francisco State University. She has been a phone sex operator for two years and plans to own her own business as a psychologist. She also sings and writes screenplays.

Siobhan Brooks: How do you deal with the stereotype of Black women historically being portrayed as whores and sexually aggressive while being a sex worker? Is this ever a conflict for you?

Sonya Roberts: Not really, because all of my sex work is done on the phone. I am not portraying myself as a Black female; I'm portraying myself as a white female, so I'm dealing with that side of the issue. Because the truth is, you get more requests from customers if you portray yourself as a white female. Usually, the men who call me want to speak to a white woman, preferably a blonde woman, but I usually say that I have black hair when I am asked by a customer to describe myself. There have been a few fantasies about race; usually, they want to compare themselves to Black men.

SB: You mean in terms of how they measure up sexually?

SR: Yeah, like, they want to know how good they are in bed. They say things, like, "Oh, I bet you would really want him over me." So, I don't really deal with my sex work as a Black woman; I deal with it as a white woman, which is kind of strange.

SB: So since you mostly play the role of a white woman, do you ever feel like you are getting a glimpse as to what it must be like to be a white woman, or a white person?

SR: I think that I get a glimpse of how white men would like to deal with white women sexually. Because it is fantasy work, they're going to be more honest about what they want, as opposed to if I were this white woman sitting across from them. Would they really say the things they say to me on the phone? Would they really demand these things? I really doubt it, unless I were a prostitute and we made an agreement that I would do whatever it is that they want.

It does give me a glimpse into white male psychology and how it works. Because a lot of the role-playing that I do has power issues involved, they want to be subordinated, which is interesting because most of the customers are white men in power. I really think it's interesting that they have fantasies of forfeiting the power that they spend most of their life trying to obtain and uphold. But than again, if one looks at this on a deeper level, their not yielding any power. They are paying me to give them a fantasy, and it always goes exactly the way they want.

SB: That's interesting.

SR: Yeah, so, I guess, I got a glimpse of the role-playing games of dominance and subordination that run through the customers' minds when they call me. There's a range of men who call me though. Mostly, they only want physical relief, with no emotion involved. Others are just lonely, or depressed and lonely, and it's easier for them to call a woman on a phone sex line than to have a relationship. A lot of them talk about problems they have with previous or current relationships. Some of them are kind of emotionally unstable too, like they don't have a sense of boundaries; they want to know how to contact me in real life, stuff like that. In some ways, it reminded me of when I worked on a crisis line—it was the same kind of behavior.

SB: Do you view men differently after doing the phone lines?

SR: Ummm. You mean in terms of the customers?

SB: I mean men whom you bring into your real life, your own world.

SR: I guess it has changed my view of men a little. I would be lying if I said, "Oh, no. Of course not." So, yes I think it has, but I think in a positive way. Because I have talked to different types of people, and I have gotten a glimpse into their mind-set, I can get little signs of where they're coming from. So, when I'm speaking with other men, I can get a clue as to their mind-set if we were ever to engage in a sexual relationship, and not be surprised if certain things come up and they're sounding like some caller I've had. Because the calls I get are not all sexual; many of the men just want conversation. That can actually be harder because those types of calls, devoid of role-playing, are going into intimacy where the customer wants to know me. So I'm like, "Hey, that's not what I'm here for. I'm here to play a role." But I've noticed that I'm developing my character's own personal life. When a customer does want to know me personally, I talk about my character's life.

SB: [Smiles] So what is your character like?

SR: Dena is 5'10" with black hair, brown eyes. She's Italian, with an olive complexion; she's the same age as me, twenty-two, also a college student. I try to keep her kind of close to who I am because you can't remember every person you talk to. So, if you keep the character similar to you, you won't mess up with a caller and tell the person that you are 5'8" and have the customer say, "Last time you told me you were 5'10"!" And they have the nerve to act like they've been lied to, when that's all a fantasy is: a lie. Another thing about Dena is that she is a fun-time kind of girl, but very compassionate and caring; usually, that is what's asked of the sex worker: to be very fun and extremely sexual. You know, you have to be so sexual that anything turns you on; you're sexual twenty-four hours a day— you wake up in the morning and your bed sheets are steaming!

SB: [Laughs]

SR: So, you're playing that up, while also giving off the air of compassion. You have to give the illusion that you actually do relate to them, even though it's just some white guy in Boston who's in his office and wants to get off for fifteen minutes. I can't relate to that in real life, but I have to act like, "Oh, Wow! That's great! You're in an office."

SB: It's interesting that most of the customers have a white middle-class existence, so, of course, white women are on this pedestal. Does it ever make you angry that, out in the real world, the way Black women are treated on a daily basis is much different from the way your character Dena is treated on the phone?

SR: Yeah, from working on the phone to my actual daily life, there is such a contrast in the level of attention men give me. Many times, I could be walking through a door and a man won't leave the door open for me—a white man. But supposedly, for Dena, the red carpet is rolled out for the little whore—basically, that's all she is. Most of the men I speak to, if I were to meet them in real life, wouldn't give me the time of day. But on the phone, I have them quivering and gasping for air—that's funny!

I don't think it makes me angry that this goes on; it makes it very evident of the role that I play, and the alleged attention I would receive if I actually were this person. I know I would get a lot of attention if I actually looked like that—a slender, tall girl in college—men would probably treat me better. I guess, at this age, it doesn't make me angry, but when I was younger, being a larger-sized woman was hard for me. I was constantly aware of the treatment of slender women as opposed to larger women, it didn't matter what race the woman was. Being a larger woman, constituted a lot of pain for me growing up. But now, at twenty-two, I look at my invisibility as more of a good thing. Because all eyes are not on me, I can maneuver to places people wouldn't expect me to show up at. It seems like, for a lot of women, being "beautiful" gets in the way of living their lives, because they are constantly aware of their appearance. In a way, I feel kind of lucky that I am outside of the beauty standard because I don't have to deal with that. I mean, I can dress up, I can put on makeup, but it doesn't mean the same thing as a woman who is considered beautiful in the standards of America.

SB: Do you have men of color call, and if so, what do they usually want?

SR: I've only had one man of color, one whom I knew about anyway, and it was an interesting experience [smiles] because I dealt with him as a white woman. He was a brother from Boston with a nice deep voice, and as we were talking, it became obvious that he had a plantation fantasy—that's what I call fantasies of this nature—someone wanting to be a slave up in the master's house with the mistress. I came off as this white girl who had never been with a Black man before. You know, Dena has never been with a Black man, ever. So as he was masturbating, he wanted me to call him "nigger." I kept having this vision of Mandingo and the woman in Victorian garb lifting up the ruffles of her skirt, saying, "Come on. Come on, Mandingo. Time to service the mistress!" [Laughs]

SB: That's funny!

SR: Really, you have to have a sense of humor on the phone because if you don't, you won't last that long.

SB: You're writing screenplays, right?

SR: Yes.

SB: How is working on the phone encouraging your creativity?

SR: I notice that I incorporate some of the traits of the callers into male characters that I'm creating. So, it has its benefits other than financial.

SB: What are your characters' personalities like?

SR: The characters are usually based on the sum of the phone Johns' personalities. The character that I'm working on now is very passive on the outside, but aggressive on the inside. That's how I would view someone who called phone sex lines, that it's an act of being passive-aggressive because you're so far removed from the person. Not so much they're being aggressive, but the situation is aggressive, the fact that they're paying someone for a service puts them in a position of control. Even when they are calling to be dominated they're not really being dominated, because there's already an agreement that I'm going to please them.

The other thing is that a lot of times they're not clear about what fantasy they want. I'm constantly trying to figure out where people are coming from on the phones. You almost have to be psychic and read their minds to figure it out. Yet they get irritated if I don't do what they want. They'll say things, like, "That's not very good" or "That didn't sound real." So here they are switching right in the middle of a scene, going from wanting to be dominated to controlling the situation when it doesn't go their way, when they were never clear about what they wanted in the first place! That's what makes them passive-aggressive. And then they hang up on me instead of communicating about what they want. So, this character I'm working on is passive-aggressive, and people always have to try to figure out just where he's coming from.

SB: And men say we're hard to understand.

SR: The only reason men can't understand women is because there is a breakdown in communication. Most men do think this is a war between the sexes; they're already coming from a defensive stance. If you are coming from a defensive stance, how is there going to be any communication and understanding? The only type of understanding you're going to have is how to win the game. This is a common theme from the callers too: I'm such a breath of fresh air. They say they've never met a woman who understands them the way I do. I think that's really sad; that's one thing that makes me say, "This guy is sad." If someone who is pretending to be someone else is the only person who can understand you, then that's pretty sad.

SB: Most men are running away from responsibilities in one form or another anyway. Most of these men have wives or girlfriends who they're not communicating with in real life.

SR: That's right. Many of them are afraid to say to their lovers, "Hey, look, this is my sexuality, my honest sexuality." They think that the women they're with won't understand them. Well, if she can't accept your sexuality, then what are you with this person for? You need to find a partner that will understand. It's that's simple; why is that so hard? I think how I look at the sex industry as a whole is as a lack of maturity on the males' part. Because that's the only reason that the industry exists. They can't find a woman in real life to do these things for them, which, obviously, there are women out there who will do these things for them. It's so much easier to look at a porn magazine, sit up in the closet, and get the pages all wet. That's simple. But to actually get to know someone. . . . Yeah, that's complicated because it takes maturity. You have to be secure with who you are, and there's a lot of men who aren't.

SB: So, in the future, you see yourself having your own business in psychology?

SR: Yes, eventually, I would like to have my own practice. Right now, I'm getting an internship helping battered women, and I'm being trained to counsel them on the phone. After I get my BA I plan to go to graduate school in psychology.

SB: Well, I wish you good luck. I know your experience as a phone sex operator will help you a lot in your field. I'll look forward to seeing your business in the future.

SR: Thanks. I will too.

37

Infernal Dreams

Kerwin Kay

Spring 1986. My breathing is shallow, my hands a little too tight on the wheel. It is late, or rather early in the morning, and I am pulling into a parking lot near a downtown porn shop. I didn't want to come here; in fact, I hate myself for coming, but I can barely think about that right now because I have to get inside. I have to see this stuff no matter how bad I feel about it. I cannot say no. I've never believed that bull about people not being able to control their behavior, but right now I don't know how to stop myself. I feel powerless. I am afraid.

What makes this whole situation worse is that I know about porn: I can see how sexist it is; I know about its noxious influence in our world. I am an activist, *a feminist!* I take Women's Studies classes in school, and for the most part, I "get it." Maybe because I grew up a "wimp," I identify with women's oppression in a more tangible way. I know what it's like to be bullied, to be made to feel small. I hate the swaggering, "cocky" attitude of most of the jocks, or rather I hate *them*. Of course, I'm way too afraid to say that to their faces, or even fully admit it to myself, but it's true.

That's what makes these trips to the porn shops—and strip clubs—all the worse. Most women trust me. They tell me I'm different from other men, more sensitive, "better." What's more, in my activist life, I often speak in favor of feminist causes. I even challenge other activists about the way women and women's issues are treated within our own community. I'm a good ally, or rather I would be if I weren't such a hypocritical slime.

Deep down, I know I'm a piece of shit. Sometimes I barely feel like I deserve to live. Maybe I don't. Right now I still can't think clearly. I leave the porn shop and get back in my car. I've spent $40 on magazines that I'll probably throw away before I get home. I pull out of the parking lot and pull over into a nearby residential area. I quickly unzip my pants. I hope to God no one sees me.

*   *   *

One of the times while taking a thirty-minute, shame-filled drive toward the strip show, I take some time to simply observe my feelings, trying to gain some insight into my (evil) motivations. I see my anger, the rage that lies behind my compulsion. I hate the strippers. I hate women in general. I want them so badly—I want to fuck them—but I can't. I *never* can. No woman *ever* wants me—I am a failure. I want to rape her/them. I want to take what I can't have. I want the beautiful woman to be sucking my cock, to be telling me how wonderful I am, how much she enjoys doing it.

But while the dancers move and undulate, tantalizing me, my desire is never fully satisfied. I leave the show, climb into my car, and quickly masturbate. I want a woman to want me, or at least to fuck me, but this will obviously never happen. I'm too much of a loser, *a wimp*. My sexual failure serves as a symbol of my overall failure in life. I am a failure as a man, as a person. My social inadequacy is clear proof of this, and my penultimate social failing is my inability to find a girlfriend.

The next day, I go to my classes. I move through my activist world and Women's Studies classes with apparent ease, though on the inside I am deeply terrified of being found out, of being identified with "the bad man." I tell literally *no one* about what is going on and instead carry on with my sexual double life. I feel ashamed of my sexual misdeeds, ashamed of my compulsive desire, but I continue to feel unable to fully control myself. All of my sexual attractions seem to be permeated by this same sense of unease and obsession, so I work hard to avoid almost any sort of intimate sexual situation, though underneath I know I am desperate for love/affection/sex. I hide my desire in the darker crevices of my psyche, sometimes so successfully that I am unaware of it myself. Incapable of initiating contact, I search yearningly for that one mythical woman who will sweep into my life and rescue me; the *she* who can somehow transform my desire into something good and wholesome. I wait, but even the women whom I do manage to get close to seem to lack the magical power I need.

Finally, I quit going to the strip clubs and porn shops. I simply quit. Throughout the whole ordeal I kept telling myself never to go back, but this time, for some reason, I've reached a place where I don't have any more options—I'm driving myself nuts. I finally manage to muster sufficient willpower to resist my compulsive behavior, at least initially. Two months later, I once again find myself back outside the porn store, late at night. I drive by twice, fascinated, obsessed, hating myself, but oh so turned on. Eventually, I simply head back home, relieved and happy that I didn't go inside. I know that I have succeeded. After that final incident, things at last became easier.

*   *   *

Radical feminist writings on pornography come as a revelation into my life.
No doubt about it, these women have my number. They have intimate knowledge of every sexual malignancy that lurks within my psyche. I read all the
anti-porn material I can, trying to glean information about the unspoken desires
that still haunt me. Susan Griffin's *Pornography and Silence* is an early eye-
opener:

> We must understand . . . that the nude woman in the pornographer's
> mind is really only a denied part of himself which he refuses to recog-
> nize. But this is a part of himself which has a will to live, a will to
> expression, to being. . . . Even the desacralized and humiliated images
> of pornography must remind the pornographer of his lost self. Even by
> his means of control, the images he has created, he feels himself losing
> control. . . . Fearing that he will be transformed if he looks on beauty,
> the pornographer takes possession of a woman's body . . . he destroys
> her soul and makes of her an object. (1981:34-35)

Griffin suggests that the repressed part of the pornographer's self is "the
feminine," those elements of soul that are rejected in the course of creating a
conventional masculine identity. I'm not *entirely* positive this is what happened to me, but it's at least plausible. She's definitely on target in describing
the loss of control I feel and my vengeful desire to take possession. It's also
hard to deny Griffin's analysis simply because I sometimes get so shamefully
turned on while reading her descriptions of pornographic degradation and
humiliation. I can't stand myself for that! It makes me feel sick *and* turned on
to read this stuff. I mean, what she's describing is horrible! I *must* change.

A few years later, I read an account in Tim Beneke's *Men on Rape* that
tells me even more about my confusing feelings:

> If sex is an achievement, then the presence of an attractive woman may
> result in one's feeling like a failure. One's self-worth, or "manhood"
> may become subtly (or not so subtly) at issue in her presence. And how
> does one feel toward someone who "makes one feel like a failure?"
> Like degrading them in return. (1982:20)

Beneke's comments strike home, *hard*. As I trace my sense of inadequacy
back into my life, it becomes obvious that I've desperately sought validation
through women, and that I feel angry about not getting it. My sense of
deficiency as a human being clearly has a lot to do with my failure to "make
it" as a man. My history as a geek won't go away.

I try to change the messages going on in my head. I tell myself it's all just societal pressures, and that helps, sometimes. I try to develop my social life, to put more emphasis on my friendships and less on some mythical "happily ever after" scenario, and that also helps, some. *Finally,* I try talking about my feelings. It's incredibly difficult to admit what I'm feeling, but I manage to open up in a men's group I'm in. It helps that there's no women around, and several of the other guys share similar feelings; for some, it's for the first time in their lives too. Talking about it is an enormous relief and allows me to feel less shame than ever before. But no matter what, I still seem stuck in the same compulsive patterns—getting turned on by the sight of a woman in a short skirt, and having this fact immediately drive me into shame and obsession—even though I'm no longer going to the porn shops. I even manage to have a few relationships with women, but despite the grace and healing I experience, the deep feelings of connection, nothing seems to alter my less savory emotional desires.

*   *   *

"Objectify me, *please!*" jokes the man who would become my first boyfriend. It's the first time I've ever heard anyone say anything positive about objectification, and I still remember the moment vividly. I don't know what to think of it, but I make sure to store it in a mental filing cabinet for future reference. Of course, he *is* a man—a very attractive, funny, and intelligent man, in fact—so I can't assume his opinions mean much in terms of women. Maybe he's twisted and is trying to justify his warped psychology, but he sure seems to be having fun in the process.

It's not the last time I hear something like that either. Moving in the lesbian/bi/gay community is a new experience; it's a little topsy-turvy for me at first, but I like it. I like the openness people have about sexuality within the community as well, and it's not just the men. Perhaps because my lesbian friends don't have to deal with all that macho bs, they're able to be more exploratory than most of the straight women I know. In any case, there are a few women around who are into S/M, and although I've heard of people who are into that, it's an entirely different thing to talk with a leather jacket-wearing S/M dyke, especially when I realize she's not a mean or scary person! I mean, she seems *at least* as together as anyone else I know. So what gives?

I start having a few flings with different guys. It's pretty fun, and happily for me my sexual compulsiveness seems to be relatively sex specific—I feel *much* more open and free in relating with men than with women. I also start getting involved in queer politics, joining Boulder's version of Queer Nation, *Queer Cosmos.* I do drag at rallies and, increasingly, for fun. I learn about hiding and not hiding, and about the liberating power of anger. I learn about how angering it is to have others make false assumptions about who you are or, just as bad, to simply erase your existence. I smooch at kiss-ins. I speak at rallies. Maybe I even learn a thing or two about courage—there are many fine people leading the way on that one.

Queer culture definitely blows open some doors for me, but it can't seem to make my sexual compulsions toward women go away. I continue to feel shame concerning this, especially when the occasional thought of raping a woman flashes through my mind. I know that I'm not going to actually rape anyone, but I know I must be pretty fucked up to even have that desire. Being seen as "queer" makes it easier for me to hide my feelings, but I know the game I'm playing, and I hate myself for it.

*   *   *

After years of trying everything to eliminate my feelings, I begin to think about the possibility of approaching the issue from a different perspective. I reflect a great deal on the coming-out process I underwent as a queer man and start looking to that as a model for coming to terms with my other desires. Reading sex-positive feminists, such as Susie Bright and JoAnn Loulan, helps me see the *unnecessary* quality of my shame, and hearing of performance artist Annie Sprinkle's sexual antics encourages me even further. None of these people give me the same types of psychological insights I gained from reading antiporn feminists, but their words speak to new potentials for which I long. It's all new and scary though. Not only am I on shaky political ground, but I'm afraid of feeling out of control again. I certainly don't want to spend a whole lot of money on porn and strip shows again, but I do decide to go back. I lay down a rule that if I start to feel out of control, I will stop until I feel more comfortable. So with this guideline, and a strict monetary limit, I prepare to reenter the world of pornographic sex.

My first forays back into the world of porn are quite tentative. I spend a lot of time *not going,* to convince myself that I am in control. But as I grow more confident, I begin to go more frequently and start pushing through the shame that held me before. My trips to strip shows begin to feel more liberatory than enslaving, and I actually am enjoying getting turned on. Finding women attractive in my daily life seems like less of a big deal now too, and I find a girlfriend who has some emotional space for my sexual proclivities. She and I experiment once or twice enacting rape scenarios; it turns me on a lot, and I don't feel the same shame that I always have before. The whole thing—the lust and passion, the emotional openness we share—draws me enormously close to her. I still go through intense bouts of shame concerning all this, but a door is definitely opening.

Within a year, I move to that haven of sexual libertinism, San Francisco, and get a job in a female-run strip club. My job is to mop up the ejaculate left on the floor of the booths, and I'm definitely not paid enough. On the plus side, I'm able to talk to many of the dancers, get a better look at the men who are into strip shows, and generally learn what this scene is about. The dancers are generally quite intelligent, and many are feminists, so the conversations are often interesting. Many of the customers, on the other hand, are jerks who have no respect for the dancers, and from time to time, we have to kick some of them out. Generally, however, the men are well-behaved, and I learn from the dancers that at least a few of them are quite nice. Frequently, a guy gets so entranced by the whole environment that he loses an awareness of his immediate surroundings. I often get bumped into by unaware, meandering men, and every once and a while, some guy leaves his quarters behind after asking for change! It's good to see this feeling from the other side, for once.

My next job is working in a porn shop in a very run-down section of the city. The men who come in are usually alone and don't say much, though a few are friendly and open. A *very* few men ask me questions about various movies, vibrators, or butt plugs, which I happily answer. A small number of women visit the shop as well, mostly in search of dildos, though there was one brave woman who came in to search for videos of men masturbating (we had several of these, but in our "gay" section).

I begin exploring a number of the other sexual avenues that are open to me in this great city as well. I go with some friends to a few of the gay sex clubs in town, receiving some of the most incredibly delightful oral sex imaginable (anatomical familiarity makes a world of difference!). True to male stereotype, no one talks much before their sex adventures, but people are surprisingly friendly afterward. Still, the sex itself is almost always very serious business, and the atmosphere is heavy, especially in the back room where the sex happens. This all changes around Pride Day, the holiday commemorating the Stonewall riots. People PARTY and CELEBRATE and FUCK and SUCK and have a great time! It's *fabulous!*

I decide to visit a few prostitutes as well, having the most fun with a playful transsexual hooker I meet in a bar. I become friends with a few other prostitutes I meet in more "ordinary" social circumstances, so I get to hear about sex work from their perspective as well. I start to think about becoming a whore myself, but for now, I decide against it. Basically, I'm a little too emotionally vulnerable to try it; I still go through periodic attacks of shame, though these are less frequent and intense than before. It helps that I have several good friends to talk with about all this.

But it's when I start getting into S/M, even just a little, that I feel the biggest change in my life. I go to a few play parties, which is fun, but it's really the "theoretical" implications that make the difference. S/M shows me that I don't have to feel ashamed of my sexual desires, no matter how aggressive or "degrading" they are. S/M places my concerns about "sexual objectification" within a much different framework, one in which particular types of desire are not inherently evil and "consent" actually has some meaning. S/M takes away my ideological justification for feeling ashamed—a great gift.

So what's the upshot of all this exploration? Well, I'm definitely *much* less ashamed of my desires than I ever have been. I am overwhelmingly less compulsive, more able to talk about what is going on for me, and more able to seek and find what I want. I continue to experience some sexual shame, but I now take this to mark those places where I am emotionally vulnerable, not those places where I am a terrible person. I learn to listen to my fear and shame and to set sexual limits based on these vulnerabilities—when I don't, I get drawn into my old patterns of feeling out of control and ashamed. So my sexual obsessiveness has certainly not been entirely eliminated, but I've also given up the attempt to find perfect solutions to this problem; what I'm doing is good enough and it's definitely moving me on the right path.

Politically I've changed my tune too, and now disagree with the antiporn analysis. Although I think it's right in many ways—most porn clearly is sexist—it ignores other contradictory elements that are *also* true, such as the enormous impact of sexual repression (itself a tool of sexist control). In my own life, I've seen firsthand how the anti-porn material can reinforce damaging shame-based behaviors. And while in some ways the changes in my sexuality parallel what an anti-lust feminist might predict—my fantasy life does indeed contain much more explicitly aggressive material than before—"surprisingly" I am much better able to intuit and respond to others' needs having reduced my own desperation and compulsiveness. I can imagine others who might be spinning more out of control than I was, men who might benefit from hearing that rape is *not* acceptable, but that their desire—as a fantasy or consensually shared enactment—is fine. This relationship between unlearning shame and leaning how to handle one's desires in a responsible and respectful manner is a connection most anti-porn feminists entirely ignore, much to their own detriment.

Today, when I think politically about male sexuality, about male lust, I get frustrated with people who won't see the complexity of the situation. If ever there was an arena that requires a multidimensional analysis, this is it. Most of the issues concerning sex are too complex to allow for simpleminded "this is good" or "this is bad" kinds of statements. In our own lives, I think we have to take careful note of all the *conflicting* demands that live within our hearts. We are vast, containing mountains. Our ethical framework must reflect this multitude.

REFERENCES

Beneke, Timothy. 1982. *Men on Rape: What They Have to Say About Sexual Violence.* New York: St. Martin's Press.

Griffin, Susan. 1981. *Pornography and Silence: Culture's Revolt Against Nature.* New York: Harper & Row.

PART III:
POLITICS

38

Why Men Are So Obsessed with Sex

Steve Bearman

Have you ever encountered a baby whose gender is unknown to you? Not knowing can feel profoundly uncomfortable. We barely realize how great the differences are in how we treat male and female people, in what we expect of them. These differences are by no means subtle, but they are so much the air we breathe that we can't even see them. We have almost no experience of relating to human beings not on the basis of their gender. If we did, we would be at ease with someone whose gender we didn't know. Instead, the first question we ask about a new person in the world is whether it's a boy or a girl. Maybe if we can't tell the difference, it's because there isn't one!

Nonetheless, from the moment of our birth, if not earlier, we are treated as gendered beings. We are not merely considered to have a gender; we are conditioned to have it. Moment by moment, day by day, and persistently over long stretches of time, the ways boys and girls get treated shape their identities. And the way boys learn to be male almost inevitably leads them directly to some kind of obsession with sex as they grow older.

All babies are considered okay to smooch and squeeze and hold close, female or male, but when they get old enough, boys stop being held and cuddled and stroked. If they reach out to adults for intimacy, we refuse them in the name of "self-sufficiency." Though this promotes independence, it does so at the cost of intimacy. This isolation is reinforced by early sexist conditioning. Boys are taught that they are different from, and better than, girls, even that they should shun or hate girls. If they are fortunate enough to escape this particular piece of the conditioning and continue to have equal relationships with girls, they are quickly marked as "sissies" and called "girls" themselves. Loving or tender relationships with other boys get them similarly marked as "faggots" and put them in danger of violence and being ostracized.

Instead, boys are encouraged to develop relationships with other boys that are primarily competitive: playing sports, jockeying for higher rank in social hierarchies such as teams, clubs, and later on, gangs and fraternities. These groups often come together to do violence to other groups, either by "beating" them in competitions or in less symbolic forms of violence. In the armies in which most of the world's men at some point participate, we learn to kill and to be prepared to go down fighting, and this model repeats itself in gang wars of all kinds. These violence-based communities fulfill some of our needs for companionship and connection, when nothing gentler is available, and so they might not seem to contribute to male isolation. However, competitive and adversarial groups offer solidarity within the group at the cost of turning everyone else into an enemy. They breed fear of other people, even of the others within our group, with whom we also must compete for rank. We may not be alone when among the group members, but the internal isolation is intense. Relationships between group members buckle and break from the pressure of having to defend, protect, and prove ourselves. This is very different from the nurturing ease and satisfaction of a mutual, equal, fear-free relationship.

A systematic enterprise of denied contact, humiliation and name-calling, being ostracized, sexist conditioning, homophobia, competition, and training for violence leaves boys more and more on their own. This habit of being "on our own" becomes familiar. Isolation is a piece of the heritage of our conditioning as boys that we carry with us into our manhood. This description of male conditioning will not exactly match every boy's experiences. But certain factors are almost universally present in one form or another for boys growing up in our present society. Isolation is one of three primary factors in our early conditioning that later leaves us vulnerable to sexual obsession.

Young people naturally seek out other people for help and support when they are faced with painful feelings. When they get hurt, feel scared, become outraged or embarrassed, frustrated or sad, they seek and expect attention. The loving attention of another human being is necessary to feel these feelings and to heal the hurts that caused them. The isolation of boys keeps them from seeking out the attention they need, prevents them from even believing it's okay to ask for help. They are left to deal with feelings themselves. Even worse, they are loaded down with messages that feelings are not something "real men" experience. They learn that "Big boys don't cry." The process of crying is interrupted, and the tears are responded to by being ignored, laughed at, or answered with threats of violence.

Being scared is yet another thing boys are told threatens their maleness. They are expected to leap into any activity, no matter how dangerous or unfamiliar, without appearing fearful. Other feelings are in similar ways denied them, and they quickly learn that expressing emotions actually makes their situation worse. Over time, the only way boys keep from showing their feelings is to train themselves not to feel them, to dull their awareness of their own experience, numb themselves to emotions. In the course of doing so, they decrease their ability to feel any feelings, joyful, painful, or otherwise. At the same time, we become disconnected from other people; we are cut off from our own feelings.

As a subset of all the feelings we are forced to numb ourselves to, we "lose touch" with how our bodies feel. We learn, sometimes literally, to harden ourselves against pain, strain, and physical effort. The training to "act like a man" is present when young boys are encouraged to ignore physical injuries, not to cry, to bear the pain and go on as if nothing happened. This is exactly the training needed to convince men to work ourselves to the point of abuse, in both the workforce and the military. The sensuality of being alive in our bodies, aware of our senses, and breathing full breaths has been written off as an unmale attribute. Sensuality has been replaced with routine. Though we notice extremes, we are unable to perceive subtleties of feeling. Tenderness and gentleness, subtle and slow as they are, have been lost. Born into bodies marvelously equipped to feel, we are forced to shut down and accept numbness.

This description may sound quite extreme. Yet it is only a picture of what is considered normal to impose on boys, what we take for granted. We don't like to believe ourselves to be in such an extreme state. We think anything we made it through must not have been that bad. If it doesn't seem, as men, that we are really so separated from one another, from women, from our feelings or our bodies, this may be because we have lost our memory of being that integrated, that connected. For most of us, the joy that is possible in our daily lives is so outside the scope of our experience that we have difficulty even imagining it. So consider here for a moment that most men alive have been through some form of this systematic conditioning. What happens to human beings who have been, since early in life, isolated from intimate connections with other people, cut off from their own feelings, and numbed to bodily awareness?

There was a time when we could perceive a loss of vividness, when it was clear that what was being offered us in our adult lives was far less than the abundance we knew was possible. As we stood facing the possibility that we would have to cope with the loneliness of isolation, the emptiness of lost feeling, the dullness of disembodiment, just then, intimacy, passion, and sensuality were all offered back to us in one, solitary form. *Sex*, we were told, is the answer. Everything you have lost can be found through sex. But here's the catch: sex is the only way you can get it back! Imagine yourself in this scenario. The urgent need to pursue sex would bear down with great pressure.

Adolescent boys are exposed to a social imperative to get laid in order to prove their maleness, long before they even know what "getting laid" means. They are bombarded with sexual images through television, advertising, and pornography. These images are very compelling, somehow conveying to them that the great mystery of life can be experienced through sex. Every story of "true love" in the cultural mythology implies that relationships are built on sex, that sex consummates love, that feeling sexual feelings is the same as being in love. Directly and indirectly, we are handed sexuality as the one vehicle through which it might still be possible to express and experience essential aspects of our humanness that have been slowly and systematically conditioned out of us. Sex was, and is, presented as the road to real intimacy, complete closeness, as the arena in which it is okay to openly love, to be tender and vulnerable and yet remain safe, to not feel so deeply alone. Sex is the one place sensuality seems to be permissible, where we can be gentle with our own bodies and allow ourselves our overflowing passion. Pleasure and desire, vitality and excitement, seemingly left behind somewhere we can't even remember, again become imaginable.

This is why men are so obsessed with sex. We are born sensual creatures with an unlimited capacity to feel and an effortless propensity to deeply connect with all human beings. We are then subjected to continuous conditioning to repress sensuality, numb feelings, ignore our bodies, and separate from our natural closeness with our fellow humans. All of these human needs are then promised to us by way of sex and sexuality. This is an effective lure because sexuality genuinely can be a potent source of love and pleasure, intimacy, sensuality, and beauty. But in no way can sex completely fulfill these needs. Such needs can only be fulfilled by healing from the effects of male conditioning and suffusing every area of our lives with relatedness and aliveness.

It's as if a being of extraordinary power and passion had been reduced and dulled and diminished over many years. The memory of passion was put to slumber deep within this being, and the being walked through life with an elusive sense of something missing, something wrong. One day, a billboard appeared, and on that billboard, surrounded by images of naked bodies and erotic acts, were the words "PASSION AVAILABLE HERE!" So excited was this being to get at even the possibility of passion, which he could feel awakening deep within, that he rushed impulsively forward, never taking the time to read the small print at the bottom of the ad. This is what the small print said:

> If you follow this path, be prepared on your way to reawakening passion to pass through a land called Obsession. Be aware that most men never make it out the other side. Sex, which will feel like the answer to your loneliness and deadness, will turn out to reinforce those feelings. You will come to feel more alive when thinking about or engaged in sex than at almost any other time. When you do experience sex, you may come closer to another human being than you can remember ever being. Sensing the safety to do so, you will begin to care deeply, and to feel all the joy and pleasure and every other feeling that has been trapped inside of you for so long, including all the fear you have never been safe enough to feel. And so the closer you get, the more scared you will feel. And you

will find ways to pull back, and you will begin to believe that it is not safe and that you are just as alone as you have always felt. You will come to blame your partner or yourself for the inadequacy and for the inability of sex to make you back into the great, vulnerable, courageous, and free being you were born to be. But because some taste, some glimpse is available through sex, you will be driven to seek it out as the solution to your life-sized dilemma. If you escape the self-condemnation of sexual repression, you will desperately search for new kinds of sexual contact, real or imagined, to make you feel whole or to make you feel anything at all. But no matter how much sex you encounter, it will not be enough to fill your enormous need to love and be close and express your passion and delight in your senses and feel life force coursing through your muscles and your skin. All sexual desire will become tainted with your desperation. Passion and desperation will begin to seem one and the same. You will be Obsessed.

Sex quickly becomes addictive for most men. Like all addictions, it offers what feels like temporary relief from difficult circumstances, only to leave us more thoroughly immersed in those circumstances, and feeling as if more of it is the only way to even come up for air. Even if we do not engage compulsively in anonymous casual sex, pornography, masturbation, or fetishistic attempts to recover what has been forgotten, sex nevertheless takes on an addictive character. When we automatically fantasize about sex and sexualize people we meet in passing, when we are sexually engaged and feel an urgent need to have intercourse, to "get off," to orgasm at all cost, we are being driven by these addictive impulses. It is difficult to accept that such attempts to get back what we've lost will always ultimately fail. Even if we accept it, we can't find our way out. An addiction this persistent occurs for very definite reasons, and until those reasons are addressed, escaping the addiction may not be possible. In the absence of healing, the addiction serves necessary functions.

Men are frequently believed to be fundamentally malevolent and untrustworthy, particularly because of our "uncontrollable" sexual desires. In light of the compulsive form sexuality often takes, we attempt to repress all of it. Yet repression is exactly the wrong idea. If sex really is one of the few areas of our lives where we can still feel, can still tell that another person is actually there with us, can still sense the joy of inhabiting a body, then repressing sexuality, vilifying it, or sublimating it into work plugs up one of the few remaining springs of vitality. Repression is not the solution. Repression is, in fact, the origin of the problem, and additional repression squelches our vitality even further. Passion, not repression, is our greatest ally in the battle to liberate our complete humanity. The message being offered us by our sexual obsession is that we are reaching for something we know we so badly need. The passion and the desire for closeness behind the obsession are our guides, despite the fact that they have kept us isolated when followed without reflection or awareness. Sexual obsession, when turned inside out, holds the key to our liberation.

My vision for myself and for all men is that we reclaim every piece of our humanity that has been denied us by our conditioning. Obsession with sex can be healed when we reclaim all the essential aspects of the human experience that we have learned to manage without: our affinity for one another, caring connections with people of all ages and backgrounds and genders, sensual enjoyment of our bodies, passionate self-expression, exhilarating desire, tender love for ourselves and for one another, vulnerability, help with our difficulties, gentle rest, getting and staying close with many people in many kinds of relationships. If sex makes us feel more alive or less alone than anything else, this is an indication that vitality and closeness are glaringly missing from every other part of our lives. Because of the nature of male hurts, our healing requires that we get in close, and stay close, with other men and women whom we choose as our allies and to whom we choose to show ourselves. It requires that we find our way back to every feeling that we never got the chance to feel fully as boys and that we feel them in their totality now. It requires that we move back into our bodies and care for them deeply. Because we have been alienated from other people, our feelings, and our bodies, we must now reclaim each of these in order to take back our humanness, and in doing so, end the desperation and the lack that keeps us obsessed.

The instruction manual for men reclaiming our full humanity, recently unearthed, contains the following highlights.

Reclaim Intimacy

Begin by directing the unconditional, loving admiration you used to reserve for people you're attracted to, outward toward all kinds of people in all kinds of relationships. Start ten new kinds of relationships with people you never imagined could be your dearest friends and most dependable allies. Who are the people in your life who are ready to receive your trust and vulnerability? Give your trust to them and ask the same in return. Since there are no limits to the closeness possible with another person, what fears do you have to face to get even closer? Share those fears and ask for help instead of trying to manage them alone. Let the people in your life know what it's really like for you, and enlist their help to bring closeness back into your daily existence. If you choose to have a primary partner, please remember that no matter how strong the relationship, one person is not enough for any human being to be close with. It is in your nature to desire closeness with all people, closeness that rarely has anything to do with sex. We have yet to discover what it will be like to have so much and such varied closeness in our lives.

Reclaim Feelings

The passionate intensity you've saved only for sexual encounters can fire up all areas of your life. What else besides sex ignites that much passion? What dreams and desires for your life would you need to rekindle in order to burn as brightly about your daily existence? Take on the challenges that make waking up exciting, that fill you with a sense of wonder and magic. Expand the envelope of who you think you are. Find feelings long buried and set them free. Cry wet tears and laugh with your whole voice; tremble with fear and giggle with embarrassment; storm with outrage at the cruel ways we've been hurt; weep with tenderness at the beauty of our existence. We need one another to feel these glorious feelings, so ask for all the help and love and attention you need. And you do need it. We just can't do this alone, and we should never have had to in the first place.

Reclaim Your Body

Sensual pleasure is our birthright, and it is available in thousands of forms besides sex. Take off your shoes and walk barefoot through the grass, the mud, the rain. Learn to breathe freely, so that every breath reminds you that you are alive right now! Dance, finding and releasing the movement within you, reveling in the gorgeous organism that you are. Touch your body freely and frequently, reawakening your senses. Take joy in the movement of your muscles, the feel of your sheets sliding on your skin as you lie down to rest, the splash of cool water on your face, and the swish of that coolness in your mouth as you drink. Become aware of the food you take in, not only savoring the taste, but also cultivating a sensitivity to how it makes your body feel long after it is digested. What would it take to slow yourself down enough to notice how much feeling is always available for your awareness? As you rediscover your senses and your infinite, creative range of movement, play like you did as a boy, when no one had to teach you how. Play hard and play soft, inventing ways to be in exuberant contact with everyone in your life.

* * *

If sex is expected to be our primary source of contact, feeling, pleasure, and love, our main connection with the memory that life is exciting and mysterious and joyful, then of course we will be obsessed with sex. Luckily, the conditioning that has put us out of touch with all these things is completely reversible. Every quality we have turned away from can be reclaimed. The passion that narrowly fixates upon sex can lead the way to a wide-open life vibrant with passion. The desire to be close that has been confused with sexual desire can motivate us to create closeness everywhere. When we fill our lives with the things we previously expected only from sex, our lives are richer, and even our experience of sex is transformed.

It is possible to be completely relaxed about sex. When sexual desire is purged of desperation, urgency, loneliness, and fear, then sex can be inspired by joy and sexual relationships can be healthy and whole. When sex is a choice, one of many choices, with no rush to get to it and no cost in missing it, it's possible to be at ease with sex and sexuality. Sex can be an exquisite celebration of intimacy and expression of love, a place for healing, a time to play with all the vigor and enthusiasm we had as children. Sex can be a place to express the passion cultivated by living a vibrant life and to delight in the ecstasy we all deserve. Sex can be separated out from all things that it is not. It can stop being the sole source of all the things that it is. We are making the long journey out the other side of the Land of Obsession. On the other side is a rich, full life beyond our conditioning, where passion takes new forms each day and we are deeply related, never alone. A new paradigm is possible for men, wide open for us to explore.

39

On Pornography's Faces

Allan Creighton

my relating to an image
my relating to an image of a woman
my relating to an image of sex that is silent, doesn't touch me
    doesn't relate to me
    an image from which my body has been effaced
my relating to images everywhere,
    on the street, in the sky, at the market, in the office, on the train, in the bar,
    at the store, on the stairs, on the stand, on the mall, off the wall, on the
    tube, on the Net, in the lunchroom, locker room, pool room, chat room,
    classroom, boardroom, down the alley, 'round the corner, 'round the bend,
    'round the barn, 'round the back, on the air, on the job, on the field, on the
    slope, on the surf, on the couch, on the line, online, sitting down, walking
    along, looking up, looking down, not looking at all
my relating to images on packages, magazines, papers, billboards, posters,
    soup cans, soapboxes, toy boxes, cereal boxes, milk cartons, comic
    books, textbooks, playing cards, postcards, get-well cards, birthday
    cards, CDs, videos, at parties, sessions, clubs, meetings, gatherings,
    groups, events, retreats, in songs, lullabies, top 10, top 40, oldies, clas-
    sics, classifieds, personals, the funnies, stories, sermons, op-eds, lectures,
    jokes, gags, routines, punch lines, all over the checkout line
my relating to an image that tells me what to do
my relating to images that measure,
    that flatten me, up, vertical, upright, erect, one dimension, in inches
my relating to images that tell me I've got to measure up
my relating to images that picture women
    that show them to be weak, vulnerable, cunning, wicked, luscious,
    secretive, willing, dangerous, back-stabbing, all alike, replaceable, bitch
    and virgin, young and hot, naive, available, yielding, surrendering

my relating to images of the woman without defenses
    fists or muscles, speech or rage
    images of women who don't talk back
my relating to images that picture me,
    that show me in charge, in the power, in muscle, in shape, on the track,
    in gear, in leather, in a jeep, on a bike, on the edge . . .
my relating to images that instruct me in sex
my relating to images that alone instruct me in sex
my relating to images that tell me she gives it, she gets it, she takes it, she
    wants it, she loves it, she needs it, she has to have it, she can't get enough
    of it, she's dying for it
my relating to images that tell me she deserves it
my relating to images I fuck
my relating to images whenever I fuck
my relating to images I can't let go
my relating to images I won't let go
my relating to images that teach me to select
    to line women up, one by one: too short, too tall, too fat, too thin, too pale,
    too dark, too flat, too full, too strong, too weak, hairy, bald, different,
    indifferent, hot, cold, overdeveloped, undersized, overdressed, undersexed,
    not white enough
my relating to images that assure me I'm mysterious and remote, aloof and
in command, on the edge and in reserve
    that hint I'm too slack-jawed, pot-bellied, wide-eyed
    that tease I'm too wimpy, too weak, flabby, skinny, I've got to shape up
my relating to images that imply I can be overcome by desire, that overcome by desire
    I cannot be held responsible
    that she's responsible
my relating to images I'll be shocked by, I can take offense at, I can loudly
    abhor and denounce
my relating to images I can blame and scapegoat, images that will take the
rap for me
    and for us
my relating to images I am fascinated with
my relating to images I don't make, don't create, don't develop, don't love
my relating to the same images
my relating to the same images again and again
my relating to images as repetitious as this

my relating to images as a child, as a boy, as a kid, as a youth, as a teen, as a
  young adult, as a man of age, as son, brother, father, single, husband,
  open lover, one of a kind, one of the boys
my relating to images that I can't forget, that I won't forget
my relating to images everywhere, every day, every hour, every season,
  every moment, to the point where I've *had enough*

And I take this rage, go out, and find

a woman

40

G.I. Joe and Barbie K-I-S-S-I-N-G: Competitive Economics, Competitive Sex

Steven Hill

When I was eight or nine, like most boys my age, I received one Christmas the obligatory G.I. Joe doll, complete with combat fatigues, M16 rifle, and a ruddy scar slashed across his cheek. My G.I. Joe was one rough, tough hombre; so rough, in fact, that one day he beat up my eleven-year-old sister's Ken doll and absconded with Barbie. My G.I. Joe carried off Barbie like a prized Helen of Troy. She was my (G.I. Joe's) prize for besting that wimp Ken, who could hardly defend the beautiful Barbie with only his tennis racket, dressed in those limy green Bermuda shorts.

Now, looking back on my dramatic play, I wonder how it was possible that a nine-year-old had figured out the role without ever having read the script. It's too simple to say that I was imitating the behavior of my peers or family, since I don't recall that any of them were into the Neanderthal style of courtship. Chances are, by that age, I'd seen something like it on television, but I cannot accept that this influence alone could have turned me into a nine-year-old version of John Wayne or Rambo. Raging biological impulses? Perhaps—but how can a gene or a chromosome instruct me which piece of plastic should beat up or snatch the other? There was entirely too much ritual and nuance involved in my act of aggression followed by my act of rough romance to be simply a result of biological programming. Let's face it, at the age of nine, before I even knew what sex was, I knew that Joe was supposed to take Barbie and do something with her to make her his—er, that is, mine.

In trying to understand (my) gender, I have returned often to the "G.I. Joe Puzzle," as I call it. The nexus between aggression, competition, and the sexual ritual known as romance has been extensively written and sung about, glorified and celebrated in movies, novels, and song. But it is still, from my observations, greatly misunderstood, particularly the central role that our highly competitive and individualistic economic system plays in the development of our sexuality. Simply stated, men and women are set up, like Barbie,

227

Ken, and G.I. Joe dolls, as one of the many prizes and rewards for each other that we can "win" if we best the competition. Ideals are established—a beauty image for females, a success image for males—that both genders are exposed to through culture, in a multitude of ways, from the earliest ages. These are the images our culture tells us we must become if we are to win acceptance and approval from our peers, family, and society.

To understand certain qualities of modern gender, it's necessary to combine a feminist analysis of gender with an analysis of the competitive and individualistic nature of our economic system. Such a hybrid analysis can provide a theoretical framework for women and men to work together to end the dual exploitation of patriarchy and our competitive, hierarchical economic system, which coexist like two sides of the same coin.

WINNERS AND LOSERS

As much as most boys and men may imagine ourselves to be like G.I. Joe, our actual lives are more similar to that of Ken. Paradoxically, despite the fact that we live in a patriarchal society, the common, everyday experience of many men is hardly one of mastery or feeling dominant. It's not surprising that feminist theory, the most cogent modern analysis of sexuality and gender, has not dwelled very much on this point. The feminist point of reference, quite rightfully, is women's experience, which has been subordinate to that of patriarchal males. But when the point of reference is the common male experience, the story can appear quite different. Despite men's real patriarchal privileges, as wage laborers, most men—even patriarchal men—spend our time getting squashed in the competitive free marketplace by bosses, supervisors, owners, and landlords. This prevents most men from recognizing the male privilege that sustains us daily, even while we're being economically exploited. Men's undirected feelings of economic powerlessness have bleak repercussions when our very masculinity and self-esteem are intricately linked to our role of breadwinner. For some men, after a day, a month, a year, or a lifetime of getting kicked around in the free marketplace, how tempting it must be to go home and act out a smoldering anger, an urge to kick around something or somebody else.

The first thing that strikes me about my G.I. Joe play is that Joe beat up Ken to win Barbie. The key notions here are "beat up" and "win." Aggression, competition, winning—win what? Why, the prize, of course. What else does a winner win, but the prize? And what is the prize? It's Barbie—feminine, thin, shapely, busty, and smiling. In the carnival game of sexual economic relations, women are one of the prizes offered to us heterosexual men for achieving our success. But the prize must not be just any woman—she must be a certain type of woman. She must be a woman who is highly desirable, one worth striving and competing for. She must be the carrot dangled at the end of the stick; she must be a worthy prize. She must be—a Barbie doll.

But, as a prize, she must be practically unattainable, perpetually out of reach and elusive, so that the man will never stop competing, never stop climbing the ladder, never stop following orders, whether on the battlefield of the military or on the corporate battlefield. G.I. Joe is primed to fight in either arena, as long as he's offered his prize for winning.

So G.I. Joe fights Ken for his prize, Barbie—she's beautiful, she's cosmopolitan, she's desirable. She's a twelve-inch replica of a Playmate or a movie star. That nine-year-old had learned the role somewhere. But where? Just think of it: what must be done to turn a bouncing, bright-eyed baby boy into a soldier who kills on command, a paid killer who is willing to pull the trigger or push the button from 10,000 feet to drop bombs of terror on civilian populations? Or to turn the young boy into an obedient worker, routinely falling out of bed, day after dreary day, trudging off to work, following his boss's orders for nearly one-half of his waking life? An observation of modern society produces the answer: you must offer that boy-growing-into-a-man a series of rewards and punishments, of triumphs, fears, and insecurities, to motivate him. No wonder that prior to bombing raids during the Persian Gulf War, U.S. pilots were shown films of scantily clad, disrobing women. These films were called "motivational" films ("Now I know why I'm fighting," said one grinning, enthusiastic pilot).

In such a sexuality, power/control issues are entangled with something as basic, vital, sensual, and infantile as human touch. This sexuality then becomes a very potent force in our society. Themes of competition, conquest, and domination are eroticized. Via a socialization process that is both blatant and subtle, females and males are assigned roles, not only as particular genders, but also in the sexual drama, popularly known as "romance." This sexuality is widely advertised and is very conducive to producing a "warrior" gender—men, in whose hands are posited the mechanisms of political, social, economic, and military power—supported by a subordinate gender—women—in a world that is still viewed as hostile, competitive, and conquerable.

LET THEM EAT IMAGES

Inevitably, not all the boys-growing-into-men, nor the girls-growing-into-women, will be able to live up to the demands of a competitive society. In a competitive society, there are winners and losers: a few end up at the top, some end up at the bottom, and most end up in between, desperately clawing for the top to keep themselves from sinking to the bottom. They feel the constant steamroller of competition nipping at their heels, stalking them, ready to devour them if they ever stop climbing to the top. This dynamic drives the economy: men and women trying to win, producing and consuming the goods and products that make the elite owners of the economy extremely rich. The media ads selling those products whisper sexy messages, hinting to us how to soothe the gap between our ambitions and our actual status.

For boys and men, one of the ways we learn to soothe ourselves is by imagining ourselves "winning" one of our prizes—the so-called "beautiful" woman. The heterosexual male search for the beautiful woman has acquired legendary dimensions; it is part of folklore, Hollywood cinema, and song. Men long for a beautiful woman—a sign of our success—who will stroke our egos and seduce us with sexual reveries that make us forget about our hard days in the workplace.

Through this gap slithers the seduction of pornography, as well as mainstream media images, and generally any sexualized beauty image, including any real-life woman who attempts to conform physically to these idealized images. With these images dancing in our heads, we men can fantasize that we possess the beautiful woman. In the privacy of our fantasies, we can temporarily reconcile our socialized craving to win and feel dominant with our actual experience of powerlessness. These sex-beauty images, which are commonly accepted as "normal" heterosexual physical attractions, or as an appreciation of women's "beauty" and "sex appeal," are the fabricated images that satisfy a man's socialized need to win against the competition. Possession of the sex-beauty image—of the Barbie doll—is a sign, a measure, of the male's success, achievement, and dominance. Contrary to claims of a cathartic effect resulting from the use of pornography, this vicarious process of relating to a sexualized image acts as rehearsal for real-life behaviors and relationships with women.

These sex-beauty images—whether they are produced by *Cosmopolitan, Ladies' Home Journal,* or Christy Hefner's *Playboy,* or embodied by well-manicured, long-maned Third Wave feminists such as Naomi Wolf or 'sex-positive' Madonna wanna-bes in leotards and Doc Martens—are the historical legacy of gender relations under the patriarchy, with a modern-day twist: "beauty" has become a commodity to be traded, bought, and sold to consumers. Such gender relations reinforce women's historical reliance on their physical appearance to win Mr. Right. A male viewer can fantasize that he possesses the sex-beauty image, and because it is a photograph, or a written image, or even a memory of a Barbielike blonde that sashayed by on the street, he literally may control and dominate the image in his mind. He can take up and put down the image as he pleases with the alacrity of a digital camera. He can experience sexual pleasure, but at his own discretion, protected inside his fantasy against the vulnerability and feelings associated with bodily pleasure.

Most significant, this dynamic is true of real-life sex-beauty images as well. A man can see a flash of a Cindy Crawford-like mane out of the corner of his eye, the painted red lips and mascaraed eyes from afar, a smooth leg or a bit of cleavage pushing out of a low-cut blouse, the female "shape" crammed into tight jeans walking down the street and, all in an instant miracle of his brain, imagine that he owns the favor of that woman, that he possesses that sex-beauty image, and that, therefore, he must be a virile, successful man. It makes little difference that up close, he realizes that the sex-beauty image is not as perfect as the first glance suggested, and he is no longer attracted to her, since she has too much upper lip hair, a crooked nose, an unsmooth complexion, or a thousand other features common to human beings but not common to sex-beauty images. For that brief moment, he was able to fantasize that he possessed that image, that he was successful and respected. After all, he can fantasize that somewhere out there is the perfect blonde or brunette, just waiting for him, right?

In a single day, this sort of experience can happen a hundred times: a flash of breast here, a profile there, a magazine cover in a grocery store checkout line, prime-time television, a World Wide Web Site, the way the hair falls, the "shape" parading across a stage—all of this in an instant conveys to his cranial synapses the crude message "Sex-beauty image. I have her. I am a successful man." Relating to sex-beauty images for one's self-approval and psychological bolstering is a subtle process, as well as an addictive one. As with all addictions, these "attractions" feel instantly pleasurable and have a "high" associated with them. The high includes a momentary fix of approval and acceptance and eroticized feelings of power and conquest that are invested with the authority and approval of the culture. Considered "normal" sexual attractions, these "highs" are a common experience, forming the cornerstone of nearly every heterosexual male's sexuality. They are, consequently, very difficult to give up.

Tragically, the magical powers of fantasy, which ideally should serve to open us up to new and more possibilities, instead become a brainwashing exercise in service to an ideology, acting to reduce our world and limit our possibilities. Like a woman's craving to be thin, sexy, and "beautiful"—to be a Barbie—the man's "physical attractions" and his attempts to become the man—the G.I. Joe—who wins this beauty are an exercise in an ideology that instructs both men and women, boys and girls how to act, how to talk, how to relieve frustration and tension, how to succeed in the free marketplace, at school, and in the rough posturings of the streets. The man learns how to approach his own physical body, how to channel his sexual desire. It is a kind of propaganda that the boy learned as he got older—after his sexual energy had been successfully blocked and then rechanneled—telling him under what conditions and with what mental images he may masturbate to release his sexual energy. Indeed, this is the key to how that nine-year-old had already learned his role so well. That nine-year-old had been totally immersed in the womb of his culture, which informed him as to his sexual identity.

Underneath the skin of a man's civility is a human wish for fulfillment, acceptance, love, and affection and a sense of immediacy, to no less extent when he is an adult than when he was a child or adolescent. Except that as he grows older, it is society itself that acts as "parent," withholding the reward of sexual fulfillment, that is, bodily feeling, sensuality, sensation, affection, and vulnerability, until certain criteria are met. From the earliest age, the boy-growing-into-a-man learns that he must wait for fulfillment until he has performed adequately, until he has proven himself against the competition. As an adult, he must prove himself as a successful man in the competition of the free marketplace. Yet, at the same time, he is told that without this fulfillment, he is nothing. No wonder, then, that this desire may become aggressive, even violent when denied. It is a classic double bind, acting as the carrot and stick to motivate men who live under the strictures of a hierarchical and competitive culture.

With his sexual fulfillment and approval withheld from him, the male's orgasm to these sexualized beauty images functions as a tremendous release for him. All these anxieties in his life are temporarily soothed by the ejaculation. But this orgasmic release comes in the service of an ideology, at the climactic end of a complex ritual in which he has made his conquest and captured the sex target, the beauty image of his desire. The tensions in his life are, for a short time, resolved, much like water bursting through a dam—until the waters back up again. G.I. Joe has his Barbie, but Ken is plotting to win her back again. G.I. Joe will have to defend his turf.

It is important to recognize that we men acquire a relationship with these sex-beauty images. The images talk to us, they whisper to us and soothe us, they make us feel good, they get us high, and they help us to escape. The relationship with these images is compounded by its masturbatory nature. Men masturbate to the sex-beauty images found in magazines and movies and to the images and memories of the "beautiful" women they know or have met, however briefly. In fact, porn is referred to as "stroke" magazines. Thus, the message and lifestyle of these images are being positively reinforced with the physical, pleasurable sensation of masturbation and orgasm. Masturbation and fantasy are indeed powerful pleasures, for in the act of climaxing to these images, the male consumer momentarily bolsters his ego and simultaneously gives himself physical gratification. In fact, he has been informed from the youngest age that he may not have such physical gratification unless certain conditions have been met. These conditions amount to nothing less than being a winner— either real or imagined. G.I. Joe gets his pleasure while Ken skulks off shamefully, settling for his porn sites on the World Wide Web and rental videos.

What would masturbation and fantasy be like without these contrived, ideological images in our heads? Can we imagine it?

THE WAY FORWARD

The insidious message of these sex-beauty images is that sexual objectification of women is being sold as a commodity to gratify men who are receiving a daily dose of humiliation and frustration, courtesy of the free marketplace. Recognizing this allows a fresh assessment of "sex-positive" proponents such as Madonna, Susie Bright, and Camille Paglia to reclaim this genre of images. Their putative efforts to "empower" women are a trap that will ultimately fail, though they themselves are enriched in the process. These images are irredeemable—not by a lofty banner of free choice, not by well-meaning feminists, not by lesbian or gay libertines, not by women pornographers—as long as they operate inside a hypercompetitive male-dominated milieu. The hierarchical gender relations of such a society will ever be distorted, dividing people into winners and losers who console themselves with various images, for which the relationship between the viewer and the viewed is exploitative, voyeuristic, and vicarious. It is a trick of mirrors, a subterfuge that can be manipulated by the wealthy elite who own and manage this competitive economic system and its corporate media outlets. They designate which women will get to speak and appear on TV and the silver screen, bigger than life in our consciousness, effectively silencing other women without the means to offer contrary perspectives. Because women such as Sharon Stone and Cindy Crawford have found success in such a system does not mean they represent liberation. The list is endless of the models and actors who are elevated to the status of cultural heroes, well paid for titillating us. The grandiose images they fabricate with the backing of an entire industry constantly reinvent the convoluted reality behind the popular hoopla we call "physical attraction" and "romance."

But this analysis suggests that truly these attractions aren't "physical" after all. Instead, they are more like mental mirages, the product of a historical socialization process in a highly competitive economic and patriarchal system. Our sense of inadequacy contributes to a self-esteem that is easily channeled toward competitive, exploitative, even militaristic values. The consequence of our "pursuit of happiness" has become an extremely narrow and disciplined workday. Perhaps the extent to which we rely on Hollywood, MTV, *Playboy,* and World Wide Web images to excite, thrill, and "liberate" us is the extent to which we have become less free. At the end of the movie, the images stop, the houselights come on, and the moviegoers walk back up the aisle, no more free or liberated than when they walked in—but you can be sure that they'll be back for more. In a world of frustrated consumers and laborers, boxed in by the vagaries of modern life, providing our fantasies for us is a growth industry.

The antidote to this state of affairs is for both women and men to bravely stop producing, dressing as, and turning on to these images, and to compassionately stop asking one another to masquerade as the same. Rather than narrowing our choice and constricting our fantasies, this antidote will allow the multifaceted nature of our human beauty to shine through, revealing a plethora of possibilities about how women and men may dress, attract, and adorn ourselves.

In my nine-year-old fantasy, G.I. Joe gets his Barbie. But, at some point, the nine-year-old must encounter the real world, and this encounter is usually devastating: He will discover that he is more like Ken, yet will still want to be like G.I. Joe. And he will have to figure out a healthy way to bridge the gap between his fantasy and his experience. We know that his culture will provide little helpful guidance. So the degree to which he succeeds will depend on his ability to carve out an understanding that our notions of physical attraction, sexuality, and beauty are the product of a complex, intertwined relationship between our competitive economic system, the images in our heads, and our patriarchal gender relations.

This type of analysis, if we have the courage to embrace it, both outside and within ourselves, combined with a feminist analysis of patriarchy, has the potential to enlist men and women as allies in one another's struggles. Women and men can work as allies to overthrow an exploitative order, constructing a safe, just world, while not giving short shrift to women's pressing issues resulting from male privilege and patriarchy.

A FINAL NOTE

Fourteen years ago, I began a monogamous relationship with a woman who was in the final stages of recovery from fifteen years of eating disorders, including anorexia, bulimia, and compulsive dieting. I had never heard of these predominantly female maladies. But what this meant was that I, who was attracted to fashionable beauty images and pornography as a way to fill up my needs for approval and reinforce my masculinity, was now involved in a relationship with a woman who had nearly died trying to embody that thin beauty ideal. In fact, when we first met some six years before our reunion, this woman was in the midst of a bulimic-anorexic mind-set and thirty pounds lighter. Upon seeing her again six years later, I had a difficult time accepting the sight of her full 155 pounds on her 5'7'' frame, now healthy and nearly recovered from the ravages of eating disorders. Over a period of two years, our relational patterns forced us to examine this phenomenon. Together, and not always peacefully, we began to unravel our inherited gender roles, beginning to perceive their sociocultural origins.

Unraveling this tangled web so that I may live a fuller life has been neither a simple nor a smooth process. It has taken a willingness to suspend my needs for control and dominance; it has meant steps backward as well as forward. My process has involved examining my "relationship" with pornography, as well as my "physical" attractions: What are my expectations of these beauty images? How do they make me feel? I have also gained insight from reading feminist literature about pornography and gender roles, both historically and today, and from living with a strong, feminist woman. Therapy has also been helpful, as has listening to the stories of other men and women. Challenging sexism and the dictates of my society, both inside and outside myself, giving voice to my unconscious experience, via poetry, dream analysis, and visual art—all of these approaches have been helpful at one time or another. It has taken a willingness to be on the road, still arriving, I'm not sure where, but I'm going there anyway.

Besides, I know where I don't want to be.

41

2 men kiss/a dollar n a dream
(or the odds of unequal attraction)

Ahimsa Timoteo Bodhrán
(for jay)

2 men kiss in a rainshower
rain coming down in small small droplets
everything fresh   clean   washed away
like roses freshly clipped   no thorns
or a morning breeze massengil commercial
birds chirping happily
gentle breeze warm n soothing
rainbows high in the sky above

2 white men lean up against a tree in buena vista park
overlooking their city by the bay
unmarked by knife wounds
leaning up against

    the loftiest of dreams

2 colored boyz kiss in a rainshower propped up against the hood of a vega
everything kosher till fists start coming down in small small droplets
then larger
    ta the beat
        ta the beat
            ta the beat of the beatings
                shower of fists coming down

2 colored boyz beaten against a windowpane of an abandoned building
south of market
eyes swollen   teeth chipped n broken   skins lacerated
stomachs cut wide open
things often seen on expensive french menus
spilling inta the street for free
mixing with oils   paint thinner   transmission fluids
gum wrappers   7-11 cups
a lotto ticket

   the loftiest of dreams

42

When I Get That Feeling:
A Conversation with Cleo Manago
About Black Male Lust

Jill Nagle

Cleo Manago is the Founder and Chief Executive Officer of AMASSI Health Wellness And Cultural Affirmation Center. He is also a longtime community activist, social architect, author, educator, and founder, in 1989, of the National Body of the Black Men's Xchange (NBBMX), an influential, innovative national organization. NBBMX was designed to educate, mentor, empower, and affirm a diverse community of Black males. A native of south central Los Angeles, where at age sixteen he began a vocation in social services, his heart, spirit, and soul have always been grounded in a deep conviction for empowering and healing disenfranchised, unattended, and marginalized communities, and in evolving human consciousness. Cleo has also been one of my greatest teachers. His career in social services and activism encompasses the four archetypes of teacher, healer, warrior, and visionary. I consider him to be among the most inspirational, truth-seeking, loving, and radical thinkers I have encountered. I am honored to make public one of our many thought-provoking and challenging encounters.

Jill Nagle: I'm thinking about the possibilities and challenges for Black male lust.

Cleo Manago: This so-called Black male lust thing is complex. The sense of self, sexuality, and erotic sensibility among Black males has been disrupted by a culture that caricatures us, thereby conditioning us to caricature ourselves. We aren't seen as simply males, but BLACK males with BLACK male lust, as opposed to being seen as male human beings of African descent. Unfortunately, some of us internalize this racist, white objectification of ourselves, which impacts our erotic sensibilities, self-imagery, and how we are perceived and treated.

JN: There is an overlap there with all male lust, in that male lust in general is framed as dangerous, out of control, et cetera.

CM: Yeah, but men are generally not perceived the same. There are great differences in the perception of males based on how they are classified by race constructs. Asian males, for example, are rarely seen as sexual or predatory, unlike Black males, who are marketed by U.S. media and social narratives as particularly sexual, virile, horny, and dangerous. No other group of males in this culture has experienced a legacy of being castrated and lynched with so much reaction to and mutilation of our penises. This is ironic, being that Black men are not known to be predatory or preoccupied with the penises of White men, castrating and mutilating them. White-dominated systems tend to actively switch around representations of reality, making the obvious difficult to recognize. Thus, Black male lust in particular is typically seen as animal, barbaric, out of control, menacing, and lust filled . . .

JN: As if an exaggeration, or, as you said, caricature.

CM: Lustful, beastlike, hog-wild. And many Whites, male and female, desire and seek Black penises for this purpose, while still seeing Black men as a caricature, as less than white. Jeffrey Dahmer is among the more known examples of a White man with such an obsession. After eating his unsuspecting victims, who were predominantly Black males, he mummified and kept their genitals.

Most are clueless about the deep normalization of "race" terrorism, normalized as etiquette and "just the way it is" in this country. Watch TV. There is no such thing as a "Black" TV show not accompanied with laughter. This and the lack of illumination about it helps determine etiquette, what's socially acceptable. At this point, it is not socially acceptable for Black people, particularly men, to present ourselves as anything but servants to the "better" good of Whites, i.e., as caricatures and buffoons. When we illuminate our essence and cultural power, our show is canceled. That's what happened to Arsenio Hall. Remember him? He stopped being a buffoon and grew into a Black man. After Minister Louis Farrakhan appeared on his show, it was canceled. The rationale was low ratings, which was complete bull. Now, again, all we have to see late at night are boring white men, who can have anybody they want on their show[s].

JN: Here are some random questions: What do you think this cultural myth is about? How did it come into being? How can it be healed/debunked? You have spent much of your life working to heal some of these wounds: establishing spaces, counseling people, raising consciousness, educating folks . . .

CM: What do I think this cultural myth is about? Okay. In a White patriarchal social system and context like the [United States], White maleness is deemed the most valuable human representation. Of course, this is a constructed "reality," created in response to feelings among this group of being inept, the opposite of what they have concocted.

JN: You mean feelings of unworthiness among white males?

CM: The constructed and institutionalized elevation of White males, through education, mass media, film, et cetera, as the highest achievers among "civilized" men, sustains the myth of White male superiority. These activities attempt to veil a profound insecurity among them. Also cloaked under this self-posturing are feelings of being threatened with White genetic annihilation, which is connected to reproductive capacity, physical power, and sexual prowess. In all of these categories, Black men then become their greatest enemy, a group with the greatest capacity to "fuck" Whites out of existence. So Black men must be subdued and made submissive and controllable through objectification, societal brutality, and stigma. They must be devalued in the larger culture. And we are! I have been in many situations where White men, including so-called heterosexual men, have felt challenged by my (apparent) sex appeal and ability to think. They literally couldn't handle being in my presence. My way of being defied and challenged their desperately needed tendency to dehumanize me, to make me less than "White."

JN: I want to go out on a bit of a limb here.

CM: Okay, but use heavy branches.

JN: [Laughter] I want to look at the threads of truth in the myths, and the consequent distortions and traps they engender. One of the costs of cultural power of certain types is a divorce from the sensual powers of the body. Economically and socially powerful bodies are controlled bodies. This is why the "bimbo factor" has cost so many male public figures their social respectability. And, as with what you were saying, the mythology that Black men and women are more "embodied" is partly how they have been kept out of such power. Detachment from the body also informs some class splits. Food preparation, toilet cleaning, waste carrying, et cetera, are all functions those with social power seek to distance themselves from. So a service class of white women and people of color of all genders is created, representing the more embodied, down-and-dirty folks.

CM: I see the commonalties, and I also see profound differences across "race" constructs as they relate to lust, having lust, and being lusted after as Black men in this society. As I said, Black males live, psychically, inside of a White-constructed "reality" that impacts us erotically, among other ways. Popular culture shows consistent examples of this. Black men portrayed as especially sex occupied and lustful are often dark in skin hue; their male or female partners often White or "lighter"-complected Blacks. The dark—particularly Black—Black man is always pursuing White and "light"—closer to White. Kinda like what's implied in Beauty and the Beast and King Kong. Get it? White and "light"—closer to White—is always being pursued by the dark—particularly Black—Black man. Get it?

JN: Because lightness, whiteness, is more socially valued. But back to the limb thread. One of the costs of power is a divorce from the body—a taboo on sexual awareness, activity, bodily knowledge, sensuality, except when well contained. Conversely . . .

CM: One of the cost[s] of pretending not to be human, to invest in social constructs of "perfection" is to become a "functional" psychotic, thus the institutionalized craziness at the core of this society.

JN: One of the perks of being in an oppressed group is that you do get to develop some taboo knowledge and integrate it into your life without immediate repercussion. But the point I was trying to make is, what if Black men really are sexier, more beautiful, more sensual, more embodied than white men, and everyone knows it? I don't know if this would have much meaning in a non-white-supremacist world, since in such a world, white men could lighten up a little and get more into their bodies and recover from their mass psychoses. Then they might be a little sexier.

CM: Ultimately, there are no perks to living a life precariously determined by the whims and neuroses of people who feel threatened by you. As you attempt to live a full and satisfying life, your friendships, associations, and even your sexuality [are] marred with the projections and assumptions of people. Sometimes, to survive, we attempt to take advantage of expectations or assumptions of high sexual capacity, for example, but ultimately, this feels contrived, dissociative, and dehumanizing. Not being seen fully and accepted as such can be very heartbreaking. Where's the perk in that? I think that perk thing is a bizarre romantic assumption made by some Whites.

There are no healthy benefits to being Black, sexy, or more beautiful in a society run by Whites who resent and feel challenged by your beauty, who are obsessed with controlling or dominating you in reaction to the self-consciousness they feel in your presence. For example, most great athletes in popular sports are Black, but almost every well-known Black marvel lives a life determined by White men (agents, owners) less capable, but more privileged, self-determined, and in power than they. This is a precarious place to be. I don't agree that Black men are more embodied than White men. I think Black people have an essence and a way of being with a different flow than White men. I think, overall, Black people are less stoic and more in rhythm with their bodies than Whites tend to be. This is a result of originating from African cultures and from the melanin that creates color in our skin and flows throughout our bodies. But people classified as White have constructed institutionalized illusions in society that create complexes, terror, and disruption of Black self-image. This makes it difficult to relax and embody one's essence or beauty. White men will lighten up, as you say, and recover from their mass psychosis when they learn to accept themselves as they are. Self-love can sometimes make one appear sexy, regardless of physical appearance.

A lack of self-acceptance among whites is at the core of what propels envy, brutal white supremacy, castration and murder of Black males—i.e., the recent beheading and burning alive of Garnet Johnson in Virginia, and the dragging alive for three miles of James Byrd in Texas, et cetera. Ironically, some Whites don't feel beautiful unless they have "ethnic" features like a tan, curled hair, generous lips, or a rounded butt. Some do want to leave or change their White bodies, regardless of delusions of superiority or "better than-ness."

JN: There's some contradiction in that whole setup.

CM: For the most part, we are all equally valuable, worthy of love as human beings. Given this fact, of course, the construct of a human hierarchy, which "our" White-biased system creates, would be full with contradictions. Contradiction is a normal aspect of the constructed supremacy of one group over another.

Despite White biases in our culture, which tend to devalue other groups in comparison, that all of us bring different and exciting specialties to the human table contradicts ideas that anyone is superior. Black men "dominate," for lack of a better term, in terms of skill, most popular sports in this country, i.e., basketball, boxing, baseball, football, et cetera. Tiger Woods and Venus Williams have made significant inroads into golf and tennis, which, overall, have been bastions for White males. It's clear that an opponent in sports wins because of superior skill. Still, after Tiger Woods won the Masters (interesting label), on public television, it was recommended that he go get some fried chicken. This comment was made by an insecure, White man (whose name I forget), whose delusions of White superiority were turned on their head so he attempted to devalue Tiger Woods as a Black man. Talk about contradiction.

I have spoken with White guys who feel inferior in the realm[s] of popular sport[s], music, art, and sexuality. Some White men, in this instance, are jealous of Blacks. It's very possible to be jealous of someone without wanting to trade places with them socially: You mimic them (by getting a tan and perming hair) and borrowing from their language and customs, and call it "pop culture."

JN: Consuming and regurgitating. . . . Is pop culture a code word for Black?

CM: Often it is! Concealing the evidence or making it vague is common too.

JN: Yeah, no footnotes or royalty checks in the mail.

CM: When people say, "Don't go there," "Chill," or "It's the bomb," they are speaking "Ebonics"; when they give high fives, et cetera, the same thing. Not only no royalties, but this is cultural theft and counterfeit.

JN: This is the only (excuse for) culture most white people know, because so many of us are so cut off from community. We are largely bereft, unconscious, disconnected. These are the tradeoffs I'm talking about. White people are like black holes, so to speak. Being a part of an oppressed community gives one a reason and a way to connect with one's fellow and sister humans that is not just about competing.

CM: I think whites are more like white holes. People classified as whites have the capacity to be conscious and connected, but have been seduced by the delusions of whiteness and false superiority complexes based on the construct of "white."

JN: We'll talk more about white people later. Back to you. You have spent much of your life working to heal some of these wounds: establishing spaces, counseling people, raising consciousness, educating, et cetera. How do you approach the psychic wounding of the sexuality of Black males in a healing way?

CM: I prefer not to dwell on Whites as well, but this interview is on Black male lust. The whole frame is not independent of White constructs. If it wasn't for the Black and White social constructs we have been conditioned to live in reaction to, this conversation might not be occurring, or at least, it would not be called Black Male Lust. If it wasn't for White racism there might be no need to even have this conversation. All that to say, one cannot talk about Black Male

Lust without at some point referring to the racialized construct, as constructed by Whites, that this dialogue is taking place in. I, like my Brothers, don't have "Black" male lust; like all males, we have human male lust, but it's often interpreted through, or disrupted by, a White-biased and objectifying lens—a lens we too often internalize ourselves. Will there be a section in the book called "White" male lust? Probably not!

But back to your question: How do I approach the psychic wounding of the sexuality of Black males in a healing way? What framework do I use instead to affirm? Well, first of all, I create space, conversation, and context in which I ask Black men to still themselves and pay attention to what they repress. I speak of black male universal concepts and ethnic and popular cultural icons that can provoke unconscious or repressed memory. Marvin Gaye's music is great for creating this space. Historically and psychically, Black men have a lot in common, particularly in the areas of pain and anxiety, dehumanization, and fear. In our patriarchal culture, regardless of our sexual preference, we are not allowed to journey into, reflect on, and really heal those spaces. This debilitates us and interferes with our capacity to psychically flow and discover our emotional continuum and our pain and joy reservoirs. This is normalized. Through my work, I abnormalize these norms and guide my dear brothers out of their constructed shell (made of glorified patriarchy, illusions of superiority over "the feminine," and a thick layer of fear).

The work, once they decide to do it, isn't difficult. Often they are like babies who long to be fed and held. The food is reveling in knowing their history, deconstructing the normalized and romanticized ways of making meaning that dehumanizes them in the culture, and destabilizing the fallacy that they are "independent thinkers" not subject to external versions of "reality" that harms their hearts, spirits, and human potential.

One of the biggest fallacies men, Black men, suffer from is that they are in total control of their lives and making their own decisions. Blacks own and run very little in this society. Clinging to the illusion of independence (from white psychic bondage) sometimes is the closest thing to independence Brothers feel they will really achieve. When the illusion falters, unprepared for "reality," many Brothers act out on each other, themselves, or their partners. Realizing they are not in control but are at the whims of White power constructs, in a culture that values "manhood" and male power, can be very disturbing. Sometimes in this instance is when some Black men take advantage of "Black Male Lust" mythology, using claims of sexual prowess and ability to find relevance in this society. To crystallize our lack of self-determination, so we can deal with it and reverse it, I often ask them if they chose to speak English, a language that deprecates the value of [Black] people of African descent and "the feminine."

JN: English? How so?

CM: Blackmailed, "fair" skin (how ironic), white slavery, white trash—in a white-supremacist culture, the words Black slavery or Black trash don't exist, implying no need to be redundant because these are "normal" or accepted conditions for Blacks. On the other hand, white slavery and white trash are common terms. Little white lies, black holes, et cetera, are also words that have white supremacist implications. And there are hundreds more.

JN: Is that intrinsic to English? Are there correlative expressions in other languages?

CM: Not absolutely, but it doesn't matter. We are speaking English, in an English-speaking context. This interview is in English, and Blacks are the only people here with no indigenous connection to affirming or African-affirming and resonant linguistics. This has a BIG impact. It interrupts our capacities for self-determination and self-love, and reinforces white supremacist delusions.

JN: How do you heal the normalized norms? What are Black male universal concepts?

CM: I'll contextualize. Do you imagine that white men in this culture universally fear the cops, have nightmares about being unfairly incarcerated, lynched, or castrated? Do you think many whites know what's it's like to go from cute little boy to social menace, suspect, endangered species, and potential rapist? These are among Black male universal concepts. Black men, relative to most, grab their/our crotches a lot, to make sure they are still there. Even Michael Jackson, a once high-profile man [was] known to grab his crotch a lot. I think it's a symptom of cellular memory residue from the mass castration of us. The concept of cellular memory is that we have memory of traumatic experiences had by our ancestors, held in our cells, our bodies. I believe this is very true. I experience it. Before I understood lynching, as early as three or four years old, I was always uncomfortable with having anything around my neck. I believe this results from cellular memory.

JN: What kind of differences does healing white-supremacist normalization make in the lives of Black men? What possibilities exist for affirming sexual connections, i.e., supportive of the whole person, not engendered by the distortions of white supremacy?

CM: Healing white supremacist normalization in the lives of Black men helps Black men to discover themselves and learn to love themselves in their own image, to live, think, and make meaning in ways that reproduce the empowerment of themselves and their legacies; instead of being Black Trojan horses for white power, they can become self/community embracing and affirmed. Regarding sex . . . I believe people who love themselves are great sex partners: less self-conscious, less codependent, and more into the mutual magic of co-satisfaction.

JN: Here's a question for you: Do you think interracial relationships are inherently destructive?

CM: Race is a construct created by people who classify themselves as white to establish a false human hierarchy based on darker and less dark skin hues, European and non-European characteristics. People come in wonderful diverse manifestations, but white self-consciousness has disrupted our capacity to value all as equally important and human. Relationships built on, or created in reaction to, race constructs, in my opinion, are inherently destructive. Until race and all of its connotations are dismantled from human life, interracial relationships, particularly between so-called whites and so-called people of color, are inherently toxic and potentially destructive. When someone Jewish marries someone gentile (white) inspired by the fact that [this] person . . . is NOT Jewish, this is self-hate motivated, anti-Jewish, and toxic.

JN: The healing that you have been working on for most of your life . . . can you speak to your visions for a transformed world? Where Black men are self-loving, safe, and relaxed?

CM: Well, I must inform you that Black men are not my only focus; the whole community needs healing and the Black male cannot be healed without the participation of his community and family. We wound each other, often not knowing it; therefore, we need to be collaborators on creating healing spaces. Healing needs to take place among all people disillusioned and psychically injured or distracted by white-dominating terrorism and sexism. People among whites need to learn to accept themselves as the melanin-challenged offspring of African people.

JN: What, if anything, would you like from your white and other allies?

CM: Whites must first realize they "benefit" materially (while suffering and dying spiritually) from the construct of white supremacy; then learn (while working toward human equity and a more humane world) to use their "privilege" and position as a funnel to guide resources to effective social change efforts. But effective must be defined in terms of purpose. Too often, including among "well-meaning" whites, effective means "it invites me in, makes me feel good about myself and comfortable." Effectiveness can't and shouldn't be determined by white comfort zones.

JN: Any final remarks?

CM: Back to the issue of Black Male Lust. I hope that my attempt to illuminate elements of the climate in which everything occurs in "our" society has been helpful. I believe everything we've discussed is relevant to the issue. Consensual lust between respectful and desired partners is a wonderful thing. Despite struggles among Black men to locate self, some of us do have the capacity to recognize and celebrate our essence and sexuality. Self-love and -discovery among Black men is part of what will better release our capacity for lust, sex, and lovemaking as a wonderful aspect of our work toward healing and being healed. Marvin Gaye, a tortured but brilliant Black man, said it best when crooning, "When I get that feeling, I need sexual healing."

43

Bangkok Story

Alison Luterman

Your story is of being alone
at twenty-four, in Bangkok,
sex capitol of the world.   Skinny, lost,
in your coveted American jeans and beat-up sandals,
you somehow thought to find a prostitute, and went with her.
Both of you young, that worthless treasure,
unasked for, unexchangeable.

In the small, sweaty room
where you'd gone with her to lie down,
you asked and she told you her story: her village,
the family she sent money to, a boyfriend
who didn't like her doing this.
Many things you didn't ask but could piece together,
knowing Bangkok—

city of a million prostitutes,
where some women are trained to slither
like brightly colored circus snakes, if that's what is wanted.
Or to lie still, for the ones who must have their way.
Or to sit astride, massage with soap, with oil, with a curried tongue,
each man who comes alone in his own sweat,
needing it that badly.

"Bangkok Story" first appeared in *The Sun,* April 1995, issue 232, p. 19.

In this country there are villages
where men come to the parents of beautiful daughters
to bargain and barter and buy a child
before it has been conceived.
In this country there are women—girls—
whose lives pass from hand to hand
like foreign money in obscure places,
beautiful and worthless.

But you two were talking.

I like to think it was a full moon.
Both of you naked,
but doing nothing,
just talking. You being you, the man I know,
only younger, and alone,
your eyes filled as you listened.
And she who had years before stopped
feeling sorry for her own sad, ordinary story,
heard again, in that moment
her young girl's voice, like a door
long unused, creaking on its hunger
in an airless little room; saw a strange man,
not of her people, cry for her.

This becomes my story as I listen to you
tell something you have never told anyone.

I listen and think about men,
their hard, hungry bodies,
and how much warmth and pain can cost.
The price of a night not spent alone,
the price of a story told,
the price of telling a story, one's own story,
to someone. The price of keeping silent.

When you told me I did not interrupt or draw away.
But for days afterward I found it difficult to leave Bangkok,
and this woman, this worn-down younger sister,
whose life you listened to but could not change.

I think of her when I order clothes from a catalog.
Clothes cut and stitched and packed
by red-eyed women and girls with black hair
from places as far away as Bangkok, and as poor.

I have never been to Bangkok,
but have my own stories of what I have done
or allowed to be done, in the name of need.
I have my own midnights
when shame beats like a hammer,
unredeemed, unredeemed.

44

Having Sex Outside the Box

John Stoltenberg

In Western cultures, the ethics of proving manhood has had disastrous consequences. Among these is a values crisis that has no name: many people experience sex and selfhood as separate, as rarely or never connected.

Representations of sex as commoditized prompt a deeply dispiriting question: Is it even possible to feel our full humanness, including our sexual humanness, in a sexual relationship with another human being where there is complete, reciprocal fairness: where each sovereign self feels safe, sustained, seen, not alone?

What would it mean to reconnect sex and selfhood—in our bodies, in our relationships, in our communities, in our lifetime? What would this eroticism be like? Who would we be to one another when we behold and are beheld as fully human, fully somebody, fully equal?

To attempt to answer these questions, I offer here some reflections about sexual selfhood, and how its experience differs—both practically and ethically—from an eroticism that is focused on embodying the social fiction of manhood. I intend this essay for anyone who has been raised to be a man and for anyone who has ever had, or has ever wanted to have, sex with one.

The decision to act relationally in selfhood mode or in manhood mode always has consequences in one's interpersonal intimacy. No sex manuals or newsstand men's magazines help people raised to be a man locate their sexual feelings in terms of that decision. Because so many of us grow up believing that all sexual feelings correspond to an experience of "real

---

Dedicated to Shere Hite, the first researcher to explore the subject of sexual feelings in a male body outside the box of "men-only-ness."

This essay contains material adapted from *The End of Manhood: Parables on Sex and Selfhood,* published by Dutton/Penguin Books, New York. Copyright 1993, 1999 by John Stoltenberg.

manhood," we do not pay as much attention as we could to the practical possibilities of sexual feelings as an experience of selfhood. Unfortunately, people sometimes deliberately turn off or turn down such possibilities. So I provide here some practical guidelines for recognizing *which mode* one is in sexually—whether, at a given moment in a sexual relationship, one is acting in selfhood mode (experiencing fully one's own and one's partner's selfhood) or in manhood mode (trying to be the man there). Knowing the difference, one is more likely to be able to change from one mode to another:

> *When I'm having sex with someone, am I feeling emotionally and physically that I belong to an affinity group of human selves? Or am I having sex as if I'm a contestant or combatant—as if sex is a qualifying round for bona fide membership in the ranks of manhood?*

Basically, for anyone to be the man there, for anyone to establish one's status as a contender in the manhood sham, someone else (someone *human*) has to be treated, at least momentarily, like an underling (not like an equal).

And basically, for anyone to feel human in a relationship—to feel sexually present *as* oneself in one's own body and *to* another self who also feels present in *their* own body—there has to be an ethical context of equality created through acts of reciprocal regard for each other's selfhood.

There are enormous pressures on penised people to stay in manhood mode during sex. Some come from inside; others, from outside. We tend to think that all the pressures from inside are biological or anatomical. Actually most of them are internalized social and political forces, such as the learned fear of other people who have also been raised to be a man. Deep inside, we feel we must always act like a man or else risk being humiliated by other men's judgment. Often, we feel—deep inside—that our manhood act is not completely credible in the rest of our life, so it had better be convincing when we have sex. Staying in manhood mode during sex can be a way to purge oneself of feelings associated with one's mother (compassion, tenderness) or to redeem one's manhood in the remembered glowering eyes of one's father. And similarly, staying in manhood mode during sex can be a way of viscerally experiencing "real and deep manhood," without which, we fear, we will cease to have a valid social existence. If the growth market for pornography and prostitution is any indication, gender anxiety in penised people—the internal terror that one is not a real-enough man—is on the increase. Having sex in manhood mode can seem to resolve that panic.

And sometimes, even those of us who try to act decently toward others, for instance by resisting the sex industry's contamination of our sexuality, feel we *must* stay in manhood mode during sex because we assume that that is what our partner expects. And indeed that may be the case, especially if our partner has never himself or herself known sex in selfhood mode.

All such pressures *feel* internal, but they are actually external. The simple truth is, in a world where only sex in manhood mode is promoted, most people raised to be a man are not consciously familiar with what sexuality in selfhood mode is or what it might be like. And the unknown can be frightening.

One of the most viscerally significant pressures to stay in manhood mode during sex is the belief that there is such a thing as a "male" sexuality—a circumscribable range of erotic sensation that can be neatly distinguished from "female" sexuality. Pick up any popular magazine marketed to men or to women and try to find an article that *disputes* this belief. To the contrary, most publications, and nearly all pornography, treat the subjectivity of sexuality as a binary: male/female, top/bottom, active/passive, inserter/insertee. Few people raised to be a man approach a sexual encounter without at some level recalling the question "How is *a man* supposed to feel during sex?" And many who fail at or reject feeling like a man during sex tend to believe the only alternative is feeling like *a woman*. The word *homophobia* scarcely hints at the grip that this false binarism has on the body politic.

Nothing about "male" sexual anatomy leads logically to the conclusion that there is a discrete set of sexual feelings that are "the male ones," which when felt can always be clearly delineated from "the female ones." A human raised to be a man might try very hard, acting relationally in manhood mode, to make certain (or make believe) that the sexual feelings he is having are only "the male ones." But he will be up against intransigent facts about human sexual anatomy that will make this effort extremely frustrating. For one thing, the nerve networks inside both penises and clitorises are both transformers and transducers—they have a similar capacity to receive and retransmit sensation from one place in the body to another and then to another and to amplify all that sensory information in an instant. For another thing, nipple eroticism is experienceable by penised humans. Moreover, in people born penised, the accompanying prostate gland is located much more conveniently for pleasurable stimulation via the rectum than is the clitoris located for pleasurable stimulation via the vaginal canal in people born vulvaed. And nonejaculatory orgasms in penised humans are not only possible; they are frequently multiple. In sum, all humans share homologous tissue structures throughout our bodies, so there is no boundary where so-called male sexual feelings absolutely end and so-called female sexual feelings absolutely begin.

Most penised folks share a passionate inner conviction that they can go looking for that boundary in their bodies when they have sex. There is no such boundary to be found. But believing that one dares not feel other than a decidedly "male" sexual feeling will surely drive one to have sex in manhood mode—and perhaps become compulsive in doing so.

To learn whether one might prefer sex in selfhood mode instead, one first needs to reexamine the social convention that coming with a penis automatically makes one feel sexually "like a real man." One also needs to reobserve one's own sexual feelings, alert to the possibility that none may be distinguishably "male," even though all are distinctly human and sexual. Because even if one believes oneself to be "a real man"—all the time, with never any qualm, no blurring—one's sexual feelings might not be containable in a canister marked MEN'S. And realizing that fact might allow one to try feeling sexual in selfhood mode for a change.

The core of one's being must love justice more than manhood.
The end of loving manhood is the beginning of sexual selfhood.

Feeling sexual in manhood mode is driven by a real desire—the desire to experience social gender sexually, emotionally and physically, so that it will seem to feel real, so that one will seem to feel real as a "real man." Feeling sexual in manhood mode is driven by the need to experience social gender on the hierarchical scale of "manhood" versus "nobody." The desire to believe and actualize this social fiction may be called *loving manhood.*

Feeling sexual in selfhood mode is also driven by desire. It is as powerful and as passionate a human longing as our human bodies were born capable of feeling. Feeling sexual in selfhood mode is driven by the need to experience our humanity emotionally and physically on the horizontal dimension of selfhood—to feel safe, to feel sustained, to feel seen and not alone, and to bestow the same human entitlement upon each one we love. The desire to honor this human reality may be called *loving justice.*

Just because one is feeling sexually aroused does not necessarily mean that one can know whether one is in selfhood mode or manhood mode, because the difference is not so much in the body's sexual feelings as in the relational context in which one is feeling sexual. The following table portrays some of these relational differences.

Relationship Clues Indicating You May Be Feeling Sexual in SELFHOOD MODE	Relationship Clues Indicating You May Be Feeling Sexual in MANHOOD MODE
There has been honesty. You have told the complete and significant truth.	There has been deceit. You have kept a significant secret or told a significant lie.
There has been beholding between you. You have been a witness to each other's subjectivity. You have recognized yourselves as two whole human beings.	There has been sexual objectification. Although one of you may have seemed to regard yourself as a subject, one of you was definitely regarded as an object.
There has been mutual respect and regard in negotiating and making all decisions that affect both you and your partner in the relationship, including sex.	There has been manipulation, coercion, duplicity, force, constraint, or some other style of one-sided, peremptory decision making in the relationship.
There has been affirmative and active consent, in every moment.	There has been a lack of consent.
There has been a context of companionship, interest in each other's interests, emotional warmth and support available to each other. That context contains all sexual relating, and that context lasts after.	There has been emotional withdrawal, avoidance—e.g., after a sexual encounter when you recoil from the other person, as if denying that what was sensual between you both even happened.
There has been enjoyment, joy, exhilaration, contact energy, shared fun—before, during, and after.	There has been teasing, jokes at the partner's expense, laughter at the partner's discomfort.
You and your partner have been profoundly present to each other, human self to human self, before, during, and after.	There has been a fantasizing of the body of someone who is not there during the sexual encounter—a remembered stranger or image, having that other body do something to yours, doing something to it. There has been fantasizing so as to evade the reality of the person you are with, because equal reality with your partner has become a turnoff.
When you recognize any of the above clues in your relational life, you may expect to experience the eroticism of loving justice.	*When you recognize any of the above clues in your relational life, you may expect to experience the eroticism of loving manhood.*

Because one can switch back and forth between selfhood mode and manhood mode in an instant, from decision to decision, from relational act to relational act, even from moment to moment in the same sexual encounter, one might not always recognize which mode one is in. Sometimes one may feel sexual vis-à-vis another self-possessed whole human being—and sometimes one may feel sexual as possessor or possessee. Sometimes one may feel sexually like somebody human. And sometimes one may feel sexually like "the man there"—or like "there's a man there" on top and one is desperate to assimilate or ingest his "manliness."

Sexual feelings in and of themselves do not express either equality or hierarchy; they are not intrinsically in either selfhood mode or manhood mode. Sexual feelings do not have a one-track will of their own. *People* do sometimes, but not sexual feelings. From tender to ardent, the full range of human sexual feelings can accompany a relational act that affirms human selfhood—justly, lovingly, mutually, reciprocally.

Sexual feelings can also accompany a relational act that affirms the possession of one human's body by another. But with the sexuality of possession there is a critical, practical limit as to when such relational acts *stop* feeling sexual for the owned one, becoming pure pain, pure dread, pure nobodyness. From the point of view of the sexually owned one, negotiation of that limit is a very high priority—and very tricky, since one's limit can be crossed in an instant and all one has to go on is trust in the partner whom one might want to be sexually owned by. If one's trust was misplaced, or if negotiations break off, one may be very badly hurt. One may also feel dumb, unlucky in love, and responsible, at least until one realizes what a game of chance the eroticism of possession really is—and how slim the odds are. Some people find that sex in manhood mode is way too risky for their taste. It is a gamble by definition, and not a win-win situation by any stretch of the imagination. From the point of view of the sexually owning one, however, negotiation of the ownable's limit is not the same priority. For the owner, the only incentive to negotiate an ownable's limit is to maintain sexual access.

Feeling sexual in manhood mode can sometimes feel like a vanishing act. Especially during the act of intercourse, sexual feelings in manhood mode sometimes cannot be aroused or cannot climax unless one has mentally gone away someplace else, even though one's body is physically existent beside another human being's body. Feeling sexual in manhood mode sometimes feels as if one's partner or one's own self has had to disappear, in order to experience sexual sensations as distinguishably "male." It feels like being not so much intimate as merely adjacent.

The experience of feeling sexual as an owner in manhood mode is an acquired taste, and not everyone who tries it has successfully mastered the knack. To do it right, one really *has* to be elsewhere in one's brain, since emotional and physical receptivity and responsiveness to another human's experience is antiaphrodisiac. Feeling *with* someone tends to cancel out sexual feelings in manhood mode. And afterward this erotic disappearing act can leave both partners feeling somewhat estranged.

As a practical matter, one may feel that the coordination and physiological functioning of one's sexual anatomy requires so much concentration that one has little left over for the feelings of one's partner. One's concentration may become so intensely focused on the operational or mechanistic potential of the penis that—simply as a matter of practical expediency—one will close down one's receptivity to the transformer and transducer potential of the penis. Put more bluntly: in order to keep one's sexual motor driving, one will focus feeling on the penis as a single-chamber piston, to the exclusion of feeling the penis as a distributor issuing energizing and tantalizing signals to various points in the engine block.

Physiologically, nothing *requires* one to shut off or edit one's sensual experience in that way. It is a choice that one makes, even as one may not be aware that it is a choice one *can* make. The choice is in what feelings from one's body one wishes to give more attention to, or which feelings one wishes to give no attention to at all. One makes the choice in how much attention one gives to feeling *with* someone. The transformer and transducer potential of the penis—while by no means the only way to experience the tactile presence of another whole human being—happens to be extremely sensitive to the motion of emotions between two partners. The transducer and transformer potential of human genitals sometimes feels like circuitry central meets circuitry central, like all systems are in touch and aglow, like all systems are pulsating and all sensory systems are amplifying and reverberating back and forth.

If all one decides to feel, basically, is whether one is erect and ejaculating, and if one decides not to feel *with,* or not to feel what one's partner may be feeling, or not to feel what oneself and one's partner may be feeling together, it may be an arduous effort to become erect and to ejaculate. One may require some other sorts of masturbatory aids, some of which may be pornography recalled from memory. This may account for why one sometimes has to disappear during a sex act with someone—why one sometimes seems to go away somewhere else in order to get off on one's own. One may have to consult one's private image bank to see what could help one get up or stay hard or shoot. Having chosen to eliminate an enormous and significant range of sensory information both from one's own body and from one's partner—but not having abandoned one's anxiety about being "the man there"—one may feel one has no choice.

Not surprisingly, some people find it difficult to own their own sexuality if they are *being owned* by someone else. And some people find it difficult to own their own sexuality if they are *trying to own* someone else. Deciding to commit one's body and brain to *possession* as an erotic transaction is to decide to stay stuck in manhood mode, and not everyone feels entirely comfortable there. Throughout human history, there have been individuals who have recoiled from sexual possession—whether as possessor or possessed. This decision—a kind of "conscientious objector" stance—may be experienceable or interpretable as a preference for the sexuality of selfhood.

Over the past years, I have been told by quite a number of humans born with "male" sexual anatomy that they have opted, for the time being or over the long term, not to attempt to perform the act of intercourse. By way of explanation, they have sometimes confided in me that in order to complete the act of intercourse, they have felt they had to regard or treat their partner's body in ways that they no longer felt comfortable doing. I infer that because they conscientiously reject a relationship of possession, the erotics of that relationship have also had to be put on hold.

Some humans born with "male" sexual anatomy have realized that their preferred experience of coitus is as an embrace, not a stab. For them, the subjective feeling that one is violating another person's body is simply emotionally impossible. These are humans who, when the act becomes one of penetration past resistance (rather than explicitly invited entry and engulfment), simply cannot feel emotionally and sensually present in the physical act. So unless they feel a full participant in the sexuality of selfhood, they demure or abstain from any relational act that they sense is being driven by desire for sexual possession.

When such humans make such choices as relational acts of conscience, they may not have a language with which to communicate to their partner what is going on inside them. Some such episodes have resulted in hurt feelings, especially if the partner is inexperienced or confused about the difference between the sexuality of possession and the sexuality of selfhood. Communications can become quite botched, actually, and what was intended as a relational act to acknowledge the partner's selfhood becomes interpretable, inadvertently, as sexual rejection.

As I have listened to such stories, I cannot help but recall the range of my own experiences in the act of intercourse, in particular the pleasure I have experienced when my erotic desire to feel ownable has been met by a partner's considerate and consensual and not too clumsy desire to own somebody. Having been in the so-called driver's seat myself, I was perhaps more able to interpret some of the mysteries one frequently comes upon on the passenger's side: when, for instance, the driver might resent directions, or when, for instance, the driver seems so preoccupied with testing the speed limit that communications with the passenger are all but out of the question. I understand intimately, in other words, something of the solipsism and self-absorption that are emotionally and physically necessary, simply as a practical and physiological matter, in order to drive the point of one's manhood home. And as much as I have enjoyed being taken for such rides, I have begun to reflect uncertainly about my own responsibility for, in effect, expecting someone else to do driving under conditions of detachment and self-involvement that in conscience *I* would find hard to do. I *know* I found such driving hard to do emotionally and physically, which was why I got off the road.

Feeling sexual in selfhood mode is not at all the same as feeling sexually "possessed" or "owned." Sometimes people feel afraid that it will be, and so they avoid even the premonition of such feelings. The misconception is easily explained: If all one is familiar with is sexual feelings as "owner" in manhood mode, one might assume the only alternative is to feel sexual feelings being "owned"—and this may feel emotionally and physically impossible. And if all one is familiar with is as "ownable" in manhood mode, one might assume the only alternative is to feel sexual feelings as "owner"—and this may feel emotionally and physically impossible.

Often a sexual embrace will begin in selfhood mode, but then one or the other partner panics, because suddenly it feels as if they stepped away from the cliffside of manhood and so they are nowhere, even though both are exactly there, human to human—loving each other more than manhood. As if in an animated cartoon when characters step off a cliff into midair and it takes them a while to discover there is no familiar footing underneath, the two have time for a momentary experience together, their sexual selfhoods meeting, perhaps ardently, ecstatically. Then one or both of them get flustered at the unfamiliarity, so they reach back to the cliffside and try to hold on for dear life. They may not have known they would not have fallen into any abyss. They may not have known they would have both been fine: safe, sustained, witnessed, sexually intimate, somebody to somebody.

Sometimes people will come together as if sexually attracted to each other in manhood mode, as if one will probably be owner and the other will probably be owned, because they might have liked each other anyway, but that was the only way they knew to express their liking sexually. Then, as they get to know each other more personally, more deeply, it becomes quite impossible, emotionally and physically, to continue seeking sexual feelings together as possessor and possessed—and so they evolve or invent for themselves a sexual expression that is premised on mutual self-possession; they discover or reclaim for themselves a sexually intimate self-revelation, until it suits them, until it becomes them; and they feel whole unto themselves and even more whole together. And so begins another Revolution from Between.

Just by looking at people, one cannot tell who has begun such a powerful revolution. One cannot tell from any assumptions about their sexual anatomy, their skin pigmentation, their money, their clothes, their age, their anything, that they may have discovered or invented the sexuality of selfhood for their very own selves. Just by looking, one cannot necessarily tell who is stuck in power *from the top down* and who truly prefers the power *between* us.

45

Some Quick Screaming Notes About Male Lust

Tim Beneke

As I sit to write about male lust, I want to scream. The topic fills me with frustration, bewilderment, a flurry of disorienting insights reminiscent of powerful, newly leashed dogs speeding away from my grasp across an open field. I am not sure I have the will or the energy to track them down. And some of them might bite. There are too many truths screaming for attention. And they don't like to talk to one another.

But I can investigate why I want to scream or a little of what the truths are screaming about. I have written a lot about male lust; far more than my interest in the subject warrants. (Book contracts will do that to you.) I don't like repeating myself. I have no desire to write more than I want to write here, now. I really don't want to be earnest, wise, sensitive, or thoughtful. Honest.

Where to begin? First, as a child born into a middle-class, not well-educated family, in 1950. Growing up, mostly in the Deep South, in a family in which sex was literally never discussed, in a period in which sex outside of marriage was considered dirty and somehow low class—sex within it was somehow lustless. Yet from the age of eight or nine, sexual lust for girls and women suffused my psychic atmosphere. I was physically precocious, 5'7'' and 130 pounds and shaving by the age of twelve, and felt intense sexual longing at a young age—and intensely pained by my longing and by the torturing attractiveness of girls and women. I felt overstimulated, overwhelmed by their power as images. Later, at seventeen, when I began to fuck, fucking was a way of quieting the power of those images, their disorienting effect on my soul, images evoking an inexorable mixture of guilt, anger, overintense pleasure, and helplessness, all coexisting in mystified confusion.

Fucking had (has) many meanings, one of which was to disempower the power of women as images. (I take it as undeniable that a frequent male response to women's sexiness is to want to degrade it by aggressive fucking.) Always the undercurrent, tugging at and struggling to suffuse the meaning of sex, that it was wrong, bad, dirty, nasty, something to feel ashamed about, low class, vulgar.

Earlier, at sixteen, I was reading *Playboy,* regarding it as progressive and liberating. My girlfriend and I would sit and read the cartoons and look at the women together. *Playboy,* by being at once a magazine for middle-class consumers, intellectuals, and people who wanted to look at dirty pictures, made sex a little more high class, a little less vulgar. Reading it in 1967, the word "sexism" did not yet exist, and I could not see what I now most object to in it—the egregious overdefining of women's subjectivity in terms of male needs.

But then, at nineteen, in college, in 1969, women in the antiwar movement finally got sick of making coffee (to appropriate a feminist cliché). Women's liberation hit men hard, especially on college campuses. It certainly hit me hard. Very fast, the one thing I did not want to be (or be seen as) was a sexist man, a man who objectified women. I wanted to always treat women like full human beings, both in my behavior and in my consciousness. I wanted to be a good boy; I wanted to please Mommy. And, I had some genuine empathy for women and what they went through.

All this rattled around inside my skull, and at twenty-nine, after several years of living in Berkeley, where the war between the sexes was still going strong, I found myself writing a book on men's attitudes toward rape. I quickly saw that rape was an extension of features found, in both behavior and consciousness, in "normal" straight male sexuality. And, following the Women's Movement, I assumed anything on the continuum in the direction of rape—anything sexual in thought and deed that contained objectification, anger, or vengefulness—to be bad. (I was too ideologically enmeshed to acknowledge that sex may often contain features of anger and love mingled indecipherably together.) I began to see male lust as vengeful and mean and saw much that was manipulative and psychically coercive in male dating patterns as little different from rape. Immersed in an effort to acknowledge and vivify the reality of violence against women, I had days when I saw male heterosexuality as virtually evil.

On an emotional level, it is impossible to separate the guilt-ridden, puritanical attitude toward sex that I absorbed from my family from the guilt-ridden, feminist attitude toward sex that I absorbed from feminism and my own politics.

I saw our most basic conception of sex, fucking, as aggressive degradation, implicitly containing a conception of women as property. A woman who had been fucked by a lot of guys was regarded as "cheap"; she could only be cheapened by fucking if the act of fucking degraded her, and the act of fucking could only degrade her if there was some preexisting conception of her as property. Sexist sex was built into our conceptual system, into our cognition, and therefore into the structure of male lust and our sexual emotions as men (or something like that). As straight men, our most basic sexual reflexes were not to be trusted. I assumed that any anger in my lust for women was somehow bad; sex was supposed to be loving, cuddly, "nonobjectifying." And I was inspecting my sexuality for continuities with rape, taking mental notes as I had sex, on a quest for insights about rape. Self-distrust piled upon self-distrust. Straight men were always/already damned.

The simple fact is that I like certain women's bodies, especially when I experience them as bodies with a consciousness full of lust toward me. (See the section on subjectified bodies in my *Proving Manhood,* 1997.) No amount of feminist analysis or diffuse residual puritanical guilt from my childhood will change that. I am like this, I now am inclined to believe, not so much because I have been socially constructed to be this way by a patriarchal, sexist culture, but more as a matter of being a strongly heterosexual male constructed by evolutionary forces to respond to certain kinds of stimulation. None of this is meant to justify or deny sexism, to legitimate harassment or rape or the oppressiveness of the male gaze in women's lives. Rather, it is to suggest a reasonable starting point for antisexist men to address sexism as it relates to sex: avoid making "the perfect" the enemy of the good.

There is much to think and write about. I think of all the images of male stupidity in lust that pervade the culture, all of the commercials of guys falling over themselves in embarrassed self-conscious lust—male lust as humiliated posturing. Why are there no (or so few) ennobling images of male lust? Typically, to be lusting is to be a fool, made incompetent by desire—lust as psychically disabling.

When is lust respectful? What does it mean to respect a woman? Is there such a thing as antisexist lust? What does it look or feel like? What are the connections between sexism and sexual repression? Where is the antisexist pornography and what should it look like? And does anyone much care about any of this?

46

Fuel for Fantasy:
The Ideological Construction
of Male Lust

Michael S. Kimmel

My boyfriend and I are on a deserted island. The palm trees flap in the soft breeze; the sand glistens. The sun is warm, and we swim for a while in the cool blue water and then come back to the beach and lie there. We rub suntan oil on each other's bodies, and soon we are kissing passionately. Then we make love in the sand.

My husband and I are at a ski resort, in a cabin, and it's late at night. It's snowing outside, so we build a fire in the fireplace and lie down on the fur rug in front of it. We sip champagne by the roaring fire, and then he kisses me and takes off my blouse. Then we make love.

These two scenes represent composite sexual fantasies offered by young women in an ongoing research project I've been developing with a colleague. Notice the rich descriptions of the scene, its moods and textures. Note the well-developed geographic and temporal settings, the elaborate placement of props such as rugs. Note that the partner is a man with whom the woman is having a long-term relationship. Note also that explicitly sexual description is minimal and usually involves vague references to lovemaking. One has no idea who does what to whom.

Sections of "Fuel for Fantasy: The Ideological Construction of Male Lust" originally appeared as " 'Insult' or 'Injury': Sex, Pornography, and Sexism," in *Men Confront Pornography: 25 Men Take a Candid Look at How Pornography Affects Their Lives, Politics, and Sexuality,* edited by Michael S. Kimmel, published by Meridian/Penguin, New York, 1990.

Here's a composite rendition of the men's sexual fantasies:

> I'm walking down the street, and these two unbelievably gorgeous blondes are walking toward me. Our eyes meet, and we realize we have to have each other. One of them kneels in front of me and unzips my fly and begins to give me the best blow job I've ever had. The other pulls down her shorts and begins to play with herself. Then I do her while the first one gets eaten out by the one I'm fucking. We do it every way we can imagine, and then they get it on while I'm resting, but watching them turns me on, so we start up again. Then we all get up and walk away with these big smiles on our faces. We never see one another again.

Here, we know exactly who does what to whom, and in precisely what order, and we know exactly what the women look like—typical men's fantasies involve famous models or actresses. Scene setting is entirely absent (if they are on the street, I wonder who is picking out the gravel and shards of broken glass from their bodies?); mood and affect seem to be lifestyle options, not necessary for the turn-on. And we have no idea who these women are.

Male sexual fantasies are idealized renditions of masculine sexual scripts: genitally focused, orgasm centered, and explicit in the spatial and temporal sequencing of sexual behaviors. We might say that women's *sexual* imaginations are impoverished at the expense of highly developed *sensual* imaginations; by contrast, men's sensual imaginations are impoverished by their highly developed sexual imaginations. (These differences hold for both heterosexual and homosexual women and men.) While there has been some evidence of shifts in women's fantasies toward more sexually explicit scenes, and increasing comfort with explicit language, these fantasies do reveal both what we think and what we think we are supposed to think about sex.

Where do such dramatically different mental landscapes come from? Men's fantasies, I believe, are fueled by two of the most central themes in American culture: sexual repression and sexism. Sexist assumptions about women's sexuality permeate our culture, and men often hold utterly contradictory notions about women's sexuality (along with cultural icons that signify these bizarre notions). Women are seen simultaneously as passive and asexual (the "frigid prude") and insatiable and demanding (the *vagina dentata* that will devour men). These images confuse men and can often paralyze women, making their struggle to claim a vital sexuality a difficult and politically charged process.

Sexual repression also fuels men's lust. (This is, of course, true for women as well, although it is often expressed differently. Though much of this discussion of fantasy shaped by sexism and sexual repression holds also for women, I will continue to focus here only on men's fantasies.) Few men would say that they are having as much sex as they want. The norms of masculinity, after all, require that men should want sex all the time and produce instant and eternally rigid erections on demand. These norms, though, contradict the social demand for sexual repression and the profoundly erotophobic thread that runs through our culture. As a culture, we abhor sex and are terrified by it because we believe that the iconoclastic anarchy of the orgasm threatens all forms of authority—political, social, economic, and familial. Thus, we associate sexual yearnings with guilt or shame, and we simultaneously understand masculinity as the constant and irrepressible capacity for desire. (In part, this helps explain Freud's opposition of civilization and sexuality, and why, in a sexist culture, women's sexuality is constructed as passive so that women can control men's sexual drive.)

Sexual repression produces a world in which the nonsexual is constantly eroticized—in fantasy, we re-create mentally what we have lost in real life. And sexist assumptions about women's sexuality provide the social context in which these fantasies take shape. Who but the sexually starved could listen to a twenty-second prerecorded message from a faceless woman over a telephone and be aroused? In what context but sexism could her message be understood? In these prerecorded fantasies, the woman's voice has a lot to accomplish in twenty seconds. She must set a scene (nurse/patient, camping trip, etc.), express her intense need for sex with the listener, vocally simulate her arousal and orgasm while pleading for his orgasm, and, finally, close the encounter with gratitude for such frenzied pleasure and bid a fond farewell to her caller, inviting him to call again or call a different number "for a live girl." All this in twenty seconds! On the telephone! On tape! And still it turns men on, easily.

Men's consistent complaints of sexual deprivation have no basis in biology, although it is comfortingly convenient to blame our hormones when we want sex. To always seek sex, to seek to sexualize relationships with women, to never refuse an offer of sex—these are crucial elements in the normative definition of masculinity. Sexual pleasure is rarely the goal in a sexual encounter; something far more important than mere pleasure is on the line, our sense of ourselves as men. Men's sense of sexual scarcity and an almost compulsive need for sex to confirm manhood feed each other, creating a self-perpetuating cycle of sexual deprivation and despair. And it makes men furious at women for doing what women are taught to do in our society: saying no. In our society, men being what men are "supposed to be" leads inevitably to conflict with women, who are being what they are "supposed to be."

Certainly, women say no for reasons other than gender conditioning; they may not be interested, or they may be angry at their partner for some reason. And, certainly, men are also angry at women who are sexually voracious and who fully claim their sexual appetites. But, in general, this dynamic of men wanting and women refusing is established early in our adolescent sexual socialization and has important consequences for both male and female sexualities.

Men's consumption of pornography is, in part, fed by this strange combination of lust and rage. Pornography can sexualize that rage, and it can make sex look like revenge. Pornography occupies a special place in the development of men's sexuality. Almost all men confess having had some exposure to pornography, at least as adolescents; indeed, for many men, the first naked women they see are in pornographic magazines. And pornography has been the site of significant political protest—from the erotophobic right-wing who consider pornography to be as degrading to human dignity as birth control information, homosexuality, and abortion to radical feminist campaigns that see pornography as a vicious expression of misogyny, on par with rape, spousal abuse, and genital mutilation.

While the right wing's efforts rehearsed America's discomfort with all things sexual, the radical feminist critique of pornography transformed the political debate, arguing that when men looked at pornographic images of naked women, they were actually participating in a culturewide hatred and contempt for women. Pornographic images are about the subordination of women; pornography "makes sexism sexy," in the words of antiporn activist John Stoltenberg. These are not fictional representations of fantasy; these are documentaries of rape and torture, performed for men's sexual arousal. Here is one pornographic director and actor, commenting on his "craft":

My whole reason for being in the [pornography] Industry is to satisfy the desire of the men in the world who basically don't much care for women and want to see the men in my Industry getting even with the women they couldn't have when they were growing up. . . . So when we come on a woman's face or somewhat brutalize her sexually, we're getting even for their lost dreams. I believe this. I've heard audiences cheer me when I do something foul on screen. When I've strangled a person or sodomized a person or brutalized a person, the audience is cheering my action, and then when I've fulfilled my warped desire, the audience applauds. (Stoller, 1985:31)

The claims of antipornography feminists—that pornography causes rape or that it numbs us to the real effect of real violence in women's lives—have been difficult to demonstrate empirically. Few studies have shown such an empirical relationship, though several have documented some modest changes in men's attitudes immediately after exposure to violent pornography (for a fuller discussion and critique of these studies, see Kimmel and Linders). Yet, whether or not there is *any* empirical evidence that pornography alone causes rape or violence, there remains the shocking difference between us: on any given day in the United States, there are men masturbating to images of women enduring sexual torture, genital mutilation, rape, and violence. Surely, this points to a dramatic difference between women's and men's sexualities—one can hardly imagine many women masturbating to reenactments of Lorena Bobbitt's ministrations to her husband. Violence is rarely sexualized for women; that such images can be routine and casual turn-ons for many men should at least give us pause.

The policy implications drawn from research on the impact of pornography square with parallel research on rape, as Nicholas Groth has stated in his conclusion to *Men Who Rape*: "It is not sexual arousal but the arousal of anger that leads to rape." He adds that "pornography does not cause rape; banning it will not stop rape" (1980:224). But such assertions beg the question "Why are men so angry at women?" Everywhere, men are in power, controlling virtually all the economic, political, and social institutions of society. Yet individual men do not feel powerful—far from it. Most men feel powerless and are often angry at women, whom they perceive as having sexual power over them: the power to arouse them and to give or withhold sex. This fuels both sexual fantasies and the desire for revenge.

In this world of constructed perpetual male lust and feelings of powerlessness in the face of women's constructed denial of desire, pornography becomes almost a side issue to the problem of men's anger at women. In one particularly compelling interview in Timothy Beneke's fascinating book *Men on Rape*, a young stockboy in a large corporation describes his rage at women who work with him:

> Let's say I see a woman and she looks really pretty and really clean and sexy, and she's giving off very feminine, sexy vibes. I think "Wow, I would love to make love to her," but I know she's not interested. It's a tease. A lot of times a woman knows that she's looking really good and she'll use that and flaunt it, and it makes me feel like she's laughing at me and I feel degraded. . . .
>
> If I were actually desperate enough to rape somebody it would be from wanting the person, but also it would be a very spiteful thing, just being able to say "I have power over you and I can do anything

I want with you," because really I feel they have power over me just by their presence. Just the fact that they can come up to me and just melt me and make me feel like a dummy makes me want revenge. They have power over me so I want power over them. (1982:81)

If men can see women's beauty and sexuality as so injurious that they can fantasize about rape as a retaliation for harm already committed by women, is it also possible that pornographic fantasies draw from this same reservoir of men's anger? If so, it would seem that men's rage at women, and not its pornographic outlet, ought to be our chief concern.

Pornography is less about the real lives of pornographic actresses than about the viewers' fantasies that their activities provide. Pornography provides a world of fantasy to male viewers—a world of sexual plenty, a world in which women say no, but really mean yes (or say yes in the first place), a world of complete sexual abandon, a world of absolute sexual freedom, a world in which gorgeous and sexy women are eager to have sex with us, a world in which we, and our partners, are always sexually satisfied. The pornographic utopia is a world of abundance, abandon, and autonomy—a world, in short, utterly unlike the one we inhabit. (I have often wondered if it is a world we would like to inhabit if only we could, or if that world is too threatening to attempt to call it into existence.) In our jobs, men's sense of autonomy and control has historically decreased. In the sexual marketplace, men feel vulnerable to women's power of rejection. Most men do not make enough money, have enough workplace control, or get enough sex. Many men feel themselves to be "feminized" in the workplace—dependent, helpless, powerless. Most men don't feel especially good about themselves, living lives of "quiet desperation," as Henry David Thoreau so compactly put it. Pornographic fantasy is a revenge against the real world of men's lives. To transform those fantasies requires that we also transform that reality.

REFERENCES

Beneke, Tim. 1982. *Men on Rape.* New York: St. Martin's Press.

Groth, Nicholas A. 1980. *Men Who Rape: The Psychology of the Offender.* New York: Plenum Publishing Corporation.

Kimmel, Michael S. and Linders, Annulla. 1986. Does Censorship Make a Difference? An Aggregate Empirical Analysis of Pornography and Rape. *Journal of Psychology and Human sexuality, 8*(3), pp. 1-20.

Stoller, Robert. 1985. *Porn: Observing the Erotic Imagination.* New Haven, CT: Yale University Press.

47

My Karma Has Just Run Over My Dogma: Addressing the Sexual Conflicts of Feminist Men

David Steinberg

Ironically enough, one of the clearest expressions I have heard of the sexual dilemma facing men who define themselves as feminist came from an outspokenly feminist woman. She was speaking about her own difficulty in integrating her feminist beliefs with her sexual desires.

"I don't know what I'm supposed to do," she said early in the 1980s, about having intercourse with her male partner. "If he's on top, he's dominating me. If I'm on top, I'm servicing him. My feminism and my sexuality are both essential to me. I'm not willing to choose one over the other. I don't know what to do."

Subjecting one's sexual desire to the rigors of ideological political analysis is both an important undertaking and a tricky piece of work. It's important because how we think of sex, and how we think of ourselves as sexual people, has real political meaning, especially with regard to how power is distributed among men and women. It is also tricky because we have such strongly ingrained tendencies to interpret sex negatively and because once the watchful eyes of the internalized sex police are mounted on your shoulder, passion and spontaneity have a way of going out the window. And, let's face it, sex, no matter how correctly micromanaged, is nowhere without passion and spontaneity.

I have a lot of sympathy for the sexual dilemmas of men who pay serious attention to feminist issues. I have strongly identified with the feminist movement since the late 1960s, not only in terms of that movement's analysis of the unjust power imbalances between men and women in society, but also for

---

An earlier version of "My Karma Has Just Run Over My Dogma" appeared in *Spectator,* September 25, 1998, *41*(2), issue 1043, pp. 5-9.

its radical redefinition of male and female gender roles. At the personal level, I have been inspired by feminism, not out of guilt over my previously un- enlightened consciousness, but because feminism offered me both the oppor- tunity and the insight to become the kind of man that I had always wanted to be, but that traditional American culture regards, essentially, as unmanly. Being rough, tough, stoic, able to leap tall buildings in a single bound, fight the good wars, be the main provider of family income, always know how to protect the poor little woman from the nastiness of the world, and die at an early age—well, it wasn't really my thing.

So I was delighted when a movement came along that called upon both women and men to see through the gender roles handed them by society and to begin to put things together differently. Rather than seeing the empowerment of women as a threat, I saw it as a relief, even if it meant giving up all sorts of male privilege. Even now, when the term feminist is more associated with man hating than with the struggle for the equal rights of women, I hold on to the notion of myself as a feminist man quite fondly. I would rather work to preserve the original meaning of the word than turn it over to the media wolves to malign. Call me sentimental. . . .

When my wife joined a women's consciousness-raising group and the lightbulbs of seeing things in new ways began going on in her head week after week, I experienced a kind of secondary redefinition of myself by osmosis. Every time she saw through some traditional definition of what it meant to be a woman, I got to see through something about traditional definitions of being a man. It was exciting. I read feminist books one after another. The liberation of women from traditional roles was aligned with, not against, my own liberation.

Eventually, it dawned on me that instead of simply envying my wife the support she got from meeting with and talking to other women about mutual concerns, I could myself get together with men who were in many ways like me and enjoy many of the same benefits. I tried to organize a men's group for the first time in 1970. After a couple of false starts, I found my way to a group of men who were actually able to talk honestly to one another about big, unresolved issues in our lives: the masculinity bugaboo, careers, fathering, relationships with women, a wide range of unacknowl- edged fears and insecurities, loneliness, loss, competition and fear of being vulnerable with other men, sexual orientation, sex. Sex for real—what we liked and didn't like, what we understood and didn't understand, how we felt good and not so good about ourselves—not simply showing off to convince ourselves we were okay. Being able to talk sincerely with other men about these issues was like taking a new lease on life, as thousands of men were about to discover.

Expanding beyond our immediate group of eight (three of us still have men's group on Monday nights), I discovered the national Conferences on Men and Masculinity and the California Men's Gatherings, where these sorts of issues were discussed and explored with a good deal of insight, innovation, caring, generosity, and mutual respect.

Unfortunately, in their early years, both the national conferences and the CMGs tended to operate in the spirit of men's auxiliaries to the women's movement, rather than bringing feminist men together around their own issues and concerns. The idea that (oppressive) men even had the right to have issues separate from those of (oppressed) women was considered controversial. There was a strong ethos that everything women did was inherently good, whereas everything men did was inherently bad, or at least severely suspect—heterosexual men, that is; the struggles of gay men were lauded in much the same spirit as were women's struggles. (At that time, both the California and the national gatherings were about equally divided between gay and heterosexual men. Bisexual awareness had not yet emerged. Indeed, one of the finer accomplishments of these gatherings was that they brought gay and heterosexual men together in a way that both groups could trust.) I was stunned when one man tried to persuade me, in all seriousness, that all women's anger toward men was justified, while all men's anger toward women constituted misogyny. This was, in fact, an accepted point of view in *Changing Men,* the main journal of the movement.

One result of this four-legs-good, two-legs-bad attitude about women and men was strong encouragement for men to distance themselves from all things masculine. Masculinity was seen, rather simply, as the culture of patriarchy, the culture that enforced male dominance and the disempowerment of women. Indeed, one of the first books of essays that came out of the men's movement was titled *Unbecoming Men* (1971). There was no sense of irony, pain, or ambivalence about what it meant to encourage all men to put themselves at odds with such a fundamental, essential aspect of who they were. It remained for Robert Bly, several years later, coming from well outside the culture of feminist men, to point out that what needed to be overthrown was not masculinity itself, but the distortion of vibrant masculinity that traditional, patriarchal gender roles represented.

The double binds created by turning so severely against one's essential nature have been devastating to feminist men in many ways, but nowhere as powerfully as with regard to their sexuality. Since all things masculine were to be discarded, or at least examined with extreme distrust, it's hardly surprising that heterosexual male sexual desire was subjected to the most intense, hostile, and devastatingly literal of critiques. If the essential error of fundamentalism, as Joseph Campbell argues, is thinking of religion literally rather than metaphorically, then heterosexual feminist men were engaged in nothing less than a fundamentalist inquisition into every corner of their sexual existence.

Constantly looking over their shoulders for evidence of power imbalance, patriarchal assumptions, male dominance, and objectification of women, how could feminist men ever relax, be spontaneous, and trust what their bodies were telling them? One man confided to me with great anguish that when he and his woman partner were making love, he actually enjoyed looking at her breasts. Was he objectifying her? he wondered. Was he being, essentially, pornographic?

At a workshop on sex addiction, I found myself paired with a man who was convinced he was a sex addict because he thought about sex almost every day—this from a man in his midtwenties who did not have a sexual partner at the time. When I suggested that it seemed quite natural to me that he would be thinking about sex when he didn't have any regular sexual outlet—that I happily thought about sex every day and I did have a sexual partner—he was both relieved and amazed. The idea that thinking about sex was natural had never occurred to him.

At one conference, I listened as John Stoltenberg, one of the foremost male antipornography activists, argued that male sexual arousal was fundamentally the same biological process as the urge to kill—both being accompanied by rushes of adrenaline, increased heartbeat and respiration rates, and a generally aggressive attitude. Hundreds of well-meaning men nodded their silent agreement.

Flagellating themselves for having any sexual desire at all, constantly on the lookout for impure images and thoughts, using gatherings of the faithful as opportunities to confess their sins, heterosexual feminist men had more in common sexually with born-again Christians than with any group of leftist progressives. Watching these conscientious men, whom I cared about so much, turn against their sexuality was excruciating. Something needed to be done.

Working with a close woman friend who was what we would now call a sex-positive feminist, I began to organize conference workshops where sexual issues and dilemmas could be examined from a more sympathetic, less fearful, less nearsighted—yet still strongly feminist—perspective. One workshop was essentially a guided fantasy in which I asked participants to envision "the most erotic man in the world," observe him from a distance, then move into his body and take on his movements, his sense of himself, his way of being in the world. It was an exercise that everyone enjoyed; it gave a clear sense that there was such a thing as an erotic masculinity with which these men could identify.

Another workshop, titled "Pornography, Eroticism, and Sexual Fantasy," was an opportunity to talk to one another about our sexual fantasies without having to worry about being judged or ridiculed. As facilitators, we emphasized the difference between fantasy and reality, reminded people that becoming aroused by an imagined sexual act did not mean that you were about to perform that act in the real world, and noted that no one gets hurt when someone has a fantasy, no matter how "politically incorrect" that fantasy might be. We pointed out that the most common sexual fantasy among women (even feminist women) was of being raped, but that this didn't mean that women actually wanted to be raped. We talked about the importance of honoring both our fantasies and our sexual feelings, even when those aspects of our sexuality came up in unexpected ways.

We then went around the circle and asked each man to describe a favorite fantasy or a favorite image from a sexual film or magazine. One by one the stories came out, cautiously at first, but growing more bold as people saw that they really would not be criticized for their honesty. When we had gone completely around the circle, we asked people to speak again, this time telling something they had been afraid to talk about during the first round.

One man, an exceedingly gentle and well-known member of the gathering's organizing committee, confessed, with considerable agitation, that his most intense arousal came from masturbating to photos of women being cut with knives and razor blades. He had never before told this to a single soul. He thought he was really sick and didn't know what to do about being so turned on by these violent images. We assured him that getting off on these pictures did not mean he really wanted to cut up women or see them harmed and reminded him that no one was hurt by his fantasy. Perhaps there was something he was deeply angry about, something that he would do well to honor and respect. If having these fantasies bothered him, he could look into it further, perhaps with a therapist, to see what was going on. After he spoke, the level of revelations by others jumped noticeably. (I later learned that this man had been severely humiliated by a group of girls in his early adolescence who pretended to be attracted to him sexually only to then publicly reject and ridicule him for imagining that they would ever be interested in someone like him.) The relief of this man, and others in the group, at being able to talk about forbidden sexual feelings was palpable. Word of the workshop spread through the conference immediately.

I began to develop a reputation at the gatherings as an advocate for the possibility of integrating a vibrant, open, expansive sexual existence with a sincere commitment to feminism. Because I had been part of the organizational core of the gatherings for many years, I had some standing from which to express such a controversial point of view. Other conference leaders disagreed with my sexual outlook, but treated me with respect. I began speaking more about my personal sexual explorations that challenged the prevailing antisexual dogma and generally encouraged people to trust their sexual desires more, to not hold their sexual existence ransom to unrealistic notions of political purity.

At one dinner conversation in the large communal dining area, I was talking with friends about consciously exploring power issues during sex as a kind of psychodramatic experiment. I told how my lover and I had experimented with tying each other down, playing sexual servant to each other, giving complete control of sexual situations over to the other, just to see what feelings were brought up. I talked about how both of us had found these times illuminating and very exciting sexually. This was at a time when information about S/M, bondage, and sexual power play was still limited to a small sexual subculture, and certainly outside the consciousness of these particular men.

By the time I was done, a circle of some thirty men had gathered around and was paying rapt attention to my every word. The idea that power imbalance could be incorporated as an acceptable part of sex play was unheard of in this group, yet all these people were obviously intrigued with the possibility. At least a dozen people later told me they were going to try this with their women partners when they got home—if their partners were willing, of course.

We put together a multimedia performance piece that combined readings of erotic poems and stories with a series of short slide shows, set to music. The readings and the images varied from sensual to sexually explicit, from humorous to passionate, from descriptive to symbolic, from playful to disturbing. The message of the show was that sexuality is politically and ethically acceptable in many different forms; that not all arousing sexual material embodies the sexist assumptions of commercial pornography; that it's possible to enjoy sexual entertainment collectively and in public, be true to one's political and ethical beliefs, and also be free of secrecy and shame.

We called the show "Celebration of Eros" and performed it at one of the California gatherings. The response was so overwhelmingly positive that we took the show to men's conferences in other parts of the country as well. As we performed the show in different contexts, we experienced, over and over again, the catharsis of men realizing that the core of their sexual desire was not a matter of wanting to harm or subjugate women, that the wish to be sexually empowered as men was not antifeminist, that there were forms of male empowerment that were not antithetical to women's empowerment. The relief and gratitude so many men (and women) felt at being released from the sexual double binds of an overly rigid, literal, fundamentally antisexual political critique were extraordinary. Encouraged by the response to "Celebration of Eros," I went to work putting the same message into book form and published *Erotic by Nature,* a collection of erotic and sexual photography, fiction, poetry, and drawings, in 1988.

The struggle of feminist men (and women) to make sense out of their sexual feelings in the context of their politics is ongoing and is also understandably difficult. The sexual imagery of the dominant culture, and that culture's very concept of sex itself, is as suffused with sexism as are other aspects of society. In many ways, the sexual assumptions we are taught from birth are intended to keep women from respecting their feelings and natures, and also from becoming strong and free from dependency on men. It is equally true, however, that the antisexual assumptions of society are also designed to keep women from realizing the power and independence that full sexual expression offers.

It is important to look at our sexual feelings and desires as men with as much political care as we examine both the other aspects of our lives and society in general. However, the erotic world cannot be understood or directed with simpleminded, rational, or dogmatic platitudes that interpret sexual gestures literally and superficially, without addressing their underlying meanings. If the spirit of Eros is to be honored, it must be addressed on its own terms, irrational and untidy as those terms may be.

48

Pornography: Addiction and Rescue— A Conversation with Caleb Armes

Simon Sheppard

Caleb Armes, a thirty-four-year-old living in Cambridge, Massachusetts, was well known as an academic. He taught at Harvard, and his book Metafictions and Mendacities *(1992) has become one of the standard texts in the field. Several years ago, he left his career to deal full-time with the issue of pornography in men's lives. He is the co-founder of Men Incorporating Decency In Change.*

On a rainy February afternoon, Caleb Armes showed me into his cluttered apartment, offered me a cup of tea, and sat down with me to talk about men and their relationship to pornography. Far from the firebrand portrayed by the mass media, Armes is actually a gentle, engaging figure, thin, sandy-haired, and bespectacled. He spoke softly, but insistently.

"I think it's important to say what I am not," he began. "I am not an antiporn activist in the Andrea Dworkin mode. While I think it's possible that consuming pornography may influence some men to harm women, there's just no hard empirical evidence to prove it. It's the harm pornography does to men themselves that I'm concerned with. My work with literally hundreds of men addicted to pornography, as well as my own experience, has shown me that the use of pornography is as much a symptom as a cause of problems." He grew more animated, stabbing the air with his forefinger for emphasis. "The men who compulsively use pornography are alienated, frustrated, lonely men. And the breakdown in our society has made them more so."

"So you don't think," I asked, "that pornography can be used for a bit of harmless recreation?"

For inspiring this piece, thanks to Leo Enzlin and to some dweeby guy from England.

"Recreation, sure. But 'harmless'? Focusing one's sexual desire on the image of a stranger in a magazine or video, or on some story that someone made up and sold—that's clearly dysfunctional. It's a substitute for relating to another person, and it drives the porn addict deeper into his isolation."

"But, Caleb, there are some who would argue that the use of pornography actually has liberating effects, providing a safe space for people to validate their own desires . . ."

"Validate?" From behind thick lenses, his blue eyes looked intensely at me. "Masturbating to pornography isn't about validation. It's about shame. That's what the men I work with have experienced. Shame. Secrecy. No one is proud of using porn."

"Caleb, earlier you mentioned your own experience. Don't you think you might be projecting your own discomfort with sex onto everyone else?"

"Oh sure, I've had some conflicts about my sexuality," Armes said. "I'm no different from anyone else. But depending upon commercially produced porn to define my sexuality only made matters worse."

I sipped my tea. "But not everyone is in a relationship. Not everyone can find a sexual partner whenever they want to."

"No, of course not. And there's nothing wrong with masturbating. I wank off." He briefly laid a hand on my knee. "I'm not ashamed of it."

An image of Caleb Armes sitting alone in a darkened room, hard-on in his hand, flitted through my mind. "But you don't use pornography when you . . . wank off?"

"No, of course not, not anymore. I try to get in touch with myself, with who I am, instead of depending on some pornographic crutch. Who needs to read about somebody else masturbating, when I can focus instead on my own pleasure?" He smiled. "I like to take my time, strip down, rub my body with oils, lie back with my eyes closed, stroke myself, get in touch with my own body."

For the first time in the interview, I realized that Caleb Armes was, in fact, a rather attractive man. Not my type, perhaps—I usually go for bigger, more masculine types—but I found myself picturing his slim, nude body gleaming with oil.

"When I masturbate, I celebrate my own sexuality. Without shame, without guilt." I noticed that Armes's right hand had moved to his torso, was stroking his chest through his light blue shirt. "How do you like to wank? Do you use pornography?"

I was nonplussed, not least because I found myself beginning to get aroused. "I didn't come here to discuss my own sexuality," I said weakly.

"There's no reason to feel ashamed," the slim man said, still stroking his chest. "We've been brought up in a society full of puritanical, Judeo-Christian crap. We're trained to feel sexual guilt. But the answer to that, to all the pressures in our lives, isn't to compulsively escape through pornography. More tea?"

"Yes, please." My dick was getting hard.

"What I want is not to pathetically sit there, my trousers around my ankles, and look at mass-produced imagery," he continued. "What I want is to feel the actual warmth of another person's flesh. The smell of sex, real sex. Don't you?" His hand began to move perilously close to the waistband of his trousers.

"But not everyone can have that, right?"

His fingers had slipped into the waist of his trousers. Was he aware of what he was doing? ". . . is powerlessness. Pornography disempowers men. Men use porn when they're bored, frustrated. Whether we're having sex with ourselves or with another person, it's important to . . ."

This interview wasn't going precisely the way I'd anticipated it would. I slipped a hand into my pocket and rearranged my swelling dick. I tried to be subtle about it, but Armes caught my move, his myopic blue eyes sliding down toward my crotch.

"I'm not saying porn is evil. I'm not saying we should ban pornography. I just want to create a space where we can look critically at how men use pornography, the reasons we turn to it, the place it occupies in our lives." His eyes still hadn't left my crotch.

What a little cock tease. What an opinionated, argumentative, cute little cock tease. He leaned back in his chair and shut his eyes. "I'm not after some quick, furtive wank. I want to luxuriate in who I am, in my body, my desires. It's only since I gave up the compulsive use of pornography that I truly learned to masturbate."

I'll bet, I thought.

"Caleb, if we could steer the conversation back to the group you work with . . ."

But his hand was deep inside his loose-fitting khaki trousers now. "No guilt," he moaned. "No shame. No . . . no alienation."

I gulped down my second cup of tea. I wasn't going to be able to stand this much longer.

"Would you like to see what I learned?" Armes asked.

"What?"

"Would you like to see what I've learned about masturbation?" But he was already unbuckling his belt.

I turned off my tape recorder.

He unzipped his pants, revealing snowy white boxers. Reaching into the fly, he brought out a beautifully hard, surprisingly large cock. With just two fingers and his thumb, he began stroking the swollen shaft.

"Come unbutton my shirt," he said.

"What?" But I'd heard what he said.

"I think you heard what I said." He was right. "You like watching me play with myself, don't you? Now come over here and unbutton my shirt." I did as he asked, standing over him, going down the row of buttons until my fingers were just inches away from his hard dick.

"What are you thinking?" asked Caleb Armes.

"I . . . I don't know. . . . I'm thinking about what a nice dick you have." He smiled, eyes still closed. "Good answer. Now, stroke my chest."

I pulled open his blue cotton shirt and ran my hands over his chest, the patch of sandy brown chest hair, circling my fingertips around his flat pink nipples. Then my touch headed south, down over his flat belly.

"That's fine, but don't touch my cock. Not yet." I wouldn't have dreamed of doing so. "You see what I mean. What we men need is touch, not some page of pornography. Now suck on my nipples."

My lips quickly nuzzled the hair on his chest, seeking out, finding, teasing Caleb's nipple.

"Mmm." He moaned. "Harder."

I started to unzip my fly.

"I didn't tell you you could jack off, did I? Not yet. Not yet." I was pissed off, kind of, but I obeyed. "Now help me pull my pants down—but don't touch my dick."

My hands got so close to his crotch that I could feel the heat radiating from his big, hard cock, but I did as I was told, pulling his pants and underwear down to his ankles, revealing trim, hairy legs.

"You see that bottle of oil on the table? Hand it to me."

He flipped open the cap and let a trickle of oil roll down over his naked torso, all the way down to his pubic bush.

"Now, take the oil and go back to your chair. Take your dick out, get some oil on it, and jack off—while you're watching me."

And so I sat there in the book-filled living room of Caleb Armes, antiporn activist, and jacked off while I watched him playing with himself. He was right: he did seem to be enjoying himself immensely, stroking his chest, his belly, his thighs, always circling back to his big, hard dick, luxuriating in its thickness, its swollen heft. Every time my own hand made contact with the head of my cock, I felt like I was going to shoot.

"Now, isn't this better than masturbating to some picture of a total stranger? Don't you like the way my body looks, so close to you, all oiled up and hard and hot?"

"Yeah, Caleb, I like it a lot." It was the truth. I could feel my cum-filled balls tightening, all ready to blow a load.

"You want to come?" he asked.

"Yeah, yeah, Caleb, I want to come."

"And you see what I mean about porn alienating us men from ourselves?" His hand was stroking furiously away at his cock.

"Yeah, I do." I could barely get the words out.

"And you like watching me?" One hand was down between his legs now, playing with his hole, pushing slippery fingers into himself, his eyes shut tighter.

"Yes, Caleb. Yes, I do."

"Then come on. Give me that load."

And I squeezed down hard on my cock flesh, till I could feel myself going past the point of control, until one last load of precum oozed out of my cock, until my hips bucked upward, until I shot streams of spunk high into the air.

"Fuck," yelled Caleb Armes. "FUCKFUCKFUCKMOTHERFUCKER!" And, fingers deep inside his ass, he shot thick ropes of cum all over his oiled-up belly and chest.

When he'd stopped panting, he opened his eyes and said, "C'mere." I knelt beside him. He took his spunk-wet fingers and gently rubbed cum over my face, on my lips. I licked my mouth clean. He reached around the back of my head and drew my face to his. Our mouths met in a long, deep, very male kiss. It seemed to last forever, though it might have only been a minute or two.

At last, Caleb Armes drew his lips from mine, leaned back, and, glasses still on, looked deeply into my eyes.

"Any more questions?" he asked.

49

Uncomfortable Questions: Black Men and Heterosexual Commercial Sex

Larry M. Gant

I must say, however, with regards to the SF [San Francisco] street scene, I experienced something that really pissed me off. Since I was staying down on Market St., I walked to the O'Farrell—a good walk, but not unmanageable. Along the way, I passed the main streetwalker areas as described in earlier posts. However, both on Tuesday night and Wednesday night, I couldn't even get a hooker to talk to me. I am a professional African American, late twenties, over 6′ and 200 lbs., pretty good-looking and well-spoken. However, each time I even made eye contact with a woman, she turned her back, and not even one acknowledged my presence when asking if they were going out.

I've had extensive experience with the street scene, so I'm pretty sensitive to not trying to look or act like vice, and not coming off like a pimp. I've even had women in some cities tell me straight up, "I don't date black men." Most of them have told me they have had bad experiences with them, and refuse to take a chance. While I think it sucks that they put me in the same category as some assholes who treated them poorly, I can at least appreciate where they're coming from. But in SF, there must have been over twenty very attractive streetwalkers I saw on Tuesday and different ones on Wednesday (trying to stay away from Thursday, as others have advised it's vice night), and not one even spoke to me. While this could be an aberration, it seemed pretty clear to me that black men were not going to be served. I saw women coming out of hotels still fixing themselves, I saw white men walk up to the same women and take them to hotels, I saw their pimps exchanging conversation with them, and there is no doubt in my mind that this was a classic case of racial prejudice.

I know WSG [World Sex Guide] is not about these types of issues, but I think it's important for other African Americans to know the deal before you head out in SF. In 1996, in arguably the most liberal city in arguably the most liberal state in arguably the world's most liberal country, it might as well have been the 1950s in Alabama, and I might as well have been asking Governor Wallace for a college scholarship. I'm used to dealing with this type of stereotypical prejudice in every other aspect of daily life, but this was shocking.

anonymous comments
from an African-American male participant
in the World Sex Guide (www.paranoia.com)

Since before the founding of the American republic, miscegenation laws have been created and enforced, black women have been routinely raped by white men as part of the spoils system of both legal and de facto slavery, and black men have been regularly lynched, castrated, and murdered at even the slightest imagined suggestion that they wanted sex with white women. In modern pop culture, as well as in congressional debates concerning welfare and the like, black men are portrayed as ravenous sexual beasts who'll fuck any "ho" they can and who father as frequently (and irresponsibly) as possible. With all the controversy surrounding sex and race, it's quite interesting to observe the extreme lack of discussion addressing race and racism in commercial sex. It's also curious to note the near total absence of black male voices on the topic, despite the fact that African-American men do indeed buy pornography, pay for phone sex, and hire prostitutes (or at least attempt to). The brother cited at he chapter's start is to be commended for his courage; however, his is one of the few voices raising the issue of black experiences with the sex industry.

In many ways, the dearth of black male voices talking about commercial sex highlights the difficulty African-American men have in talking about *any* type of sex outside of the traditionally bounded monogamous couple. The deliberate portrayal of black men as hypersexual thugs has convinced most black men to remain silent on these matters, lest they reinforce the stereotype. Speaking out on such a taboo topic as commercial sex entails great personal as well as cultural risk: who wants the burden of being branded as a lust-obsessed threat?

Yet, although black men may be reluctant to write about black sexuality and commercial sex for fear of being identified as another example of an oversexed black man, the stereotype can cut both ways. Some brothers may also get a thrill at being perceived as so sexually powerful, particularly as black men have so few other pathways to prove their "manhood" and self-worth. At times, some brothers consciously and unconsciously work this stereotype to their advantage (to the extent this gets them anything). Being perceived as "from the 'hood"—even when you're not—automatically turns one into a powerful and dangerous entity, particularly in the eyes of many whites. This image, although frequently damaging, is not without its uses. Black men may feel that paying for sex or buying pornography detracts from this black male sex stereotype; after all, how many "sex studs" have to pay for it? So then, there are at least two reasons for the lack of African-American male voices: fear of being stereotyped and fear of being removed (partially) from the limited image of power that this stereotype communicates.

A third reason black men may be reluctant to talk about commercial sex has to do with the racial realities of the sex industry. Although women of color are much more frequently arrested and incarcerated for prostitution than white women, white women dominate the sex industry at all levels except in massage parlors and (perhaps) on the street. Due to both the greater number of white women in the United States and the differential harassment of commercial sex workers of color, most prostitute women are white, as are most strippers and most porn stars; meanwhile, phone sex operators of all ethnicities are typically told to sound as "white" as possible. Thus, unless a black man is particularly motivated in seeking out women of color, it is likely that he will find himself having sex with, or gazing desirously at, a white woman. Lusting for a white woman is a potentially dangerous venture for black men, as the savage beating and lynching of Emmett Till in 1955 in Mississippi for allegedly "whistling at a white woman" attests.* The good brother is not likely to boast too loudly about his commercial sex escapades; after all, he never knows who is in the audience.

The horny brother who finds himself lusting for a white woman is vulnerable to challenges from within the black community as well. The line of reasoning goes something like this: "If he desires or has sex with a white woman, then he prefers white women in general, which means he

---

*Emmett Till was a fourteen-year-old black male staying in Mississippi. In 1955, he made international news when he was discovered dead in a river, beaten so severely that he resembled a floating log more than a human being. Several white males claimed responsibility for the act, citing his flirting and whistling at a white female as the rationale for the act. In reality, Till, a friendly, almost naive teen visiting from the North, was likely just waving and saying hi to the white female. Despite the fact that his killers were well known, no one was ever charged with his death, and the coroner's report listed the cause of death as "accidental drowning."

doesn't like black women, which means he doesn't like black people, which means he doesn't like himself, which means he will never contribute anything to the struggle for black liberation; the brother is truly lost and a traitor to his race; he can never be trusted by black people." This line of closed-loop thinking is very difficult to unravel, but in truth, the links simply do not follow one another. Many black men have some version of this thinking running around in their brains, leaving them feeling confused and shamed if they start seeing too many white women to whom they are attracted. Even if the good brother is relatively unconcerned with race and is simply playing the odds, he is vulnerable to being condemned for his choices.

If, on the other hand, our lusty brother happens to desire only black women, he, nevertheless, may be deemed too perverse or "politically unaware" to be accepted by the black community, a community he likely relies upon dearly. I sometimes notice a tendency to demand more noble and "politically virtuous" behavior from members of oppressed communities than their nonoppressed counterparts. Concomitantly, there is a tendency to judge members of oppressed communities more harshly when they engage in exploitive behaviors. Hence, Mike Tyson becomes more of a monster than Marv Albert, and a black man talking about commercial sex becomes more "sexist" than a white man doing the same. Leaving aside for the moment the question of exploitation in the sex industry (a reality for many, if not all, sex workers), it is nevertheless true that this double standard places a greater burden on black men than white.

For all of these reasons, it is extremely rare to find writings such as this one, in which a black male discusses commercial sex in the United States. In fact, I hope I'm wrong, but I fear this essay may be close to the only black male voice discussing commercial sex in recent years. A pretty extensive literature review from 1970 to 1996 yielded no published articles, manuscripts, or essays on the topic, not even in *Players* magazine (the self-proclaimed "*Playboy* for black men"). White men simply do not have to question the racial consequences of their sexual acts so minutely; they can easily fetishize racial difference and still embody the image of a powerful (white) masculinity; no one will even raise an eyebrow as long as the all-white family is not "disgraced" by the suggestion of marriage. Although white men may experience shame in speaking about commercial sex, they simply do not have to engage in any of these same mental gymnastics concerning race. For black men, however, the simple process of "gettin' some" through commercial sex can raise a very painful and difficult set of racial problematics.

Most black men I have spoken with, in fact, prefer black women. Yet go to any adult magazine shop, and at least 90 percent of the material focuses exclusively upon images of white women. Both soft-core and hard-core magazines are dominated by images of white women, as are the fetish and S/M-themed magazines. Black women are only occasionally featured in mainstream adult magazines, and one can count the number of black-themed magazines on one hand and have fingers leftover! This lack of diversity means that pictures and models are recycled continuously. *Players* magazine, for example, routinely runs pictures that, shall we say, are "classics." None of the black-themed magazines include images of actual sex, while the "mainstream" (i.e., "white") hard-core magazines feature an interracial couple at most, never an all-black duo or trio. If a black man prefers fetish or S/M material, he has virtually no choice but to view white women.

Most of the adult videos that are available either focus exclusively on whites or include racial messages that insult the sensibilities of black men. The representations in most porn movies remind many black men of the social fallout from slavery that still characterizes much of U.S. life: the racist interior life of whites; the lack of interior life for blacks; the racially degraded yet always available black women; the supremely worshipped white woman; and the sexually superior but socially inferior black man. Many black men make great effort to ignore these racial messages as they view pornographic videos and try instead to focus their attention upon the sexual behavior. Their other possibility is to view the more limited selection of "urban" (i.e., "black-directed") videos; however, these again have lower production values and draw on a limited number of models.

In relation to prostitution, black men face the potential for outright rejection, just as the brother at the beginning of this essay discovered. The reluctance appears to be due less to unpleasant experiences with black customers (no one has any negative experience with white clients, right?) than to racist beliefs. In my discussions with both prostitutes and prostitute researchers, I have repeatedly heard derisive and racist comments made concerning black tricks. We also know—if only by anecdotal report—that female sex workers of nearly all nationalities tend not to want to service African-American males. In other discussions I've had with former street-walkers, many of them told me of the unpleasant repercussions they would face from both pimps and colleagues alike if it was known they had paid sex with a black man. In the absence of an open conversation concerning these issues, black men will find themselves without any guidance as they enter the world of commercial sex, guidance that might in fact tell them some important things, not only about the racial realities of the sex industry, but about the need to treat sex workers of all nationalities with respect.

Black males have a need to develop and expand their voices on the issue of sexuality and sexual expression in general, with commercial sex being one aspect of that conversation. The voices need not reflect some mythical "black consensus," but should open up an authentic dialogue, one that is long overdue. If black men continue to allow these issues to be defined and written by others—white males, white females, black females—the result will not accurately reflect the experiences of black men, or—more likely—will entirely ignore black male experience. As black men, we have to find our voices, express them, understand the risks, and continue the dialogue, risks be damned. Otherwise, we collude in the erasure of our actual sexual lives in favor of the myths and silences that currently exist.

PART IV:
INSPIRATION

50

Rings of Orgasms

Frank Moore

rub me deeply into you
lose myself into you
rub my cock, hard or soft,
on your pleasure bone,
feeling hairy prickling pleasure
clicking up the intensity
deep inside my balls,
a deep laugh is tickling
its way from deep inside my belly,
a heart sob is pushing outward from my throat.
rings of orgasms,
each melting into the next . . .
not climaxes . . .
not charlie horse ends
with a shared cigarette . . .
but a daisy chain of orgasms
everlasting, neverending.
smell your skin
breathe you deeply into me.
suck me deeply so i am now a part of you,
so we are no more,
so we are one body
rubbing melting skin
goose bumps chills skin orgasms.

"Rings of Orgasms" was originally written in 1993 for *Orgasm Scrapbook,* a video by Annie Sprinkle (not yet completed). It has also appeared in *The Flashing Astonisher,* Spring 1998, and *Lucid Moon,* June 1998, volume 22.

orgasm is death within pleasure
where control . . . even who we are . . .
vanishes,
and we float skin rubbing at
the heart of the universe,
our combined body orgasm pumping out
visions and dreams and life and light.
within the rings of orgasm,
we are the universal heart
pumping magic,
nursing everything.
we were conceived within orgasm.
we were brought into this world
within the birth orgasm.
we were nursed from mother's orgasm.
we will go out in the orgasm of death.
live within, dream within, love within
the rings of orgasm.
rub me deeply into you
lose myself into you
rub my cock, hard or soft,
on your pleasure bone,
feeling hairy prickling pleasure
clicking up the intensity
deep inside my balls,
a deep laugh is tickling
its way from deep inside my belly,
a heart sob is pushing outward from my throat.
rings of orgasms,
each melting into the next . . .

51

Passionate Love for Christ: Out of the Closet, into the Streets

Robert E. Goss

From my earliest memories as a child, I always felt different and could not name my feelings. I loved boys as a boy. When I read Homer's *Iliad,* I found myself moved by the emotional depth of Achilles' relationship with Patroculus. In class, my teacher pointed out the virtue of their friendship. Friendship! Yes, they were best friends, but there was more than friendship. There was a passionate connection, a model of passionate love between two men. Somehow, I intuited, this love story named me.

I was raised with the normal Catholic guilt about sex. The Church perfected its rituals and social mechanisms for transmitting guilt about the body and sexuality. It encouraged a regimen of bodily control and a vigilance for any sexual feelings. Confession served to reinforce and underline Catholic control of sexuality, symbolically restoring sinful individuals to the community. The confessional was the dark box where God's surveillance was intensely encountered, and the ritual was an instrument of terror for pre-Vatican II Catholic youth.

As puberty arrived, I experienced my first orgasm, with all its terrifying feelings of pleasure and guilt. I learned to masturbate with neighborhood boys in ritual circle jerks, the older boys demonstrating. I imitated their actions, and my first orgasm felt wonderfully pleasurable. Nothing that pleasurable was without a price. The downside of what appeared to be pleasurable was the accompanying Catholic guilt.

No sin was more terrifying to confess to the priest than impure actions. The confessor would ask further probing questions. "Alone or with others?" If I said "alone," the confessor would ask what I did. I, begrudgingly, would tell him. He would lecture me how much God loved me and how much I saddened God with my sin. Priests were experts in making you feel guilty, blaming Christ's death on your masturbation.

Despite my sinfulness, I sensed that Jesus loved me. And I genuinely loved him and felt his presence also. The Church, however, represented him as the crucified savior who would judge all sexual transgressions. I loved Jesus and wanted to follow him. I wanted to be at one with him. What I really wanted was to make love with him, but I was too guilt-ridden to admit this to myself. I knew I was not attracted to women, nor did I want to marry. As a Catholic, the only option I had was the religious life.

I entered the Jesuits a very emotionally conflicted and guilt-ridden young man. The battle for control over my body intensified throughout college and my years in the Society of Jesus. The ideal Jesuit was to cultivate a lifeless body by repressing passions. When I started Jesuit novitiate, I immersed myself in the body-negative attitudes and practices of mortification preserved by the Jesuits. I was introduced to the flagellum, or the whip. There were nights in which the novice master or his assistant would place a sign on the bulletin board reading *hoc nocte,* which means "tonight" in Latin. The sign indicated that you were to whip your body with the flage. I took flagellation seriously, since I was young and naive. I would strip naked, and I would whip my shoulders and back in devotion and love to Jesus. I never drew blood, but did leave bruises on my back. I whipped myself in identification with Jesus and in love for him, but my piety subverted the practice. In prayer, I imagined a naked Jesus as a muscular, handsome, bearded man embracing me, and I became easily aroused. I envisioned burying my face in his hairy-matted chest and then desperately fought my sexual fantasies. Catholic asceticism aimed at repressing sexual impulses, maintaining flaccid penises, and creating lifeless bodies, but Catholic piety stimulated an erotic love for Jesus.

The body was the Catholic site of temptation and sexual pleasure, the gateway that Satan could use to tempt me away from God. Medieval body-deficit or body-mortified attitudes were still in place during this formative period. We were still permitted to use the "chains" *(catenulae),* a chain-link device with barbs and spikes turned inward, very much like barbed wire fence. The chain was worn either around the upper thigh or around the waist under the belt. The barbs pricked the flesh, but normally not enough to break the skin, only to irritate the affected skin.

One morning, I left the chapel from morning visit while still wearing the chain. A novice friend violated another novitiate rule—"don't touch"— grabbing me and picking me up around the waist. I screamed! The chain painfully broke the skin around my waist. My body was punctured. This first experience of bodily penetration left me questioning the value of the chain and the mortification of the body. Why does God hate the body? Why have Catholic attitudes and practices refused sensuousness and the pleasures of the body? The Church felt that it was necessary to deaden the body and its affectivity for the spirit to flourish and live.

Little did I realize that there were many men like myself, not attracted to women, in the Jesuits. Oftentimes, another novice would ask if I wanted a backrub. The first time I agreed, I naively did not realize that a "backrub" was a euphemism for a sexual encounter. As a youth, I idealized priests as men in control of their passions. Entering the Jesuits was like a kid going into a candy store, for many Jesuits were like myself, attracted to other males. Later, I noticed a pattern that emerged with other Jesuit sexual partners. I call it the "Gee, I was drunk last night and don't remember what I did" syndrome. This denial mechanism allowed many of my Jesuit sex partners to deny their human need for sex and love, bodily affection, and warmth.

Such sexual experiences countered the traditional dualist theologies and practices that opposed the body against the spirit. There were a number of Jesuits who mentored me to a sexual and a spiritual maturity. They taught me that the erotic was a meditative gateway to the sacred. The body was not to be deadened by austere practices of self-abnegation, but enlivened by its affectivity and even sexuality. The body was sacramental, the locus of revelation and the site of spirit. I began to experience the connection between body and spirit, sexuality and spirituality. I engaged in meditative sex, becoming mindful of its deep connection to God and harnessing the sexual energy into interconnectedness with the people and the world. I came to know Christ in my most intimate relationships. I realized that orgasmic bliss had many of the subtle qualities of intense but sublime, nonconceptual experience of Christ.

More important, I began to heal the split between my spiritual self and bodily urges. I began to tackle the internalized homophobia within me that blocked spirit. The erotic is the embodiment of the spirit's spontaneity. To eradicate sexuality would be, for us as bodily persons, to permanently block the spirit. I realized sexuality was neither destructive nor peripheral to my spirituality, for sexuality is involved in the center of my life. Sexuality is a means of communication and communion; it expresses a human need to connect physically and spiritually. My drive to link sexuality and spirituality enables me to understand not only their connection but their bond with justice as well.

During my theological studies for the priesthood, I found many more Jesuits open to sexual encounters and lovemaking. Jesuits in training, priests, superiors, and spiritual directors taught me how to love men sexually. They mentored me into human love and justice. I woke to the goodness of the body and the beauty of the spirit, and my relationship with Jesus the

Christ was evolving. The physical description of the beloved disciple's head on the breast of Jesus at the Last Supper attracted me. Like many gay Christians, I sensed that Jesus and the beloved disciple not only freely expressed their love physically but also celebrated it sexually. I found confirmation of my call to priesthood and service in my awakening to bodiliness. I found the Eucharist to be significant part of bodily love. Jesus said, "This is my body which is given to you." Eating Jesus' body and drinking his body were physical acts of sexual participation, intercommunion. I was falling in love with Jesus in a new and erotic way, and Jesuit spirituality thus provided me with the resources to "come out."

After ordination as a Jesuit priest in a parish in Oswego, New York, I remember, vividly, one morning celebrating the Eucharist. While in prayer at Eucharist, I envisioned Jesus in meditation and felt sexually aroused. My initial feelings of sexual arousal triggered a residual internalized homophobic reaction. I felt guilt over my erotic arousal for Jesus. Then, a feeling of wonder and of beauty, mixed with erotic excitement, swept away the internalized homophobic mechanism that I developed so well as a Catholic child. This erotic arousal for Christ became a quantum leap in my spiritual life; I finally understood that connection between deep sexuality and deep spirituality. I finally admitted to myself that I loved Jesus because he was a male, and that it was okay to love Jesus passionately and erotically as a man. I came out to God and named myself gay. It was more than just coming out as gay; my spiritual journey and my sexual journey were really one path. This envisioning was a profound experience of what Catholic spirituality calls "infused contemplation," the self-communication of God to a person in prayer. It had a deep impact both on the directionality of my life and how I would view the Eucharist. The Eucharist and the erotic became thoroughly enmeshed in my spirituality. I analyzed my sexual feelings that summer in specific examinations of conscience and continually thought about the experience of infused contemplation in prayer. I spoke with my spiritual director to discern the movement of God's Spirit in my prayer, and I also continued to masturbate, allowing myself to make love with Jesus in prayer and contemplation. My technique of meditative prayer was to envision Christ with me and experience him as a lover. I had sexual intercourse with Jesus numerous times, both as "top" and as "bottom." Jesus became the first male lover with whom I felt thoroughly comfortable being sexual.

That summer in Oswego, I glimpsed a small proportion of the fullness of the erotic grace of God and the grace of being born gay. I allowed my prayer to become sexual, abandoning narrow self-images to discover who I really was in the presence of God. I envisioned making love to Jesus, felt myself become sexually aroused, and climaxed in an orgasmic union with Jesus the Christ. That Jesus became my deep sexual partner felt right in prayer. I could no longer keep the erotic presence of God in the closet, and God came out in my life in an orgasmic explosion of interconnectedness of love and justice. Thus, I first "came out" and admitted being gay to Jesus the Christ. Jesus was my gay lover.

In coming out, my life was forever changed. I realized that erotophobia and homophobia alienated me from the most creative and loving power of the universe. God was at the root of my deep sexual longings. I made authentic connection with the source of my erotic power and my vocation to priesthood. I moved from fear toward joy, a desire to authentically connect with other men, love women, humanity, and the world. The closet controls homoerotic desire; it restricts sexual desire to the furtive and the secretive. Following Christ meant becoming who I am in erotic connection with other men and humanity. My coming out meant stepping into the light and becoming a target of violence and exclusion. It also meant that I entered a space where I was socially deviant, closing doors once open to me as a white, straight-appearing priest. Openly gay, sexual priests are dangerous to a closeted church and hierarchy. As long as I kept the secret of the closet, I was safe. Or, as a Jesuit superior said to me, "As long as you do not become public or settle down with anyone, you could be promiscuous."

I met a Jesuit, Frank, five months after ordination, and we instantly fell in love. Frank was handsome, sensitive, spiritual, fun, full of life, and committed to issues of social justice. We engaged in erotic prayer and lovemaking. Our sex was Eucharistic, intensely passionate, and intensely spiritual. During passionate lovemaking, I felt Christ in way that I only experienced in my solitary erotic prayer. I felt Christ in our lovemaking and did not want to give it up.

I found Christ in my lover, and I began with Frank to create our family of choice. We formed a family with an extended network of close friends. The model for our relationship, and even for our extended family of friends, was the Jesuit model of community. We formed an openly gay, Christian community of apostolic love. Our community remained inclusive of those who were alienated and harmed by the churches. For fourteen years, we prayed, made love, supported ourselves, founded a business, created a major AIDS service organization, and worked in various ministries for the queer community. The Jesuit ideals of prayer, generous service, and justice love infused our household. Frank and I found our community service to be strongly empowered by our lovemaking and prayer.

Each Sunday morning, Frank and I made sexual love, followed by Eucharist at the dining room table for the two of us. Both sexual love and

Eucharist were intimate and sacred moments of lovemaking. In our love-making, we choreographed our bodies in an ecstasy of pleasure and prayer. In sexual ecstasy, we celebrated deep love and deep spirituality. There was a sense of oneness with each other and a deep sense of Christ's presence in a dynamic energy flow embracing our bodies. There was a letting go and a surrender to rapture that transported us into a meditative realm of consciousness where boundaries dissolved and where the body of Christ was experienced in intimate touch, taste, smell, play, and so forth. There were times when I saw Christ's face within Frank's face as I pene-trated him in intercourse. As I was penetrated, I felt penetrated by Christ. As I tasted Frank's body, I tasted Christ's body. We experienced a ménage à trois and the inclusionary love of God.

I cannot imagine a more intense spiritual experience than to make love with your lover and see Christ's face in your lover's face while fucking. The letting go was carried into our prayer around the table as we broke bread and shared the cup of Christ's love. The intimacy of communion infused both the bedroom and the altar. We embodied love as God embod-ied love for us in word and sacrament. Eating the consecrated bread and wine was as intense a communion as our intimate lovemaking. How could I not taste Frank's body and life force in the body and blood of Christ?

Our passionate yearnings for each other did not selfishly enclose us, as some critics stereotype gay relationships, but turned us outward to engage in our communal obligations in following Christ. We grew in compassion as we learned to live passionately and act justly with each other. We took into our household ministry the throw-away people of our society: the developmentally disabled, alienated gays and lesbians, and people living with the painful realities of HIV illness. We created an apostolic communi-ty of love for the marginalized and the disenfranchised.

When Frank was diagnosed HIV positive, my ministry catalyzed into AIDS and queer activism. For some time prior, the genocidal indifference and hostility by an array of public institutions against people with HIV as well as the increased incidences of violence against queers and women had affected me. Too many of my friends had died of HIV complications, and too many of my friends had been the targets of violence, harassment, and discrimination because of their sexual orientation or gender. I wanted to do something to change the injustice of AIDS apathy and queer discrimina-tion, and in a holy anger born out of solidarity with loved ones, I joined the justice groups of ACT UP/St. Louis and Queer Nation.

I saw Christ's face within Frank's as HIV ravaged him and as AIDS service bureaucrats treated him as a victim. I found the bedroom to be the best training site for prayerful solidarity with other people because solidarity is the erotic drive to make compassionate and just connections with those who are oppressed and suffering. Solidarity is making erotic connections with lover, community, and the world, and Christ is in the midst of those erotic connections. Deep, spiritual, sexual lovemaking helped us learn about justice love and grow in solidarity.

In 1992, I knew that Frank's T-cell count was less than two hundred; he easily tired and slept a great deal. On my birthday in May, we celebrated my mailing off the first draft of my dissertation to my directors at Harvard University by going out to dinner. When we came home, we took a bath together and poured ourselves a glass of wine. Frank said to me, "Robert." I knew it was serious because he called me Robert only when I did something wrong or he had something troubling him to discuss. "Two things that I want for you. I want you to go into teaching; I think that you will be a good teacher. Second, I want you to fall in love again." I started to cry because I didn't want to hear those last words. Frank tried to console me, and we made physical love for the last time in that bathtub. I experienced pain in the depths of lovemaking; we were being pulled apart by a disease over which I had no control.

The next day Frank threw up more blood than I could ever imagine. I was extremely alarmed and drove him immediately to our physician. In our physician's office, he vomited again, filling up a quarter of the wastebasket. I looked at our physician's face, and I knew then that this was the beginning of the end. He was hospitalized in intensive care. Two nights later, Frank was placed on a respirator against his wishes, as stated in his living will, and without my permission. I fought with the hospital and internists over the decision to place him on a respirator for five days. Finally, when I threatened legal action, the hospital moved him into a private room with the respirator. I sort of slept at his bedside, as if I could really sleep with the pounding sound of the respirator and knowing how Frank felt about it. I felt that the hospital and doctors raped his body. I massaged his heels with lotion because they were bruised and bloodied from fighting against the respirator. The hospital staff finally took him off the respirator, but he continued to live. That night, in the late hours, he woke and asked what was happening. I said, "My love, you are dying. I will always love you." He said, "I love you." Those were the last words that he would speak. I took him home the next day, where he would receive hospice care, to die in our bedroom with our dogs around him. I kept a promise to him that I would be there for and with him when he died.

Throughout that summer, I was numb from grief at Frank's passing. This numbness was as deadening as the ascetic practices of my earlier seminary days. I remember that I cared little about living. My numbness and grief over losing Frank was so intense that I was most at risk for seroconversion. One of Frank's greatest gifts of love that night in the bathtub was that he freed me to love again. I also would add that the ménage à trois spirituality that placed Christ in the midst of our lovemaking kept me open to love again. At the end of summer after Frank's death, I began to recover from my depths of grief. I found I was able to celebrate Frank's life and smile at very vivid memories of our life together. The pain of loss still remained in the background, but I was able to place in the foreground our past love to celebrate in prayer. I regained the sense of Christian mission and was determined that I would never abandon my brothers and sisters who were HIV positive. I began again to engage myself in self-sexuality, remembering lovemaking with Frank and Christ. Prayer included the reclamation of my own sexuality. Through sexual prayer, I reaffirmed my belief in the living God and the life that Frank now shared with the resurrected Christ. I now realize that reclaiming sexuality is integral to personal healing, survival, and a vision for justice love in this time of AIDS.

Six months after Frank's death, I met David at a leather bar. We initially became sexually intimate without any expectations. Healing, for me, included recovery of a healthy sexuality. When I met David, my present life partner, I certainly was not looking for any relationship beyond friendship. I didn't want anyone to replace Frank, nor could anyone. Actually, we were both well-defended and not looking for an intimate relationship. We mutually slipped under each other's defenses and discovered something more than an intimate friendship. I found that sacred connection or flame in our ecstatic lovemaking. Our Eucharist sex became a communal orgy that included the presence of Christ and vivid, loving memories of Frank.

One of the extraordinary qualities about David is his loving ability to give me the space to continue to love Frank and to love him as well. I have not met many individuals who escape jealousy. One of the first things that David did as we became serious was to visit Frank's grave by himself and to speak with him. He won my heart. He has not expressed the slightest jealousy, never objecting to pictures of Frank, nor to my feelings. Frank and David have taught me the inclusiveness of Christ's love, and their procreative love empowered me as a priest-lover to enter uncharted territories, and my commitment to compassion and justice continues to express itself in my teaching, mentoring, activism, and ministry.

—52—

Hungry Suckle

Jim e Sparkle Pants

As a child, licking off the pasta dishes and ice cream bowls. Being scolded for licking countertops in public. Happy in my room with a giant jaw breaker, licking until my tongue began to bleed. Thirty years later, I find myself resting with an aching *lingual frenum* from cocksucking and endless licking. I remember the first time I sucked a friend's penis. We were teenagers tripping in the woods. I came with his dick in my mouth, with nothing but night air touching mine.

Now I sit nursing my *lingual frenum,* purring with my vision of heaven. In my heaven, where there is no risk of disease, the dualities of the human mind merge into the oneness of voracious cocksucking: big/little, dark/light, straight/curved, cut/uncut—may they all be welcomed by my hungry suckle. May they spurt and may I savor and swallow come that's blessed with a hint of mint, or buttered almonds with a pinch of cinnamon, or slightly salty with whisky and lime. In my heaven, late nights are spent with my devoted lover, the flavors of all the cums we've tasted, intermingling with the wetness of our kissing, as we glide inside each other, melting.

The Nether Eye Opens

Don Shewey

When Jerry called, I knew from his name and his tense, timid voice that I'd given him a massage once before. I found him in my client log, but the entry didn't churn up any detailed memories. The creature who arrived at my door might as well have been a total stranger. He was short and nearly bald on top, an out-of-shape blob of a middle-aged man, with reptilian slits for eyes. My notes reminded me that he was "overweight and ashamed of it."

He didn't seem to recognize me or remember that he'd seen me in the past, so I pretended I didn't know him either. We had the standard first-time preliminary chat. Did he have any injuries I should know about, or sensitive spots, or places he didn't like to be touched? He told me he'd just gotten a bunch of shots to go overseas, so I should avoid working on his arms. The control freak in me gets cranky when people say things like that. How are you supposed to get a massage if the masseur ignores key limbs?

I suspect that when someone says, "Don't touch my legs" or "Leave my neck alone," there's something else going on. Some fear of pain is being masked, or some shame, or some drive to control or to pretend to have some control. I often suspect, though, it's an indirect way of saying, "Let's skip the massage charade; I'm here to bust a nut." Trying to determine which of these factors might be at play without getting unnecessarily confrontational is a delicate matter.

"Did you get your shots earlier today?"

"No, yesterday," he said, "but they're still a little sore."

I didn't point out that yesterday was Sunday, an unusual day for in-oculations.

He went to the bathroom and came back wearing only his white button-down shirt. He slipped off the shirt and wanted to hop right onto the table. I said, "I'd like to have you do some stretching before we put you on the table,

---

"The Nether Eye Opens" first appeared on <www.erotasy.com>.

to loosen you up." He looked at me like I was crazy. Reluctantly, he took a step away from the table. As I directed him to close his eyes, take some breaths, and become aware of his body, he followed my instructions, but he acted like a little kid annoyed at having an adult make him do stupid things, like walk down the stairs one step at a time.

When I had him stretch him arms up to the ceiling, I noticed he was holding something in his right hand.

"What's that in your hand, Jerry?"

He showed me the white plastic inhaler.

"No," I said, feeling shaky. "I don't use poppers."

"You don't have to."

"I don't mix poppers with massage," I replied.

"They help me relax."

"I'm really a good masseur. You'll be plenty relaxed."

He dutifully deposited the tiny bottle on top of his clothes, which he'd left on the chair next to the massage table. As he lay on his back and I stretched out his arms and legs more, I tried to lighten the atmosphere. I mentioned that I lived in Japan when I was young and the shots we had to get before moving there. He didn't respond. He kept his lips pressed together tightly. He seemed to be pouting about having his poppers confiscated. It made me nervous. I felt guilty for shaming him about using poppers.

He resisted a lot of the massage. He seemed restless and impatient with my slow tempo, scratching himself and coughing. He never sighed and sank into the pleasure of being touched. I got the picture that he's someone who's used to going to masseurs for a half assed backrub and a hand job, no questions asked. Perhaps at the beginning I could have broached the subject of his real desire and made some accommodation. Often I do say something, like, "What's the experience you'd like to have today?" Not that anyone ever says, "A half-assed backrub and a hand job, please."

Guys like Jerry who crawl around in a snail shell of sex-shame rarely have much experience at asking for what they want. They either expect you to read their minds or they're masochistically resigned to whatever you want to dish out. In my desire to be conscious about sexual touch, you'd think I'd have developed a smooth routine by now of letting shy, sexually undernourished guys like this know what they're in for with me. For instance, I could say, "I'll get around to focusing on your erotic body, but first I'm going to spend about forty minutes massaging the muscle tension out of your back and your legs and your feet." I refrain from being that direct because I want to avoid sounding too much like one of those wholesome Danish sex education films. Rather than tease clients up to my level, I suppose I tend to sink down to their level of inarticulateness.

In any case, now I was launched into my usual massage routine, and there was no way of stopping it gracefully. I knew giving him a thorough massage had value. I also suspected that he couldn't give a shit.

Everything changed when I got around to his butt. My notes told me I had done butt work on him before, so I felt confident moving in for close butt touch. When I spread his cheeks and lightly brushed the coarse black hairs and the shiny pink skin around his stretched-out butt hole, he twitched as if shocked by an electric current. When I rested the palm of my hand against his pelvic floor and rocked him back and forth, his erection swelled out from under his ball bag, the snail poking its head out of its shell, antennae first. Even if I'm pretty sure that someone wants butt massage, I like to check. Sometimes people have hemorrhoids or loose bowels or some other condition they'd prefer to conceal. I leaned in close to his ear and said, "If you like, Jerry, I could put on gloves and do some more massage around your butt."

"Okay," he said.

I reached back to my supply cabinet and grabbed a pair of gloves and a tube of K-Y. When I turned around, he was reaching for the inhaler he'd left on top of his shirt.

I was on him in a flash. "If you insist on using poppers, Jerry, I can't continue with the massage."

"What?" he asked. I couldn't tell if he was hard of hearing or just selectively so.

I retreated from my ultimatum. "I'd rather you not use poppers during the massage."

"Okay," he said again. He returned his head to the faceplate like a scolded child.

"I want to invite you to keep breathing and taking in all the sensations you're feeling, Jerry. Does that sound okay to you?"

He shook his head yes, face down, buried in his shame.

I climbed up on the table and knelt between his spread legs. The sight in front of me—the hairy back and flabby butt of a middle-aged man—wasn't the most appetizing I'd ever encountered. I wasn't turned on, but I wasn't turned off either. Some people can't imagine touching, let alone giving an erotic massage, to somebody they're not attracted to. For a lot of young gay men, having anything to do with a guy like Jerry would be absolutely unthinkable. I don't mind. In fact, I like it. I like the feeling of control, of being entrusted with another human being's vulnerability. I have a hard time only when clients assume that because I'm touching them erotically, we've suddenly moved into some kind of reciprocal sex mode and they're free to grope me.

I guess that sounds awful. Don't kid yourself. I'm the attractive one around here. I'm the one who gets to touch and have power. Well, it's true. I want it to be clear that I'm in control. I want them to behave. There's definitely arrogance on my part. But no contempt. Anyone who presents his tender butt for loving touch gets a big gold star in my book. He can rest assured I'm going to take good care of him.

With Jerry, I felt like a spelunker ready to hunt for treasures in the secret cave. I pulled on first one white vinyl glove, then the other. The latest box of surgical gloves I bought were the smallest size, and they're skintight on my hands. They make me look like Mickey Mouse in evening wear.

In contrast to his lassitude during the back massage, the man on the table now began to respond to my every move—the cool breath on his tight butt hole, the firm pressure of three fingers over the opening, the cool slipperiness of lubricant being rubbed rhythmically over the folds of skin covering his sphincter. He jerked and twitched whenever I hit an especially sensitive spot. I knew I wasn't hurting him. I knew he was flinching because he wasn't breathing smoothly enough to distribute the intense sensations. So I coached him to breathe all the way down to his toes.

I went into him easily, one finger, then two. I brought him up onto his knees with his head resting on the table, his butt in the air. He wrapped his feet around my calves. When I slid the length of my middle finger across his swollen prostate, he groaned with pleasure. "Deeper," he requested. I adjusted my posture so I was a little higher and slid a third finger into his ass all the way up to the last knuckle, held it there, and vibrated it. With the other hand (whose glove I'd peeled off), I stroked his inner thighs, circled his balls, and tugged on his hard cock. Then I reached around and put my left hand on his lower belly just above his pubic bone and pressed inward, so his prostate received pressure from both sides.

To be this deep inside a man is about as physically intimate as you can get. The quality is so different from fucking, in some ways much more intense. Articulate, multijointed fingers can reach places inside the body that a hard cock cannot. They can increase or modify pressure on the sphincter or the prostate at will. And while someone who's fucking often has to keep sliding in and out to receive pleasure and to stay hard enough, a hand can stay put when it hits a spot that produces moans. I know, when I'm fucking, I can get very mental about the state of my erection, wanting to please my partner and prolong my own pleasure at the risk of losing it altogether. Doing butt massage, I'm liberated from that anxiety.

Touching Jerry, fiddling with his erotic knobs like an engineer tuning up a delicate machine, I felt detached, distant, powerfully in control. Like the most beneficent of gods, at once servant and master, giving exquisite pleasure and requiring nothing in return.

Once he was accustomed to being penetrated, I picked up the pace. Now I was fucking him—with my hand, anyway—in and out, pumping his butt. Inarticulate murmurs issued from his throat. He raised his butt higher. With my free hand, I slapped his big rump hard, first one cheek then the other, again and again. He jerked and cried out with each slap. His cry did not say "Stop." The sound of bare hand against bare butt excited me. I escalated the strength of my slaps. Then I paused and ran my fingertips lightly over the reddening skin. I reached down and wrapped my fist around the base of his bulging cock and balls and pulled them toward me.

"Do you have your whole fist in me?" he suddenly asked.

"No, not quite," I said. "Three fingers."

"Can you fist me?" His voice was quiet, not timid, but hopeful.

"Have you ever been fisted?"

"No. But I'd like to try."

"Let's see how it goes," I said. I put some more lube on my hand and slid all four fingers inside him. He groaned with satisfaction. I could feel his belly, his bowels, his rectum, his insides breathing with me, letting go. When I slid my hand back, a few bubbles of air pressed their way out, relieving the interior pressure. Without clenching or clamping, his ass wrapped itself around my hand, like a starfish on a rock.

I got off the table and stood next to him. I ran my free hand up his back and stroked his shoulders, his neck, the scaly top of his bald head. I leaned into his butt, which opened slightly wider. He sighed. Now I slid my thumb into his manhole, so my hand formed a wedge that pushed all the way in until my knuckles rested against his sitz bones.

I noticed that he was no longer hard. It occurred to me that he might be hurting. He might have had enough. But the gurgles he released whenever I bore down on his prostate told me he had entered a deeper zone, that altered state of erotic experience that is beyond erection and ejaculation. It's a mystical place, akin to dreaming or nearly dying, where the membrane that separates matter from spirit becomes very thin. Memories and emotions slither up from the murky depths. The nether eye opens to what's usually hidden. The roof of the planetarium slides open, and the infinite beckons. I knew he was traveling through space, like those scenes in *2001: A Space Odyssey* where suddenly the spaceship would be hurtling through a blur of stars. Only this was inner space, a tunnel of quiet dark. Vaulted ceilings, Echoey stairwell. A horse's eye. I hung out there with him.

Almost an hour and a half had passed since he got on the table. "I'm going to slow down now and start coming out of you, Jerry," I told him. One finger at a time, I brought my hand out, cupping my palm over his hole before releasing it entirely. Then I laid him flat on the table again and cleaned his butt with a baby wipe and toweled off his back before turning him over.

"How are you doing?" I asked him.

He looked up through his slit eyes and said, "Good."

I knelt at the end of the table looking at his face upside down. I saw his stubbly chin, his thin lips (relaxed now), his fleshy ears.

"You've been on a little trip, I think."

"Uh huh," he said.

"Uh huh," I confirmed. I rested my hands on his shoulders and looked down into his steely green eyeballs. They were the eyes of someone on a trip, who has seen something from the other world and not averted his gaze. He didn't seem confused or shy or embarrassed.

"Did any images or memories occur to you during this session?" I asked.

"Yes," he said immediately. I was surprised. I like asking the question, but usually people don't relate to it.

"Tell me," I said.

"I remembered that my father used to take me over his knee," he said slowly. "He would pull down my pants . . . and pull down my underwear . . . and spank me."

"And that was exciting to you?"

He nodded.

"Did your father know it excited you?"

"No."

"Did you get a hard-on?"

"No, not at the time."

"But later when you thought about it . . . ?"

"Uh huh."

I let that memory sink in. Inside me something large and dangerous moved, like a giant octopus tentacle flopping across the room. When I started slapping his big hairy butt, little did I know that I was stirring up his oldest erotic fantasies. Or mine: the forbidden Daddy love touch.

"There's something about an older man, your father, taking an interest in your naked butt that's very exciting and forbidden, isn't there?"

"More forbidden," he said.

"Ah. Many things that are forbidden are exciting."

He was quiet for a minute.

"Anything else?" I inquired.

"Yes."

I was overjoyed. More!

"I was in Morocco once," he began. "Have you ever been to Morocco?"

"No," I said. "I'd like to go."

"This was many years ago," he said. He spoke slowly, as if in a trance. "I was there with some other people on business. . . . and we were all taken to this bathhouse. . . . There were men and women there. . . . I got separated from the people I was with. . . . I saw some stairs. . . . I went up there. . . . It was a little room. . . . I met a Moroccan guy. . . . He was big. . . . well, not big. Stocky."

He paused.

"Then what happened?" I said, barely controlling my impatience to hear the whole story.

"There was a bench there. . . . He pulled it over to the middle of the room. . . . He had me get up on it . . . the same way you had me do . . . with my butt up."

Aha.

"And then. . . . you know, he fucked me. . . . And there were two other guys . . . Moroccans. . . . Three of them altogether."

"All three fucked you?"

"Uh huh."

"One right after the other?"

"Uh huh."

"That sounds hot," I said. My dick grew in my pants. To tell the truth, I was jealous.

"It was," he said immediately. "The other guys were walking around the place. . . . I didn't know where they were. . . . Men and women . . ."

"Oh," I said, "It was a place where everybody was there having sex, men and women?"

"Yes," he said.

"But they could have walked in at any time and seen you?"

"Yes."

We both quietly took in the thrill of that scenario.

This guy had more going on inside him than I ever would have suspected by looking at him. I got up and sat on the table next to him. I picked up his arm and let it rest against my chest as we continued talking.

He wanted to know more about fisting. "Do you think you could get your whole hand inside me next time?"

"I don't know," I said. "For fisting, it's a lot easier if you're in a sling because your whole body is able to relax. When you're on a table, your muscles unavoidably maintain a certain tension."

"Do you have a sling?" he asked eagerly.

"No," I said. "Some people have them in their private playrooms, and some sex clubs have them."

"I couldn't see myself doing it in a sex club with just anybody. But I could do it with you. What if I lie on my back?"

"That might be easier," I conceded. I started feeling slightly apprehensive. I'd never fisted anybody. This session was as far as I'd ever gone in that direction. I didn't want to set myself up as an expert. But his eagerness to explore touched me. He didn't seem like a numbed-out thrill seeker. From the stories he told, I understood that intense body play connected him to his deepest erotic fantasies and memories. What else can you call these things but experiences of God, memories of heaven? In those moments, brief and eternal, you feel most alive in your body and most spiritually connected to the tempestuous energy of the universe, that mystery at once so physical and so invisible. How many saints and monks, legendary for meditating days at a time on their dusty mats, have dwelt on just this, remembered or wished-for episodes of ecstatic butt fucking?

"We need to stop for today, Jerry," I said.

"Can you help me get off?"

"You want to squirt?" I asked, a little dubiously. I thought he'd gone way beyond it. I thought he'd had a sacred-sex breakthrough and realized that you don't always have to ejaculate to have a powerful erotic experience.

"Sure," he said. I looked at his dick, which he'd been idly toying with during our conversation, and I saw that it was stiff and dark pink. I oiled him up and stroked him. He had a medium-sized dick, maybe five inches long erect, circumcised, with a big split down the middle, a thick frenum. Pressed flat against his belly, his cock looked like an arrowhead—or a devil's tail. As I worked on his cock, he started running his hands over my body. I found myself tensing up, afraid that he was going to start invading me and grabbing my cock. I didn't invite him to touch me, and I wasn't at all turned on at the moment. I wanted to finish up the session and get rid of him. Sacred sex is sacred sex, but after an hour and a half, your time is up.

I pumped his cock with one hand and reached my other arm under his neck and around his shoulders. He lifted his arm to pull me down to his face. I resisted, but eventually, I allowed him to press some stubbly kisses against my face.

As I pressed my hairy chest against his, his thin lips smacking against mine pressed closed, I became for a moment that angry daddy pulling down his underpants, that stocky Moroccan towering over him and swallowing him up, the horned god appearing by magic in the forest clearing where the chubby boy lay on mossy grass pleasuring himself. The world turned upside down with a lurching sound like a train pulling out of the station. Blossoming flowers erupted from the earth. Waves of air pressed into his lungs until he burst.

54

1972

Terry Kelly

Funny there should be a bunch of junkyard dogs lounging around their gas station on Market and Castro at the birth of the gay revolution. On the day the Twin Peaks bar went queer, they were hanging out as usual, watching all the fine women pass by.

"Damn! I'd like to-to-to-to kiss the back of her knees. I've g-g-g-*got* to kiss the back of her knees!"

"Bill, you're not kissin' her knees," said the boss. "I'm going to peel those shorts off and fuck her in the ass." He adjusted his shades.

"Now that's appropriate behavior."

"Jesus, it's hot today." Roy wiped his forehead.

"Taint fair. Why are they so goddam beautiful. Look at that little bra thing she's wearin', with that bow on the back. One little tug on that thing. . . ."

"It just hurts, don't it?"

"They're here on earth to make us miserable."

"I'll drink to that."

"There's another one!"

The new guy leaned against the tire shelf and drank his beer. He showed up at the station a few months ago in an old Chevy pickup looking for a job. A cute, big-breasted, wide-eyed blonde sitting next to him. They saw him kiss her good-bye for fifteen minutes. He had his hand in her pants and everything. Right on the lot in broad daylight. Then he came to work with a skinny girl that twined around him and wouldn't let him out of the truck. Jim had to come over and tap on the window to tell him that his shift had started. They kidded him when he came in all rumpled and bitten. "Damn! You are gonna get in a shitload of trouble, boy. When that blonde finds out . . ."

"We all live together."

"Yeah, but does she know that you're playing around with the other one?"

"It's not like that."

"Well, what the hell's it like?"

"We sleep together."

"Guess I found out what it's like. Pretty damn good."

A black-haired, freckled, blue-eyed Celtic woman came into view. "Man, she's got long hair."

"I like 'em skinny, but curvy, like that."

"She's a dead ringer for that girl who showed up at the station last Friday night. It's her! The blow job artist. Right, Danny?"

"Too much teeth. It hurt."

"Okay. But it really did happen, right?"

"Goddam right it happened. My dick's still sore. She went down on both of us."

"Why would she suck you off for free?"

"I don't have a clue. She took us on in the supply room one at a time. I'll never forget it. Ty put some jackets on the floor so she wouldn't hurt her knees."

The boss drained his ale and got serious. He looked at the new guy.

"Kelly!" He nodded toward the lube room. They walked out and closed the door behind them. The boss leaned forward.

"Kelly, there's a lot of queers in this neighborhood. So treat 'em nice, Okay? I'm telling all of the guys to watch it."

"Sure, boss. No problem." The boss got another ale and joined the boys.

Kelly strolled to the back of the lube room. He took off his shirt with the company logo. Then he stripped off his T-shirt. He was a strong man with big hands and shoulders and lots of thick black hair on his chest. He put his company shirt on and tied it across his belly, Marilyn Monroe style, with the top unbuttoned.

A white Mercedes pulled up to the pumps. Kelly walked out through the lube room and zeroed in on the gentleman in the Mercedes, who was zeroing in on him. The guys were astonished.

The sun and the gas fumes and the white fenders were dazzling. The man faced a hard, flat belly with the company shirt tied across it in a most provocative manner.

"You need something?"

He was fifty-eight and he needed to have his brains fucked out. He'd pee all over himself to spend an hour in bed with this grease monkey god. But it was so easy. He gave Kelly his business card with his fingers trembling, and they made a date. A very expensive date. Then he drove away without his gasoline.

Kelly stuck the card in his shirt pocket and came back in the office to finish his beer. Nobody knew what to say.

55

Anodigital

Robert E. Penn

I have a love that protects us. I have a hate: it fucks me over. I can't live with a barrier to feeling; can't live without a 97 percent guarantee. Condom sex changes everything.

I try to make the most of it. Foreplay gets better. It is best when the thrill, which formerly lay only between my legs, migrates to other appendages. They are new erogenous passages and protrusions that palpitate, surge physical, and merge throughout my body. My libido focuses now on digits, that prod gently, placing love deep inside you.

Nothing can compare to the feeling and tactility of being inside someone; of feeling someone inside. It is a combination of so much: fluids, secretions, textures, shapes, force. I so loved to fuck before condoms. Now it is just a matter of cumming into a bag. Except when I find someone as delighted as I when cum tightens on my chest, my mind pulled back from fantasies of the man beside me by its gentle, reminiscent tug.

My body longs for the penetration, the warmth, the silken tissues that moisten all invaders.

At home, I play with myself and tingle inside and out. I control how deep. My sphincter controls how wide. My fingers and hands wander over nipples, inside thighs, around sides and under feet, tasting as only touch can, constructing mental pictures from sequential spaces felt.

I want to know the inside of another man. I put out a call to my leather friends, my bondage acquaintances: top seeking bottom, fisting only. An experienced bottom sought: muscles relaxed, open. One who knows his limits and will ask me to respect them. One who is not trying to harm himself, but wants his share of enchantment.

I go to a bathhouse and find you, your room filled with the huge dildos. Your ass greeting. We don't know each other. I don't need to know you. It is our pleasure that we seek. I will take care of you and you of me. My eyes tell you: Yes, I want to travel your passages and sense the pulse of your muscles and the flow of your blood. I want to give you bliss and let your body envelop me with fluids up to my elbow.

A delirium chants softly throughout me: I want to feel that, excite my tactile desire. I learn to transfer the mental image constructed from points of pleasure at my fingertips, bending my arm into the other bodily senses and responses: flexes, extensions, and erection.

I quake and cum inside of you, yet we are safe: My digits caress and quiver among the folds of your evacuated intestines. My full body spirals in orgasm, jism spurts, spirits of its own accord, and lands beside me; between us on the clean sheet.

Anodigitalecstasy!

56

Midwife

Matthew Simmons

When I know who I am I am You.
When I don't know who I am I serve you.

Gandhi

Keep breathing—it works, plays in the back of my mind like a mantra as I sit next to Ted's bed. I feel like a fascist twelve-stepper willing him to inhale. His ragged breathing adds another layer of sound to the other sounds floating around his apartment: Mozart playing on the stereo, the aquarium, the clock by his bed, children playing outside his bedroom window. And to think I had just fucked him last week.

I sit awkwardly wondering what to do with my hands. Caught between grief and anxiety, I imagine myself gesticulating madly like Medea wailing over the death of her children. Of course, what does it really matter what I do with my hands? Ted is completely comatose from the morphine drip. Jenny, his sister, has stepped out for fresh air and we share this private moment alone.

I arrived earlier in the evening, exhausted, not knowing that Ted was in a coma and approaching death. Sitting next to his bed, I am confronted by the waning of a client who became a lover, who became a friend; what was an unremarkable day has become extraordinary. I am now wide awake, playing the role of midwife, witnessing his last moments. To pass the time, I count the seconds between each breath, his and mine, as if through the counting of seconds, I can remember the moments of forgotten intimacy.

With the tenderness of a lover, I begin preparing the room as if we are going to make love, lighting candles and incense—the incense I was burning the very first day he showed up at my door as a client seeking some erotic companionship. I surround his wasted body with paper cranes and special objects from his childhood. I place mementos of his departed lover Bill close to his hands. My silhouette dances on the wall above his head like Peter Pan in the glow of candlelight as I caress his body with my fingertips. The body that I have washed and held, kissed and fucked, the body that has held his soul for a brief glorious lifetime. I place my hand on his heart; my other hand rests softly on his genitals, and I close my eyes to pray for his mind to find peace.

My thoughts wander to my friend Annie who had told me some time ago that on her deathbed she wanted someone to be giving her cunnilingus. She wanted to ejaculate into her death rather than simply expire. My mind plays with the thoughts of dying. Instead of weeping and wailing, how about a circle jerk? How about father anointing his son with come and wishing him an ecstatic death? Or, son washing his father's body with his semen, returning to father what was the beginning? Of course, I'm sure it is hard for us to imagine our fathers standing by our deathbeds masturbating while family and friends look on. I chuckle to myself at this John Waters-like vision and wonder mischievously if Ted would like a blow job. I slowly lift my hands off his body, assured that he is calm, returning to my chair next to his bed. I fold paper cranes, singing to him softly, contemplating my own death.

My thoughts are interrupted by the tea kettle howling in the kitchen. I watch myself going through the motions of fixing a cup of tea, aware that Ted is in the other room grasping for just one more minute of life. Each moment has become an eon of movement, as if the elasticity of time has stretched itself beyond hope of ever returning to its resilient self. I am temporarily blinded by the steam fogging up my glasses as the smells of peppermint and chamomile fill the medicine-cluttered kitchen.

The smell of peppermint invokes a memory of my grandmother, who started losing her eyesight around the same time as Ted did. All she sees now are shapes, blurred as if someone smeared Vaseline over the lenses of her eyes. One wintry afternoon, as I was massaging her arthritic hands with peppermint lotion, the apartment stilled by the loss of my grandfather, she described her eyesight as shimmering aspens. The shapes were soft, sometimes indistinguishable, sometimes merging with one another, sometimes glowing like apple blossoms in the spring. I stand immobilized in the middle of the kitchen, holding tight to the memory of my grandmother, knowing that Ted is beginning to leave his no longer essential body.

I try to maintain a sense of calmness as I put down the cup of tea I so longed to sip. I know what to do; however, panic starts to engulf my entire body. The kind of heart-racing panic when you are standing in the middle of a living room during an earthquake and vacillating between saving the Lalique about to leap off the bookshelf or your grandmother's antique flower vase pirouetting on the coffee table. Moving into the hallway, sadness sets in, with the understanding that Ted is about to bungee jump without a cord and all I can think about is eating chocolate cake.

I stand in the doorway of Ted's bedroom watching him, no longer conscious, only his body living the memory of breath. His vacant eyes stare beyond the upper corner of the bedroom above the darkened window, fixating on something I cannot perceive. A place, a destination, as if the journey to this moment was a brief respite. I notice how vibrant his skin looks in the glow of candlelight, and I imagine for a moment that he is asleep from a long day.

Tonight was intended as a sleep over. Jenny had once remarked to me that Ted enjoyed the nights that I had slept with him, cradling him like his lover Bill, soothing his fear. I slowly undress and crawl into bed with him, trying not to disturb the special objects that I have placed on his bed. Each breath he takes is a struggle now, and I think that each will be the last one.

I support my head with my hand, the elbow resting on the pillow, and gaze at Ted's profile. The flickering light makes his lips move as if he is praying. I imagine he is conversing with Bill, or his mother, or one of the many friends that he has lost over the years. I imagine we are talking like we did after many of our lovemaking sessions on my bed. As I gaze upon him, I start to reflect about the first and last time I fucked him.

Ted had remarked on several occasions that he felt shamed by his doctors for wanting to be sexual even when he had full-blown AIDS (this, of course was before the discovery of the cocktail). He was also embarrassed about his gaunt body, that he felt undesirable and had essentially no libido. Over the months, as his health declined, his opportunities for sexual intimacy were limited. His attempts at hiring escorts fizzled as they (the escorts) freaked out once they showed up or were not interested when he explained his situation over the phone. He came to me because I was his last attempt to find intimacy.

Over the course of several months and weekly appointments, Ted and I became very close. The intimacy we shared together was enough to take us away from the confines of "services rendered" to becoming lovers. Every session brought out unexpected desires in Ted and a surprising willingness in me to fulfill them. It was during one particularly emotional session that Ted talked about being penetrated. The last time he was fucked was by his lover, Bill, who had died several years ago. He wanted to have that experience one more time. We talked about it as an opportunity for him to reclaim his sexuality, which had been demonized because of his illness.

The week before he died, I entered his apartment on a bright San Francisco afternoon and immediately sensed that something was wrong. He had been told by his doctor that his body was deteriorating at such a rate that he had only several months to live; little did we know that he had only a week. I reached out and pulled him into my arms. I had expected him to unleash a lifetime of tears, but much to my surprise, he did not. He simply received the hug, thanking me quietly for my concern and invited me into the living room. We sat on the sofa next to each other for several minutes, without saying a word, the afternoon sun painting the living room with brilliant pieces of white crystal. The silence between us, profound.

My mind raced with the thoughts of what he must be going through. I tried to imagine what my experience would be, knowing that I had a short amount of time to live. Whom would I share my last moments with? What would be my priorities? What would be my salvation? I could not even begin to fathom the enormity of the situation. It reminded me of the times as a child when I lay on the earth and looked up at the sky imagining everything upside down. I would start to fall into the sky, my heart racing at the thought of descending forever, my eyes bulging at how huge the universe was and how small I was.

I gently coaxed him to lay his head on my lap, allowing him this moment of stillness. I stroked his head gently, trying to calm his thoughts. He began to speak after minutes had passed and the sun had begun to make its trek across the wall. I was the first person he had spoken with after hearing the news. He noticed that he was not as scared as he had thought he would be. He had come to terms with his death weeks before. His only hope was that the final moment would be quick and painless. He did not want to linger.

His words flowed through my soul like the snow-melted water of a mountain river. Never before had I heard such quiet acceptance, his courage astounding, reminding me of a quote: "The Way we live our lives is the Way we die." The words started to unfold in my mind, as if I were trying to understand the intricate nature of folding paper cranes. When we live with grace and compassion—embracing the preciousness of each breath as life itself and acknowledging the beauty of the divine that is in us—our death does not become a tragic event, but the ecstatic grace of time.

When he had finished speaking, I suggested we not precede with our original plan; I recommended that I massage him instead. He responded without hesitation, and with a bit of humor, that he wanted to get fucked, regardless of the news because his life depended on it. Of course, I did not share with him how performance anxiety was setting in. Knowing that someone has several months to live can wreak havoc on your erection.

I took his hand without saying a word and led him into the bedroom. As we walked down the hallway, I imagined I was Bill, alive and well, and we were about to make love at the end of the day. After entering the bedroom, I pulled down the shades and turned down the bed while Ted put on some

music, his favorite, Mozart. I began our session by holding him, letting
him know that at any time we could stop what we were doing. As we stood
embracing each other in the middle of the bedroom, surrounded by soft
music, the words of a friend, Oscar, who was a classical pianist, came to
mind. Oscar told me once that Mozart wrote such divine music because the
notes loved one another. Inhale. Thank god for schmaltzy sentimentality to
relieve performance anxiety. Exhale. I undressed Ted slowly as he stood
with his eyes closed, knowing that I would be fine.

I whispered words of encouragement into his ear and lightly kissed the
nape of his neck. My hands, without any sense of direction, softly caressed
his skin, stretching taut over his body, exposing the fragile bones. He would
occasionally let out a moan, a sound of pleasure. There was so much vitality
still left in him that each sound he made encouraged me to provide him with
more delight.

We lay down in his bed, giggling like boys discovering familiar treasures. We spent long moments fondling each other, slowly becoming
aroused. I paid careful attention to touch his lesions and sores and lightly
kiss his entire body, aware that parts of his body were contagious. My hands
carefully stroked the skin around the intravenous tube that was now a part
of his body and had only been touched by nurses and doctors. I started to
become excited each time his body reacted to my touch; every time he
whispered my name, I would let go of my fear concerning disease.

My gloved hands slowly worked their way down to his butt, squeezing
each cheek roughly, which was how he liked it. I asked him if there was
anything he wanted to add to the excitement of the moment. He asked me to
put on Bill's leather boots and his jockstrap. I found the boots in the closet
next to the bed, quite happy to put them on. There is nothing like a pair of
black motorcycle boots to turn a man on. I grabbed my jock-covered dick
and starting pumping my hips into my hands as Ted watched from the bed.
I had to fight the urge not to laugh out loud at the absurdity of trying to do a
hip-thrusting, erotic dance to Mozart, but Ted seemed to be enjoying it.

I came around to the side of the bed closest to him so he could have
access to my dick. He crawled off the bed and kneeled in front of me, his
hands resting on my butt cheeks as he pulled my dick and jockstrap into his
mouth. I pumped my dick into his face gently at first, then as he became
excited by the action, I started to thrust harder. Each time I rammed my dick
into his face, the movement caused the intravenous tube to swing. At this
point, he was so excited by my rock-hard erection trying to push its way
through the jockstrap, that he asked me to fuck him. I was amazed by how
quickly the excitement melted away the fact that he was dying. He watched
me intently as I slowly stripped out of the jockstrap, my stiff cock falling out

for him to see. I asked him to put the condom on, giving him the pleasure of feeling my hot dick.

At that moment, my erotic-altered vision saw his body vibrating with energy, free of disease—no longer gaunt and rigid, but supple and luscious. I wanted to plunge my dick into his ass. I wanted him to feel alive. I wanted him to moan so loud that the neighbors could hear him screaming in ecstasy. I helped him off the floor and onto the bed and laid him on his stomach.

At first, I lay on top of him lightly, finding the right amount of pressure so that I wouldn't crush him. I began by grinding my crotch into his ass, teasing him, making him hungry for my cock. His hips, pushing up, wanting me in his asshole. His body expressing desire that had been long forgotten. Never had I seen Ted so awake and alive in all our meetings. His passion, his longing to be united with God, his wanting to be healthy, the craving to hold his loved ones again raced through my mind as the tears of realization welled up in my eyes. Could this be God's work? Take away the crassness of fucking, the selfishness of lust. Could fucking be an act of Divinity? Would I endure ridicule for asking those questions? Yes. I push my cock into Ted's anus with the tenderness of a father, the affection of a lover, and the adoration of God, praying that all beings could understand this act of compassion. When we are finished, I take Ted into the bathroom and bathe him as he cries softly on my shoulders. Wiping the lube and the shit off of my hands, I cry softly with him. I cry out of gratitude for having this moment with him.

Ted's breath, rattling like seeds in a plastic jar, pulls me out of my reverie and brings me back into the moment. His lungs are filling up with fluid, making it difficult for him to breathe, and I realize that he is slowly drowning. I whisper to him softly and urgently to let go, not to be afraid.

I describe to him a vision of us standing at the edge of a cliff, overlooking a valley of aspens shimmering in the fall wind. The sky above us is a translucent blue that flares like forever. I describe the wind that envelops us like a favorite worn coat, the crisp air exhilarating as it rouges our cheeks.

I move closer to Ted; as his body battles for more oxygen, my words are barely audible. I tell him that we are standing on this cliff with our arms stretched wide, turning like whirling dervishes; the world spins in a kaleidoscope of blue. I take Ted's hand, which is cool, and hold it in mine, whispering with as much love as I can, "Imagine that the world is upside down and we are falling into the universe. When I know who I am I am You. I witness. I watch. When I don't know who I am I serve you. I lay my body down."

57

Kiss Me

Ray Schnitzler

"Kiss me."
But I won't.
Hovering over you,
my mouth above yours,
my breath hot on your face.
You reach for me,
lunging, sucking, needing,
pleading,
"Kiss me."
But I restrain you,
holding your wrists, your hips,
your hair.
You arch up toward me,
but I keep my distance.
And I tease you,
whispering, nibbling on your ear,
"I can tell how much you want to
kiss me."
"Yes. Pleeease kiss me."
"Count to ten, slowly;
when you get to ten, you may kiss
me."
You count very slowly.
You writhe;
You reach;
You count.
For an hour.
My eyes say,
"Get to ten, already!"
But you don't.

And I have to restrain you,
prevent you from having what we
both want,
until you get to . . .
"Ten."
"Now you may kiss me.
You can kiss me now.
Kiss me."
But you don't.

58

Holy Fuck

elias farajajé-jones

On Manhattan Island (New Netherland Colony), June 25, 1646:
Court proceedings. Fiscal [public prosecutor] vs Jan Creoli, a ne-
gro, sodomy; second offense; this crime being condemned of God
(Gen., c.19; Levit., c. 18:22, 29) as an abomination, the prisoner is
sentenced to be conveyed to the place of public execution, and there
choked to death, and then burnt to ashes . . .
   Sentence. Manuel Congo, a lad ten years old, on whom the above
abominable crime was committed, to be carried to the place where
Creoli is to be executed, tied to a stake, and faggots piled around
him, for justice sake, and to be flogged; sentence executed. (Katz,
1976:22-23)

In many African traditions, it is customary to begin every important act in
life by honoring the ancestors, invoking their presence, and asking their
blessings. So, I could not begin this essay without invoking Jan Creoli,
Manuel Congo, and my friend, Assotto Saint. Assotto's written works and the
memory of his words keep him present to us. But Jan Creoli and Manuel
Congo are unfortunately largely unknown. The previously cited quote from
the court proceedings is the first mention that I was able to discover of Black
queers in what were to become known as the United States. I was overwhelmed by the fact that these ancestors of mine were mentioned in a context
that shows them as criminals, one of whom was executed by the state. I never
could find out what happened to Manuel Congo. Did he ever have sex with
another Black man?

This essay is dedicated to the memory of Jan Creoli (d. 1646), Manuel Congo
(?), and Assotto Saint (1957-1994), Haitian-American writer, HIV activist, and sex
radical.

My other African ancestors stood on auctioning blocks in this country where their bodies were offered for sale. They were subjected to the white "gaze" quite literally; their genitalia were touched and inspected in a very public way. The bodies of my First Nations (Tsalagi/Cherokee) ancestors were forcibly removed, infected, massacred, locked up. They were so effectively removed and locked up that they do not even enter into the erotic fictions of the dominating culture. There is queer boy Latino porn; there is Filipino/Asian/Pacific Islander porn; there is Black porn. But First Nations male bodies and desires are not the subject of representation in queer men's porn.

What does it mean to live and desire/lust in a Black "male" (and I can only understand the term as referring to a wide variety of diverse definitions and experiences, including "female") body in a dominating culture that not only sexualizes but also criminalizes that body? And when that body is a Queer colored body, it is a body that is racialized, criminalized, and sexualized, all in potentially life-threatening ways.

We have bodies that were stolen, bodies that were marked, bodies that were property, bodies that were owned, bodies that were sold, bodies that were brutally murdered, bodies that were lynched, bodies that were supposed to be the very bodies of sexual transgression, bodies that were killed because they were putatively the site of sex crimes committed against white bodies.

The Black male body is reviled and portrayed as the "body to fear," yet at the same time used to sell almost everything, often with a not so well-disguised polyerotic subtext. The Black male body is constantly set up as the "body of crime." Our bodies can be used to scare white people enough to convince them to vote for someone for president. It is now chillingly frightening to take note of the fact that the bodies that are now being shown as the face of those who knowingly transmit HIV to (innocent) others are Black men's bodies. So, to live in a Black male body and to desire other Black male bodies is to move about daily on a physical, psychological, and spiritual battleground. I cannot talk about "male lust" without talking about all of this, without looking at how notions of race, heresy, "aberrant" sexualities, and crime have been woven together. Our bodies have been colonized and treated as though they were someone's occupied territories, with all sorts of projections and fears mapped out across them.

* * *

The roots of religious erotophobia in the particular varieties of Euro-Puritanism that came along with the European invaders go back to notions of a desexed God, a basically bodiless God, without any notion of a Goddess, a divine consort. In the cultures surrounding Israel, there was often some form of sexual practice connected to religious concepts and acts. In order to distinguish Israel from its neighbors, it was profoundly important to condemn its religious practices. To imitate them, to worship other gods/ goddesses, was to betray the God of Israel. The Hebrew Bible, according to Howard Eilberg-Schwartz's work, *God's Phallus* (1995), constructed a worldview in which God, who is to be the sole object of Israel's love, cannot have genitalia. Why? Because if God ("he") *were* to have genitalia, and if Israel (i.e., the men who doctrinally constituted the nation) were to love God, that would then place God and Israel in a "homoerotic" relationship. And that was something to be avoided at all costs.

In the formative years of many early Christianities as well, outright hostility toward the body continued to shape attitudes toward women (considered as the very incarnation of body and lust) and sex. These body-negative/sex-negative currents in early Christian thought reached their zenith in the writing of Augustine, a forth- to fifth-century (CE) African theologian whose work shaped Western Christianity's dichotomism and its negative attitudes toward women, the body, and sex. "Aberrant" sexualities were often portrayed as being linked to religious error (which was "criminal") and therefore to evil. The end result is that, today, very few people find it possible to think of sex and the sacred together in a positive way.

This all plays out in a potentially lethal way in the history of interpretation of the so-called curse on Ham, or the curse on Canaan. In Genesis 9:19-28, Noah's son, Ham, who has historically been represented as the ancestor of all Black people, is cursed by his father for having looked upon his (Noah's) nakedness. The other two brothers, Shem and Japheth, walked backward and covered Noah's nakedness without looking at him. When Noah "discovers" what happened, he curses Canaan, for Ham is the father of Canaan. Noah relegates Canaan to being the lowest of slaves for Shem, Japheth, and their descendants, in perpetuity. The changing interpretation of this passage would eventually link Ham and his descendants—Black people—not only to mandatory slavery but also to illicit, criminal sex. Aberrant sexualities and Blackness became inextricably bound together, leading, of course, to the development of essentialist notions of the Black man as sexual criminal, as the polymorphously perverse sexual predator. According to cultural theorist Sander Gilman (1985), this could happen because some interpretations of the story of Ham seemed to indicate that something "homoerotic" was being discussed. He goes on to point out that in the eyes of the dominating culture, the very identity and nature of Black people is rooted in this most foul of criminal sexual acts, in this "homoerotic" gaze.

Erotophobia, the fear of the erotic and of its power, has therefore played a powerful role in shaping institutionalized white supremacy's vision of what it means to be African, to be Black. African is wild, hot, savage, beastlike, libidinal, primal; in short, the African is the very embodiment of all that the dominating culture sees as evil and in need of being policed and controlled. Black people are therefore seen as being "sexually depraved" by nature, and any form of sex that white people find repulsive should, "logically," be practiced by Black people.

Erotophobia thus intersects with white supremacy in the investment of peoples of color as the exotic/erotic other—people who are seen as the very incarnations of the erotic (and, therefore, of evil), people who are sexually dangerous and therefore in need of domination. If we take a critical look at erotophobia, we can see the historical links between the war against women (including centuries of "witch" burnings), the hardening of Western Christian religious dogma in northern Europe, and the expulsion of the Other (Muslims and Jews) from Spain. This, in turn, is connected to the invasions of the Americas, Asia, and the Pacific Islands, to the African slave trade, and to the massacre of indigenous peoples. In all cases, the subject populations embodied "the erotic" of the European imagination. The earth, too, is being destroyed because it also is seen to be wild ("the savage jungle"/"the virgin forest")—just as desire is to be policed, just as women's bodies are to be controlled, just as all dark-skinned peoples "need" to be dominated, so the environment needs to be brought into submission. Interrupting erotophobia is thus profoundly transgressive, in that it challenges many intersecting oppressions (white supremacy, hatred of women, homophobia, etc.) that have their roots in erotophobia. In this context, the decolonization of Black queer male bodies begins with the physical/spiritual/psychological process of making our bodies and our desire our own.

*   *   *

For as long as I can remember, I have been attracted to the erotic in the sacred and the sacred in the erotic. My encounter with opposition to this way of seeing things gave me direct experience of the violence enfolded within "either/or" thinking. If I were spiritual, I could not be sexual, and vice versa. Sex was low and spirit was high. But since sex and the sacred cannot truly be separated from each other, it was necessary for Western Christianities to attempt to remove anything that even reminds one of the erotic. People are totally scandalized, for example, at the thought of an S/M reading of certain Western Christian ritual practices. This attitude has also shaped the negative ways in which people look at and study other religious traditions that do not share in this dichotomous approach. In many of these traditions, the body is not only the temple; it is also the place where the sacred manifests. In Yoruba religious traditions of West Africa and of the Yoruba diaspora in the Americas, when the divine *orisha* manifest through the bodies of the initiates, one speaks of being "mounted," a term carrying with it definite sexual imagery.

Erotophobia still figures so prominently in our thinking that often people will say that others only talk about "sacred sex" in order to justify their depravity. We often replicate this type of thinking when we say, "It was about more than JUST sex." Part of our colonized mentality has made us queers think that if we deny and trivialize the centrality of sex in our lives, in our (s)experiences, in our creativity, in our thoughts, in our dreams, in our interactions, then we will be more acceptable to the dominating culture. Erotophobia leads us to trivialize all that is just too blatantly erotic, too "flamboyantly" sexual, precisely because of the power of the erotic. Erotophobia makes us say, "Queer boys are shallow and silly: all they ever think about is dick. Bisexual people and BDSM/leather people are silly: they're preoccupied with sex." Erotophobic discourses and practices provide the tools for marginalizing, trivializing, and, at the same time, policing and criminalizing sex in our lives.

So much has told us that we are evil because we do not have sex for the sole purpose of reproduction; so much has told us that we are incarnations of evil because we like sex. As Black queer male bodies, we struggle against the image of us as too libidinal, too lust driven, too sexually criminal, and this struggle has given us other ways of viewing sex and bodies. We know that our Black bodies have always blurred the public/private split, have always blurred the boundaries of personal/political. When your body is on the line, you know that you are transgressing the public/private split by your very existence. When you can be arrested because of the color of your skin, you know that your body is political. When the dominating culture expends incredible amounts of time, money, and energy controlling and policing our bodies and the ways we decide to use them, then it is clear that our bodies are political. And that brings us back to the primacy of the body, the centrality of sex in our life experiences.

In my gut, I experience no contradiction between our sexualities and our spiritualities. If sex can be perceived as a gift, then surely the body must be celebrated. If sex is a path of the sacred, why is it so frightening to imagine placing sex toys, dental dams, condoms, lube, and so forth, on our altars? Sex is often a bodily path leading us to other dimensions of existence. It is a profound expression of wholeness, for spirit can be encountered in the erotic and the erotic in the spirit—they flow in and out of each other. The mystical imagery of many religious traditions takes us into these realms where the sexual and the sacred intermingle. Ultimately, what I am talking about are sexspiritualities, or spiritsexualities. These spiritualities are about wholeness: the art of wholeness, the aesthetics of wholeness, the paths of wholeness, the politics of wholeness. They are profoundly about the business of transcending apparent opposites. Our spiritualities point us toward right relationships with our Mother, the Earth, with our other animal sisters and brothers, and with one another. Justice and equality are crucial parts of wholeness, of spiritualities.

For me, the task of decolonizing my body and my desire has been rooted in the struggle for self-determination and self-definition. It has led me into the whole area of body piercing, a practice that I consider to be expressive of what I call transgressively inscribed sexspiritualities. Body piercing, as a path of expression of my sexuality, of my desire, has been reflective of a desire to be further inscribed in my Black body as a site of resistance. The actual act of piercing has produced experiences that lead me out of the body, only to return even more profoundly into bodiliness. The intensely interactive relationship between perceived pain and pleasure is highlighted not only in the actual moment of the piercing but also anytime that I touch the piercings. Ndlela Nkobi, queer Black South African filmmaker, sex radical, and theorist, says that if we tend to our interior life, why should we not also tend to the exterior as well? Why not spiritually care for the sexing of our bodies (personal communication, November 1995)? This is why I consider body piercing as sexual act and sexual statement; it is my inscribed transgressivity as a Black queer man. It is an act of decolonizing my body. For me, the recognition of the sacred in my sexuality and the sexual in my sacrality has become a crucial part of my path of liberation, of my journey toward wholeness. And this is no mean feat for a queer man of color living in a white-supremacist, sex-hating, women-hating, body-hating, homo-hating society.

Although I have long been fascinated by body piercing, I had found it easy to dismiss it as yet another marginal/alternative white practice. To equate aspects of radical sex culture with "whiteness" made them much easier to dismiss out of hand, even though they attracted me. Sex radical identity seemed to me to be something reserved for white people and possibly for people of color who were involved with them. As I would soon discover, self-identifying as a sex radical, as one dedicated to uprooting erotophobia and bodyphobia as sources of so many other forms of oppression, would lead to my being seen as a "nasty freak" in my community of origin and as a walking criminal nightmare in the eyes of the dominating culture. The erotophobic juxtaposition of spirituality and sexuality come up time and time again. Given the ways in which Black men have been eroticized, exoticized, criminalized, and killed for the mere suspicion of transgressive sex, there is a great amount of risk taking involved for Black queer men to publish our erotica and porn, to speak our desire, all while being under constant attack.

I came to body piercing because I was seeking a sexspiritual practice that allowed me to reclaim my Black queer body. Living in the HIV pandemic, I needed to feel that I could speak through and with my body; I could not allow erotophobia, HIVphobia, homohatred, white supremacy, and so forth, to erase my body. My early rejection of body piercing for anything other than earlobes was definitely rooted in my internalized Afriphobia, my internalized racism, my internalized bodyphobia. It was the fear of being too obviously "out there," of actually showing that I was a freak, of letting people know all sorts of things about my sex life by having a pierced body. It was the fear of blurring the (unreal) public/private split by "putting my business out in the street."

In the spring of 1992, my partner and I decided to have our nostrils pierced. That was where I was drawing the limit. I stated vehemently that I would never pierce my nipples; lip piercing was out of the question because it denoted far too much nastiness. Within the next two to three years, I had pierced my nipples, my dick, my eyebrow, my lips, navel, and septum (the partition be-tween the nostrils). The piercing of the septum caused for me to consider what it would mean to have something in my nose that would be a constant reminder of some of the peoples of Africa, the Pacific Islands, Asia, or Amazonia—a reminder that might be taken negatively. It would mean that my own people would ask me why I would want to "degrade" myself by looking like a "savage." My life trajectories allowed me to understand that, for me, body piercing has to do with the performativity of my colored body. If bodies that traditionally pierce are already considered to be transgressive because they are colored, then those bodies which are pierced and tattooed are already sexually criminalized bodies, perverted, deviant, oversexed. There is a connection be-tween erotophobia and opposition to body piercing and tattooing.

Body piercing is also, for me, a profound reaction to body shame. Given the world in which many of us Black queer men have grown up, shame—or the fear of shame—has played a major role in suffocating and erasing us. Body piercing then becomes an act of resistance to physical erasure through creating sacred erotic rituals of inscription: they inscribe us in our bodies. This is particularly transgressive in a context of HIVphobia that seeks to make us flee and fear the colored body, which has been constructed as the source and site of the Plague. To be openly and adornedly body, to be an openly sexualized queer body in the world is to refuse to be suffocated and to be erased; this act of being openly body reclaims the right to blur the public/private borderlands. Body piercing is not only a defiant queering of the body but also a deliberate sexing of it as well; piercings often augment sensations during sex. My pierced Black body creates a critical erotic geography in which public/private discourse is ultimately transcended.

In 1858, Sojourner Truth was challenged to prove that she was a woman by publicly showing her breasts. The white women present were shocked by the very idea, but Sojourner said that the shame was theirs, not hers, for she had nursed many white children—to the exclusion of her own—with those very breasts. This was such a powerful act of resistance and decolonization precisely because she did it in a context that said that Black women were sexually depraved and that white women were pure and pious. Sojourner Truth, who deconstructed with her very body, showed that she did not have to conform to Euro-Puritanical notions of purity and modesty in order to be who she wanted to be. She could have reacted by not showing her breasts, thinking that this public display of nudity would simply confirm what white people thought about Black women. She was not ashamed to show her body, even though by showing her naked breasts she would only confirm in the minds of some her sexual depravity and deviance; she was, after all, a Black woman. My understanding of this event helped me to understand once again the power of self-definition, of self-determination in the process of decolonization. I could be pierced; I could be a sex radical; I could point to the interdependence of sex and spirit, even though by so doing I would be offering to many proof of my depravity. But by doing these things, I was also breaking the hegemony of erotophobia in my life.

Sacred geography—for me, this is how I can describe my reinscription in my body. In a very simple way, this reinscription through piercing and tattooing makes me constantly aware of parts of my body that I have taken for granted or of which I have been profoundly ashamed. These piercings in my body then become powerful reconfigurations of the body as icon. They reflect my sex-spirituality, a journey back into the body. The time surrounding each piercing involves rigorous preparation, cleansing, care, and celebration. Each piercing has been a powerful ritual act, a moment of rebirth to which the ancestors are invited. Each body piercing is a constant reminder to me of my Black queer body as a site of resistance. My pierced body says that all of our bodies do matter and that even in an era of rampant erotophobia, some of us will still visibly signify "sexual deviance," showing that some of us do not want to have our bodies colonized.

In conclusion, a poem:

I'm a yomosexual a polysexual a perverted trance trickster, dancing on the edge, ruining your categories, your boxes, your party, because they don't even really exist.

I'm a sexual border bandit crawling through the toxic waste tunnels of your nightmares giving you realness in exchange for your virtual realness.

I'm a shady shape-shifting shaman fucking with your Internet 'cause I'm online all the time: 24, 7, 365, connected to modems you've never even heard of.

I'm my own girlfriend 'cause I'm a highsexual, a mysexual, a dissexual and a datsexual. My body matters to me and I'll pierce it and piss on it and I'll be clit, vagina, vulva, labia. And I'll be dick and nuts and I'll be whatevah. I'll be 4-legged and I'll be 2-legged and I'll still fuck with your supremacy, whether it be white, or male, or Louis XIV lesbigayristocrat or military or pat robertsonesque.

My cum might be pink and dark, dark black, but maybe that's because the edges of the pink and black triangles inside of me are jagged, those pyramids cut; they constantly dismember me so that I am re-created in new configurations that piss on your boxes so that at least I give your boxes the chance to be transformed and disappear.

I don't need you to hear my pain. I don't need you to feel my pain. I'll make sure that you get the point the next time you decide to dance on dead bodies, and I will scream so loudly that you will hear all of those voices that you have been trying to keep out, feel all of that pain that you have been paying so dearly to feel.

I'll put my ass on the line, and if you don't like it, well, baby, we'll just have to rumble. It won't be cute, but hey: I'm a nappy happy holy hip hop homo and my body matters.

Does yours?

REFERENCES

Eilberg-Schwartz, Howard. 1995. *God's Phallus: And Other Problems for Men and Monotheism.* Boston: Beacon Press.

Gilman, Sander. 1985. *Difference and Pathology: Stereotypes of Sexuality, Race and Madness.* Ithaca, NY: Cornell University Press.

Katz, Jonathan Ned. 1976. *Gay American History: Lesbians and Gay Men in the USA.* New York: Thomas J. Crowell Company.

Resurrection of the Penis:
A Political Poem

Alison Luterman

like the clapper of a silent bell
its cleft mushroom head tender
the scrotum loose as the scruff of the neck
of a puppy you hold up, young and sleepy
the long purple vein down the underside
a raised riverbed, mapping the territory of touch
the elegance of the whole, its innocence
rising out of the bush to look around

who crushed and remolded you in the shape of a weapon
I will never accept this version
who turned you upside down and nailed a murdered god to you
you who used to point the way for sacred rites of Eros at Pompeii
the christians do not own christmas, I do not cede
the rebirth of light to them
not one holiday, nor shred of meaning
reversed, lost, stolen, lied about
nor will I allow you in your passion to be diverted into violence

the egg doesn't sit there like a bull's-eye
the sperm is not a dart thrown by a missile launcher
every living thing struggles to connect
in its own way, the egg moves
toward the sperm in strong, undulant, enveloping waves
they find each other
it is not a question of conquest

"Resurrection of the Penis" first appeared in *Green Egg: A Journal of the Awakening Earth,* Spring 1994, *27*(104), p. 44.

the penis, slick and silky, diving like a gull
into the reflecting pool, over and over
looking for something
unkeepable
these gifts
I will never accept their version
everyone knows nothing
stands still in life, we all move
instinctively toward the other, there is no
other, there is only ourselves
with our eyes of spirit and our eyes of flesh
every living thing struggles to connect

ABOUT THE EDITORS

Kerwin Kay is a freelance writer and activist living in San Francisco, California. His articles have been published in *Z Magazine,* the *San Francisco Bay Guardian,* and *Anything That Moves,* among others. During the past eleven years, he has been active in antiracist, anti-imperialist, feminist men's movements, and bisexual/queer politics. In 1988, he organized the first Rocky Mountain Men's Conference in Boulder, Colorado. Kerwin's work experience includes jobs at strip clubs and porn shops, and most recently he has become active in the movement to decriminalize prostitution. He is currently a graduate student in cultural anthropology at San Francisco State University, where his thesis work focuses on runaway youth engaged in prostitution. Kerwin can be reached through his Web site at <www.mlust.com>.

Jill Nagle is a writer in San Francisco, California, whose most recent book is *Whores and Other Feminists* (1997). Her essays and fiction have also appeared in *Guilty Pleasures* (1999), *Oyrotica* (1999), *PoMoSexuals* (1998), *Looking Queer* (1998), *First Person Sexual* (1996), *Bisexual Politics* (1995), and *Closer to Home* (1992, as Vashti Zabatinsky), as well as in the periodicals *Girlfriends, On Our Backs, Curve, Anything That Moves, Black Sheets,* and *Spectator.* Ms. Nagle is currently working on *The Female Fag,* a magazine-like collection of her own and others' writings by "females" who identify with man-on-man sexuality. Ms. Nagle is also working on two new books about race in the United States and about flirtation and sexual communication. In addition, she is preparing several screenplays and is involved in a number of smaller projects. She has been politically active for many years in Jewish, antiracist, queer, and sex-radical communities.

Baruch Gould holds a Masters of Divinity degree and has a career in public health policy and program development in San Francisco, California. He is a student of Jungian psychology and formally worked in the sex industry. An AIDS and queer activist and father of three children, Mr. Baruch is currently involved in writing his memoirs.

CONTRIBUTORS

Greg Abrams is a pseudonym.

Tommi Avicolli Mecca is a longtime writer and agitator whose lifelong dream is to see demonstrators shut down the stock exchange in every major city, every day at the same moment, until the wealth is redistributed and no one has to go without food, clothing, shelter, jobs, and health care. He resides in San Francisco with two cats and hopes someday to make a name for himself as a great playwright/novelist (if someone will ever produce/ publish his works!).

Steve Bearman, based in San Francisco, has been leading groups of men for the past eight years. He leads workshops for men and women on relationships, sex, healing, and building community. In his work as a counselor, he helps people to heal from the limiting effects of oppression and unhealed hurts so they can reclaim their power and intelligence and realize their deepest dreams. He envisions and works for a day when men are free and sex is no big deal.

Tim Beneke has published widely on issues related to sexism, violence against women, and masculinity. He is the author of *Men on Rape* (1982) and *Proving Manhood: Reflections on Men and Sexism* (1997), in addition to many articles. He lives in Oakland, California, where he works as a freelance writer and editor.

Ahimsa Timoteo Bodhrán was born in 1974 on El Día de la Madre in the South Bronx. A mixed-blood Zwei-Alma'd Sefardí/Arab artista, activista, y académica, his work has appeared in numerous publications, including *LUNA; Mizna; maganda; The Evergreen Chronicles; Response: A Contemporary Jewish Review; Journal of Gay, Lesbian, and Bisexual Identity;* and the *FTM International Newsletter.* A member of both Radius of Arab-American Writers, Incorporated, and the National Association of Sephardi/Mizrahi Artists, Writers, and Intellectuals, he is currently working on three books: a brothers loving brothers anthology, a collection of testimonies by men of color who are survivors of violence, and a queer multiracial leaders interview book. He is the prize-winning author of the forthcoming *Yerbabuena/Mala yerba, All My Roots Need Rain: mixed blood poetry & prose.* Bodhrán has also helped coordinate the *Tranny Fest: Transgender and Transgenre Cinema* film festival and has taught classes in Creative Writing, Literature, and Queer/ Ethnic/Women's Studies at various Bay Area institutions. Bodhrán es un sobreviviente, curandero in training, and (grand)father/mother-to-be.

Siobhan Brooks is a union organizer at the Lusty Lady exotic dance theater, which unionized with SEIU Local 790. She is a writer and holds a BA in women's studies from San Francisco State University. Her writings have appeared in *Z Magazine, Women's Hastings Law Journal,* and the anthology *Whores and Other Feminists* (1997). She is currently at work on an interview book about people of color in the sex industry titled *Dancing Shadows: Interviews with Men and Women of Color Sex Workers,* from which her interview with Sonya is taken.

Steven E. Brown and Lillian Gonzales Brown are Founders of the Institute on Disability Culture, located in Las Cruces, New Mexico. The Institute can be contacted at 2260 Sunrise Point Road, Las Cruces, NM, 88011; (505) 522-5225 (Voice/FAX/TDD); <stebrown@juno.com; www.dimenet.com/disculture/>.

W. C. believes a playful, soft side to Dominance/submission play (D/s) deserves to be heard, one not as scary as the blood lust its detractors would like to clothe D/s in. Those who don't understand the romance of BDSM in its many forms prefer to characterize this "whips and chains" play as extreme. Readers familiar with tradition know the history of poetry and literature is filled with such expression. W. C. feels blessed to be able to write poems about the rich way humans choose to manifest their consensual love.

Justin Chin is the author of *Mongrel: Essays, Diatribes, and Pranks* (1999) and *Bite Hard* (1997). He lives in San Francisco.

Andrew Clark is a pseudonym. He writes from New York, where he is completing a memoir from which his piece is adapted.

Jorge Ignacio Cortiñas has been published in *Puerto del Sol, Socialist Review,* and *modern words.* He won first prize in the 1998 *San Francisco Bay Guardian* Fiction Contest. His play, *Maleta Mulata,* was recently produced by the San Francisco theater company Campo Santo. He is currently a Creative Writing Fellow at Brown University.

Allan Creighton was born in a farming community in Pennsylvania and raised by New Englander parents. He is married to Julie Nesnansky and lives in Oakland. He is a cofounder of the Oakland Men's Project (OMP), whose purpose is to stop men's violence against women through understanding and through transforming the socialization to "act like a man." He also cofounded and directed Men Overcoming Violence (MOVE), a counseling intervention program for men who batter in heterosexual and homosexual relationships.

Allan is staff consultant to TODOS Institute, One World Alliances, and the Diversity Leadership Training Project. In these capacities, and through the OMP, he has conducted training programs for adult professionals and youth across California and the country since 1979. His publications include *Power and Me* (with Heru-Nefera Amen), a training curriculum for foster care youth on successful emancipation from foster care; *Making the Peace* (1996, with Paul Kivel); *Young Men's Work Volumes I and II; Stopping Violence and Building Community;* and *Helping Teens Stop Violence* (1992).

Reverend Geoffrey Karen Dior Gann is a former porn star who has, in recent years, crossed over into mainstream entertainment, appearing in many movies, commercials, and television shows, such as *Veronica's Closet* and *Xena: Warrior Princess.* He is a writer, singer (with a new CD coming out soon), AIDS activist, and an award-winning director of many adult videos. He recently became an ordained minister and received his PhD in Philosophy in Religion. He is the only porn star, other than Traci Lords, to successfully cross over into mainstream entertainment, and he has done so without turning his back on the porn industry or claiming that he "didn't know what he was doing."

David Elsop and **Danielle Ephraim** are both pseudonyms. David lives in a Mid-western city, where he works at a large organization. Before this fifteen-month exploration of his sexuality, David engaged for years in various spiritual practices and therapies in pursuit of sanity. This is his first work about sexuality. He may expand it into a book someday. Danielle Ephraim has been married to David Elsop for almost eighteen years.

elias farajajé-jones is Professor of Cultural Studies at the Starr King School and is also a member of the core doctoral faculty (cultural and historical studies of religion) of the Graduate Theological Union in Berkeley, California. He is of African/First Nations (Tsalagai/Cherokee)/Ibero-Celtic ancestry. A native of Berkeley, elias is an eternal apprentice of the art of body piercing. He also works as a ritual performance artist and videographer. An honors graduate of Vassar College, he has an MDiv (magna cum laude) in Eastern Christian Studies from St. Vladimir's Graduate School of Orthodox Theology. After studying Rabbinics and Hellenistic Jewish Literature at the Pontifical Biblical Institute in Rome, he went on to earn his DThéol (magna cum laude) from the University of Bern (Switzerland). Before moving back to the Bay Area, he was Professor of History of Religions/Sociology of Religion at the Howard University School of Divinity in Washington, DC. He has been actively involved in creating rituals for queer people of color as part of a movement to transcend the dichotomous world view of Euro-Puritanism that sees sex and spirit as being in opposition. His work has helped to rediscover ways of recognizing and claiming how sex and the sacred are inextricably bound together.

Paul Fleischer is a therapist and teacher. He has a master's degree in Human Development and Learning from the University of North Carolina at Charlotte and earned his doctorate in Clinical Psychology from the California Institute for Integral Studies. Paul currently lives with his wife and son near Asheville, North Carolina.

Larry M. Gant, PhD, has over twenty years' experience in human services as a direct service practitioner, therapist, supervisor, administrator, and consultant. He has created and implemented numerous substance abuse and HIV risk-reduction programs for African-American populations, including JEMADARI (kiswahili for "wise companion"); a program targeting at-risk black men, NJIDEKA (kiswahili for "survival is paramount"); an intervention program for at-risk black women, and TABA (Teens Affected By AIDS), a program for at-risk black youth. Dr. Gant is currently an associate professor of social work at the School of Social Work, University of Michigan.

Howie Gordon is a Berkeley-based writer who spent over a decade working in adult films. As the actor Richard Pacheco, he won numerous awards while appearing in over 100 films during porn's so-called Golden Age. Gordon/Pacheco is hard at work on a memoir of his porn career and expects to publish this work, one way or another, in 1999.

Robert E. Goss is Assistant Professor in South Asian Religions at Webster University. As an activist and former Jesuit priest, he is the author of *Jesus ACTED UP: A Gay and Lesbian Manifesto* (1993) and co-editor of *A Rainbow of Religious Diversity* (1996) and *Our Families, Our Values: Snapshots of Queer Kinship* (1997). In addition, he has transferred his clergy credentials to the Universal Fellowship of Metropolitan Community Churches, where he serves as clergy on staff in St. Louis. Goss is co-chair of the Gay Men's Issues in Religion Group of the American Academy of Religion. He has an active interest in the integration of sexuality and spirituality.

Jamison "James" Green, MFA, is a writer, educator, and gender diversity consultant in the San Francisco Bay Area. He is internationally known as a civil rights advocate for all queer and transgendered and transsexual people, and especially as an advocate for transmale pride. His writing has appeared in *Anything That Moves, Transgender Tapestry,* and several anthologies.

Christopher Hall grew up in Thousand Oaks, California, a suburban rat hole located about forty miles northwest of Los Angeles. This was a deceptively valuable experience, giving him a clear vision of everything he wanted to avoid in life. The things he has done in the name of this cause include radio engineering and reporting, writing fiction and essays, and occasional political activism. In 1993, he fled the Los Angeles area for the saner region of San Francisco, where he ultimately completed a BA in Liberal Studies at San Francisco State

University. Now a resident of the Real World, he supports himself doing data entry for a local temp agency. In his spare time, he edits book reviews for *Maximum RockNRoll*, the famed punk rock magazine.

Steven Hill is a writer and political reformer. He is co-author of *Reflecting All of Us* (1999). His articles and commentaries have appeared in *The Los Angeles Times, The Wall Street Journal, The Nation, Ms., ON THE ISSUES, The Christian Science Monitor, Social Policy, Boston Review, In These Times, San Francisco Bay Guardian, San Francisco Chronicle, San Jose Mercury News, Atlanta Journal-Constitution, Seattle Times, Albuquerque Tribune, Houston Chronicle,* and many other newspapers via the Knight-Ridder and Scripps Howard news services. He has contributed to the anthologies *Making Violence Sexy* (1993) and *Transforming a Rape Culture* (1995).

Emil Keliane was born in Iran in August 1973 and was ten years old when he moved to America. He did not speak English. Within six months, he was speaking fluently, and by fifteen, was writing poetry. The diary (from which his piece was excerpted) was born when Emil was sixteen years old. Now he writes strictly in English, a language that is occasionally his nemesis, but always his passion. He did not read his work in public until the age of twenty-five, a fated day that brings him here to this anthology.

Terry Kelly, 6′1″, 200 lbs., 60 yrs, handsome, muscular, versatile. I have never lived anyplace long. The towns have drifted by our windshield. My writers are Susie Bright, William T. Vollman, Alina Reyes, Elmore Leonard, Trish Thomas, Cixous, and me.

Michael S. Kimmel is Professor of Sociology at SUNY at Stony Brook. His books include *Changing Men* (1987), *Men Confront Pornography* (1990), *Men's Lives* (1997, fourth edition), *Against the Tide: Profeminist Men in the United States, 1776-1990* (1992), *The Politics of Manhood* (1996), and *Manhood: A Cultural History* (1996). He edits *Men and Masculinities,* an interdisciplinary scholarly journal, a book series on Men and Masculinity at the University of California Press, and the Sage Series on Men and Masculinities. He is the spokesperson for the National Organization for Men Against Sexism (NOMAS) and lectures extensively on campuses in the United States and abroad.

Tortuga Bi Liberty has struggled for human rights since he was age twelve. He is now looking for over-forty persons, especially pansexual polyamorists, to write for *ElderLust,* a proposed e-zine. Send SASE by snail mail to Senior Unlimited Nudes; Department W; P.O. Box 426937, San Francisco, CA, 94142-6937.

Lou Lipsitz has been lusting, resisting lusting, and studying the matter of lust for many years. He is a poet and psychotherapist living in Chapel Hill, North Carolina. For many years, he was a political science professor before retiring to pursue his new profession. His books of poems are *Cold Water* (1967), *Reflections on Samson* (1977), and *Seeking the Hook* (1997). Some of his poems have been widely anthologized. He's been an active participant in the men's movement with a special interest in grief, sexuality, and the connections between them.

Malcolm Lowry was born to devout Latter-Day Saint (Mormon) parents in Edmonton, Alberta, Canada. At age nineteen, he served as a missionary for a two-year, self-paid tour in Japan. After his unsuccessful biofeedback therapy to become "straight," Malcolm's depression and despair caused him to lose his job as a transit driver. Over the next few years, he was admitted to hospitals several times with what seemed to be stress-induced paracarditis (inflamed sack around the heart). At age twenty-five, he took advantage of a two-year, full-tuition scholarship to Brigham Young University (BYU) to study Computer Engineering and to avoid job hunting. At age twenty-seven, however, he no longer felt able to study while enduring his never-ending inner turmoil. Feeling repressed by the antigay BYU atmosphere, he finally aborted his studies and moved to Vancouver, Canada. At age twenty-nine, and with the support of a friend with deeply held New Age beliefs, he finally chose to face the overwhelming realities of leaving his faith. Profound, crippling depression ensued. However, with medication and counseling, Malcolm's life has returned not only to a productive state but to a relatively happy one as well. Malcolm currently programs computers for British Columbia's social housing authority. This piece is the only writing he has ever published. Only now at the age of thirty-nine has he finally gained the courage to experiment with dating and love.

Alison Luterman is a transplanted New Englander currently living in Oakland. She has worked as a freelance journalist, a poet in the schools, an English as a Second Language teacher, and an HIV counselor. She has had work published in *The Sun, WHETSTONE, Poetry East, Many Mountains Moving,* and other literary journals.

Cleo Manago's essays, compositions, and ongoing columns have appeared in numerous academic journals and popular magazines, including *The Black Scholar, SBC, Whazzup,* and *Alternatives*. His writing also appears in *Atonement* (1996), a national best-seller featuring stories from the historic Million Man March. Manago is a PhD student at the California Institute for Integral Studies in San Francisco. He is currently preparing his doctoral dissertation, "Loving Oneself in One's Own Image: Recreating and Rebirthing Reality."

Reach him online at <http://home.earthlink.net/~blkembrace/index.htm> or at <www.amassi.com>.

Mark Mardon has done a lot of writing, it being the one consistent thing in his life since he was a geeky teenager writing about reptiles and amphibians. From there he went on to write about rain forests, mountains, villages, and folklore in South America, then began a long career writing and editing for one of the big conservation/environment magazines in the United States. That connected him to many great writers, activists, and adventurers, took him to many locales around the world, and sharpened both his writing skills and his perceptions about how the world works. By that time, Mark had decided he wanted to write about gay culture and the arts, so now he works for a local gay rag. He's happy doing it, because it connects him with amazingly talented and inspiring people in his community, especially the younger ones struggling to make it. He believes that the struggle itself is what's interesting and that once people make it, they can either rest on their fat laurels and be boring or remake themselves and begin struggling again. To remain young, he remakes himself often. Each time, he's happy to say, he's noticed an improvement.

Manó Marks lives with his partner in the San Francisco Bay Area, which he regards as the best place on earth for queers to live. By profession, he has been a teacher, a dishwasher, a computer geek, and is currently a queer activist and community organizer. He was one of the founders of Men Overcoming Sexual Assault (MOSA), a project of Bay Area Women Against Rape. MOSA was the first crisis line for male survivors of sexual violence in the United States. Currently, he serves as the Victim/Survivor Caucus representative to the Board of the National Coalition Against Sexual Assault. A quiet person, he enjoys computer games, science fiction, and sitting in his hot tub under the stars.

Thomas McGrath is a pseudonym.

Frank Moore, who is self-taught, has been painting since 1963. His work has been exhibited throughout the United States and Canada. In addition to oil on canvas, he also does live performances, first becoming known in the 1970s as the creator of a popular cabaret show, *The Outrageous Beauty Revue*. In the 1980s, he became one of the foremost performance artists in the United States, ultimately finding himself one of five NEA (National Endowment for the Arts) artists to be targeted by Senator Jesse Helms in the early 1990s. Since 1991, Moore has been the publisher and editor of the acclaimed underground zine *The Cherotic r(E)volutionary*. In addition to his book, *Cherotic Magic* (1993), and numerous other self-published pieces, he has been widely published in various art-oriented and other periodicals. His video works have shown throughout the United States and Canada and have won awards. Moore has a large, extensive Web site, <www.eroplay. com>, which features his and other artists' audio, video, and visual artwork. He also hosts a live weekly Internet show on <www.fakeradio.com>.

Robert E. Penn is the author of *The Gay Men's Wellness Guide: The National Lesbian and Gay Health Association's Complete Book of Physical, Emotional and Mental Health and Well-Being for Every Gay Male* (1998). His poetry and prose appear in the anthologies *Men Seeking Men* (1998), *Shade* (1996), *We Are Everywhere* (1997), *Milking Black Bull* (1995), *Sojourner* (1993), and *The Road Before Us;* in the magazines *Essence, Shooting Star Review, Thing,* and *COLORLife;* and in the literary journals *The Portable Lower East Side* and *Art & Understanding.*

Martin Phillips is a teacher. He has worked as an editor and writer for a variety of small magazines. He has also published stories and articles under a different name.

Carol Queen is a writer and cultural sexologist. She is the author of *Real Live Nude Girl* (1997), *The Leather Daddy and the Femme* (1998), and *Exhibition-ism for the Shy* (1995). Visit her at <www.carolqueen.com>.

Jack Random is a bisexual pagan, poet, pornographer, and leather daddy. He lives, works, and spanks people in San Francisco, California and can be reached for almost any purpose at <randomj@earthlink.net>.

Thomas S. Roche's more than 100 published short stories and essays have appeared in such anthologies as the *Best American Erotica* series (1996, 1997, and 1999) and *The Mammoth Book of Pulp Fiction* (1996), and in such magazines as *Black Sheets, Blue Blood, Cupido,* and *Paramour,* among others.

Sandip Roy was awarded a Good Conduct Medal in school that will surely be revoked if they find out he is included in an anthology of *Male Lust.* He grew up in Calcutta as an Indian version of the Best Little Boy in the World and now lives in San Francisco trying to shed that stigma. He is the editor of *Trikone Magazine,* on South Asian lesbian, gay, bisexual, and transgender issues, and has been published in anthologies such as *Men on Men 6* (1996), *Quickies* (1998), *Queer View Mirror* (1995), *Contours of the Heart* (1996), *My First Time* (1995), and *Q & A* (1998).

Sy Safransky is editor of *The Sun,* a magazine he started more than twenty-five years ago. He lives in Chapel Hill, North Carolina.

Lawrence Schimel is the author of the short story collection *The Drag Queen of Elfland* (a finalist for the Lambda Literary Award, the Firecracker Alternative Book Award, and the Small Press Book Award) and of *The Erotic Writer's Market Guide 1999,* among others. He is also the editor of more than twenty anthologies, including *PoMoSexuals: Challenging Assumptions About Gender and Sexuality* (1998, with Carol Queen, winner of a Lambda Literary Award), *Switch Hitters: Lesbians Write Gay Male Erotica and Gay Men Write Lesbian Erotica* (1996, with Carol Queen), *Two Hearts Desire: Gay Couples on Their Love* (1997, with Michael Lassell), and *Things Invisible to See: Gay and Lesbian Tales of Magic Realism* (1998). His stories, essays, and poetry have been included in more than 150 anthologies, and he has also contributed to diverse periodicals, from *The Saturday Evening Post* to *Physics Today* to *Gay Scotland,* among others. He divides his time between his native New York City and Madrid.

Ray Schnitzler works as a software engineer but spends as much time as possible in the worlds of love, sex, music, dance, and radical Judaism. All the rest is commentary.

Simon Sheppard's writing has appeared in dozens of anthologies, including the 1996, 1997, and 1999 editions of *Best Gay Erotica, Best American Erotica 1997,* and *Strategic Sex* (1999). He is, with M. Christian, co-editor of *Rough Stuff: Tales of Gay Men, Sex, and Power* (1999).

Michael Shernoff is a psychotherapist in private practice in Manhattan as well as a longtime gay and AIDS activist and author. In the 1980s, he was the cocreator of "Hot, Horny, and Healthy: Eroticizing Safer Sex," one of the first-generation AIDS-prevention workshops that, for many years, became the most widely used intervention for gay men throughout North America, Europe, and Australia in the early days of the HIV epidemic. His most recent works are the edited books *Gay Widowers: Life After the Death of a Partner* (1997) and *AIDS and Mental Health Practice: Clinical and Policy Issues* (1999). From his writings and workshop presentations on male couples and gay sexuality he has been dubbed "The Dr. Ruth of Gay Sex," though he is not short and does not talk with a European accent.

Don Shewey is a writer, editor, and theater critic in New York City. His books include the biography *Sam Shepard* (1997), the Grove Press anthology *Out Front: Contemporary Gay and Lesbian Plays* (1988), and *Caught in the Act: New York Actors Face to Face* (1986, a collaboration with photographer Susan Shacter). He has written hundreds of articles for a variety of publications, from *The New York Times* to the late lamented *Steam*. He currently writes theater reviews for *The Advocate*, the national gay news magazine that published his legendary 1991 "X-rated" interview with Madonna, syndicated around the world to nineteen countries in eleven languages. Don grew up in a trailer park on a dirt road in Waco, Texas, and now lives in midtown Manhattan, halfway between Trump Tower and Carnegie Hall.

Matthew Simmons is a pleasure activist, teacher, performer, massage therapist, sex worker, drag queen, radical fairy, and a proud queer man who loves women.

Jim e Sparkle Pants lives in San Francisco where he works in the public schools. He is the author of *Sucking Bananas* (1988) and *The Rosebud Diaries* (1999), a collection of prose poems/songs written to his asshole as the beloved. Jim e has an MFA in poetry and likes to sing and dance. He is kindhearted and wacky. His e-mail address is <sparkle@sirius.com>.

David Steinberg is an author, editor, and publisher of artistic, imaginative sexual, and erotic material intended as an alternative to commercial pornography. His books include *Erotic by Nature: A Celebration of Life, of Love, and of Our Wonderful Bodies* (1988) and *Erotic Impulse: Honoring the Sensual Self* (1992). His writing has appeared in such magazines as *Playboy, Boston Phoenix, LA Weekly, Salon, Cupido, The Sun,* and *Libido*. He is currently completing a book of his essays, *This Thing We Call Sex: Reflections on the Culture and Politics of Sex in America*, and editing a second book of erotic photography, *Sex Is: Sexual Photography Comes of Age*. David lives in Santa Cruz, California.

John Stoltenberg is the radical feminist author of *Refusing to Be a Man: Essays on Sex and Justice* (1989, revised edition 2000), *The End of Manhood: Parables on Sex and Selfhood* (1993, revised edition 2000), and *What Makes Pornography "Sexy"?* (1994). A frequent speaker at colleges and conferences, he is represented by Program Corporation of America <www.speakerspca.com>.

Sara Sullivan is a pseudonym.

William Thompson is a writer and storyteller who was born in Clairsholme, Alberta, Canada. In 1974, a car accident left him completely blind, which ironically was the beginning of a lifelong love of literature. After dropping out of college in 1982, he worked as a reporter for two years, before attending the University of Alberta in pursuit of a BA in Political Science and Economics. He quickly switched to English literature, and after completing an MA in Children's Literature, he began teaching at the university level. Currently, he teaches both introductory English and children's literature, is completing a PhD, writes adult short fiction, and lives with his two children in Edmonton.

Max Wolf Valerio is a transsexual man. He is also a poet, writer, and performer who has appeared in many documentaries, including the "Max" short in *Female Misbehavior* (by Monika Treut) and *You Don't Know Dick: Courageous Hearts of Transsexual Men* (by Candace Schermerhorn and Buster Cam). He will also be appearing in Monika Treut's upcoming documentary on gender,

Gender Knots. In the meantime, Max is finishing his long-delayed memoir, *The Joker Is Wild!—Changing Sex and Other Crimes of Passion,* and hopes to have it published as soon as he can find a new publisher who will allow him to be as dangerous as is necessary. Max has also written a chapbook, *Animal Magnetism,* is working on at least one other book of poetry, and is envisioning a novel, *The Church of the Transsexual Jesus.*

John Ward is a lawyer and consciousness worker who represents underdogs. John was born in Chicago and grew up there and in suburban New York City. He currently lives in Boston with a dog and a cat and two soul friends in a big house near a pond.

Jeannie Zandi, MA, is a visionary, therapist, writer, and editor who presents gender reconciliation workshops and currently works with survivors of domestic violence in Taos, New Mexico. She is an active ally of the men's movement, a feminist, a partner, and a mother.

Index

Order Your Own Copy of
This Important Book for Your Personal Library!

MALE LUST
Pleasure, Power, and Transformation

_____ in hardbound at $49.95 (ISBN: 1-56023-981-6)

_____ in softbound at $24.95 (ISBN: 1-56023-982-4)

COST OF BOOKS_____

OUTSIDE USA/CANADA/
MEXICO: ADD 20%_____

POSTAGE & HANDLING_____
*(US: $3.00 for first book & $1.25
for each additional book)
Outside US: $4.75 for first book
& $1.75 for each additional book)*

SUBTOTAL_____

IN CANADA: ADD 7% GST_____

STATE TAX_____
*(NY, OH & MN residents, please
add appropriate local sales tax)*

FINAL TOTAL_____
*(If paying in Canadian funds,
convert using the current
exchange rate. UNESCO
coupons welcome.)*

☐ **BILL ME LATER:** ($5 service charge will be added)
(Bill-me option is good on US/Canada/Mexico orders only;
not good to jobbers, wholesalers, or subscription agencies.)

☐ Check here if billing address is different from
shipping address and attach purchase order and
billing address information.

Signature_____

☐ **PAYMENT ENCLOSED: $**_____

☐ **PLEASE CHARGE TO MY CREDIT CARD.**

☐ Visa ☐ MasterCard ☐ AmEx ☐ Discover

Account #_____

Exp. Date_____

Signature_____

Prices in US dollars and subject to change without notice.

NAME _____

INSTITUTION _____

ADDRESS _____

CITY _____

STATE/ZIP _____

COUNTRY _____ COUNTY (NY residents only) _____

TEL _____ FAX _____

E-MAIL_____

May we use your e-mail address for confirmations and other types of information? ☐ Yes ☐ No

Order From Your Local Bookstore or Directly From
The Haworth Press, Inc.
10 Alice Street, Binghamton, New York 13904-1580 • USA
TELEPHONE: 1-800-HAWORTH (1-800-429-6784) / Outside US/Canada: (607) 722-5857
FAX: 1-800-895-0582 / Outside US/Canada: (607) 772-6362
E-mail: getinfo@haworthpressinc.com
PLEASE PHOTOCOPY THIS FORM FOR YOUR PERSONAL USE.

BOF96

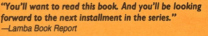